The Church in the World

A Historical-Ecclesiological Study of the Church of Uganda with Particular Reference to Post-Independence Uganda, 1962–1992

David Zac Niringiye

© 2016 by David Zac Niringiye

Published 2016 by Langham Monographs
an imprint of Langham Creative Projects

Langham Partnership
PO Box 296, Carlisle, Cumbria CA3 9WZ, UK
www.langham.org

ISBNs:
978-1-78368-119-8 Print
978-1-78368-137-2 Mobi
978-1-78368-136-5 ePub
978-1-78368-138-9 PDF

David Zac Niringiye has asserted his right under the Copyright, Designs and Patents Act, 1988 to be identified as the Author of this work.

All rights reserved. No part of this publication may be reproduced, stored in a retrieval system or transmitted, in any form or by any means, electronic, mechanical, photocopying, recording or otherwise, without the prior written permission of the publisher or the Copyright Licensing Agency.

All Scripture quotations, unless otherwise indicated, are taken from the Holy Bible, New International Version®, Anglicised, NIV®. Copyright © 1979, 1984, 2011 by Biblica, Inc.® Used by permission. All rights reserved worldwide.

British Library Cataloguing in Publication Data
A catalogue record for this book is available from the British Library

ISBN: 978-1-78368-119-8

Cover & Book Design: projectluz.com

Langham Partnership actively supports theological dialogue and a scholar's right to publish but does not necessarily endorse the views and opinions set forth, and works referenced within this publication or guarantee its technical and grammatical correctness. Langham Partnership does not accept any responsibility or liability to persons or property as a consequence of the reading, use or interpretation of its published content.

To Theodora, my wife;
and Joshua, Grace, and Abigail, our children.

Contents

Abstract xiii

Acknowledgements xv

Abbreviations xix

Chapter 1 1
  Introduction
      Ecclesiology in Contemporary African and Ugandan Scholarship 3
      The Church in the World: A Methodology 8
      The Gospel, Christian Faith and Community in the Revival 9
      The Church as a Community 13
      Faith and Narrative 16
      Sources and Research Process 17
      Research Limitations 20
      Thesis Development 21
      The World 22
      The Church 24

Chapter 2 27
  The Emerging Church in an Emerging Uganda, 1875–c1930
      The Birth of the Church in Buganda 29
      In the Kabaka's Court and Capital 32
      The Nascent Church during Mwanga's Reign 37
      Religious Rivalry 39
      Growth and Expansion 41
      An Enabling Socio-political Climate 42
      Missionary Participation 47
      Indigenous Participation 49
      Vernacularization 51
      Education and Health Services 52
      The Integration of the Church into Society 54
      Nominalism 55
      The Church and Political Institution-Building 58
      Formal Education 60
      Leadership and Ministry Formation 61
      Church Organization 63
      Reflection 66

Chapter 3 75
Schism and Revival in the Church, c1910–c1960
Ekibina kya Katonda Omu Ayinza Byona (The Society of the One Almighty God) 77
Mengo Gospel Church 79
East African Revival Movement 81
The Spreading of the Revival 84
Opposition to the Revival 89
Characteristic Features of the Revival 90
- Fellowship Meetings 91
- Singing 93
- Testimony 95
- Bible Reading 97
- Fellowship 98
- Leadership 100

Theology 101
Incorporation of the Revival into the Church 104
Mukono Crisis 105
Revival in the Church in Buganda 109
Revival in the Church in Western Uganda 110
Schism in the Revival 114
The Trumpeters 115
Okuzukuka (Re-awakening) 117
Reflection 119

Chapter 4 125
The Church in the Emerging Republic, 1960–1971
Battle at Mengo and Its Aftermath 127
The Church and the Battle of Mengo 132
Roots of the Battle of Mengo 135
The "Question of Buganda" 136
The "Question of Buganda" in the Church of Uganda 142
Erica Sabiti and the Church in Buganda – Namirembe Crisis 147
Namirembe Diocese and Cathedral 149
Housing and Land 154
Constitution Crisis 157
Resolution of the Namirembe Crisis 165
Idi Amin: The "Hand of God"? 165
Reflection 173

Chapter 5 179
The Church in the Amin Regime, 1971–1979
- The Coup and the Regime 181
- The Rise of the Military and Idi Amin 186
- The Rise of Idi Amin 189
- The Church and the Military 191
- The "Establishment" of Islam 194
- The Church in the Regime 200
- The Church in Lango 203
- Archbishop Luwum and the Regime 212
- Death of Archbishop Luwum 213
- Silvanus Wani, Successor to Janani Luwum 221
- Reflection 224

Chapter 6 233
The Church in the Obote II Regime, 1981–1985
- The "Bandits" War in the Luwero Triangle 235
- Roots of the War 238
- The Impact of the War 245
- The "Skulls of Luwero" 249
- "Desecration" of Ecclesial Centres 252
- The Church and the "Bandit" War 256
- Yona Okoth, an Obote-UPC Archbishop? 259
- The "Displaced" Church in Luwero 263
- Catechists in Luwero 267
- Worship and Sacrament during the War 269
- Namirembe-Lango "Reconciliation" 274
- Reflection 276

Chapter 7 281
The Church in the Museveni-NRA/M Regime, 1986–1992
- Archbishop Yona Okoth: A Rebel? 283
- A Divided House of Bishops? 287
- The Church and Social Concern 291
- Cattle Rustling, Rebellion and War in Teso 295
- War in Teso 302
- The "Skulls of Teso" 305
- A "Rebel" Church in Teso 307
- Ministry in Turbulent Teso 308
- The Church as a Peacemaker 313
- Bishop Gershom Ilukor: A "Rebel" and Peacemaker 317
- Reflection 320

Chapter 8 327
   The Church in the World: Toward an Ecclesiology
      The Changing Image of the Church 329
      The Church in the Pre-Independence Period 330
      The Church in the Post-Independence Period 332
      The Church in the World: An Ecclesiology 334
      An Indigenous Church 334
      An Indigenous Faith 336
      "Testimony," an Ecclesiological Paradigm 341
      The Ecclesiology of the Church of Uganda 345
         Authenticity 345
         Identity 349
         Sacrament 356
         Paradox and Mystery 358
      Conclusion 365

Chapter 9 371
   Continuing the Story: The Church in the Museveni-NRA/M Regime,
   1993 to the Present
      Continuing Turbulence under Museveni-NRA/M regime,
      1993 to-date (2015) 373
      Continuing the Story of the Church of Uganda in the
      Museveni regime, 1992 to the present 382
      Conclusion 393

Appendix A 397
   Chronology of the Creation of Dioceses, 1960–1992
         Dioceses as at December 1992 399

Appendix B 401
   Sample Questions Used in Oral Interviews
      Personal Information 401
      Personal Christian History 401
      Turbulent Periods and Areas 402
      Personal involvement 404
      General 404

Bibliography 407
      Oral Sources 407
         Spanning More Than One Era of the Church of Uganda 407
         Namirembe Crisis, 1965–1971 409
         The Church in Lango and the Idi Amin Regime, 1971–1979 409

  The Church in Luwero and the Obote II Regime, 1981–1985...410
  The Church in Teso and the NRA/M Regime, 1986–1992.......410
Archival Sources..412
  African Evangelistic Enterprise Archives, Kampala...................412
  Centre for Basic Research Archives (CBR), Kololo Kampala....412
  Church of Uganda Archives, Provincial Secretariat,
    Namirembe...413
  Personal Archives 416
Newspapers..416
Official Publications...416
  Church of Uganda Publications...416
  Uganda Government Publications 417
  Others 417
Unpublished Works 418
  Theses..418
  Manuscripts, Public Lectures and Seminar Papers....................421
Articles in Books and Journals..421
Books..426
Online Sources...433

Abstract

This thesis is an ecclesiological-historical study of the Church of Uganda, a member of the Anglican Communion, from its origins in the 1870s to the 1990s, with particular focus on the turbulent socio-political context of the post-independence Uganda. The study of ecclesiology in an African context has not attracted sufficient scholarship, in comparison to the several African church histories and church-state studies. Most church studies in a socio-political context follow the religion-in-politics or church-state methodological approaches. The present study seeks to redress this imbalance by developing an ecclesiological analysis of the Church of Uganda, utilizing a "church-in-the-world" contextual approach, which gives priority to the indigenous narrative of the history and the theological identity of the Church of Uganda.

The account begins with the social-cultural-political context of Buganda in which the Church was born, as a result of the work of the Church Missionary Society (CMS) missionaries and indigenous Uganda agents. It identifies the formative factors in its early growth and expansion throughout the whole of Uganda, and the emergence of the schismatic and revival moments. Due attention is given to the story of the East African Revival movement both as a critical factor in the indigenizing of the Christian faith in Uganda, and as the source of the methodology employed in this thesis to elucidate the "church-in-the-world" paradigm.

In the post independence period, spanning the thirty years from 1962–1992, the account of the Church follows four chronological political eras characterized by varying degrees of socio-political turbulence. The first era is the period 1962–1971 during which there was a protracted conflict over the place of Buganda in the independent republic of Uganda, focused on the battle at Mengo in 1966. The story of the Church revolves around the development of the corporate identity in an environment charged with a Buganda versus the rest-of-Uganda divide, mirrored in the conflict between the leadership of the Church in Buganda, and Archbishop Erica Sabiti and other provincial structures.

The second period, from 1971–1979, is marked by the government of Idi Amin, during which the Church had to define its ministry in the context of military dominance of civil-political life, state-sponsored violence, terror and tyranny, and the ascendance of Islam as the "established" religion. The account reflects on the life of the Church in Lango, an area that bore the brunt of the regime's terror machine, and the issues surrounding the murder of Archbishop Janan Luwum. The Church's identification with people is visible in its ministry of prayer and the word, and the subordination of its Protestant identity to a new relationship with the Catholic Church in local expressions of human solidarity.

The third era spans 1980–1985, during the second presidency of Milton Obote, when an armed rebellion in the Luwero Triangle and the government's counter insurgency measures created a displaced and traumatized population. The account examines the Church's mission and ministry in this milieu, at both the leadership and grassroots levels. The chief work of the Church was pastoral, demonstrated in the ministry of catechists and clergy, rendering dysfunctional the Anglican canonical ministerial order of bishop-priest-deacon.

The fourth period is the six years of the Museveni / National Resistance Movement government, 1986–1992, during which there was another anti-government rebellion; this time in the northern and eastern parts of Uganda. The account focuses on the leadership of Archbishop Yona Okoth, the corporate identity of the Episcopal leadership, and the issue of reconciliation that the church in Teso had to contend with and its "Pastoral-Parental' ministry.

Chapter eight weaves the account together, by reflecting on the key elements of the ecclesiology of the Church of Uganda arising from the socio-cultural-political context of the pre- and post-independence in Uganda. It offers a methodological approach to the study of the contextual ecclesiology and highlights key elements that may be considered in the development of African ecclesiology. This book is a contribution to the study of the history of the Church of Uganda in particular and African church history, in general.

Acknowledgements

One of the most meaningful metaphors of life for me is "pilgrimage"; I consider my life to be a long journey within the parameters of eternal space and time. It is the people that I have met along my pilgrimage that have brought direction and meaning to life, and made it worth journeying on. I wish to pay tribute to those I have met on this portion of the journey, as I have worked on this project, who inspired me, supported me, worked with me and believed in me. The completion of this project is a milestone, an achievement that I owe to many whose names I am unable to mention.

It was while I was studying theology at Wheaton Graduate School in the United States of America in 1985–1987 that this leg of the journey began. It is then that I first considered doing a historical-theological study on the Church of Uganda as a result of the inspiration of professors Steven Franklin, Julius Scott and Robert Webber.

The Rev Dr John Scott, affectionately known among his mentorees as "Uncle John," pledged to work with me in looking for funding for research when the time was ripe. Uncle John helped me "discover" Professor Andrew F. Walls at the Centre for the Study of Christianity in the Non-Western World, New College, Edinburgh, in 1992. Professor Walls, then the director of the Centre, through his lectures and seminars, completed the process of my conversion to history as the way to doing theology, a process that was started by Professor Webber.

I am indebted to Dr Jack Thompson and Professor Davis Kerr, my first and second Readers respectively, who guided me and continually challenged me to think historically before making theological conclusions, as they worked with me painstakingly through several drafts of the chapters of this thesis. Professor Walls also worked with me in the initial period of writing this thesis. Mrs Anne Booth-Clibborn, Dr Fabian Nabugomu and

Mrs Joyce Wandawa helped me check the "is" and "was" of the draft thesis before submitting it.

The community at the Centre provided a cordial and stimulating environment for reflection, academic discourse and work: Miss Margret Acton, the Centre Librarian; Mrs Anne Fernon and Mrs Ruth Scott, secretaries; and Mrs Elizabeth Leitch, Librarian for the African Christianity Project, were always willing to render assistance. Miss Crystal Webster, from the university's Computing Services Department was patient in taking me along the road of computer literacy. My fellow pilgrims, students at various stages of their research, made my burden lighter by sharing their burdens and supporting me to carry mine. I pay special tribute to Diane Stinton, who transformed my hardily legible hand-written drafts to typescript.

Many families and friends enabled me to feel at "home" in cold and windy Edinburgh. The Rev and Mrs Roger and Mushy Simpton provided a home and became family for me during the first year, and made more endurable the experience of being away from my family in Uganda. Fabian Nabugomu, then pursuing his doctoral studies at Edinburgh University, became a true brother and soulmate; his experience as a researcher and his passion for the Church of Uganda were also a source of encouragement. Eric and Velerie Allan and son Keith accommodated me during my last year, and provided the occasional social break for a good meal and to watch football. 21 Jeffrey Street was "home" because Keith Allan made it so, making more bearable the reality of being away from my home in Kampala.

I am indebted to the staff and archivists of the archives that I visited several times: Africana Section of Makerere University Library, Bishop Tucker Theological College, Mukono; Centre for Basic Research, Kololo-Kampala; Church of Uganda Provincial Secretariat, Namirembe; Africa Evangelistic Enterprises, Kampala; Namirembe Diocese, Namirembe; and the Department of Religious Studies, Makerere University. I owe special tribute to Archbishop Yona Okoth and his successor Livingstone Mpalanyi-Nkoyoyo, who granted unencumbered access to the Church of Uganda archives at Namirembe. Fred Mukungu, the Church Archivist and Librarian of Bishop Tucker Theological College Library served me well.

I owe tribute to my first two research assistants, Aryantungyisa-Aharikundiira Kaakaabaale and Mary Sonko Nabachwa, who combed the newspaper holdings in the African Section of Makerere University Library and helped me to begin the arduous task of researching the Church of Uganda Archives at the Provincial Secretariat. Kaakaabaale continued with me to the very end. Bishop Girshom Ilukor, Mr Zebulon Kabaza, Rev Canon Peter Kigozi, Rev Canon Charles Odurukami and Rev Canon Daudi Serubidde, helped to locate the valuable sources on Teso, the East African Revival, Mengo, Lango, and Luwero accounts, respectively. I am grateful to all those men and women who found time to be interviewed. Mr Zebulon Kabaza, Canon John Bikangaga, Revs Odurukami and Serubidde, and Bishop Ilukor read through the first draft of the relevant chapters, to help me ascertain the accuracy of the names of informants and facts recorded.

This project would have been impossible without the financial support of the Christian International Scholars Foundation (CISF) and the Langham Research Scholarships, who awarded me scholarships towards tuition and research expenses. The International Fellowship of Evangelical Students (IFES), my employers, not only provided financial support for my family, but also gave me time off work to pursue studies; Mr Lindsay Brown, the General Secretary, was most supportive.

In any journey, it is the closest companions that matter most. Theodora, my dear wife, was true to her name – "gift of God." She has been the most cherished of all my companions as she not only had to deal with my absence from home for several months, but has also had to become "father" and head of the household. Joshua, Grace and Abigail, our children, were not embittered by my regular absence from them, but encouraged me to journey to the end. Kaakaabaale deserves special tribute because she relocated to be where I could not be, and became part of the family during my absence; and Stella Kasirye was available all the time as "elder daughter." Peace Mugobera, my "sister" ran my office effectively during the last year; and members of Thursday Fellowship, and the Family Fellowship, who proved that in Christ we are family.

To God Be the Glory

Abbreviations

BD	Bachelor of Divinity
CMS	Church Missionary Society
COU	Church of Uganda
CSCNWW	Centre for the Study of Christianity in the Non-Western World
DP	Democratic Party
DipTh	Diploma in Theology
FRONASA	Front for National Salvation
FOBA	Force Obote Back Again
KJV	King James Version
KOAB	*Ekibina kya 'Katonda Omu Ayinza Byona*
KY	Kabaka Yekka
n. d.	Not dated
MA	Master of Arts
MLitt	Master of Letters
MTh	Master of Theology
NSA	National Security Agency
NRA	National Resistance Army
NRA/M	National Resistance Army/Movement
NRM	National Resistance Movement
OI	Oral Interview
PA	Provincial Assembly
PAE	Provincial Assembly Executive
PhD	Doctor of Philosophy
UMSC	Uganda Muslim Supreme Council

UNLA	Uganda National Liberation Army
UPC	Uganda Peoples Congress
UPA	Uganda People's Army
UPF	Uganda People's Front
UPM	Uganda People's Movement

CHAPTER 1

Introduction

This work is a historical-ecclesiological study of the Church of Uganda, whose genesis is associated with the visit of the explorer-journalist, Henry Morton Stanley, to the Kabaka (king) of Buganda in April 1875. Subsequently, the Kabaka extended an invitation to Christian missionaries, and the first Church Missionary Society (CMS) missionaries arrived in Buganda in 1877. From those small beginnings the Church of Uganda has grown immensely and is, to date, the second largest church in Uganda, with a membership of over six and a half million people.[1]

The study focuses particularly on the socio-political context of post-independence Uganda, 1962–1992,[2] a period that was characterized by crises, and rapid, turbulent and often, violent, social-political changes that brought untold suffering to the peoples of Uganda. The aim of the study is

---

1. According to *The 1991 Population and Housing Census (National Summary) Uganda*, Entebbe: Statistics Department, Ministry of Finance and Economic Planning, Uganda, April 1994, 20–21, the membership of the Church of Uganda in 1991 stood at 6,541,830 (39.2% of the population) compared with 7,426,511 (44.5%) Roman Catholics, 1,758,101 (10.5%) Muslims and 934,908 (5.6%) classified as "other." The latter includes other Protestant groups such as the Seventh-Day Adventists, Baptists, Pentecostals and those who adhere to primal religions. The remaining 0.2% did not state their religious affiliation.

2. There are several publications that were released, focusing on this period of thirty years: Khiddu E. Makubuya, V. M. Mwaka and P. G. Okoth, eds., *Uganda: Thirty Years of Independence, 1962–1992 – Assessments* (Makerere University: The Committee for the Workshop, 1994); Alex Mukulu, *Thirty Years of Bananas* (Nairobi: Oxford University Press, 1993), a drama production that the author produced to coincide with the thirtieth anniversary of Uganda's independence; Phares Mutibwa, *Uganda since Independence: A Story of Unfulfilled Hopes* (Kampala: Fountain Publishers, 1992); James Tumusime, ed., *Uganda 30 Years, 1962–1992* (Kampala: Fountain Publishers, 1992).

to answer the question, "What did it mean to be 'church' in the historical socio-cultural-political context of Uganda?"

The question is answered firstly by narrating the story of the life and experience of the church in that socio-political context, and then, reflecting on how the story authenticates the Church of Uganda as "church." The first task of the study is therefore historical. It is to elucidate how the Church of Uganda adapted, accommodated, confronted, resisted, reformed, interacted with, survived, and acted as a faith-community. The second is theological. It is the task of reflection, grappling with ecclesiological questions: What it is about the Church of Uganda that authenticated it as "church" in the historical cultural-socio-political context of Uganda, and why it reacted the way it did to the various life situations that the context presented. The separation of the two tasks should not be construed as implying a split identity of the Church, one historical and the other theological. They are separated merely for methodological clarity.

Although the bulk of the original research was confined to the turbulent socio-political context of post-independence Uganda, the account begins with the origins and early growth of the Church of Uganda in the context of the kingdom of Buganda and an emerging Uganda, prior to independence. The issues and factors that impinge on the story of the Church in the post-independence period were latent in the pre-independence era. This thesis is therefore an account of the Church since 1875, with particular focus on the post-independence period, 1962–1992.

The study is limited to the Church of Uganda, hereafter referred to as the Church, a member of the worldwide Anglican Communion. An attempt to cover the entire church in Uganda in its diverse denominational expressions, though desirable, would be too extensive and unmanageable.

The year 1961/62 is a convenient starting point for original research because it was a watershed for both the Church and the country, Uganda. For the Church, 1961 marked the beginning of self-rule because it was the year that the Archbishop of Canterbury formally relinquished his authority over the eight dioceses in Uganda, Rwanda and Burundi. He installed Bishop Leslie Brown, the first Archbishop of the Province of the Church of

Uganda and Ruanda-Urundi,³ thereby granting administrative autonomy to the Church as a separate province. One year later, in 1962, Uganda gained her independence from Britain, after more than sixty years of colonial rule.

The criterion for determining the endpoint of our study, 1992, was based on the need for a long enough period for the original research in order to make a comparative longitudinal study possible. With this period of thirty years, key motifs, trends and milestones can be identified in the life of the Church of Uganda, making it possible to reflect on ecclesiological issues in the historical development of the Church of Uganda in post-independence turbulent context.

Ecclesiology in Contemporary African and Ugandan Scholarship

There are four identifiable approaches in ecclesiological studies in African theological scholarship: mission and church history; religion and politics or church-state relations; indigenous mission and ministry; and, thematic contextual ecclesiologies. In the first category are church histories, particularly of historic mission churches, and others that focus on the missionary heritage and its impact.⁴ While these studies contribute to an understand-

---

3. The name "Church of Uganda" is used throughout this thesis, to refer to the section of the Province in Uganda, even prior to the time when Uganda became a separate Province, after the creation of the Francophone Province, covering Rwanda, Burundi and Boga-Zaire in November 1979. See Appendix 1a, Chronology of Creation of Dioceses chronicles the creation of dioceses from 1960 to 1992.

4. Among the more notable mission and church histories are: J. F. Ajayi, *Christian Missions in Nigeria 1841–1891* (London: Longmans, 1965); E. A. Ayandele, *The Missionary Impact on Modern Nigeria, 1842–1914: A Political and Social Analysis* (London: Longmans, 1966); Ogbu Kalu, ed., *The History of Christianity in West Africa* (London: Longman, 1980); Zablon Nthamburi, ed., *From Mission to Church* (Nairobi: Uzima Press, 1982); Zablon Nthamburi, *The Methodist Church in Kenya* (Nairobi: Uzima Press, 1982); Lamin Sanneh, *West African Christianity: The Religious Impact* (Maryknoll, New York: Orbis Books, 1983).
Works on the Church of Uganda in this category include: M. Louise Pirouet, *Black Evangelists: The Spread of Christianity in Uganda 1891–1914* (London: Rex Collings, 1978); Tom Tuma, *Building a Ugandan Church: African Participation in Church Growth and Expansion in Busoga 1891–1940* (Nairobi: Kenya Literature Bureau, 1980); Tom Tuma and Phares Mutibwa, eds., *A Century of Christianity in Uganda* (Nairobi: Uzima Press, 1978); K. Ward, "A History of Christianity in Uganda," in *From Mission to Church*, ed. Z. Nthamburi (Nairobi: Uzima Press, 1982), 81–112.

ing of the missionary impact, and the historical roots and development of the churches in Africa, they do not develop contextual ecclesiologies. They seem to assume that the ecclesiologies of the "daughter" churches in Africa are the same as those of their founding mission churches in Europe or North America.

Church-state studies[5] focus on the nature and role of the church, and the state, and their relationship, and contribute significantly to an understanding of the interplay of Christianity and politics at the institutional level. This approach is what has dominated the study of the Church of Uganda in the pre- and post-independence socio-political turbulence of Uganda.[6] In this regard, Hansen has distinguished three levels of analysis: the ideological, the sociological and the institutional. At the ideological level, the presupposition is that a "certain religion by its doctrine and ethos

---

5. Some of the Church and State studies are: C. Hallencreutz and A. Mayo, eds., *Church and State in Zimbabwe* (Gweru: Mambo Press, 1988); Eliewaha E. Mshana, "Church and State in the Independent States of Africa," *African Theological Journal* 5 (1972); Zablon Nthamburi, "The Donatist Controversy as a Paradigm for Church and State," *African Theological Journal* 7, no. 3 (1988): 196–206;

6. The following works have handled the study of the church in Uganda from the religion-and-politics approach: Holger B. Hansen, "Church and State in a Colonial Context," in *Imperialism, the State and the Third World*, ed. M. Twaddle (London: British Academic Press, 1992), 95–123; Holger B. Hansen, "Church and State in Early Colonial Uganda," *African Affairs* 85, no. 338 (January 1986): 55–74; Holger B. Hansen, *Mission, Church and State in a Colonial Setting, Uganda, 1890–1925* (London: Heinemann, 1984); Holger B. Hansen, "Religion and Politics in Independent Uganda: The Role of the Religious Factor in Ugandan Politics and a Discussion of the Conceptual Framework," University of Copenhagen: unpublished paper prepared for the Workshop on Religion and Politics, E.C.P.R. Joint Session, Brussels, April 1979; Kathlene G. Lockard, "Religion and Political Development in Uganda, 1962-72," University of Wisconsin: unpublished PhD dissertation, 1974; Dan Mudoola, "Religion and Politics in Uganda: The Case of Busoga, 1900-1962," *African Affairs* 77, no. 306 (January 1978): 22–35; Edward B. Muhima, "Church and State," Kampala: unpublished paper presented at Salt and Light Conference, Kampala, November 1992; Akiiki B. Mujaju, "Church and State Relations in Rapidly Changing Societies," Makerere University: unpublished public lecture in memory of Archbishop Janani Luwum, Kampala, February 1989. Kevin Ward, "The Church of Uganda amidst Conflict: The Interplay between Church and Politics in Uganda since 1962," in *Religion and Politics in East Africa*, eds. H. B. Hansen and M. Twaddle (London: James Currey, 1995), 72–105; F. B. Welbourn, *Religion and Politics in Uganda 1952–62* (Nairobi: East African Publishing House, 1965). Edward Muhima's study, "The Fellowship of His Suffering: A Theological Interpretation of Christian Suffering under Idi Amin" North Western University: unpublished PhD thesis, 1981, is unique in its approach. It is historical-theological, and therefore has a similar approach to this study. However while Muhima focuses on the theme of suffering only, and limited his study to the Idi Amin era, this thesis examines the corporate life of the Church in a wider historical context.

inspires a socio-political ideology or attitude, which again is reflected in a specific secular behaviour."⁷ The sociological approach "emphasises the capacity of religion to form social groupings, mainly manifesting itself in pluralistic situations."⁸ The religious divisions "constitute [thus] the major grouping principle, and religion serves as a means to express group identity, while the objectives may be purely secular or a mixture of religious and secular elements."⁹ The institutional approach is "concerned with the organisational expression of religion. Frequently this dimension is identical with what is normally termed the Church-State problem."¹⁰

The demerits of the religion-in-politics approach, and its church-and-state variant, accrue from its theoretical premise of the secular-sacred Cartesian worldview, and the preoccupation with the institutional model of the church. By positing the church and the state or Christianity and politics as two separate arenas, church-state studies do not address the theological issues in the interplay. Hansen himself has acknowledged the limitations of the approach. He has observed a methodological dilemma, that although, at the sociological level, the approach helps to identify three religio-political groups – Catholics, Muslims and Protestants – during the early period of the planting of Christianity in Buganda, the difficulty is to isolate "what is religion and what is politics in this configuration."¹¹ The preoccupation with institutional elements of the church detracts from other aspects of "being church."¹²

Most of the works that address indigenous church mission and ministry describe the status of the mission and ministries of particular churches and then assess to what extent they are indigenous.¹³ Indigenization is interpreted to mean:

---

7. Hansen, "Religion and Politics in Independent Uganda," 16.
8. Ibid., 17.
9. Ibid.
10. Ibid.
11. Ibid., 5.
12. Avery Dulles, in his book *Models of the Church* (Garden City New York: Image Books, 1978), has identified four other models or aspects of the church in addition to the institutional one. They are: mystical communion, sacrament, herald and servant.
13. Among those that describe and evaluate particular churches' missions and ministries are: Efraim Andersson, *Churches at the Grass-root* (London: Lutterworth Press, 1969); Bolaji Idowu, *Towards an Indigenous Church* (London: Oxford University Press, 1965);

To Africanise Christianity, that is, give it an indelible African character . . . a type of Christianity here which will bear the imprint MADE IN AFRICA, and which is not a cheap imitation of the type of Christianity found elsewhere or a periods in the past. This involves Africanising Church structures, personnel, theology, planning, commitment, worship, transaction of its mission, and financial independence.[14]

The methodology of the majority of the essays on mission and ministry is to prescribe what "ought to be" by reflecting on "what is." These essays elucidate the need and the direction of Africanizing forms and structures. Their limitation, however, is that by making it their goal to prescribe "what ought," they do not sufficiently grapple with "what is."

Thematic studies have generally followed the contextualization-inculturation approach, whereby distinctive features of the primal religio-cultural African context provide the theological starting point for constructing what may be called African ecclesiologies. Themes like community,[15] clan,[16]

N. N. Getui, "The Family, the Church and Development of the Youth," in *The Church in African Christianity: Innovative Essays in Ecclesiology,* eds. J. N. K. Mugambi and L. Magesa (Nairobi: Initiatives Publishers, 1990); B. Kisembo, L. Magesa, and A. Shorter, eds., *African Christian Marriage* (London: Geoffrey Chapman, 1977); John S. Mbiti, *The Crisis of Mission in Africa* (Kampala: Uganda Church Press, 1971); Anne Nasimiyu-Wasikye, "African Women's Legitimate Role in Church Ministry," in *The Church in African Christianity: Innovative Essays in Ecclesiology,* eds. J. N. K. Mugambi, and L. Magesa (Nairobi: Initiatives Publishers, 1990); D. W. Waruta, "Towards an African Church," in *The Church in African Christianity: Innovative Essays in Ecclesiology,* eds. J. N. K. Mugambi, and L. Magesa (Nairobi: Initiatives Publishers, 1990).

14. Mbiti, *Crisis of Mission in Africa,* 2.

15. Those that have utilized the theme of community include: Manas Buthelezi, "In Christ - One Community," *Africa Theological Journal* 7, no. 1 (1979); and John Mbiti, "The Ways and Means of Communicating the Gospel," in *Christianity in Tropical Africa,* ed. C. G. Baeta (London: Oxford University Press, 1968), 329–347.

16. Those that have utilized the theme of clan include: Josiah Kibira, *The Church, Clan and the World* (Upsala: Almenist and Wiskell, 1974); Roland J. Payne, "The Influence of the Concept of the Traditional African Leadership on the Concept of Church Leadership," *Africa Theological Journal* 1 (February 1968): 69–74; Abisai Shejavali, "The Influence of the Concept of the Traditional African Leadership on the Concept of Church Leadership," *Africa Theological Journal* 1 (February 1968): 75–82; John M. Waliggo, "The African Clan as the True Model of the African Church," in *The Church in African Christianity: Innovative Essays in Ecclesiology,* eds. J. N. K. Mugambi and L. Magesa (Nairobi: Initiatives Publishers, 1990).

and ancestors[17] are some of those that have been utilized. The merits of these thematic-inculturation studies accrue from the fact that they take seriously the assumption that a church must be indigenous to its context if it is to function effectively as a faith community. Starting with the primal religio-cultural context accords credibility to both the church and the context. The church is not portrayed as a resident alien, nor is the context judged as inconsequential in impacting the church. On the contrary there is recognition that the church "becomes" in context. However the major pitfall with contextual African ecclesiologies so far is that they have tended to limit "context" to the primal religio-cultural background.

The present study is a historical-contextual-theological account of the Church of Uganda, combining a historical approach with contextual-theological reflection. "Context" is not limited to the primal religio-cultural milieu, but also to the socio-political context. In both pre- and post-independence periods, there are both religio-cultural and socio-political aspects that impacted the Church in varying degrees. The contextual-theological approach dictates that attention is given to considering indigenous perspectives to the notion of "religion," the indigenous apprehension of the gospel, and to the church as an indigenous community. In order to handle and interpret the whole experiential reality of the Church, in its "becoming" in the multifaceted historical context of the pre- and post-independence Uganda, a contextual theoretical paradigm is utilized; it is "the church in the world" approach.[18] This paradigm enables us to elucidate an indigenous contextual-ecclesiology.

---

17. Among those who have utilized the ancestral theme are: Benezet Bujo, who has devoted a large section entitled "The Theology of the Ancestors as the Starting Point for a New Ecclesiology" in his book *African Theology in Its Social Context* (Maryknoll, New York: Orbis Books, 1992); E. Fashole-Luke, "Ancestral Veneration and the Communion of Saints," in *New Testament Christianity for Africa and the World*, eds. M. Glasswell and E. Fashole-Luke (London: SPCK 1974), 209–221; Charles Nyamiti, "The Church as Christ's Ancestral Mediation: An Essay in African Ecclesiology," in *The Church in African Christianity: Innovative Essays in Ecclesiology*, eds. J. N. K. Mugambi and L. Magesa (Nairobi: Initiatives Publishers, 1990).

18. I owe my first interest to this approach to Robert E. Webber, *The Church in the World: Opposition, Tension, or Transformation* (Grand Rapids: Zondervan Publishing House, 1986). Later my study of the East African Revival convinced me of its value as an approach to the study of the church.

The Church in the World: A Methodology

"The church in the world" approach to the study of the Church of Uganda has four features. First, it is coherent with the primary understanding of the church as a theological entity, a community of faith. The assertion that it is *a community* relates to those elements of its self-hood that identify it as part of human society; and the assertion that it is a community *of faith* implies a distinct identity which delineates it as "church" in society. The two concepts – "church in the world," and "community of faith," have the same logic.

Second, it builds on the basic assumption that both the church and the world are the arena for the sacred-secular drama. So it cannot be said that the construct "church in the world" posits two realms, one sacred and the other secular. On the contrary, it emphasizes the common heritage of the church and the world. To illustrate: when a natural disaster strikes an area, or civil chaos and turbulence wreck a community, the church as a community that shares in the ordinary life of the here and now, will also share in the suffering resulting from the disaster. The faith of the church community will be expressed in the context of that turbulence.

Third, unlike the church-state approach that tends to limit its analysis primarily to the institutional aspects of the church, the "church in the world" approach has the capacity to handle the total life of the church. For, while it assumes essential continuity and convergence between the church and the world, it demands that a critical distinction be maintained. The idea of a distinct community posits an institutional dimension because, as H. Richard Niebuhr has stated, "no community can exist without some institutions that give it form, boundaries, discipline, and the possibilities of expression and common action."[19] Thus the "church in the world" framework requires that consideration be made on the institutional aspects as well as the communitarian, in the process of examining the symbiotic relation and distinction between the church and the world.

Fourth, the approach is rooted in the Church's story. It is implicit in the whole of the Church's story and explicitly enunciated in the East African

---

19. H. Richard Niebuhr, *The Purpose of the Church and Its Ministry* (New York: Harper and Brothers, 1956), 22.

Revival, otherwise called the *Balokole* Revival.[20] The Revival, discussed in chapter 3, was a movement of renewal and reform, originating from among the indigenous lay people of the Protestant Church in Uganda, and members of the Ruanda Mission, a small mission formed out of the Church Missionary Society (CMS)[21] in the late 1920s. The Revival is particularly significant for this thesis because of its impact on the story of the Church and as the source of the "church in the world" methodological paradigm. It is the way the gospel was appropriated in indigenous categories in the Revival that provides a starting point for conceptualising the approach.

The Gospel, Christian Faith and Community in the Revival

The East African Revival has been credited, by both internal and external sources, to be one of the most significant movements in the history of the Church of Uganda.[22] Its impact is recognized at two levels: first,

---

20. In most literature the two names "East African Revival" and *Balokole* are used synonymously; "East African" referring to the geographical extent of the movement, and *Balokole* as reference to people internal to the movement – *Balokole*, technically less correct than *Abalokole*, is a Luganda word which literally means the "saved ones." "East African Revival" is most commonly used among the *Balokole*. They use "East African Revival" to refer to the movement and *Balokole* or "revival brethren" or just "brethren" to refer to the people. See for example Dorothy W. Smoker, *Ambushed by Love* (Fort Washington: Christian Literature Crusade, 1993); James Katarikawe and John Wilson "The East African Revival Movement," Fuller Theological Seminary: unpublished MTh and MA Thesis, 1975; and Bill Butler, *Hill Ablaze* (London: Hodder and Stoughton, 1976), all accounts by *Balokole*. In this thesis the name used to refer to the movement is "East African Revival," or just "the Revival," and *Balokole* to refer to its adherents. The movement spread to the Eastern Africa Countries of Kenya, Tanzania and Southern Sudan.

21. The Ruanda Mission was founded in protest to what was perceived by its founders to be liberal and modernist theological influence in the CMS. Three principles were affirmed in their constitution:
1) The Ruanda Council and the missionaries of the Ruanda General Medical Mission stand for the complete inspiration of the whole Bible as being, and not only containing, the Word of God.
2) Their determination is to proclaim full and free salvation through simple faith in Christ's atoning death upon the cross.
3) They are satisfied that they have received from the CMS full guarantees to safeguard the future of the RGMM on Bible, Protestant and Keswick lines. Stanley Smith, *Road to Revival* (London: Church Missionary Society, 1946), 42.

22. This view expressed by, for example: Archbishop Leslie Brown, *Three Worlds: One Word* (London: Rex Collings, 1981), 115–118; Archbishop Janani Luwum, in his "Foreword"

in increasing the degree of involvement and commitment to the Church; and second, in making the gospel "become incarnated more deeply and radically into African patterns of thinking and action, a genuinely African expression of Christianity."[23] The latter gave rise to the former. It is because the Revival ethos emanated from the integration and blending of the gospel with the core elements of traditional culture that it led to a greater commitment of its members to the Church.

The identity of the Revival hinged on the two motifs: the cross of Christ – a central motif of the gospel, and the clan-community – a defining element of traditional-cultural society.

According to the Revival, the core of the gospel is the Christ-event; that is, the historical birth, life, death, resurrection and ascension of Jesus of Nazareth, and the "coming" of the Holy Spirit at Pentecost. The hinge of the Christ-event is taken to be Jesus' death on the cross, the defining moment of his salvation mission. The *Balokole* believe that:

> The death of our Lord Jesus Christ on the Cross is the focal point of history. The books of the Old Testament point to it. The Gospels describe it in detail, and the Epistles look back to it. The Salvation of mankind is bound up with the Cross of Christ.[24]

Therefore, authentic Christian faith, in Revival terms, is a function of the relationship of an individual, and by extension, of a community, with the cross of Christ.

The discussion of the validity of positing Jesus' death on the cross as the soteriological hinge of the Christ-event is beyond the scope of this thesis. What is significant for our study is that the *Balokole* focused on the Christ-event as the ground of faith.

---

to Tom Tuma and Phares Mutibwa, eds., *A Century of Christianity in Uganda 1877–1977* (Nairobi: Uzima Press, 1978), xiv; John V. Taylor, *Processes of Growth in an African Church* (International Missionary Council Research Pamphlets 6), (London: SCM Press, 1958), 15–16; Archbishop Silvanus Wani, "How to Make Christ Relevant to My People: The Story of the Church of Uganda," a seminar paper, n.d., 5, 12.

23. Kevin Ward, "'TukutendererezaYesu': The Balokole Revival in Uganda," in *From Mission to Church*, ed. Z. Nthamburi (Nairobi: Uzima Press, 1982), 113.

24. J. E. Church, *Every Man a Bible Student*, rev. ed. (Exeter: Paternoster Press, 1976), 54.

Although faith was understood to be an individual's experience, in the Revival it was recognized that personal faith could only be sustained in the context of the community, "the fellowship," in which and through which, faith was expressed. Describing the centrality of "fellowship meeting" in Revival spirituality, Stanley Smith wrote:

> The Fellowship Meeting: Every revived Christian stands in need of fellowship with some fellow believers with whom he can meet regularly . . . It does not take the place of the ordinary services and meetings of the Church . . . its essential feature is that it is a time of sharing spiritual experiences in the presence of Christ, where all meet in Him on a level of equality.[25]

It is in "the fellowship," the community of those "at the foot of the Cross," that the individual identity found its basis. This echoes John Mbiti's axiomatic statement about the primacy of the community in defining individual identity in African traditional culture: "I am because we are; and since we are, therefore I am."[26] Like the African clan-community, based on blood kinship, the "fellowship" is the *faith*-community based on the kinship engendered by "the cleansing blood of Jesus."[27]

Thus, the Revival provides the theological point of departure for this thesis: that the church is a Christo-centric social entity. In other words, the entity "church" is defined by two realities: the Christ-event, that is, the historical birth, life, death, resurrection and ascension of Jesus of Nazareth, and the "coming" of the Holy Spirit at Pentecost; and the historical, religio-cultural and social-political *sitz im leben* of a particular community. The church is both a *faith* community and a *community* of faith. It has a dual origin but a single identity.

Faith originates in the gospel. The historical Christ-event is the kernel of the gospel: Jesus, who was born in Bethlehem, lived in first-century Palestine, died at Calvary, resurrected and ascended. But the Christ-event

---

25. Smith, *Road to Revival*, 143.
26. John Mbiti, *African Traditional Religions and Philosophy* (London: Heineman, 1969), 108–109.
27. 1 John 1:7. This is a very frequently quoted portion by the *Balokole*.

is also rooted in eternity – past, present and future. The incarnate Christ is he who "was with God from the beginning,"[28] who "was, and is, and is to come,"[29] – he is God's self-revelation for the salvation of created order. The proclamation of this gospel among a people in a particular historical, religio-cultural and social-political context, yields a faith-community, the church. Faith is therefore a category of relation between the church and the Christ-event.

The church embodies the gospel in experience and transmission, as the church proclaims it in any particular context. As the community that embodies the gospel, the church is itself not external to the context, but is a participant in it. John Mbiti expressed this well:

> The church as the Body of Christ is herself the living channel, par excellence, of communicating the Gospel. Not only does she teach and proclaim the Gospel but she is the embodiment of that gospel; and her voice goes forth not only in audible words but in her very existence and life. As she makes her numerical expansion and spiritual growth, there the Gospel is being proclaimed and communicated. She cannot be severed from her message, and neither can that message become meaningful except within the embrace of the church.[30]

A history of proclamation has therefore evolved a tradition, rooted in the proclamation by the apostles of Jesus, recorded in the New Testament and continued in various forms throughout the centuries. The church is the bearer and conveyor of that tradition, the custodian of the Christ-narrative, the subject of the narrative and locus of faith praxis. Since the Christ-event is rooted in eternity – past, present and future – to be related with the Christ-event is to be connected to eternity. Thus the roots of the church's being are in eternity, and her future in the eschaton. This is the span of the faith-life of the church.

The authenticity of the Church of Uganda as "church" is therefore to be judged on the basis of its corporate relation with the Christ-event. This

---

28. John 1:2.
29. Rev 4:8.
30. Mbiti, "The Ways and Means," 337.

was essentially what the Revival movement was about, in its emphasis on salvation in Christ as the only legitimate basis for being a real Christian. Without subscribing to the legalistic and external demands that the distinction "saved" and "not-saved" entailed among the *Balokole*, it has to be recognized that the essence of that distinction was faith, the relation with the Christ-event.

The Church as a Community

The assertion that the church is a *community* points to a relationship between the church and the society in a particular epoch. At the primary level, the notion of "community" assumes shared temporality: that the church is a historical reality, in space and time. "Community" is what describes the church's being in the world.

The complex question of the character of "Christian community" in particular, and "religious community" in general, has attracted much discussion in sociology and theology. In his study of the relationship between the gospel and culture, Richard Niebuhr has suggested that there are five types of relationships that span the Christ-Culture spectrum. They are: opposition – Christ against Culture; agreement – Christ of Culture; synthetic – Christ above Culture; polarity and tension – Christ and Culture in Paradox; and, conversionist – Christ as transformer of Culture.[31]

Roy Wallis, in elaborating how religious communities relate to the wider society in which they are, has developed a triangular typology within which the orientation to the world of any new religious community can be placed.[32] Wallis' triad-polar is constituted by: first, the "world-rejecting" orientation, whereby the religious community "views the prevailing social order as having departed substantially from God's prescriptions and plan";[33] second, the "world-affirming" orientation, in which spiritual potential can be realized without the need to withdraw from the world;[34] and third, the

---

31. H. Richard Niebuhr, *Christ and Culture* (New York: Harper and Row Publishers, 1951).
32. Roy Wallis, *The Elementary Forms of the New Religious Life* (London: Routledge & Kegan Paul, 1984), 10.
33. Ibid.
34. Ibid., 22.

"world-accommodating" orientation, in which religion "provides solace or stimulation to personal, interior life" in the world.[35]

Robert Webber has proposed a similar typology to Wallis', arising from church history and the historical mission-orientation of the church to the world.[36] Webber has argued:

> First there is the witness of the church *against* the world, such as that in the early church; second, the model of the church and the world in *paradox*, which has antecedents in early Constantianism; and third, the model of the church in *transforming* culture, which is rooted in Augustine and elaborated in the medieval period. However, the classic expressions of these three theological models are found among the Reformers . . . by the Anabaptists (church and world in antithesis); second, . . . Martin Luther (church and world in paradox); and finally, . . . John Calvin (church transforming the world).[37]

Niebuhr's, Wallis' and Webber's typologies are present in the history of Church of Uganda, as it was "formed" in the "world" of Uganda. The Revival ethos provides an approach to reflecting on the story of the Church that acknowledges the presence of all the types in the one historical community. The approach is hinged on the way the Balokole perceived the world.

The Balokole perceived the "world" as a complex blend of at least three realities. The first reality is the "world" in its created form – the world as the universe, people, and the arena of human existence. The second, is the "world" of adverse spiritual agencies at work in people, institutions, and through people; manifested in acts of lust of all sorts, hatred, selfishness, greed, murder, violence, and perversion. This is the "world" whose god is Satan, "the prince of the power of the air" (Eph 2:2). This "world" is to be shunned and rejected. The third reality of the "world" accrues from the individual and community's praxis in created world in relation to the "world" of adverse spiritual forces. The people and institutions whose character and life is shaped by those forces are characterized as "worldly." "World" here is

---

35. Ibid., 35.
36. Webber, *The Church in the World*.
37. Ibid., 81.

used as a label of the social reality unlike "them," a distinction engendered by the faith-relation with the Christ-event. In Revival terminology, it is the distinction between the "saved ones" from the "not-saved": a distinction that the Balokole deduced from the biblical exhortation to "be in the world" but "not of the world."[38] Although many of the Balokole perceived the idea of "separation from the world" to connote a rejection of the world, an in-depth study of Revival ethos indicates that "to be separated from the world" primarily meant a disposition to the world that sought to maintain a distinct identity and life-style based on the faith-relation with the Christ-event, and the consequent perpetual existential tension of the faith-life in the world.

What the Revival emphasized is that Christian faith distinguishes the created world from worldliness, affirming the former and shunning the latter. For them the calling of the faith community is to be in the world without being worldly. Without subscribing to every thing that the Revival espouses, what is significant for this study methodologically is the Revival premise that the distinction between the church and the world is based on faith. The perspective employed in this thesis is that a history of the Church of Uganda is a history of a *faith*-community; an account of the manifestation of its faith-relation with the Christ-event in the historical setting of Uganda.

Part of the thesis of this study is that any account of a church is incomplete without an account of the world where it explicates its faith-life. In order to narrate the story of a faith community, one needs to narrate as well the story of the society in which the community explicates its faith. The point here is that the process of being and becoming "church" is shaped by the "world." Herein lies the intersection of history and theology, in the fact that it is only in a concrete historical context that the church becomes. History here should not be understood as referring only to ecclesiastical history but the ecclesial-contextual history as well. It is therefore imperative that a study of the Church of Uganda takes serious account of the context in which it is becoming church. Hence, the historical-theological approach to the study of the Church that is the feature of this thesis.

---

38. John 17:13–19.

Faith and Narrative

It has been postulated that the essence of being and becoming "church" is faith, visible in a concrete world. The world in which the church lives out its reality is always subjective. It is the "world" as "it is" not as "it ought to be"; the world as it is apprehended by those who live in it. Therefore the task of the researcher is to "name" that world according to the perceptions of those who live in it, to capture its nuances, contradictions, challenges and opportunities, as they are perceived by those who dwell in it. It is "in this world" that the church as a community of faith is being formed.

The way to apprehend that world and the faith engendered in it is by description. Bolaji Idowu has asserted:

> The cogent fact (here) is that no one has ever seen or touched "faith." Faith only becomes known as it realises or actualises itself in expressions. And expressions of faith by persons must reduce themselves into forms, which can be described in categories.[39]

H. Jackson Forstman has echoed the same argument in clarifying the nature of the Christian faith, that, "Christian faith is a relationship between a man and his God brought about in response to the proclamation of Jesus Christ . . . it cannot be argued; it can only be described."[40] Narrative is the category of description that is adopted in this thesis because of its capacity to elucidate faith. The merit of narrative as a descriptive tool is its capacity to combine event and interpretation together. Stanley Hauerwas and Gregory Jones have made the case well for narrative as a method:

> Narrative is neither just an account of genre criticism nor a faddish appeal to the importance of telling stories; rather it is a crucial conceptual category for such matters as understanding issues of epistemology and methods of argument, depicting

---

[39]. Idowu, *African Traditional Religion: A Definition* (London: SCM Press, 1973), 27.
[40]. H. Jackson Forstman, *Christian Faith and the Church* (St Louis, Missouri: The Bethany Press, 1965), 32.

personal identity, and displaying the content of Christian convictions.[41]

What constitutes a narrative are: people, events, places, and the network of relations and issues about them. What gives credibility to a faith-narrative is if a person of faith tells the story in which he or she is a participant – gives an oral testimony. The parameters for determining the sources for the narrative are therefore based on "testimony." The distinction between subjectivity and objectivity of the source is irrelevant because the subject of inquiry – faith – belongs to the realm of experience, which combines events and their interpretation from the perspective of an existential faith-relation.

Sources and Research Process

The necessity to access existential perspectives demanded that primary attention in the research was given to internal sources; sources that originate from active players, those who were part of the unfolding drama, so that they were telling not someone else's account but their own. This was crucial since the project depended on an accurate "naming" of their world. It is those who were active participants in the events that they narrate, that are most able to name their world as they experienced and lived in it; its nuances, struggles, hopes, fears, and prospects. First-hand experience accords credibility to the narrator as source of a faith narrative.

This is what distinguishes the genesis account of the Church, covered in chapter 2, from the rest of the thesis, in that the former relies primarily on second-hand narrators. But even then an attempt has been made to tell the story from the perspective of the indigenous players.

The nature of the study demanded that the research was qualitative rather than quantitative. The primary sources accessed may be categorized into five types. First are the publications by authors who were present, as participants and not merely as observers, in the events they describe. Second are the numerous unpublished papers by students and critics whose heritage and historical involvement in the particular area or conflict they write about precludes a merely "objective" narrative or assessment. These were

---

41. Stanley Hauerwas and Gregory Jones, eds., *Why Narrative? Readings in Narrative Theology* (Grand Rapids, Michigan: Eerdmans, 1989), 5.

found in several archives and in personal holdings. Of particular benefit were the numerous unpublished dissertations, most of them by students of Bishop Tucker Theological College.[42] These dissertations contain primary material, as they are a result of primary research done in the various areas in Uganda. The majority of them are a fruit of interviews with eyewitnesses.

The third type is government-orientated newspaper articles[43] and published government position papers. The merit of these sources does not lie in objectivity or accurateness of record, but rather in the fact that they portray the government version of the incidents reported, a perspective that is necessary for understanding the whole socio-political context of the Church.

The fourth category of sources comprises official documents of the Church, such as records of proceedings of meetings and correspondences, most of them found in the Archives of the Church of Uganda, housed at the Provincial secretariat at Namirembe. The significance of these sources lies in the fact that they are the deposit of the institution's perspective and memory of the events and the issues as they unfolded. They are therefore a critical source for elucidating the institutional narrative.

The fifth category of sources is oral interviews of leaders who were present as eyewitnesses or players in the drama of events in the Church. The thesis draws heavily on these interviews as the best way of telling the story of the Church; an approach based on the premise that their story is the part of the story of the Church.

Prior to going to the field, a questionnaire was developed that was intended for circulation and as a guide in the interviewing process. The initial filled questionnaires that were returned gave a very unsatisfactory response both in percentage returns and content. I decided therefore that rather than circulate a questionnaire, the questions would serve as a guide in interviewing informants.[44] Although this involved much more expenditure

---

42. Most of these are held at the Bishop Tucker Theological Library Archives, and at the Department of Religious Studies, Makerere University.

43. Newspaper reports were accessed from the newspaper holdings in the Africana Section of Makerere University Library, which have retained material from the 1960s to the present day.

44. The sample of questions that were used as a guide in the interviewing process is provided in the Appendix 1b.

in terms of money and time, I found it to be a more effective way of accessing the oral sources because I was able to determine more concretely the integrity of their account.

The discussion of the place and the management of oral sources in a historical study like this one is beyond the scope of this thesis.[45] The one issue that warrants a brief comment here is the reliability and integrity of oral sources for a historical account. In my view there are two critical factors that determine the reliability and integrity of oral sources. First, the contextual structures of custody and transmission of memory; and second, the mnemonic and transmission capacity of the particular source selected. In communities where the primary custodian and conveyor of the corporate memory is oral tradition, oral sources are deemed as reliable as written sources are in a print-tradition context. It should be noted that the substance of corporate memory is not just events as they happened, but rather events as they were interpreted from the perspective of their significance to the community, which is what constitutes tradition.

The integrity of oral data, in an oral tradition context, has to be judged on the basis of the capacity of the source to retain the memory and pass it on, rather than on the basis of orality. The same is true of the integrity of written sources within the written tradition; the reliability of the written material should be judged on the basis of the credentials of the source, rather than merely on literacy. For in a community where information is conveyed orally, not everyone has the capacity to preserve the memory and articulate it, the two crucial elements that determine the quality of an oral source. The third element is time. The farther away, in temporal terms, the source is from the events described the less credible is the source singularly, and hence the need to collate the evidence from many sources to establish the existence of a tradition. In the case of contemporary events, the oral source is more reliable when the data given is not hearsay but an eye-witness account.

---

45. Some of the works that deal with oral historiography are: David Bebbington, *Patterns in History: A Christian Perspective on Historical Thought* (Leicester: Apollos, 1990); David Henige, *Oral Historiography* (London: Longman, 1982); Jan Vansina, *Oral Tradition: A Study in Historical Methodology*, trans. H. M. Wright (London: Routledge and Kegan Paul, 1965); Jan Vansina, *Oral Tradition as History* (London: James Currey, 1985).

The contemporary nature of the issues and events that were the subject of the research for this thesis was advantageous in according to the sources a higher degree of accuracy of their accounts, because the events were still in living memory. Moreover, for many of the people interviewed, their accounts were their life histories. In order to ensure an even higher degree of reliability, a deliberate choice was made to select informants who were recognized as leader-elders in the community, because it is they who were perceived and perceive themselves as the custodians and transmitters of the community's memory. In oral cultures, community leadership is conferred on the basis of seniority in experience and ability to pass on that experience to succeeding generations; those who are able to recall the past into the present. An indispensable quality to community leadership is the capacity to articulate the tradition of the community, a reference to the narrative that has formed it. Even though there are other conveyors of tradition such as cultural institutions, symbols and events, they still require an oral commentary. Again, it is the elders that are the custodians of these commentaries. For example, among the Baganda, the *Bataka*, as the leaders and elders of the different clans of the Baganda, are expected to "be knowledgeable in the history and traditions of the clan"[46] and to pass on that knowledge and heritage to succeeding generations.

Research Limitations

The experiential element in the sources and the contemporary nature of the issues and events that were the subject of the research posed some limitations. The fact that the events are contemporary and many of the people that were involved are still alive, led some people to decline being interviewed for concerns of safety and privacy. In two instances informants declined being interviewed, and in one an informant requested to remain anonymous. Thankfully all the major archives, at the Diocesan centres and at the Provincial secretariat at Namirembe, granted me unrestricted access.

The challenges and limitations that the Church archives presented arose from lack of organization and loss of records. At the time of field research, the materials in the main archives of the Church of Uganda at the

---

46. Waliggo, "The African Clan," 123.

Provincial secretariat at Namirembe were not catalogued in a manner that would make them easily accessible. They were all stuffed in boxes, generally classified as: "Provincial Assembly Papers," "Archbishop's Papers," "House of Bishops Papers," and so on. This made the task of accessing the material arduous and sometimes frustrating.

Lack of archival organization was compounded by loss of records. After several attempts to locate the Church newspaper, *The New Day*, renamed *The New Century* in 1977, I was informed by the Church archivist that they were not available in any of the two main Church archives; the one housed at the Provincial Secretariat, and the other in Bishop Tucker Theological College Library. The situation was even harder with diocesan archives. One entire morning spent in the Archives of the Diocese of Soroti, in Teso, did not yield much because, according to the diocesan secretary, the records were either lost or misplaced. In the case of Namirembe diocese archives, where I searched for material associated with the Church in Luwero during the Luwero war in the Obote II regime, no data was found because, apparently, it was destroyed during the war.

Though there were not many secondary sources on the Church of Uganda, especially during the post-independence period, many authors have discussed some of the issues that relate to the methodology of the thesis, the socio-political history of Uganda, the Church of Uganda and the theological questions that the study raises. These sources are acknowledged where they have had a direct bearing on the study.

Thesis Development

The "church in the world" methodological approach dictates that in dealing with ecclesiastical material, space is given to elucidating the historical-material context of "world" in which the Church was formed. It is highlighting the features of the "world" of the Church that gives content to the preposition "in" in the paradigm "church in the world." The account in each chapter therefore has a dual focus, on the world and the church, which elucidates the symbiotic relationship between the two as it chronicles the distinctiveness of the church.

The World

Rather than begin the account of the genesis of the Church, in chapter 2, with the missionary origins in Europe, the chapter begins with a brief description of the cardinal elements of Kiganda society, the "world" to which the missionaries came, and in which the Church first took root. The religio-cultural and socio-political structural relations of pre-colonial Buganda influenced the process of evangelization and the growth of the Church. In each of the succeeding chapters space is given, first to explicate the critical features of the socio-political "world" of the Church in the different periods and areas under study, as part of narrating the story of the Church, before dealing with ecclesiastical material. The socio-political narrative belongs as much to the Church as does the ecclesiastical.

What makes post-independence Uganda a significant "world," is its characteristic feature of social-political turbulence.[47] In a period of thirty years, 1962–1992, Uganda had no less than ten governments, ranging from military dictatorship to elected multiparty democracy; and no less than five civil wars, affecting all four regions at different times, in particular Buganda, Northern and North Eastern regions. It is reckoned that during these periods of internal violent conflict, over half a million people were killed and a total of over two million people displaced at different times. This, together with all the associated social and political upheavals, caused immense suffering to the Ugandan people, in their families and communities.

In an attempt to explain the roots of the cycle of turbulence in post-independence Uganda, political scientist Gingyera Pinycwa has postulated that:

> Generally, in Africa today, to have a president from a given sector of a country always results in other people taking it for granted that that particular sector is as a whole dominant in

---

47. All the socio-political analysts of post-independence Uganda are agreed on this: A. G. G. Gingyera-Pinycwa, *Northern Uganda in National Politics* (Kampala: Fountain Publishers, 1992); Samwiri Karugire, *Roots of Instability in Uganda* (Kampala: Fountain Publishers, 1996); Eriya Kategaya in his "Foreword" to J. Tumusime, ed., *Uganda 30 Years 1962–1992* (Kampala: Fountain Publishers, 1992); Mukulu, *Thirty Years of Bananas*; Mutibwa, *Uganda since Independence*.

the political system, even if the President attempts to spread out his appointments to higher officers of state as well as development projects throughout the country. Nor is it generally taken into account that the vast masses of the people from the President's home area will generally neither come near him nor acquire, during his tenure of office, anything extra to improve their hard lot in life. Should large numbers of the security forces also happen to hail from the President's particular sector of the country, then the verdict as to the dominance of that sector is deemed verified beyond any reasonable doubt. Again the lot of the ordinary masses in the sector where such a President and his fellow tribesmen in the armed forces come from is not considered important: the particular sector of the country as a whole will be seen as in political ascendancy in the country.[48]

Accordingly, the political landscape is divided into two groups: those who are considered to dominate political power, and those who perceive them as dominant, and by default consider themselves left out. Because the former is considered to access the benefits of political ascendancy, in the same way "their misdeeds tend to be also attributed to all the people from the sector from which the leader comes."[49] This is true of the post-independence political developments of Uganda. What Gingyera-Pinycwa does not include in his postulation is the violent nature of political transition that was characteristic of post-independence Uganda. It is violence that escalated suspicion and vengeance, leading to a cycle of turbulence. Turbulence constituted the organising principal for the selection of the case studies.

The first of the turbulent-context case studies, covered in chapter 4, is Buganda during the period when Uganda was emerging as a Republic under the leadership of Milton Obote. The second is the Idi Amin regime (1972–1979) during which most of the people, but especially the people of

---

48. A. G. Gingyera-Pinycwa, "Is there a 'Northern Question'?" in *Conflict Resolution in Uganda*, ed. Kumar Rupesinghe (Oslo: International Peace Research Institute, 1989), 51.
49. Ibid., 61.

Lango and Acholi, who were perceived as the beneficiaries of the Obote era, suffered at the hands of the regime's violence. This is the context of the story of the Church, covered in chapter 5. Chapter 6 narrates and reflects on the story of the Church during the second Uganda Peoples Congress (UPC) government, 1980–1985, again under the leadership of Obote, when most of Buganda was engulfed in civil war as a result of the bitterness created during the first Obote era. The last of our case studies is set during the first six years of the National Resistance Army/Movement (NRA/M) government, 1986–1992, under the leadership of Yoweri Museveni. During this period civil war was concentrated in the North and the Northeast regions of Uganda which were associated with the previous regime of Obote II. Chapter 7 discusses the life of the Church during this period, focusing on the experience in Teso.[50]

The Church

It has been evinced that narrative is an effective genre for elucidating the faith-life of the church. Since a narrative is constituted by people, events and places, and the network of relations and issues about them, each chapter focuses on some of the key players in the unfolding drama of the events in the Church, relating portions of their biographies and the events and issues surrounding them. A comprehensive narrative emerges, that elucidates the nature of faith and the church, for it is the total sum of the biographies that form the story of the church.

To begin the account of the Church of Uganda with the arrival of the missionaries would be to truncate the narrative. The story therefore begins, in chapter 2, with the Buganda narrative, prior to the advent of the CMS missionaries, in order to appreciate the direction of the ensuing story of the rapid growth and spread of the Church. Space is given in chapter 3 to another story, the development of schisms and renewal in the Church, and in particular to the East African Revival movement, highlighting the key individuals and events that formed it. The Revival story provides coherence

---

50. Personal security considerations did not enable me to research the account of the Church in the turbulent context of West Nile and Acholi because there was civil war going on during the period of research.

to the whole thesis by tracing the historical roots of the theological influences and orientations of the biographies of the major players of the post-independence narrative of the Church. In the process of deciphering and building a coherent narrative of the whole Church in its diverse life, the Revival narrative was found to have an inbuilt capacity for providing a descriptive-interpretative paradigm for the whole narrative.

As a narrative of a corporate body, it is crucial to zero in on individuals, events and places that focus on the life of the community. A church as diverse and extended as the Church of Uganda makes arduous the task of selecting the areas, individuals and events that are central to the community's narrative. However the identification of turbulence as a defining element of post-independence Uganda narrowed the spectrum of areas for the study to those where turbulence was most concentrated. Feasibility of research and amount of space limited the research further to those areas where the turbulence was considered typical, spanning the time frame from 1962 to 1992 and giving a wide geographical coverage. The stories of the churches in Buganda, Lango, Luwero and Teso, covered in chapters 4, 5, 6 and 7, respectively, reflect aspects of the Church's corporate faith-life in the context of the social-political turbulence at the grassroots. The need to trace the historical development of the Church in post-independence Uganda, and the flow of the account, led to narrating and reflecting on the relevant portions of the biographies of Archbishops, Erica Sabiti, Janani Luwum, Silvanus Wani and Yona Okoth, who served the Church during this period.

The last chapter employs the theoretical framework of "the church in the world" as a paradigm in reflecting on the whole narrative of the Church in context, and in providing building blocks for a contextual ecclesiology. By utilizing the Revival motif of testimony, four major motifs are identified for an ecclesiology of the Church of Uganda. They are authenticity, identity, sacrament and mystery.

This study is a contribution to the study of the history and ecclesiology of the Church of Uganda. It offers a new approach to the study of the Church of Uganda in its historical-cultural-socio-political context. It outlines how that context has shaped it and gives fresh insights into its ecclesiology. It is seminal in its attempt to deal with the story of the Church in the post-Idi Amin era and in reflecting on the ecclesiological issues raised by story of the Church, in the context of the civil-political-military insurgencies of post-independence Uganda.

It is also a contribution to the study of church history and ecclesiology in an African context. It gives fresh insights in understanding the nature of the church and its mission in context, particularly in contexts of civil strife, turbulence and war. It offers a methodological approach that could be adopted in other indigenous ecclesiological studies, particularly in its insistence on indigenous sources. I hope it will stimulate further interest and research in the uncharted territory of contextual African ecclesiology.

CHAPTER 2

The Emerging Church in an Emerging Uganda, 1875–c1930

When Christian missionaries set foot on Buganda soil in 1877, the geo-political entity "Uganda" that is today, was nonexistent (See Map 1, Uganda: International Boundaries and Districts, p 28).[1] The role of Buganda and of the Baganda,[2] who were the first to receive European missionaries and to constitute an indigenous Christian community in Uganda, was pivotal. The way the Baganda, as a religio-cultural and social-political community, received the faith and later became its transmitters, shaped to a large extent the meaning of being and becoming a Christian, and of being and becoming "church" in Uganda.

There were four elements in Buganda society at the time the missionaries came, whose significance in determining the kind of church that was being born is examined in this chapter. The first element is the *Kabaka* (king of Buganda), who was the primary mover of the missionary project in as far as Buganda was concerned. The second is the place and role of "religion" in Kiganda society. The third is the clan, the defining element of group and individual identity. The fourth is the impact of Islam, the

---

1. The international boundaries of Uganda, as they are today, were finally concluded in 1926 after a long process of "cutting and pasting" that begun in 1894 with the declaration of Buganda as a Protectorate of the British Government. *Documentary History of the Boundary of Uganda and Administrative Divisions 1900 and Those of 1976*, Entebbe: the Republic of Uganda, 1976, 1–41. Buganda's boundaries, though not as precise as they are today, extended to cover the present districts of Kalangala, Kampala, Kiboga, Luwero, Masaka, Mpigi, Mubende, Mukono, and Rakai.
2. "Buganda" is the Kingdom; "Baganda" the people – plural, "Muganda" is singular; and "Kiganda" or "Ganda" an adjective. The adjective used in this thesis is "Kiganda." This follows Bantu language orthography.

first foreign religion to find a footing in Buganda. The latter might be considered external but in my view it has to be categorized among the internal factors at the time the Christian missionaries came because it was already one of the socio-economic and political parameters of the kingdom of Buganda.

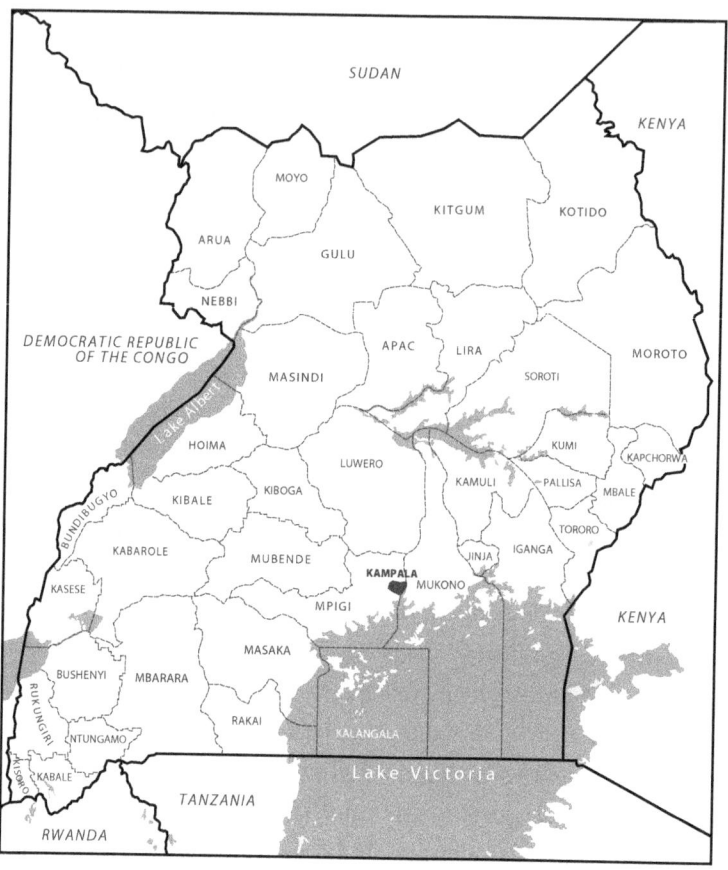

Map 1: Uganda: International Boundaries and Districts, 1992

There are four external factors that defined and embodied Christianity as it was apprehended by indigenous recipients: the catalytic role of Stanley, the explorer-journalist; the Church Missionary Society (CMS) missionaries that came to start the work in Buganda; the coming of the White Fathers to plant Roman Catholicism and their subsequent clash with the CMS mission (herein after referred to as the Mission); and the introduction of colonial rule. The interplay of these external factors with the internal, in the birth of the Church in Buganda and its expansion beyond, is considered.

The planting of churches beyond Buganda was simultaneous with the extension of the Protectorate borders. The patterns of response in Buganda were taken by the missionaries as yardstick for the evangelization of the rest of Uganda. This chapter outlines the positive and negative impact of this scenario in the growth of the Church, as both missionary and indigenous agents evangelized the different areas of Uganda. It highlights the factors that promoted growth and the challenges that were encountered in that process.

The chapter concludes by reflecting further on the interplay of the internal and external elements in the process of evangelization, and the features of the indigenous church that emerged and extended all over Uganda. What initially came to Buganda as a foreign religion, was received and translated into local idiom, with the result that the Church quickly assumed indigenous characteristics from the beginning.

The Birth of the Church in Buganda

Some accounts of the genesis of Christianity in Uganda start with Stanley, his visit and interaction Kabaka Mutesa, and the now legendary letter in the *Daily Telegraph* in 1875 appealing for missionaries.[3] To start with the European origins of the Church in Uganda, however, places too strong a premium on its European heritage, and therefore undervalues the factors of African identity that were imprinted in the Church right form its inception.[4] Although the significance of the missionary impact cannot be disregarded, the only way to appreciate fully the later developments in the Church is to begin the account with Buganda at the time of the advent of the visitors from Europe.

The kingdom of Buganda had a centralized, hierarchical structure of government. At the top, and indeed the centre of the kingdom was the

---

3. For example, Tuma and Mutibwa, *A Century of Christianity in Uganda*, begins the story of the Church with Samwiri R. Karugire's essay "The Arrival of European Missionaries: The First Fifteen or so Years," 1–15, which lays emphasis on the European background.
4. K. Ward has made a similar assertion in his "A History of Christianity in Uganda," 81.

Kabaka (king of Buganda), the most powerful person, and "the symbol of social, political, economic and, to some extent, religious power."[5] Wilson Mutebi has expressed well what the Kabaka was to Buganda at the time:

> The whole land of Buganda belonged to him and all its inhabitants. He was called *Namunswa* (the queen ant) to indicate his importance. He was referred to as *Ssabalongo*. This is the title of a man who has had twins more than once, and it is the greatest title any man can get in Buganda. It was given to the Kabaka to indicate that no person could be greater than him.
>
> He was called *Mukama* (Lord), *Ssabasajja* (greatest of all men), *Mpologoma* (Lion), *Ssegwanga* (Cock), *Magulunyondo* (metal legged). He was also called *Ssabataka* which means the head of all clans in Buganda.
>
> The political system enabled him to maintain a position of power and authority. Below him were three main types of important officers. There were the *Abami Abamasaza* (the County Chiefs) some of whom were hereditary and others appointed by the Kabaka. As he appointed these officers he could sack them if and when he wanted. Even in case of the hereditary office he could sack one and appoint another, so long as he chose the replacement in the same clan.[6]

The Kabaka exercised totalitarian, though not always total, control over his subjects. Although he was supreme as the *Ssabasajja* and *Sabataka*, the chiefs and the clan heads wielded some power. The most important chiefs were the *Katikkiro*, equivalent to the modern day Prime Minister, and the *Kimbugwe*, the guardian of the reigning monarch's umbilical cord. In the royal palace and capital, the Kabaka surrounded himself with several wives, chiefs, slaves, executioners and priests. Pages, another important element of life in the court of the Kabaka, were selected youths, given to the service

---

5. Abdu B. K. Kasozi, *The Spread of Islam in Uganda* (Nairobi: Oxford University Press, 1986), 17.

6. Wilson Mutebi, "Towards an Indigenous Understanding and Practice of Baptism amongst the Baganda, Uganda," Makerere University, Kampala, unpublished Master of Arts thesis, 1982, 38–39. The three were *Bakungu* (chiefs), *Bataka* (clan heads), and the pages in the court.

of the Kabaka with the prospect that, if any proved themselves, they could become chiefs. These pages, however, could as easily become targets of the fury of the Kabaka in the event of any displeasure with them. This was the power structure of the kingdom of Buganda to which Henry Morton Stanley the explorer-journalist[7] came when he arrived at the court of the Kabaka, Mukabya Mutesa I, in April 1875 and introduced Christianity.

The notion of "a religion," as "a particular system of faith and worship,"[8] was a foreign concept to the Baganda. This is not to imply, however, that the Baganda were devoid of religious ideas, values and practices. Religious practice was so integrated in all of life that it could not be isolated as an object to be named. This total infusion of life by religious ideas is evident in the conceptual structures of life in Kiganda society. Consider, for example, the names of the national divinities, the *Balubaale*,[9] and their functions: *Walumbe*, responsible for death and disease; *Kiwanuka* responsible for lightening; and *Mukasa* and *Nabuzana* controlling fertility and childbirth, respectively; and *Kibuuka,* responsible for war. These "national divinities were controlled by the king. Their main duty was to protect the king and the country. They were not supposed to be more powerful than the king."[10] Besides the national divinities, there were also private divinities associated with particular clans and lineage, known largely by the clan members.[11] The names of the *Balubaale* and their place in society convey the fact that religious ideals and values pervaded all of life, as it revolved around production, reproduction and power. There were therefore neither believers nor

---

7. Stanley, though primarily on an exploration mission to Central Africa, was also foreign correspondent of the *New York Herald* Newspaper, which together with the *London Daily Telegraph* sponsored his expedition.
8. This is how *The Concise Oxford Dictionary* defines "religion," and it is how the term is generally used.
9. Dunstan K. Bukenya, "The Development of Neo-Traditional Religion: The Buganda Experience," University of Aberdeen, unpublished MLitt dissertation, December 1980, 19–55, for a thorough discussion of Kiganda traditional beliefs and practices. The *Balubaale* were deified ancestors, recognized because of an outstanding heroic role in the life of the nation. They were the focus of the day-to-day life.
10. Mutebi, "Towards an Indigenous Understanding," 47.
11. Ibid.

non-believers. Such distinctions were irrelevant. This is reflected further in the fact that there was no vernacular Luganda word for "religion."[12]

Clan identity is what formed the basis for the distinction "self" and "other." In the words of one elder: "*Obulamu bw'Omuganda buli mukikka*," meaning, "the life of a Muganda is in his clan."[13] This conveys the centrality of the clan as the basis for group identity. It would be impossible to discuss questions of descent, succession, inheritance, family life, and politics without recourse to the clan system.

> The clan system in Buganda determined marriage law, socio-economic relations, religious systems and political offices. Social and political mobility was possible through the clan system of relationships, which equally controlled palace and royal duties including marriage to the king.[14]

The advent of foreigners and their religions therefore represented a paradigm shift in defining group identity, and the definition of "religion."

In the Kabaka's Court and Capital

Stanley was neither the first foreigner nor the first white man in the Kabaka's court. Both Arabs and other Europeans had preceded him.[15] Four factors, however, made Stanley unique. First, he stayed longer than any previous white visitors did. Second, he aided the Kabaka in the battle at Buvuma Islands in Lake Victoria, using his firearms. This display of firepower deeply impressed Mutesa who, at the time, also had fears of an invasion by Egyptian and Sudanese forces north of his kingdom. Third, Stanley though not a missionary, taught the Kabaka some rudiments of Christianity, and

---

12. The word used *eddini*, was derived from Arabic and must have been introduced with the advent of Arab traders in Buganda.
13. S. Peter Kigozi, OI, Ntinda, Kampala, 20 December 1996.
14. Bukenya, "Development of Neo-Traditional Religion," 13.
15. Buganda had strong trading links with the East African Coast. Swahili and Arab traders reached Buganda even before Mutesa became Kabaka. They came in search of ivory and slaves in exchange for firearms and cotton-cloth. Three white men had preceded Stanley: John Hannington Speke and Captain Grant, who were on an exploration mission of the source of the River Nile, in 1862; and Colonel Chaille Long, an American, who visited the Kabaka as an envoy of Colonel Gordon, the Governor of the Equatorial Province of the Egyptian Empire.

in the same vein discredited Islam. Fourth, Stanley proposed that Mutesa should invite Christian missionaries who would teach him and the peoples of his kingdom about the new faith.

Islam, which was brought by Arab traders from the East African coast in the 1840s,[16] preceded Christianity and was the first foreign religion in the court of the Kabaka. Although Kabaka Suna received instruction in Islam he never embraced it. His successor, Mukabya Mutesa I, embraced both the Arabs' merchandise and religion, and "established" Islam. Mosques were built all over the kingdom and the Islamic calendar adopted.[17] However Islam did not root itself in the life of the people. One of the reasons for this was the cultural distaste for circumcision. It was unthinkable that the Kabaka should be mutilated. Thus, despite his zeal, he was never fully converted to Islam. In addition to the issue of circumcision, the Egyptian Muslim traders who visited Buganda in 1876 led to greater discontent with Islam because they criticized the Qibla of the court mosque and questioned the validity of an uncircumcised Kabaka leading Friday prayers.

The coming of Islam also created an atmosphere of openness. Its coming had showed both to Mutesa and his chiefs that it was possible to add to the traditional cult of the *Balubaale*. Consequently, when Stanley introduced to the Kabaka the new faith, Mutesa was as open in considering it as he had been with Islam.

The reasons for Mutesa's enthusiasm to receive European missionaries have been widely discussed by both political and mission historians.[18] Some have argued that Mutesa's motivation was not primarily religious but political. This assessment is based on an understanding of religion and politics as two separate realms, a conceptual worldview that was alien to Buganda culture. It should be recognized that in inviting the missionaries

---

16. Kasozi, *The Spread of Islam in Uganda*, 18–33.
17. Ibid., 20–39, and Michael Wright, *Buganda in the Heroic Age* (Nairobi: Oxford University Press, 1971), 6–9, on the impact of Islam during Mutesa's reign.
18. J. F. Faupel, *African Holocaust: The Story of the Uganda Martyrs* (Africa: St Paul Publications, 1984), 10–11; Hansen, *Mission, Church and State*, 12; Samwiri R. Karugire, *A Political History of Uganda* (Nairobi: Heinemann Educational Books, 1980), 60–62; Semakula Kiwanuka, *A History of Buganda*, London: Longman, 1971, 168–170; D. Anthony Low, *Religion and Society in Buganda 1875–1900* (Kampala: East African Institute of Social Research, 1956), 1–5; Ward, "A History of Christianity in Uganda," 83–84.

to his kingdom, Mutesa did so in the terms in which he understood "religion." For Mutesa "religion" was primarily utilitarian in value. This was the case in primal,[19] religious practice and his experience of Islam. The national divinities in traditional Kiganda culture-religion were controlled by the Kabaka, and were responsible for protecting the Kabaka and the kingdom.[20] The Arabs who brought Islam had participated and helped the Kabaka in various battles. In further confirmation of this utilitarian view of religion, Stanley had, in addition to teaching him about his faith, helped him in another of his battles.[21] So far his experience of other religions did not contradict this utilitarian perception.

It is therefore reasonable to conclude that Mutesa's enthusiasm for the Europeans arose from his hope that their coming would serve his immediate need for military defence and protection. He needed allies who would supply him with arms and ammunition against Egyptians. The coming of the Europeans would hopefully open new relationships that could strengthen his military defence capacity, which he so urgently needed at the time against a looming invasion from the north. Stanley's involvement in the war in Buvuma Islands and his display of superior firepower had impressed the Kabaka. With such a prospect Mutesa conversed with Stanley about the Christian faith and permitted missionaries to come to his kingdom.

Eighteen months passed between Stanley's departure from Buganda and the arrival of the first missionaries. Of the eight CMS missionaries who left Britain for Buganda, only the Rev C. T. Wilson and Lieutenant Shergold Smith arrived at the Kabaka's Court at the end of June 1877.[22] Disease and death hit the rest of the group. There was an element of surprise, dismay

---

19. "Primal religion" is used interchangeably with "traditional religion" to keep, as Andrew F. Walls has argued, "the two important facts about them [traditional religions]: the historical priority of these worldviews to all the great religions, and in all parts of the world, and their basic elemental nature." A. F. Walls, "Africa and Christian Identity," in *Mission Focus: Current Issues*, ed. W. R. Shenk (Ontario: Herald Press, 1980), 213.

20. Mutebi, "Towards an Indigenous Understanding," 47.

21. Karugire, *A Political History of Uganda*, 63, and John V. Taylor, *The Growth of the Church in Buganda* (London: SCM Press, 1958), 36.

22. The names of the other six were Alexander Mackay, T. O'Neill, G. J. Clark, W. M. Robertson, James Robertson, and Dr John Smith. T. Tuma, "Church Expansion in Buganda," in *A Century of Christianity in Uganda 1877–1977*, eds. T. Tuma and P. Mutibwa (Nairobi: Uzima Press, 1978), 17.

and even disappointment between these missionaries and Mutesa during their first meetings. Mutesa could not understand why they only wanted to teach religion and could not make, provide or trade-in-arms and ammunition. Had not the Arabs and Stanley taught religion, traded in firearms and occasionally joined him and his armies in raiding his neighbours? Nevertheless, Mutesa welcomed the missionaries. As had become a matter of policy since the advent of foreigners in Buganda, the missionaries were restricted to the Court. They were only permitted to conduct their missionary activity under the watchful eye of the Kabaka. Their first converts were pages.[23] When Alexander Mackay arrived later in 1878, missionary initiatives began to win greater admiration from Mutesa, primarily because Mackay had the technical skills of an engineer.

The arrival of Father Laudel and Brother Amans, French Roman Catholic missionaries of the order of the White Fathers, in February 1879, radically changed and charged the religious climate in the Court. First, their arrival increased the number of Europeans in Buganda. This increased European traffic sent negative signals to Mutesa and made him more apprehensive and suspicious of European intentions. Second, the White Fathers claimed that their version of Christianity was more authentic and true than that of the CMS missionaries who had preceded them. The intense wrangling, rivalry and mistrust of the two groups was evident to the Kabaka, as each group tried to discredit the other before him, in a bid to win his favour. Mutesa used this to his benefit by playing one group against the other, showing commitment to neither.

The rivalry exhibited in Mutesa's court was an importation from Europe. The two missionary groups belonged to rival Christian traditions, Roman Catholic and Anglican,[24] and hailed from two traditional enemies, France and Britain, whose relationship had been embittered by their imperial

---

23. The first baptisms took place in March 1882 when five boys who had been Mackay's pupils were baptised by Rev Philip O'Flaherty. Their names deserve mention as the first Christians in Uganda: Sembera Kamumbo, who took the name Mackay; Mukasa who was baptized Edward; another Mukasa named Firipo; Buzabaliwo named Henry Wright; and Takirambudde who was baptized Yakobo.

24. Faupel devotes a large section of his book to exemplify the nature of this rivalry and conflict among the missionaries. As a Roman Catholic author he is at pains to exonerate the White Fathers. Faupel, *African Holocaust*, 14–20.

interests. In addition to the Anglo-French rivalry, this period of the nineteenth century was marked by a recurrence of ecclesial-theological disputes between Catholics and Protestants in Europe, occasioned not least by the first Vatican Council (1869–1870) that decreed the doctrine of Papal infallibility, thus completing the process of "counter-Reformation" that had begun several centuries earlier at the Council of Trent (1545–1563).

This bitter rivalry increased as the two churches extended their influence in Buganda and it became engraved into the nascent Church as a mark of its identity. From this time, the CMS and the Church they founded were known as Protestant rather than Anglican. Since denominational affiliation became a basis for group identity, it was extended to the political arena. Therefore by 1880, there were four rival religious protagonists in the Kabaka's court and capital: Muslims, Protestants, Roman Catholics, and traditional religionists of *Balubaale* cult, which set the stage for further conflicts in the years to come.

Distinct Christian communities developed when Mutesa relaxed his restriction against any religious instruction taking place in his Court, and allowed the missionaries to move into two large houses at Nateete. This enabled the missionaries to have households, with retainers and servants – a lifestyle like that of the chiefs. The adoption of this indigenous social structure made the Christian presence less foreign. A community of believers was thus established, meeting regularly at Nateete and in various homesteads of converted or sympathetic chiefs, learning and sharing their faith. The facility of Mackay's Swahili and Luganda translations of hymns and gospels catalysed the understanding of the new faith, to the extent that some of them volunteered to teach others.[25] It is important to note that all these converts were either of the chiefly upbringing or nurtured as potential chiefs in the court and capital of the Kabaka.[26] This became important in the subsequent growth of the church, since the missions converted future chiefs of Buganda, the men of influence in Buganda's state system.

---

25. Taylor, *Growth of the Church in Buganda*, 52–53, mentions Firipo Mukasa, Henry Wright Duta and Mackay Sembera as the first native teachers.
26. Wright, *Buganda in the Heroic Age*, 21, 22. Wright outlines the elitist background of some of the early converts, who were later killed.

The Nascent Church during Mwanga's Reign

As already noted the increase in traffic of Europeans in the kingdom of Buganda and the growing rivalry between the protagonists of the different religions was increasing Mutesa's apprehension and suspicion of the foreigners in his kingdom. His death in October 1884 and the accession to the throne of his youthful, inexperienced and headstrong son, Mwanga, heightened the impact of these factors. In the shadow of his highly revered and experienced father, Mwanga sought to assert his position and power. He was also known to be a narcotic smoker and a homosexual,[27] and did not care for any religion. According to Michael Wright, Mwanga's "fundamental weakness on his accession in 1884 was that he was an unbeliever in an age of faith."[28] His character, personality and lifestyle coupled with the latent context of rivalry, resulted in a head-on collision with the missionaries and their converts.

The teaching of the Europeans seemed to be the cause of increasing insolence and insubordination among the pages who had become Christians, as manifested by their apparent allegiance to their missionary teachers and their refusal to acquiesce to Mwanga's homosexual desires. Those in the capital who opposed the ascendant influence of Christianity, notably Muslims and Mwanga's Katikiro Mukasa, took advantage of the Kabaka's fury with the missionaries and pages to agitate for decisive action against them.[29] On Mwanga's orders several pages were executed. In the first two years of his rule, over fifty Christian pages and minor chiefs were brutally killed. Some were maimed, others cut to pieces, and others were burned, both Catholics and Protestants.[30] The CMS missionary, Bishop Hannington, was also killed during that period, in Busoga in October

---

27. Faupel, *African Holocaust*, 82.
28. Wright, *Buganda in the Heroic Age*, 11. Wright shows how Mwanga had no respect or sympathy for any of the religions at the Court at his accession.
29. Many commentators and scholars have highlighted the role of Muslims and chiefs in fueling Mwanga's animosity against the Christians, notably Faupel and Wright in their accounts, *The African Holocaust*, and *Buganda in the Heroic Age*, respectively.
30. Lists in Faupel, *African Holocaust*, 207–222 and Samwiri Karugire, "Arrival of European Missionaries," in *A Century of Christianity in Uganda 1877-1977*, ed. T. Tuma and P. Mutibwa (Nairobi: Uzima Press, 1978), 13–15. It should be noted that these were not the first religious martyrs of the period. During Mutesa's reign, about seventy young converts to Islam were burned at Namugongo for refusing to participate in prayers

1885. Hannington had ill advisedly used the Eastern route to Buganda, a route that was considered a back door and therefore dangerous for the security of Buganda. Besides, Mwanga had learned that Hannington was to be the leader of the Protestants,[31] a fact that increased his suspicion. Mwanga therefore ordered his killing.

The period immediately after the martyrdom of 1886 was turbulent.[32] Tension between Mwanga and the Muslims, traditional religionists, and Christian chiefs, increased. In a bid to strengthen his standing, Mwanga developed a strong army, subdivided into regiments, led by chiefs.[33] By this time the religious allegiance of these chiefs was divided along the different religious factions and therefore the regiments were built along the same lines. The leaders of the three religious groups (Muslims, Protestants, and Catholics) began to bring in large quantities of arms. This increased Mwanga's suspicion that they were becoming too powerful but his attempt to get rid of them sparked off a series of battles.

A rebellion led by an alliance of the regiments of Christians and Muslims routed him out of the palace in September 1888. Mwanga fled, but the Muslim-Christian alliance did not last. One month later, the Muslims with the assistance of Arabs fought and defeated the Christians and installed their own Kabaka, a Muslim. The Christians fled westwards, and while in exile they marshalled their forces. Two years later they fought and defeated the Muslims. Mazrui has rightly observed that in the entire pre-independence period this was the "time of maximum amity between the Protestants and the Catholics in Uganda."[34] The Christians restored Mwanga to the throne. But the Roman Catholic and Protestant alliance did not last either. In 1892 they fought each other for the control of both

---

conducted by him. See David Kavulu, *The Uganda Martyrs* (Kampala: Longman, 1969), 12.

31. James Hannington was consecrated in London in 1884 to become the first Bishop of the diocese of Eastern Equatorial Africa.

32. For a full account of this period: Wright, *Buganda in the Heroic Age*, and Kiwanuka, *A History of Buganda*, 192–270.

33. Michael Wright discusses the rise of a standing army during this period and its command, Wright, *Buganda in the Heroic Age*, 24–28, and details the wars that followed. In fact Wright's book is essentially about this period in Buganda's history.

34. Ali Mazrui, "Religious Strangers in Uganda: From Emin Pasha to Amin Dada," *African Affairs* 76, no. 302 (January 1977): 25.

the capital and the provinces. The Protestants, with the help of Captain Lugard of the Imperial British East Africa Company (IBEAC),[35] defeated the Roman Catholics.

Religious Rivalry

Religious rivalry was not new, but this time it took on overtly political dimensions. While in the late 1870s and early 1880s it was the missionaries and Arabs whose bickering and rivalry was overt, it was not long before their converts, the Baganda, emulated this conflict. All the religious groups had concluded that their survival depended on the acquisition of military and political power. It was the desire to control the centre, including the Kabaka, which continually bred suspicion among the leaders of the different religions and therefore heightened their conflicts. Religious affiliation became the basis of group identity and therefore the new way of ascending the ladder of political power.[36]

Political partisanship developed along religious lines. By the beginning of the 1880s Buganda had been divided into two parties – the "Bakatoliki" and the "Bapolostante," otherwise called "Bafalansa" and "Bangeleza" respectively, both referring to the Christian traditions and countries of origin of the two missions.[37] Religious divisions became the most important mechanism for allocating resources within the political system and therefore membership of a religious group served as the obvious means of securing one's share.[38] For example, the distribution of chieftainships, among Christians and Muslims after their joint victory against Mwanga in September 1888, was made on the basis of a rough equality between their forces. The same thing happened between Roman Catholics and

---

35. The IBEAC had arrived in Buganda only in 1890 mandated to secure British interests in the region following the signing of a treaty, in Europe, between Britain and Germany that placed Buganda under the British sphere of influence.
36. Holger B. Hansen's discussion of the restructuring of power in *Mission, Church and State*, 12–20.
37. Welbourn, *Religion and Politics in Uganda*, 5–9.
38. Hansen, *Mission, Church and State*, 18.

Protestants after defeating the Muslims in February 1890 and after the defeat of the Catholics by the Protestants in 1892.[39]

The events of this period had far reaching implications in shaping the Church in Uganda. The balance of power was tilting in favour of the young Protestant church, and entrenched it, as Louise Pirouet has pointed out, as the "established church."[40] This is comparable to the "established" position of traditional religion prior to the advent of Christianity, with the difference that while the traditional religionists had a recognizable power base, they did not control the political power structures. This time religion controlled the centre. Furthermore, these religious feuds instilled in their converts intense mistrust and animosity toward each other, thus setting the stage for continuous rivalry. The rivalries between the Protestant and Roman Catholic missions in Buganda were perpetuated throughout the process of planting churches in Uganda.

It is noteworthy that during this entire period, the Baganda converts, most of who were chiefs, led the nascent Church. In July 1885 when the CMS missionaries saw the increasing hostility of Mwanga against the Christians, they formed a church council consisting of twelve leading Baganda Christians, to act as leaders of the young church in the event of the missionaries being suddenly expelled from the country.[41] Their names deserve to be mentioned as the first leaders of what would later be the Church of Uganda. They were: Nikodemu Sebwato, Zakariya Kizito Kisingiri, Paulo Nsubuga Bakunga, Mackay Sembera, Tomasi Senfuma, Isaya Mayanja, Nuwa Walukaga, Semu Bekokoto, Freddy Kizza, Henry Wright Duta, Samwiri Mukasa and Mika Sematimba.[42] These men were respectable heads of households and therefore well suited to lead the small clusters of Christians. This marked the birth of an indigenous church.

---

39. Kiwanuka, *A History of Buganda*, 254. The Protestants were allocated the major chieftainships, the Roman Catholics were to be in charge of Buddu and the Muslims were sandwiched between them in Gomba, Busunju and Butambala. See ibid., 108–130, and D. Anthony Low, *Religion and Society in Buganda 1875–1900* (Kampala: East African Institute of Social Research, 1957), 9.
40. Pirouet, *Black Evangelists*, 67.
41. Tom Tuma, "Church Expansion in Buganda," in *A Century of Christianity in Uganda 1877–1977*, eds. T. Tuma and P. Mutibwa (Nairobi: Uzima Press, 1978), 20.
42. Ibid.

The absence of the CMS missionary leaders must have increased the confidence of the indigenous leaders and reduced their dependence on the missionaries. This may have been a factor in the increase of the number of conversions. Far from deterring conversions, the killing of Hannington and the Christian converts in 1885–1886, and the so-called revolution of 1888–1892, motivated many to approach the church leaders requesting baptism.[43] The decision to move out from the capital into the country and beyond did not come from the missionaries but from the African Church leaders.

Growth and Expansion

The expansion of the Church beyond the capital to the rest of Buganda and to the various parts of the emerging colonial state of Uganda, was in three thrusts.[44] The first, spanning the period 1890–1905, was into Buganda and the neighbouring kingdoms of Busoga, Ankole, Bunyoro, and Toro; the second, around 1905–1915, extended Christianity to the less centralized peoples of Acholi, Lango, Teso, and Bukedi as it was known then; and the third thrust moved into the peripheral areas, of West Nile, Kigezi, and Karamoja in the 1920s. This followed more or less the same path of colonial incorporation of these areas into the Uganda protectorate, declared over Buganda in 1894.[45] A number of factors led to this tremendous growth and expansion: an enabling political climate; increase in the number of missionaries; indigenous ownership and participation in missionary work; vernacularization and evangelization through formal education.

---

43. Ibid., 21.
44. Two very incisive works that review the growth of the church during this period are: Taylor, *Growth of the Church in Buganda*, and Pirouet, *Black Evangelists*, Although not as detailed, the essays in Tuma and Mutibwa, *A Century of Christianity in Uganda*.
45. The *Documentary History of the Boundary of Uganda and Administrative Divisions in 1900 and those of 1976*, Republic of Uganda, 1976, traces the extension and demarcation of the Protectorate boundaries up to 1926, which is the same period that the missionaries were starting work in the peripheral districts.

An Enabling Socio-political Climate

The rapid spread of the Church in Buganda and to the rest of Uganda was propelled by a conducive socio-political climate in Buganda, the pioneer recipient of the missionaries. The climate was advantageous at two levels: first, at the level of the kingdom government of Buganda, and by extension local administrations in the other kingdoms and districts; and second, at the colonial government level. Once the Protestants controlled the centre, all the important chieftainships in Buganda were allotted to leading Protestants as chiefs.[46] Most of the chiefs combined the roles of church leadership and chieftainship. Some were members of the Mengo Church Council, and others even among the first to be ordained.[47] These men actively supported evangelization and Christian teaching. In fact, the missionaries worked at first entirely through these chiefs, regarding them as the natural leaders of the church, as indeed they were.[48] These chiefs provided housing and feeding for the missionaries.[49] They mobilized material and financial support for the catechists and teachers in their areas, and very often, it was at the initiative of these chiefs that teachers were commissioned to serve in their areas of influence.[50] The missionaries were so pleased with the way these chiefs contributed to the growth of the Church in Buganda that it became for them the *modus operandi* in the rest of Uganda with some success.

However this strategy did not always work as well in all the other areas of the Protectorate as it did in Buganda, for two reasons. First it was based on a hierarchical centralized social-political structure, and not all the communities were organized this way. It succeeded to some extent in

---

46. Notable among them were Apolo Kagwa, the Katikiro, and the important chieftainships of Kyadondo, Singo, Kyagwe, Bulemezi and Busiro, which were occupied by Paul Nsubuga Bakunga, Yona Waswa, Nikodemu Sebwato, Zakaliya Kizito Kisingiri and Yoswa Kate Damulira respectively. See Tuma, "Church Expansion in Buganda," 23, and Taylor, *Growth of the Church in Buganda*, 59.

47. Nikodemu Sebwato and Zakariya Kizito were chiefs and also ordained in the Church.

48. Taylor, *Growth of the Church in Buganda*, 68.

49. Pirouet, *Black Evangelists*, 12.

50. Pirouet's account of the planting of the church in Buddu and the pivotal role of the Protestant chief Nikodemu Sebwato is just one example of this. Pirouet, *Black Evangelists*, 19–20.

Toro,[51] Bunyoro,[52] and Busoga,[53] which had hierarchical structures, but not in Acholi,[54] Lango[55] and Kigezi[56] whose peoples were organized around clan leaders who occupied leadership positions due to their capacity to provide military leadership and protection for their clans and chiefdoms. Although chiefs in all cases played an important role in providing leadership and helping in the establishment of Church centres, they did not always have the kind of influence over their people that the chiefs in the other hierarchically organized communities enjoyed. But even this could not be taken for granted in all kingdom areas. Ankole is a case in point, for although it had a centralized structure of government, the strategy did not succeed because of the ethnically based *Bahima-Bairu* cleavage, and the socio-political organisation of the kingdom.[57] The *Bahima*, the ruling class of Ankole at that time, and a cattle-herding community, constituted a smaller population than the *Bairu*, whose livelihood was by land cultivation, and were ruled by the *Bahima*. The latter were not well regarded by the *Bairu* because they took the *Bahima* hegemony as an imposition.

Second, Baganda who initially implemented the strategy, were not always welcome because they were perceived as imperialist agents. The protectorate government had elected to use Baganda in administering the rest

---

51. Pirouet, *Black Evangelists*, 39–46, for fuller account.
52. Ibid., 76–84, for fuller account.
53. Tuma, *Building a Ugandan Church*; and Tuma, "Church Expansion in Buganda," 45–56, for fuller account.
54. Pirouet, *Black Evangelists*, 144–154, and J. K. Russell, *Men without God? A Study of the Impact of the Christian Message in the North of Uganda* (London: Highway Press, 1966), 1–25, for fuller account.
55. The story of the coming of Protestant Christianity to Lango is not as well documented as that of its northern neighbour Acholi. Russell has suggested that the reason for this is the late entry of CMS missionaries into Lango, influenced by their attitude to the Lango as inferior to the Acholi, in Tuma, "Church Expansion in Buganda," 61. Tom K. Olal in his study "Church and Politics in Lango-Uganda (1971–1981)," Makerere University, unpublished Diploma in Theology dissertation, 1982, has a brief section on it.
56. The planting of the church in Kigezi is usually covered as part of the story of the Ruanda Mission. It is covered in Patricia St John, *Breath of Life* (London: The Norfolk Press, 1971), and Stanley, *Road to Revival*.
57. David Weeks, "The Growth of Christianity in the Kingdom of Nkore (Ankole) in Western Uganda before 1912," University of Aberdeen, unpublished M Th Dissertation, 1979, for full account; Also Trevor Williams, "The Coming of Christianity to Ankole," *The Bulletin of the Society for African Church History* II, no. 2 (1966): 155–173, and Pirouet, *Black Evangelists*, 110–119.

of Uganda. The missionaries assumed that the appointment of as many Baganda Protestant chiefs as possible throughout the protectorate would help the cause of the Church like it had done in Buganda. But for the Baganda this would expedite the extension of Buganda's influence. So evangelistic motives were entangled with the desire to increase the influence of Buganda. This provoked resistance in the initial stages of evangelisation in Bunyoro, Toro, Ankole, Busoga, Bugisu, Teso and Bukedi. A little digression here is appropriate to the Bunyoro, Bugisu, Teso, and Bukedi stories as illustrations of this.

Kabalega, *Omukama* (king) of Bunyoro, had always been a threat to Buganda. When the British declared a Protectorate over Buganda in 1894, and sought to extend the Protectorate government to Bunyoro, Kabalega resisted them. Both the colonial government and Buganda fought him, and drove him across the Nile. He took refuge in Lango, from where he continued his military resistance. The hostility between Buganda and Bunyoro made the Mengo Council hesitant in sending teachers to Bunyoro. It was not until Kabalega was decisively defeated, and a new *Omukama* (king) installed, that some measure of progress was registered.[58] Moreover the Bunyoro Church Council sought autonomy from Buganda, to the surprise of the CMS missionaries.[59] But this should have been expected, since to continue under the Buganda Council would be to perpetuate domination of Buganda even in ecclesiastical matters.[60]

---

58. The situation changed when *Omukama* Kitehimbwa, considered by the Banyoro to be a stooge of Buganda and the colonial government, was removed by the Protectorate government and replaced with Andereya Duhaga. Duhaga was a more acceptable leader to the Banyoro than his predecessor was, and he was more committed to the Christian cause. It is noteworthy that most of the early Christians were previously those who were part of Kabalega's raiding bands, *basurura*. Pirouet, *Black Evangelists*, 89.
59. Pirouet, *Black Evangelists*, 101–106.
60. Ibid. This desire of the Banyoro for independence from Buganda surfaced more clearly in the *Nyangire* ("I have refused") uprising of 1906–1908. It is Fisher who persuaded the *Omukama* to call for a special meeting of the *Lukiiko*, to quell the rebellion.

Bugisu, Teso and Bukedi[61] were ruled by Kakungulu.[62] Kakungulu was given the region north of Lake Kyoga to administer by the Protectorate administration as a reward for his role in the defeat and capture of Kabalega. It was from there that Kakungulu launched his successful conquests of Teso, Bugisu and Bukedi. Lawrence summarised Kakungulu's conquests:

> The pattern of occupation was everywhere the same; first an armed expedition would be made from an established fort to a new area; the pretexts were often obscure, sometimes a request for help from a warring faction or sometimes a threat of attack by local inhabitants; after skirmishes or pitched battles a new fort would be established and a garrison of armed Baganda installed. This garrison would then extend its influence over the surrounding countryside, by establishing armed posts or minor forts. When local opposition had been overcome the region would be proclaimed as *saaza* and the smaller areas controlled by outlying posts would be defined as *gombololas*. Baganda chiefs were appointed down to *Muluka* level.[63]

The Baganda chiefs that Kakungulu appointed to administer the whole region were predominantly Protestants who also actively promoted evangelization.[64] Those who were part of Kakungulu's occupation force[65] attempted evangelizing this region. They did not make much headway among the people, however, because in addition to the cultural barrier, they were associated with Buganda conquest and colonization. So the initial response

---

61. These three are taken together because the story of the planting of Protestant Christianity in the three areas was connected with Semei Kakungulu, the Muganda Protestant chief-turned military general and imperialist, and his conquest and occupation of a vast area of eastern Uganda. In fact the whole area was known to Buganda as Bukedi, the land of *Bakedi*, the "naked ones." See Pirouet, *Black Evangelists*, 172.
62. For full account of Kakungulu's conquests and rule see: Michael Twaddle, *Kakungulu and the Creation of Uganda, 1868–1928* (London: Currey, 1993).
63. J. C. D. Lawrence, *The Iteso: Forty Years of Change in a Nilo-Hamitic Tribe of Uganda* (London: Oxford University Press, 1957), 18.
64. For example Sedulaka Mwanga, the Gombolola chief of Buwalasi, personally conducted evening prayers for his household; Rachael Sweeting, "The Growth of the Church in Buwalasi-I," *The Bulletin of the Society for African Church History* II, no. 4 (1968): 338.
65. Among them was his Chaplain the Rev Andereya Batulabudde.

was resistance.[66] The situation only changed when local evangelists were deployed and with the arrival of CMS missionaries who introduced education and the growing of cotton.

At the colonial level the declaration of Buganda as part of Britain's sphere of interest and subsequently as a protectorate, in 1894, provided an enabling political environment for the missionaries. They had welcomed the intervention of the Imperial British East Africa Company. In fact, Bishop Tucker and the other CMS missionaries were foremost in calling for the declaration of an Imperial Protectorate over Buganda, to replace the company, for fear of a repeat of the 1885–1887 persecution and massacres. D. A. Low observes:

> Thereafter the British missionaries continued to support the Protectorate Government. The reason is clear. There was perhaps a natural tendency for British missionaries to support the protectorate government, but the main point was that without the law and order that the British administration was introducing, mission work on the scale which was being opened up would not have been possible. It is the Old Story. The Church was glad of the stable arena that the state provided.[67]

Moreover it was the stated policy of the colonial government to guarantee missionary freedom in their mission because Christian missionary activity was seen as a dispenser of western civilization.[68] There was an unwritten collaborative agreement between the Mission and the colonial government.

---

66. Sweeting in her essay, "The Growth of the Church in Buwalasi-I," 334–349, and also Part II of the same essay continued in *The Bulletin of the Society for African Church History* III, no. 1–2 (1969–70): 15–27, has suggested that the evangelization of Buwalasi by the Baganda proceeded in four sequential stages: resistance, caused by associating Christianity with Buganda imperialism; consolidation of Buganda's rule which involved the routing out of indigenous customs and forms of government and replacing them with Buganda forms, together with the introduction of teaching in the church and school; "Gandaization," which involved the popularization of chiefly lifestyle through education for the sons of chiefs and potential chiefs; and the desire for self-assertion of the Bagisu by reviving their own forms and taking full responsibility of church and local government.

67. Low, *Religion and Society in Buganda*, 15.

68. Hansen in his article "Church and State in a Colonial Context," 95–123, traces the genesis and development of a differentiated application of the colonial policy of religious tolerance and neutrality in favour of Christian missions because of this civilising objective. He has shown how this was the case in Uganda.

An issue that constantly recurs in the story of the spreading of the Church is its rivalry with the Catholic Church, a matter that had its roots in the religion-political feuds of the late 1880s and early 1890s in Buganda. Religious rivalry, prejudice, and partisanship also fuelled zeal for planting churches,[69] but also meant that a lot of energy was expended trying to denigrate the Roman Catholics. The planting of the Church in Ankole provides a typical scenario. The arrival of the Protestant church missionaries in 1899 preceded the Roman Catholic missionaries, who arrived in 1901, introducing a new dynamic to the scene, to which the Protestant missionaries responded by disparaging the Roman Catholic faith.[70] It should be pointed out however that political dominance did not always work to the advantage of the Protestant Church. The fact that the Roman Catholics could not count on an enabling political environment that the Protestants took for granted meant that the Roman Catholics put in more energy in grassroots evangelization. Consequently in most areas the Roman Catholics won more converts than the Protestants, even where Roman Catholics were latecomers.[71]

Missionary Participation

Another factor that accounts for the rapid growth of the Church is the increased number of missionaries. It was crucial that as the protectorate government was extending its borders beyond Buganda, there was an available missionary force to open up new mission stations in the new regions. As several more missionaries arrived into the country in the 1890s and the first decade of the twentieth century, there was manpower to do this. Prior to the Christian victory the presence of missionaries in Buganda had been

---

69. Ward, "A History of Christianity in Uganda," 84. The haste with which the missionaries embarked on establishing a CMS mission station in Busoga was because of the desire to prevent the Catholics from starting work there. Tuma, *Building a Ugandan Church*, 21–31.

70. Trevor Williams discusses the rivalry introduced by the arrival of the Roman Catholic Missionaries in his essay "The Coming of Christianity to Ankole," 164–166.

71. In fact by the time of independence, the Catholic Church commanded 28.5% compared with the 27.7% for the Protestants. F. B. Welbourn records these figures of the census of 1959 as the share of Uganda's population by the two faiths. Muslems were recorded at 4.7%. Welbourn, *Religion and Politics in Uganda*, 8–24.

sparse and sporadic.[72] However from 1890 their numbers swelled.[73] Each one of new missionaries made a significant contribution to the growth of the church, as they were sent to open mission stations across the country.[74]

Three of the CMS missionaries that arrived around this period deserve further attention because of the catalytic role they played in the spreading of the Church to all the regions. First was Bishop Alfred Tucker whose leadership had a significant impact on the process of building an indigenous Church. Bishop Tucker believed in developing a self-supporting, self-extending indigenous-led church. For as early as January 1891 Tucker commissioned the first lay-evangelists, six of them, and later in 1893 ordained some to the diaconate. Those six deserve mention as the first commissioned ministers of the Church of Uganda: Henry Wright Duta Kitakule, Sembera Mackay, Yohanna Mwira, Mika Sematimba, Paulo Bakunga and Zakariya Kizito Kisingiri.[75] Tucker did not believe in missionaries dominating the leadership of the Church but rather the development of trained indigenous leadership who would be equals with the missionaries. Tucker was so committed to this that he tried to include it in the constitution establishing the Native Anglican Church.[76] Taylor notes that, "he tried in vain to persuade his fellow missionaries to accept a constitution by which they would become equal fellow workers with their African colleagues, under the same legislative body."[77]

The second was A. B. Fisher, who was posted to Singo where he opened up centres all around the mission station for teaching and reading

---

72. In October 1888, when the Muslims forced the Christians out of Buganda the missionaries were also expelled. And in February 1890, Mackay died after twelve years of unbroken service to the young church in Buganda. The next batch of missionaries arrived at the end of 1890.

73. Bishop Alfred Tucker arrived in 1890. At the beginning of 1893, after a short period of absence from Buganda, Bishop Tucker returned with Revs J. Roscoe, E. Millar, Mr G. L. Pilkington, R. H. Leakey, who were stationed at Mengo. Also with Revs L. A. Gunther and A. B. Fisher, who were sent to open a station in Yona Waswa's Singo province. Already in the country were Archdeacon Walker, C. T. Gordon, Rev George Baskerville and Rev R. P. Ashe.

74. Tuma, "Church Expansion in Buganda," 23.

75. Pirouet, *Black Evangelists*, 20.

76. This was henceforth the constitutional name of the Church in Uganda, until 1960 when it was changed to the Church of Uganda.

77. Taylor, *Growth of the Church in Buganda*, 72.

– dubbed "synagogues" – under the leadership of young trained converts.[78] This "Fisher-scheme" was a combined operation by the Christian chiefs, as heads of local clusters, and the new catechists. The adoption of the scheme by the Church Council speeded up the recruitment and deployment of catechists in Buganda and beyond.[79]

The third was G. L. Pilkington, who was a linguist and, together with Henry Wright Duta, undertook the work of translation and by 1897 had completed the translation of the Luganda Bible. Pilkington's instrumental role is also associated with what has come to be known as the "Pilkington Revival" of 1893. In that year, Pilkington, while on holiday on the island of Kome in Lake Victoria, had a "revival" experience, which he shared with his fellow missionaries at Mengo. He interested them in the idea of holding a series of special services to enrich the spiritual life of the Church. People flocked to these services and for many church members this was a time of spiritual awakening, and of a new commitment to Christian service.[80] Many of those who committed themselves volunteered as catechists and "missionaries" to unreached lands in Buganda and beyond. Every month "missionary meetings" were organized by the Church Council at which some evangelists reported on their work and called for fresh recruits. The impact of the fruit of the Pilkington revival was strengthened by the adoption of the Fisher-scheme by the Church Council. It is reported that within one year of the beginning of the revival 260 new evangelists were at work, occupying eighty-five stations of which twenty were beyond the borders of Buganda.[81] The evangelists to Toro, Bunyoro, Ankole and Busoga, were a fruit of the revival.

Indigenous Participation

Indigenous participation in the leadership of the nascent Church and in the evangelization of Buganda and the rest of Uganda was crucial for the growth of the Church. The training and deployment of indigenous catechists and

---

78. Ibid., 75.
79. Tuma, "Church Expansion in Buganda," 24.
80. Ibid.; and Pirouet, *Black Evangelists*, 22, 24–35.
81. Taylor, *Growth of the Church in Buganda*, 64.

evangelists was a characteristic feature of Church in its formative years. Tuma has observed that by the end of 1893 there were five categories of church leaders in Buganda: European missionaries, ordained Baganda, lay evangelists, Baganda Christian chiefs and the Church Council.[82] Of these five categories, four were indigenous. In part, what accounts for the success story of the planting of Christianity in Uganda is the rapid transformation of receptors to becoming transmitters.[83] Roland Oliver also observed:

> In nearly all these vast developments, the foreign missionary expansion both Catholic and Anglican, had followed and not preceded the expansion of the faith through indigenous channels. In most of the new districts the missionaries came to consolidate bands of neophytes already gathered by unordained, very often unbaptized, African enthusiasts, who had been in contact with Christian teaching at the older centres.[84]

It is instructive that even at this early time the Church Council recognized the critical role of women's leadership, and commissioned women leaders as teachers and counsellors for women converts.[85] A unique feature of the growth of the Church in Toro was the deliberate training and deployment of women catechists, as a result of the arrival of two women missionaries in 1901 – Ruth Hurdith and Edith Pike. Pirouet has recorded a total of thirty-six women who were licensed catechists by 1910.[86] Some of these women were among the pioneers of the work in Ankole.

Christianity became more credible and acceptable to the recipients as a result of the fact that it is indigenous people who transmitted it. These "black evangelists," as Pirouet has called them,[87] certainly had an advantage over their "white" counterparts, the CMS missionaries. Their being black offset the fact that the majority of the earliest catechists were Baganda. But

---

82. Tuma, "Church Expansion in Buganda," 23.
83. Pirouet's study *Black Evangelists* is an account of the growth and spread of the church by indigenous agents. Tuma's study, *Building a Ugandan Church* also shows that the growth of the church in Busoga was a result of indigenous participation.
84. Roland Oliver, *The Missionary Factor in East Africa* (London: Longmans, 1952), 182–183.
85. Pirouet, *Black Evangelists*, 25–26.
86. Ibid., 73–77.
87. The title of her book is *Black Evangelists*, a reference to the indigenous evangelists.

it was necessary that training and commissioning of local catechists, evangelists and teachers follow the baptism and conversion of the first converts in any place if there was to be significant growth in an area. For example, the dependence of the young Acholi church on Banyoro evangelists, and the domination of Baganda catechists in Teso, accounts, in part, for the poor response in both areas.

Vernacularization

The extent to which the transmitters of the faith, whether CMS missionaries or indigenous catechists, used indigenous forms determined the quality and often quantity of the response. The production of vernacular translations of the whole or portions of the Bible, *The Book of Common Prayer*, and other educational materials yielded results. One such tool that was used widely during the early years was the *Mateka*, (literally "commandments"), a first reading book containing among other things the Ten Commandments. The early translation of the Bible into Runyoro-Rutoro certainly propelled growth in Toro and Bunyoro.[88] There is also evidence that Kitching's translations[89] of the gospels and some hymns into Ateso had a positive impact.[90] A similar story is repeated all over Uganda.

The obverse of this story is illustrated in missionary attempts to make Luganda the official language of mission work, which was met with resistance everywhere. The beginning of the work in Ankole is a case in point, where the Banyankole resisted the introduction of Luganda as the official language of the mission. Subsequently, they preferred Batoro catechists to Baganda. The main factor in their favour was the proximity of their vernaculars. Added to this was the fact that Luganda as a language had an imperialist feel to it.

---

88. The translation of the Bible in Runyoro was completed in 1912.
89. Kitching, with the assistance of three Iteso, Ogwang, Okurapa and Okusai, devoted his time to learning the language and reducing it to writing. He updated the *Mateka* and produced portions of the gospels, prayer book and hymns.
90. "How Christianity came to Teso (1900–40) with Special Reference to the Church Missionary Society," Makerere University, unpublished Diploma in Theology dissertation, n.d., (and no author named) 15,19, shows how this influenced the reception of the Christian message in Teso.

Acholi is another case in point. J. K. Russell has discussed at length the negative impact of the failure to use a local word, *Jok,* for God, instead of adulterating the Runyoro word for God, *Ruhanga,* to create a new Acholi and not so meaningful word, *Lubanga*.[91] It is the leadership of indigenous people like Muca Ali that helped to win some trust among the Acholi, leading to some conversions.[92] Certainly, vernacularization enabled the receptors to feel at home with their new faith making them more receptive.

Education and Health Services

The missionaries employed "reading" as part of their evangelistic strategy. "Reading" centres were among the first to be established in any place where a mission was starting. These reading centres were later transformed into formal schools as more missionaries were called, whose primary assignment was the development of social services, particularly education.[93]

In Lango, the introduction of formal education as part of the evangelization programme had a similar impact. Kenneth Olal observed that the opening of schools increased membership in the Church in Lango. By 1914 the presence of the faith was evident all over Lango as a result of the introduction of formal education:

> Naturally the faith gained prestige and monopoly among the Langi. The little education that the catechumen received (reading and writing) enabled converts to occupy key positions in the administrative sector of the district. They also formed the nucleus of opinion leaders and the society elite. By 1914 virtually all chiefs had identified themselves with the new faith.[94]

---

91. Russell, *Men without God?*, 1–6.
92. Pirouet, *Black Evangelists*, 163. One of the reasons for any positive response to Sira Dongo's leadership was the proximity of his vernacular *Alur* language to *Luo,* the language of the Acholi.
93. In 1897, Bishop Tucker invited C. W. Hattersley to Uganda to build up a system of primary schools. And in the same year Dr Albert Cook and Miss Timpson, a nurse, arrived at Mengo and opened a hospital. Their work was strengthened by the arrival of two other medics, Jack Cook and Ashton Bond in 1901.
94. Olal, "Church and Politics in Lango-Uganda," 7.

In some instances Church teachers and Christian chiefs allied together to coerce the people into reading. In places where the Protestant chiefs played the dual role of Church and civic leadership, forcing people into Church and school became a matter of course.[95]

These pioneering initiatives of the Church in the field of education bore so much fruit that education grew to become the largest department of the Mission. The provision of education swelled the numbers of adherents everywhere in the protectorate and dominated the focus of the Mission. Patricia St John's account reflects this in Kigezi:

> The aims of the old missionaries were simple, too: education not for its own sake, but as a means of evangelisation and teaching the Christian faith. "Our aim is not an educated African aristocracy, but a consecrated ministry of teachers, clergy and civil servants," wrote Jim Brazier in 1930. "We do not want a religious distinction to exist between government workers and mission workers. We want to exercise the ministry of evangelism through both." And how well they succeeded in those early years, as one after another went out, content with the merest pittance of pay, to open little out-schools all over the district.[96]

However, with the development of education came new challenges. Although the missionaries intended education for evangelization and incorporation into the church, the provision of literary education became an end in itself. The type of education being offered by the mission was also a gateway to economic advantage. To the receptors reading became one of the marks of "conversion," and a passport to becoming a member of the new society that the "*eddini*" represented. Even at its basic level of "reading," education not only got people into the Church, but also provided them the possibility of employment within the local administration. The social standing accorded by reading increasingly became the greater

---

95. Rachael Sweeting, in her research in Bugisu, found that quite often the chief would bully the people into attendance at Church and school. Sweeting, "The Growth of the Church in Buwalasi – I," 345.
96. St John, *Breath of Life*, 165.

motivation for associating with the missions and the Church, and becoming a Christian.[97] In her research among the Bagisu, Sweeting observed:

> The administration relied heavily for its Gisu personnel on the early generation of Christians. If anyone wanted a good post, he had to be a Christian. Anyone who wanted to marry a man with a good post had to be a Christian herself. In every case the first step was admission to the Church school. The catechumens and other readers were to be seen at Church worship, but not the baptised. Some immediately upon their baptism were found to have dropped all pretensions at Christian living according to the teaching of the Church. The tendency was to regard baptism as the be-all and end-all of Christian instruction.[98]

Thus, reading as the primary means of evangelization, though successfully bringing into the Church many converts, led to a significantly large membership that had little or no understanding of Christianity.

Though development of health services was not to the same degree as the development of schools, they were also intended to serve the evangelization project of the CMS Mission, and contributed to bringing more of converts into the Church's fold. Health centres were started at major Mission centres, which expanded to become hospitals: at Mengo near the Kabaka's palace, in 1897; at Kabarole in Toro, in 1903; and, at Ngora in Teso, in 1922.[99]

The Integration of the Church into Society

The integration of Christianity and the Church into Buganda and other societies, as the CMS and indigenous missionaries evangelized them, happened at two levels: first, at the level of reception, as converts adapted their

---

97. Pirouet, *Black Evangelists*, 29.
98. Sweeting, "The Growth of the Church in Buwalasi – II," *The Bulletin of the Society of African Church History* III, no. 1–2 (1969-70): 19.
99. Roy Billington, "Early Years of Medical Work in the Church of Uganda," in *A Century of Christianity in Uganda 1877-1977*, eds. T. Tuma and P. Mutibwa (Nairobi: Uzima Press, 1978), 90–93.

new faith into the indigenous structures, which gave birth to what the missionaries called nominalism; second, at the level of institution building, as the CMS missionaries and African leaders sought to build structures to accommodate and promote the growth of the Church. This resulted in the restructuring of the societies in which the churches were planted and indeed of the whole country.

Nominalism

By the turn of the century, the Church had already become a part of Buganda society. Protestant Christianity had already been accepted as a religion of Buganda. This is what had given rise to what the missionaries perceived as nominalism in the Church. It has been observed that among the Baganda it had become a social imperative to belong to a particular Church. This motivated many of the people to seek baptism, swelling the membership of the Church. What caused concern in the CMS missionary circles, was the lack of evidence of conversion in the moral life of the adherents. The majority of the converts continued to live in their old ways, and some of those who had abandoned them at baptism, relapsed back to them. So grave was the concern of the missionaries that Bishop John J. Willis, on succeeding Bishop Tucker as Bishop of Uganda in 1911, found it necessary "to institute a searching inquiry into the state of Christian morals and to introduce the threat of excommunication at the Synod of 1913."[100]

Although the missionary reports interpreted the lack of Christian moral standards in the Church as a result of decline in commitment,[101] it can be better understood by considering the notion of religious commitment from the perspective of its adherents and the function of ritual in traditional custom. For the Baganda, as all the other people of Uganda, in traditional culture-religion there were two broad categories of religious practitioners, distinguished by their professional involvement, not by religious zeal or

---

100. Oliver, *The Missionary Factor*, 209. The situation does not seem to have improved because Hewitt also records that "the worldliness of the Church" remained a recurrent theme of missionary reports in the 1920s and the early 1930s. Gordon Hewitt, *The Problem of Success: A History of the Church Missionary Society, 1910–1942* (London: SCM Press, 1971), 239.
101. Taylor, *Growth of the Church in Buganda*, 61, 82–83.

commitment. The first category was priests and mediums, the experts, who acted as human intermediaries with the spirit world. The second was the ordinary people.[102] Since the ordinary people did not have much direct business with God except in times of calamity and other special needs, their normal "religious" commitment was nominal. Religious commitment was about fulfilling clan rituals associated with birth, harvest, death, and contributing to clan obligations to the kingship. The idea of individual commitment was alien.

Some of the religious practices in Christianity had similarities in traditional custom and culture. In appropriating them, the Africans related their significance to that of their parallels in traditional culture. Take for example baptism, the Christian ritual of incorporation into the church. Among the Baganda, baptism was similar to *Okwalula*, "to hatch the children," the rite of incorporation into the clan.[103] Mutebi explains:

> The idea here is that the children were born physically to their families, but as far as the clan is concerned they are still not yet born until the rite is performed. Therefore when they are born again at the rite of incorporating in the clan they are really new children as far as the clan is concerned, and that is why each one of them gets a new name.[104]

Thus, though for the missionaries, baptism was a symbol of both incorporation and commitment, to the Baganda it was like *Okwalula*, just for incorporation, a passport for group identity. Membership to the clan, though central and primary to the identity of the Baganda, was also nominal. Therefore the nominalism that perturbed the missionaries was for the indigenous adherents "real religion."

Nominalism was the result of the process of adaptation of Christianity into traditional culture-religion. Though the missionaries were distraught by the polygamy, drunkenness, and adultery that were prevailing among the Christians, the Africans did not seem to see the contradiction, because

---

102. Mutebi, "Towards an Indigenous Understanding," 50.
103. S. Peter Kigozi, OI, Kampala, 20 December 1996. Also, Mutebi, "Towards an Indigenous Understanding," 130–141, 207–208. Mutebi's cardinal argument is that *Okwalula* and baptism are parallels since both are incorporation rites for group identity.
104. Mutebi, "Towards an Indigenous Understanding," 207–208.

these practices were not prohibited by traditional culture-religion. As one analyst has characterized it, Christianity was for them a new "fetish in the place of the old."[105]

The missionaries sought to transmit a faith that would lead to moral conviction and conversion. As the people received Christianity, to be a Christian was much less a matter of conviction than of social propriety. So while the missionaries saw nominalism as a negative indicator of reception, for the indigenous people it was a positive sign of having incorporated Christianity into their religio-social-political structures. The development of a cadre of experts, the catechists and clergy, further enhanced nominalism because it tallied with the "orders," in traditional religion, of priests and mediums. In my view, the professionalization of the ministry advanced further the idea that "nominal" Christianity was "normal" Christianity, in the perception of the indigenous adherents. Nominalism was a result of integrating Christianity into indigenous society.

At the institutional level, the integration of the Church into society revolved around its formal and informal linkages with the traditional and colonial institutions.[106] If the pre-1900 period is taken as the genesis period of the Church, then the first two and a half decades after 1900 were a period of consolidating the Church to become a permanent member of Buganda society and, later, the rest of Uganda. The Mission worked with the indigenous Church leadership, and was often supported by the colonial establishment in building infrastructure and structures that would entrench the Church in society. At least four elements are observable that constituted that process: the influence of the Missionary and indigenous Church leaders in the restructuring of political institutions; a focus on education as the backbone the work of the Mission; the professionalization of the ministry; and the development of church organization.

---

105. Quoted in F. B. Welbourn, *Religion and Politics in Uganda*, 7.
106. Hansen's monumental work, *Mission, Church and State*, is an analysis of these linkages in various areas such as land, labour, education, legislation and administration, and the resultant relationships. He has dealt in detail with the institutional growth of the Church of Uganda resulting from the interplay with the other two institutions, the Mission and the State.

The Church and Political Institution-Building

In order to understand the role of the Church in the political developments after the declaration of Buganda as a protectorate in 1894, a distinction needs to be made between the attitude of the CMS missionaries to political institutions and that of the African members of the Church. The missionaries' experience was of a legally established church – the Church of England. The evangelical heritage of the CMS mission seemed to dictate against establishment of a state church on the mission field.[107] But the need to protect the Mission from a repeat of their experiences in Buganda in the second half of the 1880s, and in order to secure freedom in the exercise of its mission work, it was important for the missionaries to influence political institution-building.

Reference has already been made to the instrumental role of the Mission in calling for the declaration of a British Protectorate on Buganda. Bishop Tucker and Archdeacon Walker were active players in the negotiations that gave birth to the Uganda Agreement of 1900.[108] The treatment of the full impact of the Agreement on the restructuring of Buganda society and on the emerging Uganda as a whole is beyond the scope of this thesis. But there were two outcomes, which stand out as pivotal in shaping the identity of the Church, that warrant brief comments. First, political power in Buganda was now, *de jure*, to be disposed according to affiliations based on religion, with the Protestants in a pre-eminent position. This was mirrored in subsequent agreements and settlements as the colonial administration extended the Protectorate boundaries beyond Buganda. Second, the stipulation that the CMS mission was allotted land "in trust for the native churches"[109] meant that it was the Mission to continue the process of negotiating with the colonial authority over the revision of the land

---

107. Max Warren makes this point in "The Missionary Expansion of Ecclesia Anglicana," in *New Testament Christianity for Africa and the World: Essays in Honour of Harry Sawyerr*, eds. Mark E. Glasswell and Edward W. Fashole-Luke (London: SPCK, 1974), 138.

108. Anthony Low account of the negotiations for the Uganda Agreement shows how pivotal the involvement of Walker and Tucker was in shaping its structure and content. D. A. Low and R. C. Pratt, *Buganda and British Overrule 1900–1955* (London: Oxford University Press, 1960), 25–159.

109. "The Uganda Agreement of 1900" in *Buganda and British Overrule 1900-1955*, eds. Anthony D. Low and R. Cranford Pratt (London: Oxford University Press, 1960), 360.

policy set out in the Agreement. Land ownership was central to the development of the educational enterprise that dominated the work of Mission and the Church.

Hansen has identified another objective of the missionaries' involvement with the traditional and colonial political authorities: the establishment of a Christian country, by which the Christian factor becomes "a guiding principle in the formulating policy."[110] The establishment of a Christian nation is to be distinguished from the establishment of a Christian state. The latter "implies the Christianisation of institutions in the state and the establishment of institutional linkages between church and state."[111] Establishing a Christian state would entail the "establishment" of the church, a status the CMS missionaries did not desire for the Church. Therefore they sought, under the leadership of Bishop Tucker and his successor Willis, to establish a Christian nation by influencing social legislation. For example, the Mission worked hard at ensuring that the marriage laws that were instituted were based on Christian values.[112] The other area through which the Mission sought to build a Christian nation was education.

It has already been argued that the distinction between religion and politics did not exist in the worldview of the Baganda and the other nationalities that were incorporated to form Uganda. For example, in Buganda, as it has already been indicated, the "religious professionals," the priests and mediums of the *Balubaale* cult, had the "political" responsibility of protecting the Kabaka. Politics had a religious dimension and religion had a political dimension. What Mbiti said of Africans in general is true of the Baganda: their religiosity affected all areas of life and they looked at life and experienced it through this religiosity.[113] Therefore the goal of the African leaders of the Church was the "Christianisation of political institutions,"[114] seeking to establish a virtual Protestant monopoly over the

---

110. Hansen, *Mission, Church and State*, 299.

111. Ibid.

112. Ibid., 206–279.

113. John Mbiti, "Christianity and Traditional Religions in Africa," *International Review of Missions* 59 (October 1970): 432.

114. This is how Hansen characterizes the process by which the indigenous political institutions became controlled by the Protestants. Hansen, *Mission, Church and State*, 318–358.

traditional political institutions. Once the process had been accomplished in Buganda, it was extended to the other kingdoms and areas of Uganda through the agency of Protestant Baganda chiefs, in alliance with Baganda catechists and evangelists.

Formal Education

The schools were initially started for the daughters and sons of chiefs and clergymen. They were also considered to be the breeding ground for potential chiefs and administrative assistants in the colonial administration. But as education expanded – horizontally in extent, and vertically in levels – it took on a character of its own. The CMS mission began consciously to make education an essential part of its work and increasingly turned most of its resources. It became the primary preoccupation of the Mission. As Asavia Wandira observed:

> The pace of expansion of the Church and its quality became inextricably intertwined with the expansion and quality of education. To the outsider it looked as if there could be no education centre without the Church and equally there could be no Church centre without education.[115]

Schools became centres of Christian instruction, conversion and the formation of character.[116] Taylor notes:

> Anyone reading through the records and reports of the Uganda mission cannot fail to be struck by a change which quite suddenly comes over them about the year 1904. Up to that time there is a regular yearly account from each mission district of the missionaries' itenerations, the work of the catechists and the successes and failures in the outreach of the church. But in later reports almost all the space is devoted to the educational and medical work of the mission as a whole. They are paragraphed not according to districts but by institutions, and the

---

115. Asavia Wandira, "Missionary Education in Uganda Revisited," in *A Century of Christianity in Uganda 1877-1977*, eds. T. Tuma and P. Mutibwa (Nairobi: Uzima Press, 1978), 82.
116. Hansen, *Mission, Church and State*, 249.

catechist ceases once and for all to have any news value. This in a rather startling way reveals what was certainly a gradual, and largely unconscious change of interest in the mission as a whole.[117]

Education became the "backbone" of missionary work.[118] The Protestant and Catholic missions were seeking to out do each other in monopolizing education, as a way of propagating their "religions" and thereby ensuring dominance in society. Moreover the colonial government was hesitant to take over education from the missions, due to the size of financial commitment that it required. The colonial government therefore looked with sympathy upon the missions' educational enterprise, and was content to support it through grants.[119]

The dominant focus on education introduced professionalism within the CMS missionary ranks, and distanced the African Church workers further from them. Missionary attention was increasingly drawn more towards education and away from the concerns of evangelization and nurture of the young converts outside the educational institutions.

Leadership and Ministry Formation

The style of leadership of the first generation of African church leaders was largely chief-like. As more and more catechists and lay evangelists were deployed, there was an evolutionary shift from the chief-church-leadership to the catechist type. Moreover the missionaries were increasingly uncomfortable with the chief-church-leaders, because of missionaries' perception and tradition of the separation of church and state.[120] The missionaries therefore set out to develop an independent ecclesiastical structure. Archdeacon Robert Walker developed a training centre at Mengo, where men were sent

---
117. Taylor, *Growth of the Church in Buganda*, 91.
118. Hansen, *Mission, Church and State*, 250.
119. Hansen has analysed the historical process by which the two missions came to monopolize education, the establishment of the educational enterprise and the bargain for grants from the colonial government in his *Mission, Church and State*, 224–258.
120. Taylor, *Growth of the Church in Buganda*, 72, notes that the very idea of separate hierarchy of church and state was foreign to the Baganda, since it implied a dualism in the society.

for training as Junior Catechist, Senior Catechist and Lay Readers. In 1901 the numbers had grown so great that all Junior Catechists were trained in the county and district centres.[121] This professional ladder became, henceforth, the main and almost exclusive recruiting ground for the supply of ordained clergy.

The professionalization of the ministry had a negative impact on the Church initially. First, the chiefs were distanced from church affairs. Their enthusiasm waned and a number even began to fall away from Christian living and the support of the church.[122] The security of the catechist who had depended on the support of the chiefs waned as a result, and the catechists began to be disenchanted. Moreover as the colonial political establishment grew, it became obvious that to be a catechist was not as lucrative as being in government structures. All this led to a serious lack of catechists and a falling away of quality in the men who offered themselves. There was even a strike in 1905, when some of these catechists demanded better terms and higher wages. The net consequence of all this was a decline both in the quality and quantity of Christians.[123]

Second, there was a shift in the role of the missionaries and their relationships with the indigenous leaders of the Church.[124] While the chief-church-leaders were colleagues to the missionaries, the catechists were not. A number of them had been recruited from the pool of "boys" and "servants" in the households of the missionaries. When these "boys" became catechists and church leaders the missionaries still considered them as boys. The partnership that existed during the earlier period, with the first generation leaders, between the missionaries, the African clergy and the Christian chiefs, was gradually eroded.

Third, the parallel development of professionals to run the schools gave rise to a separation and demarcation of roles of the catechist and schoolmaster. As Tom Tuma observed in Busoga, this led to a "growing gulf

---

121. Ibid., 76.
122. Ibid., 79.
123. Tuma, "Church Expansion in Buganda," 28. The table shows a significant drop between 1904 and 1906 in the numbers of baptisms and Christian converts.
124. Taylor, *Growth of the Church in Buganda*, 73, 76.

between the catechist and the schoolmaster, which threatened to wreck the otherwise informal catechist-schoolmaster 'alliance'."[125]

The situation was exacerbated by the lack of a linkage between higher education and recruitment to the ministry. The Mission's disposition towards education as the "backbone" of missionary work was not translated into a recognition of the need for an educated cadre of clergy and catechist to serve the growing educated elite. Furthermore, the status value of formal education was raised by the fact that formal education was an essential criterion in the colonial administration's recruitment of workers. Therefore in societal standing, the catechists and clergy were of a lower status compared to that of their counterparts in colonial administration.

The establishment of diocesan theological colleges, at Mukono in 1913[126] and at Buwalasi in 1930, entrenched the professional ladder system of recruitment for the ministry. The poor remuneration of catechist and clergy could not attract the interest of those in the formal education system. The result was a perpetuation of the depressed status of the ministry in society.

Church Organization

Elements that were internal and external to the Church influenced the development of organizational structures in the formative period, from the time of the Mengo Council in 1885. Internally, the Church needed to determine the relationship between the CMS mission and the emerging indigenous church. Externally, there was the colonial administration establishing and expanding its control of the Protectorate, and the traditional cultural-political authority readjusting to the new environment. The interplay between internal and external factors also became a source of tension and further readjustment in the Church.

Alfred Tucker, effectively the first bishop of the Church,[127] was concerned right from the beginning that whatever organizational structure

---

125. Tuma, *Building a Ugandan Church*, 71.
126. Kevin Ward, *Called to Serve: Bishop Tucker Theological College, Mukono; A History, 1913–1989* (Mukono: Bishop Tucker Theological College, 1989), 2.
127. The diocese of Uganda was carved out of the diocese of Eastern Equatorial Africa in 1897 under the leadership of Alfred Tucker, its third bishop, having arrived in 1890. Its first bishop was killed during Kabaka Mwanga's reign; the second bishop, Henry P. Parker,

adopted, it should provide for "the equality of the workers [African and missionaries], and for the total integration of the [CMS] mission into the Uganda church whereby the missionaries should be at the disposal of the synod."[128] But Tucker met with vigorous opposition from his fellow missionaries, and therefore the constitution for the Native Anglican Church (NAC) adopted in 1909, vaguely linked the Mission to the Church but never under it.

Church structures were developed along the same lines as those of the colonial administration, patterned along Buganda kingdom administration that had become the colonial model for administering the Protectorate. As Bishop Brown observed:

> The Church had a hierarchy parallel to that of the state. The Bishop corresponded to the Governor; the archdeacon to the Chief Secretary; and the rural dean, pastor and evangelist mirrored the County Chief, the sub-County chief and the local chief. In many cases the area of the deanery was the same as a county, and that of a parish a district.[129]

The ecclesiastical administrative boundaries were demarcated along the same lines as the geo-political divisions of the colonial administration. It seems however, that shortage of staff in the Church made it difficult for the parallelism between the ecclesiastical and civil administration to be maintained. In each district there were three levels of Church workers corresponding to their origins. The indigenous catechists were at the bottom of the pyramid; the Baganda clergymen in the middle; and, the CMS missionaries at the top.

To match the ordered hierarchy of ministry there was a corresponding organization of the Church into a pyramid structure.[130] Uganda was divided into districts and the Diocesan Church Council was a representative organ, dominated by missionaries. In the Church Council, decision making increasingly came by democratic and representative principle, rather than

---

consecrated in 1886, managed to reach the south side of Lake Victoria in December 1887 but died of illness there in 1888, without ever reaching Uganda.

128. Taylor, *Growth of the Church in Buganda*, 87.

129. Brown, *Three Worlds*, 128.

130. Taylor, *Growth of the Church in Buganda*, 76–77.

the hitherto operative principle of corporate responsibility and consensus. The input from the grassroots was increasingly lost as the Church increasingly became centralized. Taylor observes:

> It was at the centre that the problems of the church must be faced and discussed by the delegates to the Council. It was at the centre that the needs must be known and new recruits enlisted for the work. And at the centre was the missionary.[131]

The process of centralization weakened the grassroots work since it was relegated to the periphery. But centralization had another effect. With the missionary at the centre, his role as controller became increasingly evident, and introduced the principle of tutelage. Taylor remarks:

> The principle of tutelage in the church is revealed by any clericalism which cannot trust the laity with spiritual responsibility; by any bureaucracy in which every official is supervised by the man above him; by a centralisation which only recognises as part of the church life those things that are initiated, supported and controlled from a central office; and by the imposition of "extraneous" demands which do not touch the conscience of the local churches. Above all it expresses itself with attitudes of watchfulness, anxiety and pessimism.[132]

This therefore increased the cleavage between the missionary and the native, the clergy and the laity, and gave rise to clericalization of the ministry. With the missionaries increasingly turning their energies and resources to social services, the gap between the clergy and catechist was growing. The clergy enjoyed increasing powers and the catechist suffered from increased responsibility, and diminished authority.

Tom Tuma has pointed to one positive aspect of some of these developments: the diminishing missionary influence at the pastoral level allowed the indigenous workers a lot more room for individual initiative and assumption of more responsibilities.[133] For although the lower levels

---

131. Ibid., 78.
132. Ibid., 83.
133. Tuma, *Building a Ugandan Church*, 144–168.

of church leadership did not share in the authority wielded by the middle- and higher-level leadership, those at the middle level were Africans. This instilled confidence in indigenous leadership that was crucial for the years ahead.

As a result of numerical growth and geographical spread, the Uganda diocese was partitioned in 1927 into two, creating: the Diocese of Upper Nile, covering eastern and northern Uganda and stretching from Bukedi to West Nile;[134] and the diocese of Uganda, covering Buganda, Busoga and western Uganda.[135]

Reflection

The leading role of Buganda in the political development of Uganda was mirrored in the ecclesiastical sphere. Mission work in Uganda was patterned along the experience in Buganda and developments in Buganda always produced ripple effects in most, and sometimes all, of Uganda. Hansen has summarized well the impact of Buganda, what he calls "the Buganda syndrome," on the process of planting churches and the development of institutional structures in Uganda.

> First, Buganda was an important determinant in the policy-making process. Secondly, identification with Buganda accounted in various contexts for the government's attitude and its responses to the mission's suggestions and actions. Thirdly, the Buganda factor influenced the attitude to the mission and the church in other parts of the community.[136]

This "Buganda syndrome" was implanted into the identity of the Church, and in the later years became a source of internal tension and conflict.

The planting of churches beyond Buganda followed a three-phase process. The first phase was characterized by initial resistance to the pioneer missionaries, followed either by some conversions or withdrawal, depending on the impact of the resistance. The first indigenous conversions always

---

134. The Upper Nile included southern Sudan. In 1935, the Southern Sudan became part of the Bishopric of Khartoum.
135. Uganda diocese covered also the two countries of Rwanda and Burundi.
136. Hansen, *Mission, Church and State*, 404.

sparked off a response, either of further resistance or rapid growth depending on the level of destabilization of the social and power relations engendered by those conversions. This is why the strategy for the missionaries was to begin the work of evangelism with the kings and chiefs hoping that their conversion would result in the subsequent reconfiguration of the social and power relations in favour of the missions.

Once the first resistance was overcome, it was followed by the second phase characterized by rapid growth and the building of some rudimentary organizational structure that incorporated indigenous participation and ownership of the leadership process. The pioneer indigenous leaders were selected on the basis of their standing in the community prior to conversion. Experience in Buganda had taught the missionaries that to consolidate that growth, it was crucial to incorporate the development of schools as part of the process of recruiting and developing indigenous leadership. So the third phase was characterized by the development of educational and medical services, the latter primarily for evangelism, and the former for both evangelism and development of leaders. The attraction of social services resulted in further numerical growth. The problem of this phase for the missionaries was that while numbers of baptism were often very high, the churches were empty on Sundays.

A crucial factor to observe in the progress of the planting of the Church in Uganda is the distinction between the "faith transmitted" and "faith received." The former refers to Christianity as understood by the transmitters, and the latter to Christianity as understood by the receptor in the process of reception. The receptor always indigenizes in interpreting and applying the transmitter's messages; that is, he incorporates the transmitter's message on the basis and terms of his or her own structures of understanding and existence. The result is not always as intended or desired by the transmitters. Even when certain forms are accepted wholesale without any visible adaptation, the substance and meaning attached to them will be adapted to fit in with the indigenous ones.

"Nominalism" illustrates the significance of distinguishing "faith transmitted" from "faith received." After Christianity was accepted as an integral part of Buganda society, the missionaries did not realize that the reasons for "conversion" had changed. The missionaries still believed that acceptance of Christianity would lead to conviction, conversion and commitment, whereas for the Baganda, to be a Christian was much less a matter of conviction than of social propriety. What the CMS missionaries called "nominalism" had resulted from the indigenizing of Christianity in categories of traditional religious practice. In this sense "nominalism" is a form of indigenous *Christianity*. Because the missionaries did not understand this process of indigenization, they continued using the same methods of evangelization, of "reading" and formal education, which were the very methods that promoted the "nominalism" that was averse to them.

"Nominalism" is also indigenous *religion*, in the sense that it is a consequence of the indigenization of the notion "religion," that is, religion as a basis for group identity, and not just a category of an ontological relationship with the ultimate Other. It is for this reason that the participation of indigenous catechists and evangelists in transmission was crucial, since they became carriers of an already-indigenized Christianity.

A pattern had emerged in the process of planting churches beyond Buganda. In most of Uganda the first evangelists were CMS missionaries and African evangelists, mostly Baganda, although not exclusively. The next step was the developing of local evangelists in the Church, a process that was often paralleled by the development of local assistants in the civil-administrative structure. Many who began their career as church teachers, were later appointed as administrators in the civil hierarchy, since the most literate in an area would be the church teacher, and literacy was an essential requisite for the posts of *Ssaza* and *Gombolola* chiefs.[137] The third step in developing ministerial leadership involved the promotion of some of the African teachers and evangelists to ordained ranks of deacon and priest. This also led to the building of a hierarchy in ministry. Moreover at this stage, in most of the Church centres, there was a church school and a formal school at which western education was imparted. In the larger centres there would also be a health centre. Of all these levels of ministry the role of the catechist-evangelist was most pivotal.

There are two other features of identity, arising out of the "Buganda syndrome," by which the Church knew itself and was to be known in the

---

137. Sweeting made a similar observation in the development of Church ministers in Buwalasi.

years to come: Protestant and "established." Protestant identity resulted from its rivalry with the Catholic Church. It needs to be clarified that the Protestant identity of the Church had very little to do with the Protestant reformation in Europe of the sixteenth and seventeenth centuries, because the European experience was not in its memory. True, it was part of the memory of the Mission, and occasionally missionaries referred to this historical link; but it never became a formative factor in the experience of the indigenous Church, because the most crucial "other" was the Roman Catholic Church in Buganda. This distinction was so important that it became a mark of personal identity. As Low observed:

> At the same time it is very striking indeed that in the first extant list of members of Buganda's newly constituted "native council," the Lukiiko, which dates from 1902, each member should have been primarily designated as either "P," "C," or "I" – Protestant, Catholic, or *Islaimu*. These designations were now indigenous to Buganda. They had become established amongst the most important which men possessed.[138]

This denomination-based identity was subsequently transported to all Uganda. To be Protestant was a way to distinguish the identity of the Native Anglican Church of Uganda over against the other two "religions," Islam and the Roman Catholic Church, but in particular the Roman Catholic Church. The primary connotation of the notion "religion" was not "faith" as in an ontological relationship, but rather group identity. "Religion" or *eddini* became a social categorization. It is for this reason that Protestantism was considered a different "religion" from Roman Catholicism, as opposed to considering both as belonging to the same religion but different denominations. This was an indigenization of an otherwise alien category "religion," imbued with a contextual meaning. "Religion" as a category of "faith" had never been the primary basis of group consciousness, but rather blood kinship, beginning with the smallest unit, the household, to the clan. Nations as geo-political entities were an amalgamation of various clans either through a historical process of migration or conquest. Now with the introduction of *eddini*, "religion," shaped in its three forms

---

138. Low, *Buganda in Modern History*, 48.

– Islam, Protestantism and Roman Catholicism – societal configuration became transformed and more complex.

However it should not be construed that there was no element of faith in the indigenous apprehension of Christianity. The pageboys killed by Mwanga died because of their faith. A distinction needs to be made between two perspectives. The first focuses on Mwanga and his henchmen, and the second on the pageboys. Mwanga saw them from the perspective of "religion" as a socio-political category. From this perspective, they were a threat to him and therefore Mwanga's action was intended to check their political ascendance. As Mande has put it, "Mwanga's problem was not religion *qua* religion, but fear of having power eroded."[139] However, the fact that the pages faced their death incognito in terms of religious affiliation, suggests that for them it was their faith at stake. Roman Catholic author Faupel reluctantly admits this in quoting Miti, who wrote:

> In the early days, especially during the persecution, there was no distinction of religion or denomination; we were all Christians, whether one went to Mackay or Pere Lourdel for religious instruction. All Christian converts were one family, with two internal arbitrary divisions as it were; we loved one another, and wished one another well.[140]

They died together, Protestants and Catholics. It was the missionaries who were keen on distinguishing the forms of Christianity to which they belonged.[141] The religious wars in Buganda of the late 1880s and early 1890s were essentially a struggle over group supremacy and not faith. The establishment of Protestantism was the consequence.

The notion of "establishment" has to be interpreted from the perspective of the historical, religio-cultural and socio-political context of Buganda, because it is Buganda that gave this status of establishment to the Church. It has already been argued that the notion "religion" was itself alien to

---

139. Wilson Muyinde Mande, "An Ethics for Leadership Power and the Anglican Church in Buganda," Aberdeen University, unpublished PhD Thesis, 1996, 41.
140. James Miti, quoted in Faupel, *African Holocaust*, 137.
141. Faupel in his entire account, *African Holocaust*, is also at pains to distinguish the martyrs according to their religious affiliation, and classifies them as Catholic and Protestant martyrs and not just Christian. Ibid., 207–222.

traditional Buganda, because all of life was religious. But if pre-Islam, pre-Christian Buganda is analysed in terms of "religion,"[142] where "religion" is understood to be "compounded of custom, law, outward observance, beliefs held in common,"[143] and define "establishment" as "the religion that serves the state," then the cult of the Balubaale was the "established religion" of the kingdom, a status accorded to it by custom. The cult of the *Balubaale* existed to serve the Kabaka and the kingdom. This was the mindset with which the Baganda appropriated Protestant Christianity.

If the only legitimate mechanism for "establishment of a church" was constitutional legislation, then Hansen is right in observing that:

> As regards establishment, the Church of England model could not be extended to Uganda, despite the fact that the mission and the church were in ecclesiastical communion with the Church of England; these links did not place the church in a position different from that of any religious body.[144]

In fact an attempt at legal establishment was made by some Baganda delegates at the second meeting of the new synod in 1906, when they proposed that the Church be made an integral part of the kingdom by legislation. But the head of the CMS mission pointed out that "there was no established church in Uganda, and therefore no state church, as both Catholics and Protestants were present in the country."[145] Hansen adds:

> If for no other reason, it was fully recognised that the denominational factor precluded any kind of establishment. It should be added that this did not rule out a process of Christianisation of essential political institutions like the

---

142. The notion "religion" can be misleading when applied to primal religious practice, because it has the tendency to cloud the real essence of pre-Christian traditional approaches to religion, because the popular usage of the term "religion" connotes "a particular system of thought." However when "religion" is understood in its primal African traditional understanding as referring to societal norms, rituals and values – a way of life, then we can use it to describe African experience of reality and of the "Ultimate Other." For an extended discussion on the definition of African traditional religion, see Idowu, *Towards an Indigenous Church*.
143. Taylor, *Growth of the Church in Buganda*, 258.
144. Hansen, "Church and State in a Colonial Context," 119.
145. Ibid., 109.

kingship and chieftainship, nor the projection of an image of establishment in relation to the African political system.[146]

What Hansen calls "Christianisation of essential political institutions" was "establishment" to the Baganda. Mazrui has helpfully pointed to the sixteenth-century principle of *cuius regio eius religio,* "whosoever reigns shall determine the religion of his territory," in understanding establishment in the Ugandan context.[147] With the advent of foreign religions in Buganda, it was always the Kabaka's religion that constituted the official religion of the kingdom. Although Mutesa I did not officially convert to Islam in the earlier period prior to the advent of Christian missionaries, the Islamic golden age of 1862–1875[148] was possible primarily because Mutesa I adopted Islam. During the short-lived reign of Kabaka Kalema, the "only truly Muslim king,"[149] after the resounding victory of the Muslims, Islam was the established religion for that period of time.

It was this understanding of "establishment" that motivated the Protestant or Catholic Baganda chiefs to compete for baptism of Mwanga.[150] They even restored him to the throne after routing out Muslims and Kalema from the palace, in spite of Mwanga's responsibility for the massacre of Christians in 1885–1886. The installation of the Protestant baby-king, Daudi Chwa in 1897, and his "coronation as the first Christian Kabaka" at Namirembe Cathedral, not only sealed political ascendancy of the Protestants, but also confirmed the established position of the Protestant Church from the perspective of *cuius regio eius religio.* Although the colonial government tried to preclude constitutional establishment by enforcing a policy of religious neutrality for the State, the constitutional apparatus of which would be separated from any religious affiliation, the indigenous people were engaged in finding their own ways establishing the Church. The Catholic Church attempted to claim establishment on the basis of its numerical majority but without success. As Mazrui has observed:

---

146. Ibid.
147. Mazrui, "Religious Strangers in Uganda," 21–26.
148. Kasozi, *The Spread of Islam in Uganda,* 20–33.
149. Ibid., 48. Kalema ruled for less than one year, spanning most of 1889.
150. Kiwanuka, *A History of Buganda,* 220–236.

Catholics over the years began to outnumber Protestants significantly, both within Buganda and on national scale. And yet this situation of Catholic demographic preponderance was accompanied by a Protestant political ascendance. Here once again lay the seeds of *cuius regio eius religio*.[151]

The notion of "establishment" imbued with indigenous meaning, not to be associated with constitutionalism or the "establishment of the majority," but with the religion of the ruler.

Thus the church that the CMS missionaries had participated in founding during the last quarter of the nineteenth century emerged in the early quarter of the twentieth century as an indigenous, Protestant and quasi-established church.

---

151. Mazrui, "Religious Strangers in Uganda," 26.

CHAPTER 3

Schism and Revival in the Church, c1910–c1960

The previous chapter gave a brief account of the genesis of the Church, how it grew and spread, to the extent that by 1926, when the borders of the geo-political entity "Uganda" as it is known today were finalized, the Church embraced the entire country. As the Church grew, it attracted a large membership, became "established," and was increasingly becoming institutionalized. This was especially the case in Buganda, where the Church was into its third generation of indigenous and missionary leadership. There were growing internal tensions in the CMS mission and the indigenous Church leadership which gave rise to a realignment of social forces in the Church, leading to the emergence of schismatic and renewal movements, dissenting from the "establishment" of the Church. They were a response to the Church's growing bureaucratization and "nominalism."

In addition to the internal tensions in the Church, the socio-political situation of the late 1910s and early 1920s created a catalytic environment of dissent from established order. It was a period of ferment, resulting from the restructuring of social, political and economic relations provided in the Buganda agreement of 1900.[1]

---

1. Reference is made in particular on the impact of the Buganda Agreement on land distribution and the consequent social-political tensions, particularly among the Bataka, leading to the formation of the Federation of the Bataka in 1921. Only two years before that the Young Baganda Association had been formed, in opposition to the chiefs in power. D. Anthony Low, *Buganda in Modern History* (London: Weidenfeld and Nicolson, 1971), 89; C. Robins, "'Tukutendereza': A Study of Social Change and Sectarian Withdrawal in the Balokole Revival of Uganda," Columbia University, unpublished PhD dissertation, 1975, 143–144.

This chapter examines the development and significance of three movements: *Ekibina kya Katonda Omu Ayinza Byona (KOAB)* Society of the One Almighty God, the Mengo Gospel Church and the East African Revival.[2] The greater part of the chapter is dedicated to the rise, spread and impact of the East African Revival movement beginning in the late 1920s, because of its enduring and paradigmatic impact on the Church. However, all the three movements highlight the significance of the two features in the growth and impact of the Church in Uganda at the time: vernacularization and nominalism, which have to do with the process of indigenization.

The chapter begins by considering the emergence and demise of the KOAB and the Mengo Gospel Church.[3] Then it delves into the story of the East African Revival, first by outlining its emergence and spread. Due attention is given to its characteristic features, its ecclesiological orientation and the issues that its incorporation into the Church raised, thereby elucidating the contribution of the movement to the entire story of the Church.

The chapter concludes by reflecting further on the insights that these movements bring to the understanding of the issue of nominalism in the Church. It also examines the implications of the three theological motifs in the Revival for understanding the Church. These are: the Cross, as the theological-hermeneutic for Revival *credo* and *praxis*; the fellowship, as the ecclesiological equivalent to the indigenous clan-community; and the notion of "testimony" as that which authenticates individual and community faith, the distinguishing mark of "real" Christianity from "nominal" Christianity.

---

2. The Africa Greek Orthodox, another movement that emerged during this period, is left out of the discussion because it has a long story of its own, later becoming a major denomination. But the issues that its emergence raises are essentially the same as in the case of the other two. Welbourn has placed the emergence of all three movements against this background of religious and moral decline, in his study *The East African Rebels* (London: SCM Press, 1961), chs. 1, 2.

3. Our discussion based on Welbourn's study, *The East African Rebels*, chs. 2–5, and Oral Interviews with Zebulon Kabaza and Rev Canon P. Kigozi.

Ekibina kya Katonda Omu Ayinza Byona (The Society of the One Almighty God)

Yoswa Kate, an early convert to Christianity in the 1880s, doubled as a chief of one of the major counties in Buganda[4] and a licensed catechist. Whether his disapproval of the land settlement dictated by the 1900 Uganda agreement has anything to do with his disenchantment with the Church is not certain. He is on record to have protested against the bias of the agreement in favour of *Bakungu* (chiefs) over *Bataka* (clan elders).[5] Welbourne has indicated that his dissent with the Mission and the Church began with his discovery, from reading the vernacular version of the Bible, that there was no Biblical justification for the use of medicine. One of the relevant passages is as follows:

> When thou art come into the land which the Lord thy God giveth thee, thou shalt not learn to do after the abominations of those nations. There shall not be found among you anyone that maketh his son or his daughter to pass through the fire, or that useth devination, or an observer of times, or an enchanter, or a witch, or a *charmer*, or a consulter with familiar spirits, or a wizard, or a necromancer. For all that these things do are an abomination to the Lord: and because of these abominations the Lord thy God doth drive them out before thee. Thou shalt be perfect with the Lord thy God.[6]

Kate interpreted the text to mean that in the event of any sickness the believer's response ought to be complete reliance on God Almighty for healing. The Luganda vernacular version translates the word "charmer" as *omusawo*. It is the same Luganda word used to refer to anyone in the medical profession. On the basis of this interpretation, Kate concluded that the Bible repudiated the medical doctor.[7] The irony of Kate's interpretation is

---

4. Kate was a *Mugema*, head of the Monkey clan.
5. Welbourn, *The East African Rebels,* 18–20. Kate is said to have absented himself at the signing of the Uganda Agreement in protest. He was of the view that the Agreement had curtailed the authority of the Kabaka in the kingdom. Low and Pratt, *Buganda and British Overrule* 89.
6. Deut 18:9–12 (KJV, emphasis added).
7. Deut 18:11.

that the missionaries had condemned traditional religious practices on the basis of similar biblical references, and Kate now applied it to the missionary medical practice. He formed *Ekibina kya Katonda Omu Ayinza Byona* (abbreviated KOAB) translated "the Society of the One Almighty God," to embody and proclaim the new-found truth.

One of the early converts to KOAB was another certified church teacher, Malaki Musajjakawa, who took it even further and argued that there was no biblical basis for requiring baptismal candidates to go through the rigour of preparation as was the case in the Church then. According to him the only biblical requirement for baptism was a public profession to belief in God and the resurrection of Christ.[8]

The response to Malaki's teaching was phenomenal. The readiness with which baptism was obtainable, provided all the usual advantages of being a Christian in Buganda, with no period of preparation and with a welcome tolerance of polygamy, alcohol and perhaps witchcraft.[9] Hitherto KOAB adherents were referred to as *Bamalaki*, literally translated "of Malaki," after their leader, Malaki. In 1914, KOAB broke away from the Church. The conversion of Semei Kakungulu to the movement in the late 1910s was instrumental in the spreading of the movement to Eastern Uganda. Baganda agents were also enthusiastic in spreading the movement to other regions. However, by and large the movement did not get many adherents in other regions. It remained concentrated in Buganda.

So great was the response that by 1921 there was an estimated 91,740 *Bamalaki* in Buganda alone[10]. A movement of this magnitude was bound to clash with the missionary Church leadership and colonial administration. The moment came when both the Mission and colonial government launched a vaccination campaign against smallpox. In keeping with their theological convictions the Bamalaki and their leaders not only shunned the immunization but also opposed the campaign. This prompted a decisive action from the Mission and colonial government. They collaborated and deported Yoswa Kate and Malaki in 1929, marking the movement's

---

8. Welbourn, *The East African Rebels*, 35.

9. Ibid., 50.

10. Welbourn has provided comprehensive statistics on the spread of the movement up to 1930, ibid, 54–57.

demise. It is noteworthy that the two arch-rivals, the Protestant and Catholic Churches agreed that "Malakite" baptism could not be accepted and that those members of KOAB who wished to join their churches would have to go through the baptismal preparation and be baptized again.[11]

Although the movement did not last, it is significant that reading of the vernacular Scriptures was catalytic in its emergence. The phenomenal response to its baptism shows the extent to which the natives desired Christianity. Now that Christianity had become indigenous, the Church, by insisting on rigorous baptismal preparation, was viewed as a barrier to greater incorporation of the masses into it. The formation of KOAB was a result of a search of an alternative church, one that would be true to indigenous reading of the Scriptures and transform Christianity from being a religion of a few to one for all, as was the case with traditional religion. In a sense KOAB was an indictment against the Church that it was nor sufficiently "nominal."

Mengo Gospel Church

Mabel Ensor, the founder of Mengo Gospel Church, came to Buganda on a short service with the CMS in December 1915 and was posted to work as a nurse at Mengo hospital. She joined as a full missionary after her home leave in 1920, convinced that her missionary gifts were as an evangelist rather than a nurse. She served briefly in Toro as a nurse and was then posted as an evangelist in Hoima. It was while in Hoima that her disquiet with the Church's "nominalism" began. Her disgruntlement with the Church and Mission increased when she moved to Kamuli in Busoga in 1923. She reported that, "a very large number of baptised Christians have returned to polygamy, devil possession and drinking: witchcraft is widely practised, and one is forced to the conclusion that much so-called Christianity is not the real thing but a veneer."[12] When she relocated to Gayaza 1926, she introduced a practice of making a public statement of conversion before baptism, as a way to deal with what she saw as a growing nominal membership.

---

11. Ibid., 38.
12. Ensor, quoted in Welbourn, *The East African Rebels*, 62.

The Mission administration began to be weary of her "unorthodox" ways and put some limitations to her movements, to her displeasure. She protested even more vehemently against the nominalism in the Church, and CMS policies. The head-on clash with the Mission came when she made a public accusation against an African clergyman, and refused the bishop's request to suspend work in that parish until the issue could be settled.

In March 1928, Ensor resigned from the Mission and moved to live at Mengo in the home of another missionary. It was here that she started her Bible study classes, later moving to her own home and built a church. Simeon Nsibambi, who was instrumental in the emergence and spreading of the East African Revival, was one of those who regularly attended Ensor's Bible study classes. In fact, it was at one of those Bible study classes that Nsibambi met Joe Church, the young medical missionary, who was on short leave from his work in Rwanda.[13]

Although many people attended the Bible study classes and other meetings she ran, only about 150 were baptized in twenty-five years. All the men who were ordained[14] at the beginning of the Mengo Gospel Church defected. The impact of Ensor and her church was very limited and short-lived. Her departure from the scene in 1953 was effectively the end of Mengo Gospel Church. The majority of its members rejoined the Protestant Church.

With such a track record it would be easy to dismiss Ensor and the Mengo Gospel Church as inconsequential, but the fact that Ensor attracted a following in spite of her "faith principle," dominating leadership style, and failure to identify with African lifestyle[15] demands our attention. The significance of Ensor's Mengo Gospel Church does not lie with her as an individual, but with what she represented, which attracted both missionary and indigenous enthusiasts. Although they did not agree with her forming another church, they shared her revulsion against moral relapse in the Church that was interpreted to be an indicator of "nominalism." The

---

13. Church refers to this meeting with Nsibambi as a milestone experience in Joe E. Church, *Quest for the Highest* (Exeter: The Paternoster Press, 1981), 66–68. Mabel Ensor later became a fiery critic of the Revival.
14. Ibid., 65–66. Missionaries of the Heart of Africa Mission from South Africa ordained three African leaders.
15. Ibid., 70.

emergence of the Mengo Gospel Church was a result of a perception that the Native Anglican Church of Uganda had lost its credibility and integrity as a community of faith in Christ, having become a church for all regardless of moral standing. Ensor's Mengo Gospel Church was the logical outcome of the CMS missionary perception that the Church had become nominal.

East African Revival Movement

Like Mengo Gospel Church, the roots of the Revival[16] are to be located in the growing discontentment with the moral state of the Church, and in the itinerant preaching ministry of Simeon Nsibambi. Although several accounts and studies[17] of the movement consider the encounter between Simeon Nsibambi with Joe E. Church in Kampala, in 1929, to be the "birth" of the Revival, Kevin Ward is right in pointing to Simeon Nsibambi as the prime mover.[18] Brian Stanley's argument that the Revival was a

---

16. There are four primary written sources on the Revival: Church's diary, *Quest for the Highest*; Katarikawe and Wilson's Study, "The East African Revival Movement"; the Revival hymnal *Ebyeshongoro Eby'Okujunwa*, and Joe Church's bible study manual *Every Man a Bible Student*. I consider the latter to be the systematic text of the Revival. In the Author's preface, Church has acknowledged that: "This book is rooted in revival. It took shape over a number of years as an outcome of the Revival, which from 1932 spread throughout Central and East Africa." (p. 11). These sources are considered authoritative because they are all internal to the Revival and its ethos. Joe Church is the acclaimed first generation revival leader missionary; James Katarikawe and John Wilson were both *Balokole* who were deeply involved in the life and leadership from the 1940s and 1950s respectively; and the hymnal was extensively used in the 1950s and 1960s in Ankole and Kigezi. Mr Z. Kabaza, who got saved at the Mbarara Convention, told me this in an interview with him, Kampala, 5 December 1994.
The oral sources were interviews with Zebulon Kabaza; Peter Kigozi; Geraldine Sabiti; and Yedediya Kayima, all of whom were saved between 1936–1950.

17. Narrative accounts include: Butler, *Hill Ablaze*; Church, *Quest for the Highest*; Katarikawe and Wilson, "East African Revival Movement"; H. Osborn, *Revival - A Precious Heritage* (Winchester: Apologia, 1995); Smoker, *Ambushed by Love*; Patricia St John, *Breath of Life*.
Analytical Studies include: R. Anker Petersen, "A Study of the Spiritual Roots of the East African Revival with Special Reference to Its Use of Confession of Sin in Public," Aberdeen University, unpublished MTh thesis, 1988; John Wilson, "Beliefs and Practices of the East African Revival," Fuller Theological Seminary, unpublished MA thesis, 1975; Robins, "Tukutendereza"; Most of these accounts owe their genesis narrative to the missionary sources, in particular Joe Church's diaries. For a more comprehensive bibliography see J. Murray, "A Bibliography on the East African Revival Movement," *Journal of Religion in Africa* 8, no. 2 (1975): 144–147.

18. Ward, "Tukutendeza Yesu," 114–115.

"movement so deeply rooted in an alien tradition,"[19] is based on the assumption that the origins of the movement primarily lie with Joe Church. To contend that "a true understanding of the Revival is impossible without an adequate consideration of the European religious tradition from which it sprang"[20] is to grant too strong a premium to its missionary origins. On the contrary, the Revival owes its primary origins in Uganda, with Nsibambi, in the context of a church that was perceived to have become nominal. Nsibambi's meeting with Joe Church after one of Mabel Ensor's Bible study sessions, that Brian Stanley credits to have been the genesis of the Revival,[21] only helped to take his vision of revival to Gahini in Rwanda where Church was working as a medical doctor.

It is Nsibambi's story, and not Joe Church's, that ought to dominate the genesis account of the Revival. After all Church was new on the Uganda Church scene, having arrived in the country in December 1927. He had therefore not yet experienced the Church, and could not speak of its "nominal" state with the same passion as Nsibambi. The Nsibambi-Church meeting needs to be considered from Nsibambi's perspective, and not that of Joe Church, and put in the wider context of the declining moral standards in the Church.[22]

Simeon Nsibambi had been converted as a young man at high school, but remained dissatisfied with his spiritual state and that of his church. He served in the First World War, and it was during that time that his search for an authentic life-changing experience began. Zebulon Kabaza recounts the story:

---

19. Brian Stanley, "The East African Revival – African Initiative within a European Tradition," *Evangelical Review of Theology* 2, no. 2 (1978): 194.
20. Ibid.
21. Ibid., 189.
22. Katarikawe begins his study by considering the nominal state of the Church and the issues raised by the schismatic movements. But on getting to the genesis of the Revival, he falls in the trap of telling the story from Joe Church's angle. Katarikawe and Wilson, "The East African Revival Movement," 38–51. The problem here is reliance on written sources, and ignoring the vast deposit of oral sources in the experience and memory of the Africans. The primary reason for Joe Church-biased accounts is their dependence on Church's accounts, which have been the only available written accounts of the genesis of the Revival for along time.

Schism and Revival in the Church, c1910–c1960

During the war of 1914–1918, he went into a ship to Zanzibar, and he had a lot of worry in his heart, but God taught him something. He saw that the ship was on a big ocean, but it had a captain who guided it; and he saw that he needed a captain to guide him in his life. God showed him that the captain he needed was Jesus.[23]

It was while he was working as a health inspector in the Buganda government, in 1922, that he experienced what he told his friends was his conversion, a baptism in the Holy Spirit.[24] He did not speak about it until 1926, when "God told him to tell others"[25] and hence started his preaching career, beginning with colleagues at work, members of his family, visiting people's homes and preaching on the streets, convinced that people needed to experience a life-transforming encounter with Jesus. This, he believed, would restore moral health to the Church. In his view the problem in the Church was "sin," and therefore the need for repentance.[26] Among his early converts were his younger brother Blasio Kigozi, Yona Mondo, William Nagenda his brother in-law,[27] and Yusuf Byangwa Mukasa.

When Ensor started her Bible study classes, Nsibambi was one of the first members of the class. Nsibambi shared Ensor's revulsion of a "nominal" Church, but was committed to renewing it from within rather than forming a separate one. It was at these meetings in March 1929 that he met Joe Church, a young missionary with Ruanda Mission.[28] Six months

---

23. Zebulon Kabaza, Personal Diary, 1952, 1953.
24. Ibid., and S. Peter Kigozi, OI, Kampala, 20 December 1996. Kigozi got saved in 1941, later became a very close friend of Nsibambi.
25. Zebulon Kabaza, Personal Diary, 1952, 1953.
26. Ibid.
27. Nsibambi and Nagenda married from the same family. Mondo was working at Government Printers, and Nagenda was a clerk in the colonial government, in Entebbe.
28. Joe Church was a missionary with Ruanda Mission sent by Cambridge Inter-Collegiate Christian Union (CICCU) in 1928, a group whose spirituality was heavily influenced by the Keswick holiness teaching, where he was active as a student while at university. The Keswick Convention is an annual Conference started in 1875, meeting in the Lake District of England at a village called Keswick. It emphasized the "in-filling of the Holy Spirit," "the deeper life," holiness and the "victorious Christian life." As Anker Petersen has shown in his study, "A Study of the Spiritual Roots of the East African Revival Movement with Special Reference to the Use of Confession of Sin," this double heritage shaped the ethos and teaching of the Revival right from its beginnings.

later they met again in Mengo. They studied the Bible together following themes as laid out in the Scofield Reference Bible[29] and prayed together. Although Church's account of this meeting indicates that Nsibambi decided "before God to quit all sin in faith, and claimed the victorious life and the filling of the Holy Spirit,"[30] other source close to Nsibambi indicate that this happened much earlier, in 1922.[31] If anything, this meeting was a turning point in the attitude and career of Joe Church. He admits to have returned to Gahini with a renewed sense of mission to preach salvation.[32]

Nsibambi continued for a while with his work in the public health department in Entebbe, but soon resigned to devote himself to full-time evangelistic work, based in his home in Bulange, in Mengo. His mission was to preach repentance and salvation, and urging any and all to be born again.

The two places, Mengo and Gahini, became revival centres, sources from where revival streams flowed to various regions of Uganda and Rwanda, and in later years to other parts of Eastern Africa. The decade of the 1930s saw the Revival spread to other parts of Rwanda, Burundi and to the entire Western, South Western and Buganda regions of Uganda and beyond.[33]

The Spreading of the Revival

There are a number of factors that may account for this rapid spread: prayer; the zeal of its adherents; the itinerant witness teams; missions and conventions; and the diocesan jubilee missions in 1937.

Prayer was recognized to be the primary mover in the spreading of the Revival. There was praying everywhere and all the time. Nsibambi, Church, Kigozi, Kinuka, Shalita[34] and all those involved in its beginnings

---

29. Church, *Quest for the Highest*, 67–68.
30. Ibid., 68. Evidently the Scofield Bible was Church's idea, as Nsibambi could not have had it at the time.
31. Zebulon Kabaza, Kampala, OI, 15 January 1997; S. Peter Kigozi, OI, Kampala, 20 December 1996.
32. Ibid.
33. In our study we have concentrated on the spread and impact of the Revival in Uganda only.
34. These three men, Blasio Kigozi, Yosiya Kinuka and Kosiya Shalita were working at the Gahini Protestant mission station in Rwanda. Blasio Kigozi, a Muganda, and younger brother to Simeon Nsibambi, was in charge of the boys school; Yosiya Kinuka, the head hospital assistant at Gahini, a Munyankole, had been trained by Dr Stanley Smith, and

believed that it was through prayer that God's power for Revival would be released. Church expressed this belief:

> Prayer is either a force or a farce. I believe in some mysterious way that will only be revealed to us in the life to come, prayer is the initial means by which our "material" bodies can "tune in" to God and become channels of his power to flow through to man.[35]

Conscious of the need for prayer for the "jubilee" missions[36], Joe Church sent to England a *Plea for Revival Prayer Fellowship* that was published and widely circulated.[37] Prayer continued to be a major theme and emphasis in the Revival.

The "saved ones" or *Abalokole*[38] as they referred to themselves, were urgent and zealous in telling others about repentance and the need to be born again, leading many to salvation.[39] They seemed to have not only a sense of urgency but also of obligation.[40] Robins summarizes their lifestyles well: "They travelled widely, camping on hillsides, in houses of Christians,

---

had volunteered to come with Church to start the hospital at Gahini; and Kosiya Shalita a Rwandan national had been educated in Uganda and was now a catechist at Gahini, his birth place. Church and Shalita used to share the leadership of the Daily Bible studies, which they started in early 1929.

35. Quoted in Katarikawe, and Wilson, "The East African Revival Movement," 55.

36. These were evangelistic campaigns organized to mark the fiftieth anniversary of the Church.

37. A full text of this is in St John, *Breath of Life*, 116–121. Patricia St John reckons that human effort and direction seem to have had little to do with the rapid early spread of the revival, "but the wave of prayer that went up from many parts of the world as a result of Joe Church's pamphlet, *Victorious Praying* no doubt had much to do with it."

38. *Abalokole* is plural, and *Mulokole* singular. Though technically less correct, the most frequently used word is *Balokole* instead of *Abalokole,* and it is what is maintained in this thesis.

39. The revival experience was called many names: being born again, being saved, deciding for Christ, believing, repenting of sins, yielding to Christ, receiving new life, conversion.

40. Church in *Quest for the Highest,* 82, tells the story of one Paulo, who after he was saved, asked to have three months leave to go far away to preach and witness to his home in Central Rwanda. This was common at the time. Church reports that as a result of the Convention at Gahini in 1933, twelve volunteered to go to Shyira and eight to Kigeme and twenty more to eastern Rwanda. So aggressive were they in their zeal that they were nicknamed *abaka*, which means "those on fire" or "the fiery ones." Ibid., 99.

preaching wherever they could collect an audience."[41] Their guiding principle was that "every Mulokole is a witness"[42] to the non-*Balokole*. They preached anytime, anyplace, anywhere – on buses, roadsides, in peoples homes, sometimes sleeping there, market places, church compounds and at funerals.[43] Their commitment, zeal, and sense of urgency were expressed in spontaneous evangelistic and missionary outreach. Blasio Kigozi epitomized this. His zeal and burden for the Church earned him an invitation from the then Bishop of Uganda, Cyril Stuart,[44] to address the Ugandan diocese Synod in 1936. Blasio was delighted at the opportunity. At the leaders' retreat prior to the synod, he spoke boldly against nominalism, formalism and moral laxity that were present in the Church. He could not speak at the Synod because he fell ill and died before the Synod. But his three-point message, which he had prepared, was read at the Synod, with much effect.[45]

A third feature of the spreading of the Revival was the preaching "teams." A team was any two or more Balokole meeting together for fellowship and mission. The first team consisted of Simeon Nsibambi, Yusuf Byangwa, Martin Luther Lwima and Yusuf Mukasa, based at Mengo.[46] Yosiya Kinuka, Blasio Kigozi and Joe Church were the second team of the Revival based at Gahini. The Mengo team was strengthened later in 1935 with the conversion of Yona Mondo and William Nagenda. But Nagenda had to join the Gahini team after Kigozi's death in 1936. Katarikawe's study records various preaching teams, at meetings and conventions, in

---

41. Robins, "Tukutendereza," 135. This was concurred by Kigozi, OI. Kigozi informed me that during the early years in Buganda the Balokole were not permitted to preach in the churches and so preached usually at the end of church services, in streets, markets, on buses – really anywhere there was an audience.
42. Katarikawe and Wilson, "The East African Revival Movement," 185.
43. Wilson tells stories of people saved at funerals. Ibid., 216.
44. Stuart succeeded Willis as Bishop of Uganda in 1934.
45. His three points were: (1) What is the cause of the coldness and deadness of the Church in Uganda?, (2) Why are people allowed to come to the Lord's table who are living in sin?, (3) What must be done to bring revival in the Church of Uganda? Church, *Quest for the Highest*, 122.
46. Kabaza, OI. The name Yusuf Mukasa has since disappeared in the memory and records of the Revival, because he did not continue.

East Africa and abroad.[47] A conspicuous feature of those teams was their multinational and often multiracial composition.

The Revival did not spread only through the spontaneous activity of the Balokole. Missions and conventions were planned, intended to bring renewal to the members of the Revival and as a way of evangelizing the thousands of baptized nominal members of the Church.[48] The first of the Conventions was at Gahini, soon after the Christmas of 1933. It was this convention that gave the first public platform, and set a format for the Revival message that was to become a kind of convention curriculum.

> There were addresses each day at 9, 11, and 3:30 p.m. which were arranged so as to form a sequence to last over five days, as follows: sin, the Holiness of God, the Second Birth, Repentance, Faith, Prayer, the Holy Spirit (three addresses), sanctification, the Christian walk (two addresses) and the Second Coming.[49]

It is instructive that Joe Church believes that with this Convention Revival began at Gahini,[50] even though there had been numerous conversions prior to this event. It does indicate the significance Joe Church attached to the event in propelling revival. Conventions were the major events that gave public portfolio to the Revival. The Revival leaders[51] always used a convention as a way of penetrating an area.[52] The Kabale con-

---

47. Katarikawe, and Wilson, "The East African Revival Movement," 77.
48. In the Revival accounts these two words, "conventions" and "missions" are used interchangeably because both were taken together.
49. Church, *Quest for the Highest*, 98. This is the same sequence of talks given at the Kabale Convention 1935, Mbarara 1936, Hoima 1937, and Kako 1937. The subjects were "Sin (Tuesday), Repentance (Wednesday), the New Birth (Thursday), 'Coming out of Egypt,' Separation (Friday), the Holy Spirit and the victorious life (Saturday)" were followed by a Gospel Service with eight testimonies on Sunday and a praise meeting on the final Monday. Ibid., 117. Church records that "At Mbarara they followed the same plan as we had at Kabale, but Blasio had asked for one extra subject . . . to be lost, perishing or doomed," Ibid., 121.
50. Church, *Quest for the Highest*, 98.
51. By 1936 the revival leaders were clearly J. Church, Blasio Kigozi and Kinuka, from Gahini and Simeon Nsibambi from Namirembe.
52. Similar conventions held in Mbarara in 1936, Kabete in Kenya 1937, Maseno in 1938, Bukoba in Tanzania in 1939, Juba in the Sudan 1939, Namirembe 1940, and Toro in 1941 sparked off the fires of revival in these areas.

vention of 1935 is particularly significant. It was the first time that both Mengo and Gahini streams met, and built solidarity that would lead to the rapid spread of the Revival along the Gahini-Kabale-Mengo corridor. Lawrence Barham wrote after the Kabale Convention of 1935:

> Confession of sin, restitution, apologies followed; many had dreams, sometimes receiving stirring impressions to read certain verses of the Bible, which led them to put away some sin, beer drinking for example. Preaching bands have gone out through the district; and very many are stirred . . . There is naturally a good deal of opposition and a certain amount of persecution.[53]

Bishop Cyril Stuart of the Diocese of Uganda recognized the value of the Revival in renewing the Church. To celebrate the Diamond Jubilee of the Church he planned a Diocesan-wide evangelistic mission led by the Revival leaders. The Jubilee missions, as they were called, and conventions took place in 1937 in several key centres in the diocese: at Hoima, Kako, Mbarara, and Mukono. Many were saved during these missions and were fired with zeal to take the message of the Revival to their people and beyond, as had happened earlier with the Pilkington Revival of 1893. The Mbarara, Mukono and Kako Conventions and their ripple effects produced some of the most outstanding Ugandan evangelists and churchmen. Among them: Eliyeza Mugimba, translator of the Runyankole/Rukiga Bible; Erica Sabiti, later first Archbishop of Uganda;[54] Zebulon Kabaza,[55] later the first Mission co-ordinator of the Church of Uganda; and Yoasi Musajjakawa later Archdeacon in Namirembe Diocese.

The Namirembe Convention of August 1940 must be singled out, as it was the first to bring together Balokole from the Diocese of Uganda with leaders from all over the East Africa region for instruction, exhortation and

---

53. Quoted by Church, *Quest for the Highest*, 117.

54. Geraldine Sabiti, OI, Kinoni Mbarara, 18 December 1996. Sabiti was saved after the Mbarara Convention, on 15 January 1939, as a result of the preaching of those who had been saved at the Convention of 1937. Sabiti was instrumental in encouraging Amos Betungura, Yustus Ruhindi, and Misaeri Kauma, to join the ordained ministry in the 1950s. These men later became Bishops in the Church.

55. Kabaza was saved two weeks later through the preaching of those who had been saved at the Convention, through the witness of E. Mugimba.

Bible teaching.[56] It marked the end of the first phase of the revival during which the features and ethos of the Revival were formed.

Opposition to the Revival

As the Revival spread, there was opposition to it particularly from the Roman Catholic Church, civic and political leaders, and the Church hierarchy.

The Balokole regarded Catholics as they did "pagans"[57] and "nominal" Protestants, and therefore took every opportunity to preach to them, thus creating tension. In Kigezi district, the conflicts between Catholics and Protestants that were endemic from the inception of the work of the two mother missions were exacerbated by the Revival.[58]

Opposition from the civic and political leadership arose from what was thought to be disruption, by the Balokole, of social, civic and economic order. For example, in Kigezi a curfew was imposed to stop the Balokole from their night singing.[59] In Ankole, Erica Sabiti's brother, who was a chief, opposed him. He accused Sabiti of encouraging people to disobey the authorities and to defile venerable *Bahima* traditions;[60] in Rujumbura Chief Karegyesa arrested some Balokole and sent them to gaol in Kabale[61] and in Buganda Katikiro Wamala, was opposed to any recognition of the Revival in the Church.[62]

Within the Revival itself there was tension. There was uneasiness over outward manifestations of revival that were becoming progressively more violent in the late 1930s. The weeping, trembling, glossolalia, dreams, visions and noises credited to be the work of the Spirit, caused some unease and disrepute because these dramatic manifestations were becoming

---

56. Church, *Quest for the Highest*, 181.
57. This was the way those who practised traditional religion were referred to.
58. Robins, "Tukutendereza," 240.
59. A file was opened in the District Commissioners office for these "twice born" and a strong letter written to the Archdeacon to deal with the Balokole. Katarikawe and Wilson, "The East African Revival Movement," 100–110. Also, Church, *Quest for the Highest*, 175.
60. Ward, "Tukutendereza Yesu," 121.
61. Ibid.
62. Kigozi, OI, 1996.

fashionable, leading to hysterical imitations and excesses.[63] Joe Church records an incidence when some of the Balokole in Kampala determined that with the new liberty in the Spirit, some exposure of the body, even between male and female, was a sign of victory over temptation.[64] Church adds:

> It was dealt with by prayer, and by helping these people to see that as a rule those who practice extremes (*kufuba* or striving as we used to call it) are generally those who are hiding some sin in their own lives that they won't give up. The whole thing died out within a few months, but not before it had given rise to exaggerated rumours.[65]

There was discomfort and tensions among the missionary members of the revival over the external manifestations of the Revival, and its theology. This was always a subject of discussion and contention, and often required special meetings.[66]

The opposition to the Revival and internal tensions did not stop the Revival in its growth and spread. By 1940 the Revival had spread to the whole of Eastern Africa, as far as Juba in Southern Sudan. It was now a movement with an identity of its own within the Church, with distinct *praxis*, *credo*, and leadership.

Characteristic Features of the Revival

What distinguished a Mulokole from a "nominal" Christian was evidence of a crisis conversion experience, enunciated in a "testimony," and being part of a fellowship group. These two, personal testimony and fellowship, on the one hand nurtured faith, and on the other hand, they were its evidence. It was within the context of the fellowship that one continued to experience revival and was enabled to continue in faith. The way to identify

---

63. Patricia St John tells some of the extremities of this in Kigezi that required intervention from the leaders, Lawrence Barham and Ezekeri Balaba. St John, *Breath of Life*, 124–125. Also see Church, *Quest for the Highest*, 132, 164, 169–171.
64. Church, *Quest for the Highest*, 176.
65. Ibid., 176–177.
66. The first such meeting was convened in Rwanda in 1938. See St John, *Breath of Life*, 139–144.

oneself with the fellowship was by attending fellowship meetings and other Revival gatherings at which other Revival activities were announced.

Fellowship Meetings

The fellowship meeting epitomized all that the revival stood for and became its trademark.[67] Stanley Smith has captured well the place of the fellowship meeting in Revival spirituality:

> The Fellowship Meeting: Every revived Christian stands in need of fellowship with some fellow believers with who he can meet regularly . . . It does not take the place of the ordinary services and meetings of the Church . . . its essential feature is that it is a time of sharing spiritual experiences in the presence of Christ, where all meet in Him on a level of equality.[68]

Regular attendance of the fellowship meetings was an indicator that one was continuing to be saved. There were local weekly or bi-weekly meetings primarily for devotion and mutual encouragement in Balokole homes and sometimes in Church centres depending on whether the church leadership was willing to accommodate them. Then there were monthly district meetings, often evangelistic in emphasis, at which people from the local fellowship groups came. The very large conventions organized at diocesan centres drew attendance from all over East Africa and beyond.[69] They provided an opportunity for international exchange, evangelism and Christian nurture and aimed at the renewal of churches.

The local fellowship meeting was the primary locus of worship for the Balokole. For, although their worship deriving from their dual identity (to the Church of Uganda, and to the Fellowship) had two forms, the formal and non-formal, the non-formal took precedence over the formal. Formal worship was within the context of the liturgy and order of the Church of Uganda on Sunday mornings, and non-formal worship was in

---

67. Katarikawe tells us how it all began in the early 1930s, in Katarikawe and Wilson, "The East African Revival Movement," 135.
68. Smith, *Road to Revival*, 143.
69. Dorothy E. W. Smoker indicates a similar pattern in "Decision-Making in East African Revival Movement Groups," in *African Initiatives in Religion*, ed. D. Barret (Nairobi: East African Publishing House, 1971), 97.

the context of Revival meetings and gatherings. Max Warren is right in observing that in so far as those involved in the Revival had been brought up in the Anglican tradition, the *Book of Common Prayer* continued to be valued.[70] The fellowship meeting was "to supplement the worship of the prayer Book"[71] without being a substitute. The key elements of what may be called the liturgy of the fellowship meeting were: hymn and chorus singing; extemporaneous prayer and thanksgiving; testimony and "walking in the light"; and the ministry of the word. Wilson describes the order of a typical Friday Fellowship meeting at Namirembe:

> There is singing of choruses for a quarter of an hour to the time of the meeting, because many people come by bus and others have come a bit late. Then all the brethren bow in readiness for prayer. No one is asked to pray specifically, but all feel the freedom to express their thanks and praise to God for the time he has kept them since the time of the last meeting, and also entreat Him to come down in His power and love and minister to them during the present meeting.
>
> Many people participate, until there is silence, which indicates that everyone feels that enough prayers have been given. Then they wait for those who are ready to "walk in the light" and to share with them what God has laid upon their hearts, which may take thirty minutes in all . . .
>
> The ministry of the word
>
> After this period of walking in the light one person stands up, usually on request or expressing his intention to speak by such words as "I have a word . . ." If no other person has asked before, he would give the word from the Bible. Then a few others would be free to stand up and expand or bring contribution to the message that has been given. It is often thought to be in bad taste to introduce a new subject when a brother has already spoken on another one. The ease with which they

---

70. Max Warren, *Revival: An Enquiry* (London, SCM Press, 1954), 107.
71. Ibid.

take up each other's message, expand it and bring it home to the hearers has always amazed brethren . . .[72]

However, what Warren has called the supplement emerged to be the primary, precisely because the fellowship meeting was where the Balokole belonged first. The defining moments of Revival spirituality were always at the Fellowship meeting.

Singing

Singing was a dominant feature of Revival meetings. Through singing the Balokole expressed joy, shared their testimonies, worshipped God and preached. In Kabale after the 1935 Convention, singing and dancing at the fellowship meetings is said to have gone on late into the night and even all night long. Katarikawe's remarks are worth quoting here about the development of revival hymnody:

> During this time many hymns were composed and sung throughout Kigezi. All the preaching was done mostly through hymns, followed by testimonies. Many people would burst into tears as they came under conviction through the words of the hymns, which had deep theological meaning. And as they sang they would appeal to those who had not found the forgiveness of sins through fear of losing their prestige, or fearing to confess their sins, to consider the One who had left all to come down for humankind. They sang about the love of God, the blood of Jesus, the new Jerusalem, and many other great themes. Those hymns were collected and printed under the title of 'Ebyeshongoro Eby'Okujunwa' – *Hymns of Salvation*[73]

Several of the traditional hymns were syncopated to fit with African tunes.[74] This is how the *Ebyeshongoro Eby'Okujunwa* was put together. Most of the hymns are familiar tunes but with new lyrics, and the others are old hymns sung to African tunes.[75]

---

72. Katarikawe and Wilson, "The East African Revival Movement," 166, 167.
73. Ibid., 100.
74. Church, *Quest for the Highest*, 131.
75. Of the 100 entries in the book, 3 are compositions of the Balokole, both lyrics and tune; 25 have original lyrics, with a tune adopted from *Golden Bells*, *Keswick* or *Ancient*

The Revival movement has come to be identified by a chorus which emerged spontaneously at the second Balokole Convention at Namirembe in 1944, another adaptation of a Keswick hymn, sung in the vernacular.

Tukutendereza, Yesu
Yesu Mwana gw'endiga
Omusayi gwo gunnazizza;
Nkwebaza, Mulokozi.

We praise thee, Jesus
Jesus the Lamb
Thy blood has cleansed me
I thank thee, Saviour.[76]

This chorus is sung during any and all events of the Balokole. It may be sung after one has given a testimony; or as a signal for the start of a meeting; as a greeting when two or more meet after a long time of absence from one another; or a punctuation of a sermon in a church service or fellowship meeting. It is a multi-purpose song, which would be sang expressing gratitude, joy, thanksgiving, and praise. It became the trademark of the revival and is sung throughout Eastern Africa to this day.

The hymnody of the Revival reflects an indigenous faith response engendered by the pre-Christian traditions. Idowu's has observed that "Africans are always singing; and in their singing and poetry, they express themselves, all joys and sorrows of their hearts, and their hopes and fears about the future find outlet."[77] The lyrics of the songs composed by Africans in the Revival attest to this. Celebration and story are combined in each hymn, as it recounts the message of the cross and salvation Jesus offers.

---

and Modern or *Sacred Songs and Solos* hymnals. *Ebyeshongoro Eby'Okujunwa* (London: SPCK, 1951).

76. Translation in Church, *Quest for the Highest*, 270, 271. The original is in *The Keswick Hymn Book*, London: Marshal, Morgan & Scott, no. 170. The lyrics of the chorus in English are:
   Glory, Glory Hallelujah
   Glory, Glory to the Lamb!
   Oh, the cleansing blood has reached me
   Glory, Glory to the Lamb!

77. Idowu, *African Traditional Religion*, 85.

Testimony

In the Revival, a testimony had two versions – life and oral. The quality of life is what gave content to the oral version; that is, the testimony was expected to be visible first before it was heard. Therefore authentic testimony was a combination of both. It had four dimensions to it. The first was the public confession and profession that was part of the conversion experience at the moment of conversion. Conversion in the Revival was always a crisis experience,[78] but was not complete until it was acknowledged publicly, beginning with a public confession, repudiating the past life and then followed by restitution. Reference to the past life was often a detailed confession of moral sins, such as stealing, dishonesty, sexual immorality, smoking tobacco, hatred, bitterness and alcohol abuse.[79] Restitution involved returning any stolen goods and unfaithful partners repenting to their aggrieved spouses, and seeking forgiveness and reconciliation. This was called "putting things right."[80]

The second dimension to the testimony was historical, as a narrative of the conversion experience. The moment of conversion was always looked back to as the beginning of the faith journey, and was therefore definitive of one's identity as a Christian. This kind of testimony had three sections to it: the life before conversion, characterized by disobedience against God, the evidence of which was a lifestyle dominated by moral sins; the turning point, the conviction by the Holy Spirit to turn away and surrender to Jesus; and the benefits of salvation. This testimony is what distinguished a Mulokole from an "ordinary" Christian. It was not just a statement of what happened, but an authentication of the present in the light of the past. The testimony of conversion was therefore the defining story.[81]

---

78. In fact in some instances, particularly in Kigezi in the early days of the Revival, conversions were expected to be dramatic, often accompanied with dreams and visions John Wilson's study "Beliefs and Practices of the East African Revival Movement" is an excellent account of these.

79. Church reports of much repentance of these kinds of sins during the Hoima Mission 1937, in Church, *Quest for the Highest*, 142–143, and at the Inter-mission Convention in Bufumbira, p. 126.

80. Katarikawe and Wilson, "The East African Revival Movement," 157.

81. Katarikawe and Wilson have written their defining stories (testimonies) in "The East African Revival Movement," 226–252, which serve as excellent examples of this historical dimension.

The third dimension of a testimony was a current account of the faith journey. Having been saved, the historical narrative of conversion was not deemed sufficient. A testimony was expected to be always fresh, and therefore a regular feature of life in the context of the community of the "saved ones," as evidence of continuing in salvation. Revival was understood as a "daily coming back to the cross with a broken and contrite heart."[82] Each "coming back to the cross" provided material for the oral version. The essence of this dimension of a testimony was the experience of God in daily life, enunciated orally to fellow Balokole. "Brokenness," an expression coined from the psalmist phrase, "a broken and contrite heart,"[83] was the hallmark of the continuing work of God in a life, which was manifested in the fellowship by "walking in the light."

The fourth dimension looked to the future hope in heaven. In this sense therefore a testimony is not yet complete but always provisional, awaiting and looking forward to the eternal future glory. The Balokole always spoke with disarming certainty of heaven.[84]

The oral version of the testimony served to illustrate and authenticate the reality and power of the cross of Christ and his blood in the here and now, evidence of a living and active faith.[85] In preaching, Balokole would therefore punctuate their sermons with "testimonies" – stories from their lives and faith pilgrimage. Personal testimony was an integral part of a sermon and crucial for their confidence and boldness in preaching. As Wilson observed, "When a brother preaches in a church but does not give a short time for his testimony, the brethren feel sad and challenge him, as they feel sincerely that a good gospel exposition is established by one's testimony."[86]

At the heart of it, therefore, a testimony was not just speech, but life. The entire life of a Mulokole and indeed the fellowship[87] was expected to be a testimony of the saving and sustaining grace of God. It was life before it

---

82. Church, *Quest for the Highest*, 126.
83. Psalm 51:17. This is one of the favourite texts of the Balokole.
84. Of the 25 original hymns in *Ebyeshongoro Eby'Okujunwa*, 5 emphasize heaven.
85. Ibid., 183–185.
86. Katarikawe and Wilson, "The East African Revival Movement," 183.
87. Ibid., 161.

Schism and Revival in the Church, c1910–c1960

became speech, action before words. This is why testimonies could be sang, celebrating conversion and new life, and as a form of preaching. One such:

1. I was a rebel
   In my heart
   When I heard the messengers
   Preaching the word of Jesus

2. How we could be saved
   From the guilt of sin
   And become children
   Because of the death of Jesus

3. When I thought (about them)
   I felt guilty
   Because of my transgressions
   And the sins in which I was born

4. So I beseeched Him
   Confessed my sins,
   Trusted in His death
   And I was saved

5. I began to loathe
   Those (things) I used to love
   Which will pass away together with this world
   When Jesus comes back

6. I now have peace
   And the life of Jesus;
   And the Holy Spirit
   Helps me to overcome the things of the world

7. Then I began to grieve
   In my heart,
   Grieving for those in the world
   Who are not saved

8. Let all of us who are saved
   Grieve for those in the world
   And preach the gospel to them
   It is our work.[88]

This hymn is a typical example of many composed in the early days of Revival, recounting and celebrating the story and journey of faith, and making the call to conversion.

Bible Reading

Bible reading was a primary devotion for the Balokole, both in private and in public. It was always at the heart of the revival from the beginning.[89] The title to J. Church's book, *Every Man a Bible Student,* expresses the relationship of each Mulokole with the Bible. Personal Bible reading was expected

---

88. *Ebyeshongoro Eby'Okujunwa,* Hymn No. 2 (Words and Tune original)
89. Church, *Quest for the Highest,* 61.

to be a part his or her daily routine. As outlined by Wilson, Bible reading was a central item in the liturgy of the fellowship meeting. At conventions the Balokole employed what they called "team exposition," whereby "one would come prepared with a message as a Bible Reading and then the team would follow, expounding it further, and illustrating each point by personal testimony."[90] It is noteworthy that the Revival proceeded against a background of a church in which the translation of the Bible into the vernaculars of the people had been taken as a priority.[91]

Fellowship

The notion of fellowship was central to Revival. It was understood to mean "living in transparent sincerity, and a willingness to share with one another the experiences of daily life. In this way barriers of misunderstanding are constantly being cleared away."[92] Everyone who was saved became a member of a local fellowship group.[93]

The Balokole, as members together of "the fellowship," referred to each other as "members of the same clan-family," in Luganda *aboluganda*, rendered "brethren."[94] The fellowship was an egalitarian community, in which individual identity found its basis in the community. They prayed together, shared testimonies, walked in the light and read the Bible together. The expression of common faith however was not only visible in reading the Bible together, preaching together, or praying together; it was expressed in the everyday life concerns. For example, in the matter of marriage, when a girl in the community is sought in marriage, the brethren may deny her if the suitor is not approved, particularly, if he is not a *Mulokole*. "If they agree to the marriage, the brethren in the community undertake the arrangements, provide the feast, and the transport, and attend the ceremony

---

90. Church, *William Nagenda: A Great Lover of Jesus* (London: Ruanda Mission, 1973), a pamphlet published in Memory of Nagenda, 4–5. Available in CSCNWW Archives, 52 NAG Uganda.

91. Max Warren makes this observation, in *Revival*, 95.

92. Church, *Quest for the Highest*, 194.

93. Church has outlined well the characteristics of these groups. Ibid., 259.

94. This is the same meaning in other Ugandan languages. For example among the Banyankole it is "*abeishemwe,*" "of the same father"; and among the Bafumbira it is "*bene data,*" "of our father."

in force."[95] The entire process of marriage, from courtship to marriage, is undertaken by the fellowship together and not just by the two individuals getting married.[96] Good marriage and family life were considered central in authenticating the witness of the Balokole in the wider community.[97]

Another illustration of the strong bond of community is in bereavement and death.[98] As John Wilson has observed, the Revival fellowship also has a definite part to fulfil, "arranging for the reading of the will and all things necessary for funeral and burial. The brethren feel it their duty to call on the bereaved family and some stay with them for a while, in order to express the unity and solidarity of the fellowship."[99]

That unity and solidarity was not automatic, but rather a discipline, manifested in the twin motifs of "brokenness" and "walking in the light." "Brokenness" meant a willingness to be guided and corrected by fellow Balokole. The disposition of brokenness before fellow Balokole was reckoned to be evidence of a positive response to the Holy Spirit's conviction of sin or his guidance.[100] "Walking in the light" meant having transparency and communion with fellow Balokole, as instructed 1 John 1:7. Stanley Smith has described it well:

> Walking in the light: This is taken to mean transparent sincerity, a desire to be known for what one is and not what one would like to appear to be. This may involve the confessing of faults in the fellowship meeting, a valuable test of the genuineness of one's repentance.[101]

The evidence of "brokenness" was "walking in the light" in a testimony of cleansing from sin, outlining to the fellowship the convicting work of the Holy Spirit and the journey from stiffnecked-ness to brokenness.[102]

---

95. Taylor, *Growth of the Church in Buganda*, 102.
96. Katarikawe and Wilson, "The East African Revival Movement," 205.
97. Ibid., 201–213.
98. John Wilson discusses this in detail. Ibid., 214–219.
99. Ibid., 215.
100. Osborn, *Revival*, 104.
101. Smith, *Road to Revival*, 143.
102. Wilson records two such, in Katarikawe and Wilson, "The East African Revival Movement," 172–175.

Advice or correction from the group, "putting someone in the light," may follow such confession. The recipient of the correction was expected to receive the "light" from the others in an attitude of "brokenness."

The evidence of spiritual vitality for any of the brethren was continued involvement in the life of the fellowship, especially in attending fellowship meetings, regularly announcing one's current spiritual and material pilgrimage in a testimony, and continuing in telling "others," those not-yet-saved, about Christ; for "every Mulokole is a witness."[103]

Leadership

The fellowship community was structured like a clan-family. As in any African clan-family, those who were senior in the Revival were accorded honour and acknowledged as "first among equals."[104] They were the leaders *de facto*. Although Wilson argues that the basis of appointment to the leadership team was "as a result of the Holy Spirit touching certain ones with the freedom and maturity to make some contribution to the guidance of the body"[105] this often meant the "elders" in the experience of revival. No other criterion of leadership was acceptable. This was their way of protesting against clericalism in the church and the undue emphasis on hierarchy or *obukulu*, a Luganda word for "eldership," a term which they used as a critique of the clergy who clung to the trappings of prestige, respect and power which their status gave them.[106] Decision making in the Revival was always by consensus.

A counter-cultural element in the composition of the leadership teams was the equal participation of women and men. As a matter of fact it was a requirement for those who were married to be part of the team as a couple, husband and wife together. Three factors account for this. First, within the context of the fellowship, women's identity was not confined to being wives or potential wives as was the case within traditional society, but sisters in Christ, of equal standing with the men. The relationship that defined one's

---

103. Katarikawe and Wilson, "The East African Revival Movement," 185.
104. Among the Baganda these elders in the faith are some times endearingly referred to as "*Tata*" and "*Mama*," literally translated father and mother respectively.
105. Katarikawe and Wilson, "The East African Revival Movement," 177.
106. Ward makes this point in his essay, "The Balokole Revival in Uganda," 120–121.

identity in the fellowship was the one with Christ. This became the primary basis for defining group membership and leadership.

Second, there was nothing in the criteria for identifying leaders in the Revival that discounted women. Since the marks of leadership were associated with maturity and seniority in Revival, and the gifting of the Holy Spirit, women could therefore be as much part of the leadership teams as men were.

And third, the functions of the leadership teams required that some of the elder women, the *mamas*, play that role from the front. While women leadership has always been acknowledged in the traditional societies, its place and exercise has often been behind the scenes. Among the Baganda, for example, there was a specific leadership role accorded to the paternal aunt in the process towards marriage, in her nurturing of the young bride, but it was not for her to determine the acceptable suitor to the bride. This was left to the elder-men in the clan.[107] However in the Revival where the fellowship was the context of such nurture, the elder women's nurturing responsibility was recognized not just as a behind the scenes function, but one that was crucial in leading to a decision about a suitor. These elder women in the Fellowship played a similar role to that of the "auntie" in traditional culture-religion with the difference that in the Fellowship that responsibility was exercised from in front, in fellowship with men.

Theology

The theological paradigm of the Revival was the motif of the cross and the blood of Jesus. The cross of Christ constituted their hermeneutic. In the book, *Every Man a Bible Student,* that I consider to be the theological manual of the Revival, of the forty-four topics, eight deal directly the cross and the blood of Jesus.[108] According to J. Church, the "theologian" of the Revival, as quoted earlier in chapter 1:

> The death of our Lord Jesus Christ on the Cross is the focal point of history. The books of the Old Testament point to it.

---

107. F. Kyewalyanga, *Traditional Religion, Custom, and Christianity in Uganda* (Freiburg im Breisgau: Internationales Katholisches Missionswerk, 1976), 49–76.
108. Church, *Every Man a Bible Student,* 7–8.

The Gospels describe it in detail, and the Epistles look back to it. The Salvation of mankind is bound up with the Cross of Christ.[109]

The cross and the blood of Jesus were also the central subject of the Balokole's hymnody. Fourteen of the twenty-five Revival hymns in the hymnal *Ebyeshongoro Eby'Okujunwa*, deal directly with the theme of the death of Christ, a clear indication that in the understanding of the Balokole of all the salvific events of the incarnate Christ, the cross was the pivot on which all hang. It was the centre of their devotion.

The cross and the blood of Jesus was the basis of fellowship. The cross was seen as the cohesive force that made them one. The most quoted passage of Scripture is 1 John 1:5–10, which to them delineated the ethics of the cross as: repentance, confession, walking in the light and fellowship. Patricia St John has captured this ethos well, in observing that according to them:

> There is only one class at the Cross: humble, forgiven sinners, rejoicing because Jesus has forgiven them, and this forms a bond between them that cannot be broken. "If we walk in the light as He is in the light then we have fellowship with one another and the blood of Jesus Christ His Son cleanses us from all sin."[110]

It is devotion to the cross that broke down barriers of race, nationality and sex. The experience of the cross is what led to repentance and cleansing from sin, often referred to as "being at the cross."[111] The evidence of the work of the cross in the believer and indeed the fellowship were the twin disciplines of "brokenness" and "walking in the light." The patterns of community life in the Revival are a result of incarnating the message of Christ crucified and the cleansing power of this blood in African patterns of community.

The Balokole believed that an appropriate life response to the cross demanded a "separation from the world," concerning which, Church wrote:

---

109. Ibid., 54.
110. St John, *Breath of Life*, 161,
111. Church, *Quest for the Highest*, 135.

It does *not* necessarily mean the life of an ascetic, or to shut oneself up in a monastery. But spiritually, for the true Christian it means the power to live "in the world, but not of the world," i.e. the desire for worldly things and pleasures is replaced and overcome by the new nature of Christ, which fills the heart. Compromise with evil in any form hinders blessings for the Christian.[112]

The contrast was the nominal Christian life, equated to a worldly life, characterized by preoccupation with "drink, dress, . . . and the things of the world" as communicated in the following hymn:

> You who trust in the things of the world,
> How is it you are never satisfied with them.
> Even your forefathers
> Were not satisfied with them.
>
> You eat, you drink,
> You dress, you make yourselves smart,
> You laugh, you play,
> But you forget death.[113]

The crucial point here is that the conviction that genuine Christian life entailed a shunning of the world was based on the motif of the cross.

The cross constituted the core of Balokole preaching.[114] The conviction of the Balokole was that it is the message of the cross and the blood of Jesus that the Holy Spirit uses to convict people of sin and lead them to salvation. Their confidence of an eternity with God in heaven resulted from their confidence in the finished work of Christ on the cross. On the same basis the non-Balokole, those who had not appropriated the work of the cross and the blood of Jesus in their lives, had no basis of hope but a fearful eternity without God.

---

112. Church, *Every Man a Bible Student*, 61 (emphasis in the text).
113. *Ebyeshongoro Eby'Okujunwa*, part of hymn no. 27. Translation, by Z. Kabaza. Also hymns 25, 45, 48, 53, with the same emphasis of separation.
114. Of the twenty-five hymns in *Ebyeshongoro*, nine make an appeal to repentance.

Incorporation of the Revival into the Church

Unlike the leaders of the two movements, KOAB and Mengo Gospel Church, there was no time when the Revival leaders considered leaving the Church to form a new one. There were two reasons for this. First, they were convinced that since it was the Church that needed reviving, it would be an act of disobedience to God for them to form a new church. Second, for them there was no such thing as a "believers church." They had come to appreciate the other values that the Church served, such as the administration of the sacraments and the provision of education and health services. They were content with a dual identity: as members of the Church, and the Fellowship. To them it was the Revival fellowships that were to constitute the nucleus of the Church. Incorporation and integration of Revival ethos into the Church was therefore their desire and goal.[115]

Bishop Stuart[116] recognized the Revival as a renewing movement in the Church and made attempts to incorporate it fully in the Church. The first major opportunities in the Diocese of Uganda at which the Revival message was given were key institutional events. These are the Mukono Clergy Retreat of 1936, at which Blasio Kigozi spoke; the 1936 Diocesan Synod, at which Blasio Kigozi's call to the Church to awake was read; and the Uganda Diocese Jubilee missions of 1937 led by Revival leaders. All these events had a significant impact on the Church and fulfilled in part Stuart's desire for the Revival to renew the Church. However, it was the events at the theological college at Mukono in 1941 that caused a crisis that threatened schism in the Church and drastically shifted Bishop Stuart's agenda to incorporate the Revival institutionally.

---

115. All the Revival leaders that I interviewed expressed this. They include Kabaza, Kigozi, Yedediya Kayima, Geraldine Sabiti.

116. Bishop Stuart succeeded Bishop Willis in 1934, as bishop of Uganda diocese, after Willis retired that year.

Mukono Crisis

The immediate cause of the crisis at Bishop Tucker College Mukono[117] was a contention between the college[118] administration and members of the Revival over the appropriateness of 4:00 a.m. praise and prayer meetings, and 6:00 a.m. "open-air" preaching sessions, which the Balokole had instituted. 6:00 a.m. was, according to them, a strategic hour when they would preach to the "nominal" ordinands by broadcasting the revival message to them while in their beds or just getting up. The issue at stake, however, was the whole question of the integrity of Revival in the Church. The aspects of the Revival that were considered by some in the CMS mission and Church to be extreme and divisive were the very ones considered by members of the Revival to be central to its ethos. Moreover, although Bishop Stuart himself had a warm sympathy for the Revival and was anxious to integrate it into the life of the Church, he presided over a missionary force that originated from two opposing camps at home – the Student Christian Movement (SCM) and the Cambridge Inter-Collegiate Christian Union (CICCU).[119]

The 4:00 a.m. praise and prayer meeting and the 6:00 a.m. "open-air" preaching sessions had arisen out of a determination by the Balokole students[120] to stay the tide of students' moral laxity, and what they considered

---

117. Lengthy accounts of this can be found in: Church, *Quest for the Highest*, 113–203; Kevin Ward, "Tukutendereza Yesu," 81–112; Kevin Ward, "'Obedient Rebels': The Relationship between the Early 'Balokole' and the Church of Uganda: The Mukono Crisis of 1941," *Journal of Religion in Africa* XIX, no. 3 (1989): 194–227; Katarikawe and Wilson, "The East African Revival," 105–119.

118. Bishop Tucker Memorial College at Mukono was set up in 1913 to provide training for ministers for the Church. It also had a Normal School for the training of vernacular Teachers. By 1940 it was an established training centre for Lay Readers and ordinands.

119. Church, *Quest for the Highest*, 124, and Ward, "Tukutendereza Yesu," 117. Prior to the Mukono Mission of 1936 called by Bishop Stuart in preparation for the Jubilee Missions of 1937, Joe Church corresponded with Bishop Stuart wondering "how far the SCM and CICCU should combine on the same platform" because he felt there was no way SCM's liberal theology would combine with Revival. The mission itself was disrupted by sharp disagreements between Church and Herbert, the Warden of the College. Herbert protested to Church over what he saw as excesses and theological aberrations of the Revival. Herbert had felt that the emphasis of the preachers on the blood of Jesus was unhealthy. In a bid to balance the theological forces at Mukono after the Mission, Stuart brought to the College Bill Butler, a CICCU man. But Butler never got along with Jones, an alumnus of SCM, and who had replaced Herbert as Warden of the College.

120. Stuart's strategy to train an educated clergy and incorporate the Revival into the Church had brought some graduates from Budo, among whom were Balokole, notably

to be "liberal theology" promoted by some of the tutors at the College. Thus when Warden Jones banned the meetings, the Balokole students, led by William Nagenda, now in his final year as an ordinand, defied the ban and continued meeting. They saw it as a test of their commitment to what they believed to be a calling and mission from God. The warden acted fast to deal with what in his view were acts of insolence and insubordination. He suspended Chaplain Kaggwa and twenty-six students. They were given a chance to apologize in writing, promising among other things that they would not preach or take part in any meeting in the College without the permission of the Warden. They all refused this and so were expelled as rebels, *bajemu*.[121]

The result was a clash and a protracted conflict between the Church and the Revival leadership. Bishop Stuart was away in Zanzibar over the period of the clashes between the Balokole and the College administration. On returning he supported disciplinary measures imposed by the warden. He convened an extraordinary Diocesan Council meeting in November 1941 to deliberate on the crisis. The Council published new rules that were considered necessary to curb what the Council judged as excesses of the Balokole.[122] William Nagenda was barred from preaching in Uganda Churches, and Joe Church's licence to preach was withdrawn.

The Balokole leaders met in December that same year in Kabale to review the situation. This meeting endorsed the action of the "rebels," arguing that the heart of the conflict lay in the issues of liberalism and Jones' disquiet with the Revival.[123] They also criticized the new Church rules, as an attempt to stamp out the Revival, but reaffirmed their commitment to the Church.

William Nagenda, Eliyeza Mugimba and Erisa Wakabi. The 1936 mission increased the number of Balokole students at the College, who under the leadership of William Nagenda started a meeting for prayer and praise, each morning at 4:00 a.m. The inspiration for the 6:00 a.m. sessions had come from Easter 1941 Toro Convention attended by some of the Balokole students, led by Butler and the chaplain of the College, Rev Benoni Kaggwa.

121. Kevin Ward has provided a list of all of them and their area of origin in "Obedient Rebels," 206–207.

122. See Katarikawe and Wilson, "The East African Revival," 110, for the rules.

123. Church, *Quest for the Highest*, 186.

The 1942 Diocese Synod set up a commission of enquiry into the crisis. Although Bishop Stuart still believed in the value of the Revival, he felt that its leaders had "let down the cause of the Kingdom over the Mukono troubles."[124] In February 1943 the Bishop had a meeting with the Ruanda Mission missionaries in a further attempt to prohibit what he feared might be an imminent split. At that meeting the missionaries apologized over the Mukono events and a "New Way" towards reconciliation was charted out in a fourteen-point document. Bishop Stuart felt that there was emerging a process of healing and that by following the fourteen points stipulated in the "New Way" a potential secession of the Revival from the Church would be defused, and there would be secured a reintegration of the Balokole into the Church. Among other things in the "New Way" guidelines, the Bishop asked that the distinctions *Abalokole* (the saved ones) and *Abatali abalokole* (those who are not saved) should be dropped, and instead use the term *Abakristayo* (Christians); and that public confession of sins, in particular of sexual sins, should be minimized.[125]

The Bishop's proposals were bound to be rejected by the Balokole because, in a nutshell, the proposals questioned the core values of the Revival. The distinction between the "saved" and "not-saved" was the essence of the Revival as it distinguished, from the perspective of the Balokole, a "real" Christian, *omulokole*, from a "nominal" one, *omukristayo*. The Revival message was targeted to the *abakristayo*, the "nominal" Christians, with the object of leading them to salvation, and therefore to a new status as "saved ones." The difficulty with the Bishop's attempts for reconciliation was that he was seeking to institutionalize an ethos that was diametrically opposed to the institutionalism in Church, for which the Revival was born and existed to reform. Therefore the tensions in the relationship between the Church and the Revival leadership remained.

The African Revival leaders distanced themselves from the apology of their missionary "brethren," judging that it was hurried and ill considered. They rejected the Bishop's "New Way" and demanded that the Ruanda missionaries dissociate themselves from it, an action that the missionaries took

---

124. Bishop Stuart, quoted in Ward "Obedient Rebels," 210.
125. See all the fourteen guidelines in Robins, "Tukutendereza," 436–437.

at their meeting in December 1943. Thus the Revival defied institutional incorporation and stayed as a movement among Church members, who might include the clergy, maintaining an uneasy form of co-existence with the "un-revived" hierarchy.

Confronted with the choice to be separated from the Church[126] and remain "pure" as in the Mengo Gospel Church scenario, or to remain in the Church by being institutionally incorporated, with some compromises, the Revival leadership chose neither. Wilson Lea, who invited Nagenda to his tea plantation in Namutamba after his expulsion from Mukono, urged the Balokole to form a new church, but the Balokole's commitment to what they saw as their calling to the Church as their mission field, prevailed. Sabiti's words capture the commitment and mission of the Balokole in the Church:

> The people of the Church of Uganda love their church much, and wouldn't listen to anyone who is supposed to be trying to leave the Church, and we feel that the message God has given us was for the whole Church of Uganda – the message of living the victorious life through the cross of Christ . . . The people of the Church of Uganda have seen those who failed to reform the Church of Uganda by leaving it, and they would be afraid of us if they supposed that we were trying to form a new Church.[127]

Sabiti's allusion "to those who failed to reform the Church of Uganda by leaving" was a reference to Ensor and Mengo Gospel Church. According to the Balokole, leaving the Church would be an act of disobedience against God who they believed was the Author of the Revival.

Although his attempts to institutionalize the Revival had failed, Bishop Stuart did not desire to expel the Balokole,[128] but rather continued to accommodate them. He granted them permission to hold the Revival

---

126. All the Balokole informants that were present during this period concurred that it never occurred to them that the right thing would be to secede. Kabaza, OI; Geraldine Sabiti, OI; Kigozi, OI. See also Robins, "Tukutendereza," 164–166.

127. Quoted by Ward, "Tukutendereza Yesu," 123.

128. Bishop Stuart stated this in the Synod of 1942, quoted by Ward, "Obedient Rebels," 210.

Convention in Namirembe in 1944, solely led by them, and gave his full blessing to the Kako Convention in 1950.[129]

Incorporation of Revival ethos into mainstream Church life depended on at least three parameters: the adoption of Revival ethos by missionary and African leadership of the Church; the maturational level of the churches and level of Christianization of society; and the place of some of the African Revival leadership in the hierarchy of the Church and in society. By 1950, there were two distinct modes of incorporation of the Revival in the Church of Uganda: opposition and clustering, in Buganda; and integration, in Western Uganda.[130]

Revival in the Church in Buganda

The Revival was not accepted as part of the mainstream of the Church in Buganda. Rather than Revival being the norm of church leadership and life in Buganda, it was clustered around the homes of the key leaders in Buganda. There are several reasons why this was so. First, in Buganda,[131] despite the fact that it was home of Simeon Nsibambi, Yona Mondo, Blasio Kigozi, and William Nagenda, some of the early pillars of the Revival, the Balokole were not able to assume the leadership of the Church. By 1940 there were only three ordained ministers in the Revival fold, Besweli Galiwango, Disani Mukasa,[132] and Benoni Kaggwa. The fourth, Kigozi, died in 1936. They were joined by another in 1950, Yowasi Musajjakaawa. These few could not influence the Church in this vast region.

Second, as Ward has rightly argued, the fact that the Church in Buganda "was already established with its own traditions, with a vigorous indigenous

---

129. Kevin Ward has suggested that the Kako Convention of 1950 can considered a decisive point in the growing acceptability of the Revival into the mainstream of the life of the Church, in his essay, "Tukutendereza Yesu," 123.
130. In 1926 the vast area of northern and eastern Uganda was constituted as a separate Diocese of Upper Nile. The spreading of the revival to Eastern and Northern Uganda is a distinct story occurring much later, in the 1950s and 1960s. The most influential stream of the Revival in this region was the Trumpeters, discussed in the last section of this chapter.
131. In addition to written sources, the oral interviews with Kigozi, Kayima, and Kabaza have provided the other parts of the story.
132. Disan Mukasa was brother to Nagenda.

clergy jealous of its status and rights, and an articulate laity"[133] made it difficult for its leadership to accept the Revival. The clergy regarded the forthright preaching of the Balokole as ridiculing them and the idea of a person with social standing in society repenting and confessing his sins in public was detestable and culturally inappropriate.[134]

Third, there were no significant missions and conventions targeting Buganda for a period of ten years, between 1940–1950. At Namirembe, the epicentre of the Church, Bishop Stuart had become disgruntled with the Revival leaders after the Mukono crisis.[135] Anxious to retain the Revival within the Church, but worried that the likes of the Mukono leaders could derail it away from the Church, he organized a convention on Revival lines without the Revival leaders in 1943. It was, as Joe Church reported later, organized entirely by those who were not connected with the Revival, "if not actively opposed to it including the Warden of Mukono."[136] Joe Church called it "*the Bishop's Compromise Convention.*"[137] But even this does not seem to have had a significant impact.

Thus, in Buganda, although the Revival remained, it was clustered around the leaders of the Revival: in their homes, and in parishes led by Balokole clergy.[138]

Revival in the Church in Western Uganda

In Western Uganda, in particular Kigezi, Ankole and Toro, Revival ethos became the *modus vivendi* of Church leadership and life. Revival ethos

---

133. Ward, "Tukutendereza Yesu," 125.
134. Kigozi. OI.
135. He called the Mukono Crisis "the greatest crisis of the history of the Church of Uganda." Quoted in Robins, "Tukutendereza," 154.
136. Church, *Quest for the Highest,* 201.
137. Ibid., 202.
138. Namutamba, home of Nagenda, which became the largest centre in Buganda; Katale, on Entebbe Road, home of Mondo, and later Kawempe when Mondo moved residence; Kabungo in Masaka, where Musajjakaawa was parish priest; Mukono, Kyagwe where Benoni Kaggwa was parish priest, with the support of layman, Yedediya Kayima; Kawala Parish, where Disani Mukasa was serving and Ndejje Teachers College in Luweero, where Miss Patty Drakeley was Principal. Kabaza, OI; Kigozi, OI; and Yedediya Kayima, OI, Kampala, 29 April 1997.

increasingly became the primary source of the Church's life, mission, and ministry.

The Church in Kigezi developed along the lines of the Revival movement.[139] In fact it had from its inception a separate identity from the Church in Uganda. Kigezi, Rwanda, and Burundi, although organizationally part of the Uganda Diocese, in terms of ethos, they were a separate church. The mother mission of the Church in this region, the Ruanda Mission CMS, was doctrinally conservative-evangelical, contrasted with the main CMS, which was more accommodative of various theological and ecclesiastical traditions.[140] It is this "accommodation" that the founders of the Ruanda Mission wanted to protect their Mission from, and provided for safeguards in its foundation documents.[141] This separate identity was recognized by Bishop Stuart as indicated by the fact that when he withdrew Joe Church's preaching licence in Uganda, he allowed him to continue preaching in Kigezi, Rwanda and Burundi.[142]

Revival ethos was "official" *praxis* and *credo*, because the key Church leaders, both indigenous and missionary, had imbibed it right from its beginnings. The initial apprehension of some of the Ruanda missionaries gave way to universal acceptance among them.[143] Church's relocation from Gahini to Kabale in 1938 to co-ordinate the work of the Revival full

---

139. In addition to the written sources, the other sources, for this section, include my oral informants: Z. Kabaza and G. Sabiti, who were active in the Revival at the time.
140. Within its fold CMS accommodated the liberal Student Christian Movement (SCM) associated missionaries and the evangelical Cambridge Inter-Collegiate Christian Union (CICCU) types, and missionaries of both high and low church traditions, a character that was the root cause of the formation of the Ruanda Mission within the CMS, as Stanley Smith and Patricia St John show in the accounts of the Ruanda Mission, *Road to Revival* and *Breath of Life*, respectively.
141. The Ruanda Mission was founded in protest to what was perceived by its founders to be liberal and modernist theological influence in the CMS. Three principles were affirmed in their constitution: (1) The Ruanda Council and the missionaries of the Ruanda General Medical Mission stand for the complete inspiration of the whole Bible as being, and not only containing, the Word of God. (2) Their determination is to proclaim full and free salvation through simple faith in Christ's atoning death upon the cross. (3) They are satisfied that they have received from the CMS full guarantees to safeguard the future of the RGMM on Bible, Protestant and Keswick lines. Smith, *Road to Revival*, 42.
142. Ward, "Obedient Rebels," 192–193.
143. The two most senior leaders in the Church, Canon Lawrence Barham and Rev Ezekeri Balaba, were members of the team at the Kabale Convention of 1935. C. Robbins examines in detail the nature of integration in Kigezi, OI, 140–296.

time further strengthened its standing in Kigezi. For the next eight years, Joe Church was based at Kabale, and so was Stanley Smith, then Field Secretary of the Ruanda Mission and in charge of medical work in Kigezi. In fact Kabale took over from Gahini as the centre of the western axis.[144] The successful Kabale convention of 1945, to which well over 15,000 people came, is further evidence that Kabale had taken centre stage in the life the Revival, and also that it enjoyed support of the Church in Kigezi. Joe Church reports that the year prior to the convention, local conventions "had been going on in all the five districts of Kigezi" and that teams were operating in all the Church centres.[145]

The other reason why the Church in Kigezi developed along Revival lines was, as Kevin Ward has observed, the fact that the long process of education, which in the other regions of Uganda was the means of incorporation of people into Christianity, came later in Kigezi. The Revival preceded the introduction of formal education, so it offered an immediate opportunity of identifying oneself with the new way of life, and took on the character of a mass movement from "paganism."[146] But even here to be saved was never a prerequisite for baptism. A distinction was maintained between becoming *omukristayo*, a "nominal" Christian, and being saved. The former was achieved through baptism, and the latter through a separate crisis experience.[147]

Three major factors account for the way Revival ethos was integrated in the life of the Church in Ankole. First was the Mbarara Convention in early 1936, at which several of the missionary and African leaders embraced the Revival. Those who were saved at the convention were men

---

144. Church, *Quest for the Highest*, 152, 154, 186. It was at Kabale that the 1941 meeting was held among the Revival leaders, missionaries and Africans, to discuss the handling of the Mukono crisis.

145. Since then, a similar Convention has been held in Kabale each decade, under the directorship of Church leaders: in 1955, 1965, 1975, 1985, and 1995. I have personally participated in two of these.

146. Ward, "Tukutendereza Yesu," 124.

147. Kabaza, OI. Kabaza recalls that an attempt was made to require salvation before confirmation, but this too was dropped later.

highly regarded in Ankole society, as teachers and palace workers, and this helped give credibility to the Revival.[148]

Second, was the leadership of Rev Erica Sabiti, who was saved in 1939 during a visit to Buye, the Revival centre in Burundi.[149] Sabiti was then the parish priest of the prestigious Bweranyangyi parish,[150] heartland of the *Bairu* people of Ankole. It was second to Mbarara in receiving the cream leadership of the Revival in early 1937. When Erica Sabiti was transferred to Kinoni Parish, he hosted a major Convention in 1939. Kinoni was also strategically placed on the way from Kabale to Mbarara, and therefore a convenient halfway house for the Revival leaders travelling between Kabale or Gahini and Mengo. Sabiti was one of the national Revival leaders who met in Kabale at the end of 1941 and produced a report protesting to Bishop Stuart about the handling of the Mukono crisis.[151]

The third factor was the return to Nyabushozi of one of the Mukono rebels, Edward Kakudidi.[152] Nyabushozi was the heartland of the *Bahima* people, the ruling class of Ankole at that time, who had identified themselves with the "religion" of their king, *Omugabe*. Kakudidi teamed with another early convert, Mucokoli, and developed an itinerant evangelistic ministry among them along their nomadic pastoral life pattern.[153] Kakudidi and Mucokoli's preaching from kraal to kraal, holding evangelistic meetings and fellowships, brought to centre stage the Revival ethos as the primary way of becoming a Christian among the Bahima. The genius of their work among the Bahima was the adoption of nomadic mission style akin to their indigenous lifestyle.

---

148. Among them: E. Mugimba, Kyoya, Mulumba, Mukasa, all teachers; Nyondo, working in the local government as secretary.

149. Geraldine Sabiti, OI.

150. Next to Ruharo in Mbarara, was Bweranyangyi in ecclesiastical prominence in the Church in Ankole. In 1951 it became the second deanery in Ankole.

151. Church, *Quest for the Highest*, 186.

152. John Muhanguzi, "The Spread of the Revival Movement at Burunga in Nyabushozi County, East Ankole, Uganda," Makerere University, Kampala, unpublished Dip. in Theology dissertation, October 1985, 14–15.

153. Ward, "Obedient Rebels," 218.

K. Ward has suggested a fourth factor: the linguistic and cultural links between the Bairu, the agricultural Banyankole majority, and the Bakiga of Kigezi.[154]

Although the integration of the Revival in the Church in Toro was not of the same magnitude as that in Kigezi or Ankole, it was nonetheless closer to the Ankole-Kigezi type than Buganda. What the Mbarara Convention of 1936 was to Ankole, the Toro Convention of 1941 was to Toro. One of the first ordained ministers in the Church in Toro was Yosiya Kamahigi, father-in-law to Sabiti, who was saved in the late 1930s and, like Sabiti, provided the support the Revival needed from the Church.

There are two aspects of the Revival story that are not found elsewhere in the region: the memory of the Pilkington revival of 1893 and the involvement of royalty.[155] Toro had been evangelized by Baganda catechists who had made their commitment to mission through the Pilkington Revival. While in Toro they spoke of its blessings, and this was still in living memory of the Batoro when the Revival came to Toro in the late 1930s. Several among the ruling *Babito* clan were saved, notably three leading ladies: Princess Ruth Komuntale, sister to the *Omukama*, king of Toro; Eseri Kiboga, one of the aristocrats; and Tedora Macaica, another leading lady,[156] a factor that was significant in giving credibility to the Revival in the Church, particularly among women.

Schism in the Revival

The theological orientation and practices of the Revival were often a subject of contention within and without the Revival. Some of the practices were perceived to be extremist and were often dealt with in the fellowship.[157] There are two, however, which grew to become movements within, and later separated from the mainline Revival: the "Trumpeters," also called "Strivers," led by Lubulwa, and the *Okuzukuka*, "Reawakening," led by

---

154. Ward, "Tukutendereza Yesu," 125. "Runyankole" and "Rukiga" are dialects of the same language.
155. Geraldine Sabiti, OI.
156. Ibid. Komuntale got saved in 1937.
157. James Katarikawe has discussed the tensions over visions, glossolalia, 'crucifying the old man' and 'striving after holiness' in his account, "The East African Revival," 133–134.

Yona Mondo. These two deserve some attention as they highlight how the Revival doctrine of "separation form the world" and its leadership structure became sources of tension and rifts. The Trumpeters also represent a separate stream of Revival and were instrumental in carrying its message to the hitherto "un-reached" areas of Northern and Eastern Uganda.[158]

The Trumpeters

The founder of the Trumpeters was Eliya Lubulwa, a medical doctor and a prominent, educated Muganda Mulokole,[159] one of those who was saved in the early 1940s. He became a fiery preacher. To aid him in his preaching, he had made for himself a trumpet out of an old paraffin tin and through this he would broadcast his message to congregations as they were leaving their churches on Sundays.[160]

Those who were saved through his preaching emulated his example and adopted the use of trumpets; hence the movement came to be known as "trumpeters." Lubulwa worked in several medical centres during the 1940s: Mbale, Mulago, Hoima, Toro, Gulu, Kitgum and Arua. It was during his service in Northern Uganda in 1947–1949, that he grew dissatisfied with what he considered to be half-hearted commitment of his fellow Balokole. Therefore in addition to addressing the nominal masses in the churches, he started challenging Balokole and sometimes castigating them for being worldly.[161] His message was: "*Omuntu afuukire ddala omuntu wa Katonda* – a person has to be wholly given over to God and his service"[162] He took this message wherever he was transferred to work. As a consequence of

---

158. Among the sources for this stream: Kenneth Gong, "The History of the Revival Movement in Kitgum Church of Uganda Parish, Northern Uganda Diocese," Makerere University, unpublished Diploma in Theology dissertation, 1985; Bishop G Ilukor, OI, 19 March, 1996; M. Lloyd, *Wedge of Light: Revival in North West Uganda* (Rugby: Margaret Lloyd, n. d); Obote, "Why the Revival Movement has failed in Teso," Makerere University, Dip. Th. Dissertation, 1978.
159. Kayima, OI; Ward, "Obedient Rebels," 216. Kayima knew Lubulwa very well and lived in Lubulwa's home for several years, from 1946 until the time when Lubulwa was expelled from the Revival.
160. Lloyd, *Wedge of Light*, 9.
161. Kayima, OI, *op cit*.
162. Ibid.

his "radical" understanding of godliness as contrasted with worldliness, he chose a John-the-Baptist style of dress with a tunic, raincoat and no shoes.

He went to the Kako convention in 1950 with the same mission and message, to awaken the Balokole to their worldliness, calling for radical conversion which, according to him, entailed abandoning such "worldly" pursuits like education, secular work and material possessions. While at the convention he would wake up at 4:30 a.m. and broadcast in his megaphone, calling people to repentance, to the displeasure of the other Revival leaders. It is then that the conflicts he had with some in the leadership of the Revival, notably with William Nagenda another leading educated Muganda Mulokole, surfaced. But Lubulwa was undeterred in expressing his conviction that nominalism had also crept into the Revival. The other leaders disagreed with him and asked him to repent of "striving."[163] Lubulwa did not "break" as was expected, and was expelled from the convention and the Revival.

Lubulwa's open conflict and disagreement with Nagenda and other leaders primarily resulted from leadership struggles and only secondarily, from questions of orthodoxy and ortho-praxis, as the other leaders.[164] After all, the Lubulwa-type excesses were not uncommon in the history of the Revival, but they had been resolved from within. Notably, he was one of the more highly educated African Balokole[165] with a long experience in the movement and yet was not incorporated into the leadership team. The first time Lubulwa appears in Joe Church's account is in the Namirembe Convention report of 1944; it was simply noted that "Dr Lubulwa was also there."[166] The next time he appears is at the Kako Convention, when he is associated with disrupting the convention and "having to be told to leave."[167] Lubulwa must have felt disenfranchised by the Nagenda-biased

---

163. Hence the nickname the "Strivers," given by the mainstream Nagenda-wing of the Balokole.

164. Katarikawe narrates the open conflict with Nagenda and subsequent dismissal from Kako Convention in 1950. See Katarikawe, and Wilson, "The East African Revival," 134–135.

165. Some of the Makerere graduates at the time were: E. Sabiti, Z. Kabaza, Nagenda and E. Mugimba. They were all recognized leaders in the Revival.

166. Church, *Quest for the Highest*, 209.

167. Ibid., 237.

team and therefore protested by refusing to bow to the Revival status quo. They too reasserted their authority by expelling him, a way that was contrary to Revival ethos.

Lubulwa's expulsion did not deter him. He continued to preach with his megaphone, now making the denunciation of the revivalists as cold and compromising a pivotal part of his message. He quit medical practice for a while, sold his car, abandoned paying school fees for his children and became an itinerant evangelist, taking his mission especially to the east of Uganda and the north. Despite the unconventional preaching methods of Lubulwa and his group, many people were converted in their ranks.[168] In the late 1960s he returned to his home in Buganda, opened a medical clinic, and also continued with his itinerant preaching work.[169]

Okuzukuka (Re-awakening)

A full discussion of the *Okuzukuka* (Re-awakening) movement is beyond the time frame of the discussion in this chapter.[170] A brief attention to it is appropriate because the roots of *Okuzukuka* are in economic prosperity in Uganda in the 1950s and 1960s, and the apparent upward social mobility of some of the senior Balokole. The 1950s were also a time of political ferment in Uganda, particularly in Buganda. James Katarikawe admits that the Balokole, like others, found themselves equally involved in this. He continues:

> The Holy Spirit convicted many of the coldness, which was due to *their involvement in the world*. A meeting was held in Kabale in 1960 for the leaders. There was much blessing and many returned to their homes with a new vision. The Kampala brethren went further; they held a meeting at Entebbe. They came out with a new testimony of having been "awakened out of sleep." Debts, trading of all kinds, taking of insurance

---

168. There are many trumpeters in Soroti and Gulu. In Arua it was abandoned in the 1970s.
169. Kayima, OI. Lubulwa's career ended with his death in 1969. He was shot at by robbers, and later died of the bullet wounds.
170. For a comprehensive discussion of the *Okuzukuka* see Robins, "Tukutendereza," 297–341.

and even keeping dogs was regarded as sin because it meant putting one's trust in dogs to keep him rather than in God. There was to be no buying on credit, and taking government loans to buy cars or build houses, no joining of co-operatives. All current fashions of dress, especially for ladies, and keeping hair long in any style, became preaching topics. And on top of that, it did not matter how one was or came. Unless he said that he had been "awakened" he could not be accepted as a real brother.[171]

The doctrine of "separateness" was thus taken to its conclusion. William Nagenda attended the Entebbe meetings, but began to have many reservations over "awakening," warning his colleagues against legalistic righteousness. Yona Mondo at this time was leading the Re-awakening tendency, and in his fold were the ailing Simeoni Nsibambi, and some of the Mukono rebels.[172] Mondo accused Nagenda of being out of touch with the Revival due to his prolonged absence in Europe. Here, as in the story of the Trumpeters, were signs of a jealousy.[173] Efforts to resolve and reconcile back the "re-awakening Balokole" were fruitless, and in 1971 an open organizational split occurred, with Mondo as leader of the Re-awakened group. Simeon Nsibambi, who had been at the centre of the efforts towards reconciliation, remained in mainstream Revival.

Leadership and internal conflicts aside, the most significant question that the Trumpeters and Re-awakening submovements highlight is the implications of the doctrine of "separateness," and its corollary, the issue of nominalism, in the Revival. The critical issue that Lubulwa and Mondo brought to the Revival was as to whether the movement that evolved in protest to a nominal Church, characterized by *bukulu*, a reference to totalitarianism of clerical leadership, was itself slipping to nominal revivalism. Blasio Kigozi's clarion call – *Zukuka!* – *Awake!* – at the beginning of the

---

171. Katarikawe and Wilson, "The East African Revival," 217 (italics mine).
172. They are J. Musoke, E. Musoke, Gingo Kabuliteka, Wakabi and Mwavu. Ward, "Obedient Rebels," 217.
173. It is said that Mondo felt marginalized by his fellow senior Balokole, in not selecting him among overseas teams. Kabaza, OI, and Kigozi, OI.

Revival is here re-echoed by Lubulwa and Mondo, calling the Balokole to *Re-awaken!*

Reflection

The formation of *Ekibina kya "Katonda Omu Ayinza Byona"* (KOAB) was an indictment on the Church that it was not sufficiently indigenous. Essentially KOAB's standpoint was that the Church was paying lip service to the vernacular Scriptures and hindering the full incorporation of the people into Christianity as their new faith by requiring rigorous baptismal preparation that was indefensible from the Scriptures. So, while the missionaries, on the basis of the Scriptures, were decrying the "nominal" state of the Church, Kate and his followers on the basis of the same Scriptures but of vernacular rendering, had come to the opposite conclusion, that the Church was not "nominal" enough. "Nominalism" had two meanings: the one negative from the perspective of the CMS missionaries, and the other positive from the perspective of Kate and his followers. The basic difference between the two is not so much the reading of different translations, but rather the starting point in understanding and appropriating faith. The missionaries starting point was their experience of Christianity and all its historical-cultural trappings in its CMS form, while for Kate and Malaki, it was the traditional-vernacular faith in which there were neither believers nor unbelievers. From the perspective of KOAB, Christian baptism became an indigenizing tool, a ritual of inclusion rather than exclusion.

Unlike Kate, Nsibambi perceived "nominalism" to be a negative phenomenon. But this should not be concluded that Nsibambi's perception of "nominalism" was the same as that of the CMS missionaries. This is evidenced by the contrasting conclusions that Ensor and Nsibambi arrived at: Ensor forming an alternative church, and Nsibambi starting a movement within the Church. It is different hermeneutical starting points that led Mabel Ensor and Simeon Nsibambi to different conclusions about how to deal with the "nominal" state of the Church. For Ensor, since the native Anglican Church had fallen short of what she believed a church ought to be as a community of faith, she opted for an alternative church as the solution. This was an option in her experience. Nsibambi, on the other hand, had been nurtured by the Church and accepted it as his community of faith, having taken the place of his traditional faith community. There could be no justification in his experience for another church. The other "church" he knew – the Roman Catholic Church – was according to him a different "religion" and therefore could not be an option. Sabiti expressed this sentiment well, which was really shared by the African Balokole, that "the people of the Church of Uganda love their church much, and wouldn't listen to anyone who is supposed to be trying to leave the Church."[174] Therefore for Nsibambi, Sabiti, Kabaza and the other Balokole leaders, there was one option: the revival of their church.

The way the hermeneutical starting point shapes faith-response is evident even within the Revival, especially in relation to ecclesiastical ritual and form. Looking at the literature on the Revival, the Ruanda Mission missionaries had some theological difficulties over the routinized practices of baptism of infants, the liturgy and place of Holy Communion, and the liturgy.[175] The African Balokole accepted these forms without question. First, for the African Balokole the theological debates surrounding baptism, Eucharist and the Absolution were inconsequential for faith. In fact if anything the rituals were part of the faith pilgrimage. Second, like all the other Africans, belonging to the Church of Uganda and participating in its ritual and ceremony conferred upon them some social standing in society. They did not find any ground to forego these benefits.

The identity of the Revival hinged on two motifs: the clan-community, and the cross. Revival ethos emerged in the process of blending both. This illustrates how the process of forming a truly indigenous Christian community entails integration and blending of ethos from within the peoples' historical-cultural context and the Christ-event. It is a case, as Adrian Hastings has put it, of universality being "troublesomely but necessarily embedded within a true particularity."[176] So, every community that bears

---

174. Sabiti, quoted in Ward, "Tukutendereza Yesu," 123.
175. When Joe Church and Decie his wife delivered their first baby, they preferred to dedicate him instead of baptizing him in protest at the "routine baptizing of infants" in the Church of Uganda. See Church, *Quest for the Highest*, 80. Joe Church also records an incident when there was controversy among the missionaries over the reading of the "Absolution" by a layman, and the celebration of the *agape* meal instead of a full fledged communion with liturgy. Ibid., 72–73, 90, 189, 190, 194.
176. Adrian Hastings, *African Catholicism* (London: SCM, 1989), 82–83.

the name Christian will claim to be a result of a blending of ethos from within the peoples' particular historical-cultural context and the Christ-event. However, what determines the nature and character of faith of that community are the elements of historical-social culture, and the Christ-event that are blended in the process of becoming a Christian community. What distinguishes the Revival is blending of an element central to African identity – the clan-community – with the motif of the Christ-event – the cross.

The Fellowship as the locus of Revival faith praxis and as the basic unit of organization is one outstanding feature that shows how the Revival evolved as a genuinely African experience of Christianity.[177] The leaders of the fellowships were like the elders of a traditional clan, in the sense that they were not elected, but became leaders on the basis of their seniority in the experience of those values that defined the community. Hence the adoption of family language to refer to their community, as "members of the same clan-family." The fellowship meeting was a type of a "regular clan meeting"[178] in which the members first declared their continuing membership by word of testimony, because membership to the clan depended on the continuing "cleansing in the blood of Jesus."[179] They were a community, with certain norms and practices, and with a social order and structure of community support.

But these patterns of community were not just a Christianization of African patterns but an incarnating of the reality of Christ-crucified and the cleansing power of this blood into indigenous structures, forming a new clan-family, bonded by the kinship of the blood of Jesus shed on the Cross.[180] The Revival chorus, "*Tukutendereza Yesu,*" "We praise you Jesus," became a way of greeting, as a way one was identified with this new clan.[181]

---

177. Josiah Kibira, a member of the Revival movement in Tanzania argues that the idea of this "new clan" was a unique contribution to understanding ecclesiology in an African background in his book, *The Church, Clan and the World.*
178. John Mary Waliggo discusses how central the regular clan meeting were to the way clans operated in Buganda in his essay "The African Clan," 121–122.
179. This is a common expression by the Balokole.
180. Warren, *Revival*, 78.
181. All over Uganda, one can easily identify the tribe by the way they greet.

Conspicuously *Tukutendereza Yesu* is not an address to the one being greeted, but rather to Jesus, the Supreme Head of the "new clan."

The critical issue in incorporation and integration is balance. The Balokole's disquiet with the moral state of the Church, which was called "nominalism" by the CMS missionaries, arose from their sense of the lack of distinctiveness in the Church *vis-à-vis* the rest of society. It was a charge that the Church was not distinctly Christian, that is, that the ethos that defined the Church was predominantly from its traditional heritage and the social-cultural expedience of her people. In a word, according to the Balokole, the Church was worldly. Hence the charge that *Abakristayo* were not "real" Christians. The need for revival was to transform *Abakristayo* into "real" Christians. Becoming a Mulokole was equivalent to becoming a "real" Christian, as distinguished from a "nominal" one, *Omukristayo*.

Here lies the significance of the testimony motif in the Revival. The testimony was the result of the encounter and blending of the Christ-event, which in Revival theology was centred on the cross, and the historical-social-cultural narrative, at individual and corporate levels. The result was always a transformed life, a story to be told – the testimony. The principle, "every Mulokole is a witness," clarified that what qualified one to be a preacher of the gospel was not theological education, or ecclesiastical recognition such as that conferred through ordination or the award of certificates. Rather, it was a testimony, evidence of the encounter with the Christ-event narrative, which in Revival terms is what marked the "saved" ones, from the "not yet saved." And since every testimony was 'particular', uniquely personal, it was an expression of indigenous faith. It is this that gave the Revival the edge in impacting the Church's life, as Bishop Leslie Brown's recognized when he started his work in 1953 in Uganda:

> When I started work in Uganda I was depressed by the deadness of many congregations and by the fact that the people seemed to think that if you had a *ddini* (religion) you were quite all right. Congregations were very scanty. The clergy were very depressed and very few indeed got their pay regularly from their congregations . . . This sad picture was fortunately not universal throughout the diocese. In Kigezi and in Ankole, in the West, new churches were being built and

existing churches packed with people . . . The reason why there was so much difference between the districts in the liveliness of Christian people was largely the acceptance or refusal of the East African Revival.[182]

What Brown called the "deadness of many congregations" was for the Revival a result of the absence of a faith encounter with the Christ-event at individual and corporate levels contrasted with "liveliness of Christian peoples" – those for whom the Christ-event was part of their narrative.

---

182. Brown, *Three Worlds*, 115.

CHAPTER 4

The Church in the Emerging Republic, 1960–1971

Thus far in the account of the Church, Buganda has emerged as having had a pivotal role in the growth and spreading of the Church to the rest of Uganda. During the early formative years of the Church, as borne out by the account in chapter 2, the response in Buganda to the CMS missionaries' initiatives in evangelization became a model for the evangelization of the rest of Uganda. Even in the building of social service infrastructure and ecclesiastical structures, what happened in the Church in Buganda was simply duplicated elsewhere in Uganda. Patterns of growth and decline in the Church in Buganda were also more or less repeated later in the churches in the other areas of Uganda. The story of the emergence and spreading of the East African Revival from Namirembe to most of Uganda illustrated also the central role that the Church in Buganda played in shaping the ethos of the entire Church. This pre-eminent role of the Church in Buganda had come to be taken for granted by both missionary and indigenous leaders particularly in Buganda.

Buganda was accorded pre-eminence over the other areas of Uganda by the colonial government as well – a status that was enshrined in various agreements, but most notably the Buganda Agreement of 1900. The fact that the colonial government administered the rest of Uganda through Baganda agents must have contributed to the image of a supreme Buganda in Uganda.

This state of affairs was relatively easy to maintain while the Church in Buganda remained at the centre, and the kingdom of Buganda remained with an autonomous government. However in the decade of the 1950s, as the country was running up to independence, Buganda's pre-eminent political position was increasingly being called to question. The churches in the other areas of Uganda were also vibrant and growing, with credible leadership. There was bound to be tension and conflict over the Buganda *versus* rest-of-Uganda cleavage. The events and issues that unfolded in the decade after independence over this cleavage, and in particular the battle of Mengo and its aftermath, and their implications for the Church, are the subject of this chapter.

In order to put the developments in the Church into context, the account examines briefly the historical roots of the conflicting agendas of the kingdom of Buganda and the central government of Milton Obote,[1] and particularly the crucial question to which the battle points, the place of Buganda in Uganda. The story of the Church during this period also revolves around this question, and is reflected in the tension in the Church's self-definition and understanding of its identity as an indigenous church for Buganda, and a "universal" church for Uganda.[2]

---

1. Sources on the socio-political turbulence of this period include: Akena Adoko, *From Obote to Obote* (Kampala: Vikas Publishing House, 1983); Kabaka of Buganda, *The Desecration of My Kingdom* (London: Constable, 1967); Karugire, *Roots of Instability*; Mutibwa, *Uganda since Independence*.

Each of these sources has a unique contribution to the story. Phares Mutibwa writes as a Muganda, a fact which he acknowledged to have shaped his account, Mutibwa, *Uganda since Independence*, xiv–xv. The Kabaka of Buganda was an active player – it is at his palace that the battle raged. Akena-Adoko was also an active player from the opposite side of the socio-political spectrum, as the chief of the intelligence organ of central government, called the General Service Unit, see Adoko, *From Obote to Obote*, 82–85. And Karugire writes as a political historian.

2. Sources on the Church during this turbulence are interviews with key figures that were present and active participants. They include: Bishop Yokana Mukasa, then Dean of Namirembe after succeeding Dunstan Nsubuga; Rev Can Daniel Lubwama, then Diocesan Secretary and Archdeacon of Namirembe Diocese; Rev Canon S. P. Kigozi, the controversial husband to Namasole, the mother of Kabaka Mutesa II, and a youth worker in the Church at the time; Silvanus Wani, a bishop in the Church then; Canon John Bikangaga, the chief architect of the Church of Uganda Provincial Constitution 1970, and the creation of Kampala Diocese. Extensive research was also carried out in the Archives of the Church of Uganda. Akiiki Mujaju has discussed some aspects of this and the implications to the Church in his article, "The Political Crisis of Church Institutions in Uganda," *African Affairs* 75, no. 298 (January 1976). Kathlene Lockard devotes a chapter on this period in her study, "Religion and Political Development," 174–229. The approach in this chapter is different from both Mujaju's and Lockard's because it is theological and not political in its orientation, and is a more detailed account of the events in the Church.

The chapter recounts the conflict between the Church in Buganda and the national leadership of the Church of Uganda, sparked off by the election and enthronement of Erica Sabiti as Archbishop, replacing Leslie Brown. On the one hand, Erica Sabiti and the national Church leadership were seeking to establish national institutions; and on the other, the leaders of the Church in Buganda were striving to protect their autonomy as a church for Buganda by clinging to the symbols that marked their Kiganda identity. This caused tension that developed into a crisis, a protracted tug-of-war between Dunstan Nsubuga and the Church in Buganda (the Dioceses of Namirembe and West Buganda) on one side, and Erica Sabiti and the Executive of the Provincial Assembly of the Church of Uganda on the other.

The turning point in the story is the intervention of Idi Amin, a Muslim military dictator. Although a fuller discussion of the rise to the presidency by Amin belongs to the next chapter, it is his role in resolving the crisis in the Church of Uganda that is of interest in this chapter.

The chapter concludes by reflecting on the issues and dilemma in the Church over the conflicting agendas, at the Provincial and Buganda Church leadership levels. The critical issue in the Church is how to affirm both its corporate identity and the particularity of its constituent parts. The contribution of Archbishop Erica Sabiti to this process of self-definition is appraised.

Battle at Mengo and Its Aftermath

On 23 May 1966, the three Buganda chiefs who had been prominent in the motion in the *Lukiiko* (the kingdom's legislature), asking the central government to remove itself from Buganda,[3] were arrested and detained. As the news of their arrest spread across Buganda, war drums were sounded as an indication of declaration of war.[4] The stage had been set for violent confrontation between the central government led by Prime Minister Milton Obote, and the Buganda government led by the Kabaka. Convinced that

---

3. David Martin, *General Amin* (London: Faber and Faber, 1974), 118. They were Sebanakita, Lutaya and Matovu.
4. Adoko, *From Obote to Obote*, 76.

the Kabaka had been amassing large quantities of military hardware in preparation for war, Obote ordered Colonel Idi Amin, who was the commander of the armed forces, to investigate an alleged store of arms and ammunitions illegally held in the Kabaka's Palace.[5]

In the early morning hours of 24 May 1966, central government troops, under the command of Amin, attacked the Kabaka's Lubiri palace. The Kabaka and his men were prepared.[6] The battle, which was waged within the confines of the central palace, the Lubiri, raged for most of that day, except for the interruption of a heavy rainstorm in the middle of the day, interpreted by some as an act of God.[7] As the rainstorm calmed down, the Kabaka escaped.[8] The Kabaka's first refuge home was the White Father's residence on Rubaga hill, from whence he charted his escape route through the bushes of Uganda, to Bujumbura in Burundi. It was from Bujumbura that he flew into exile in Britain.[9]

Following the escape and flight to exile of the Kabaka, the central government troops overran and occupied the palace. There were many casualties in the Kabaka's palace.[10] There were reports of "thousands of Baganda dead from 23-5-66 up to 29-5-66."[11] Idi Amin is reported to have ferried lorry loads of bodies from Mengo "thereby confirming Sir Edward Mutesa's own estimate that the death toll of the battle had been as high as 2,000."[12]

---

5. Ibid., 77. Later that week Obote explained that "the operations were not against the Kabaka, nor to place the Kabaka under custody but to check on information we had received that there were arms in the Kabaka's Palace at Mengo . . . My orders did not include the detention or arrest of the Kabaka. I was only interested to find out whether there were arms in the Palace." Reported in *Uganda Argus*, 28 May 1966, 1.

6. The Kabaka of Buganda, *Desecration of My Kingdom*, 10. Also, Rev Canon Daniel Lubwama, OI, Kampala, 13 Jan 1997. Rev Lubwama, who said he was a friend of the Kabaka, recalled that in anticipation of the attack, the Kabaka had run for safety to the Makindye Palace the previous day. He went and found him in the Makindye Palace, asked him to return to the Lubiri for safety and prayed with him at the Lubiri. That day the central government forces had already surrounded the palace.

7. Lubwama informed me that the rainstorm was confined to the Lubiri and its immediate surroundings. In his view, this was God's miraculous intervention that paved the way for the safe escape of the Kabaka.

8. The Kabaka of Buganda, *Desecration of My Kingdom*, 14.

9. There is a detailed account of the Kabaka's escape by him in The Kabaka of Buganda, *Desecration of My Kingdom*, 15–26.

10. S. Peter Kigozi, OI, Kampala, 20 December 1996; Lubwama, OI.

11. The Kabaka of Buganda, *Desecration of My Kingdom*, 23.

12. Mutibwa, *Uganda since Independence*, 39.

It appears however that the majority of the residents of the Lubiri escaped.[13] Many were detained,[14] among them the sister to the former Kabaka, Nalinya, and Kabaka Mutesa's sister, Nabageleka. A state of emergency and a dawn-to-dusk curfew were declared in all Buganda. Police and army were dispatched to all corners of the kingdom to quell rural violence and uprising.[15] The whole of Buganda was engulfed in tension and fear. Police stations and army units were targets of an outraged Buganda population.[16]

However the most significant consequence of the May events was the hatred and bitterness planted in the Baganda for Obote. They interpreted the attack on the Kabaka's palace as tantamount to an attack on Buganda as a whole, and their identity being personified in the central role the Kabaka played in the life of the Baganda. The Kabaka's government articulated this in *Buganda's Independence* published on the eve of Uganda's independence:

> Buganda is an ancient kingdom with a long history and her dynasty exceeds thirty-seven kings in an unbroken line. The history of Buganda begins with a kingdom, and continues throughout the centuries with Kingship, right up to the present day. There is not a single period in our history when the Baganda had no King ruling over them. The Baganda have a system of clans and by means of royal marriages among women of various clans, and since by custom members of the royal family belong to the clan of their mother's side, a situation has arisen in passage of time, whereby most clans have

---

13. The Kabaka in his account has two letters of people very close who escaped, in The Kabaka of Buganda, *Desecration of My Kingdom*, 22–26. Erina Kigozi (wife of S. Peter Kigozi after death of Namasole his first wife) was a teacher at the Lubiri Primary School. She escaped with all the children from the school, according to Kigozi, OI.
14. The government newspaper reported that none of the government troops were killed in the battle, while about twenty other people lost their lives there, and about another twenty were killed elsewhere in Buganda. Obote admitted that about 600 people were arrested throughout Buganda. *Uganda Argus*, 28 May 1966, 1.
15. See a description of an uprising in one of the areas in the heart of Buganda, Kangulumira, Bugerere in A. F. Robertson, *Community of Strangers* (London: Scolar Press, 1978), 218–233.
16. Obote in an address to the nation on 31 May 1966 acknowledged that police stations at Kyagwe, Bulemezi, Kayunga, Buddu, Singo, and Luwero were attacked. So were the army units at Makindye and Masaka. There was some loss of lives and damage to property. Quoted in Adoko, *From Obote to Obote*, 79.

had a ruling Monarch or an outstanding Prince as a member of their clan (sic). This custom has had a profound effect on the Kiganda society. Buganda Kings are unique in that they play two big roles during the tenure of their office as monarchs, namely that they are rulers as well as being superheads of all heads of clans in the Kingdom. As a result, the King of Buganda, bears a personal relationship to every single Kiganda family in the Kingdom. In other words it is inconceivable for a Kiganda society to exist without a King.[17]

The "inconceivable" occurred with the exile of the Kabaka, the consequences of which were confirmed by the adoption of the Republican Constitution that abolished kingdoms within Uganda.

On 9 June 1967 the government published constitutional proposals which would convert Uganda into a republic. The proposals were debated for three months, and a Republican Constitution was adopted by parliament on 8 September 1967, abolishing Uganda's traditional kingdoms.[18] Buganda Lukiiko buildings were turned into the headquarters of the Ministry of Defence, and Lubiri and Bamunanika palaces became army barracks. The Baganda interpreted all this as a fulfilment of Obote's scheme and strategy to destroy Buganda. Buganda's bitterness and hatred for Obote were sealed. Mutibwa, reflecting on these events wrote:

> Having moulded Uganda into a nation-state at the expense of Buganda, Obote went on to weaken it still further by dividing the former kingdom into four districts – West Mengo, East Mengo, Masaka and Kampala – with the same status as other districts elsewhere in Uganda. The "term" Buganda was thus removed from the political language of Uganda. To rub salt into the wound, Obote turned the former Buganda parliament building (Bulange) into the headquarters of the Ministry of Defence; the Kabaka's Palace at Mengo (Twekobe)

---

17. The Kabaka's Government, *Buganda's Independence* (Mengo: The Information Department of the Kabaka's Government, 1960), 23.
18. The Bishops of both the Roman Catholic and Protestant Churches welcomed the 1967 Constitutional proposals "as necessary to stabilise the country and promote a greater national unity." Reported in *Uganda Argus*, 30 June 1967.

was turned into Malire army barracks; and his palace at Bamunanika, some 30 miles north of Kampala, was occupied by Obote's soldiers and later used by Amin to train his own army from Southern Sudan. All these actions exacerbated the Baganda's bitterness.[19]

The Kabaka died in exile in November 1969. Rumours that Mutesa had been poisoned, although denied by the findings of the inquest held in Britain, persisted among the Baganda,[20] accentuating their bitterness and hostility toward Obote. Phares Mutibwa, himself a Muganda, expressed it thus:

> Up to this day, the Baganda and the people of the other kingdom areas have never forgiven Obote (this does not apply to Amin who they knew, acted only as Obote's instrument) for the destruction and abolition of their kingdoms which had existed some five centuries. In particular, the Baganda have never forgiven Obote for forcing their Kabaka to flee as an exile to England where he died in poverty three years later.[21]

From this time on, Obote and his central government operated in suspicion and fear of Buganda. Margaret Ford is right in observing that:

> He was afraid to travel in Buganda without an armed escort. But always at the back of his mind was the comforting thought that his army contained large numbers of his own fellow Langi and Acholi tribesmen and he knew he could count on their loyalty if the Baganda tried to take control.[22]

The assassination attempt on Obote on 19 December 1969 confirmed his fears. It was concluded that the assassination plot had been engineered by leading members of the former Buganda hierarchy, working in conjunction with supporters of the late Kabaka who were with him in exile

---

19. Mutibwa, *Uganda since Independence*, 59–60.
20. Kenneth Ingham, *Obote, A Political Biography* (London: Ronteledge, 1994), 125.
21. Mutibwa, *Uganda since Independence*, 60.
22. Margaret Ford, *Janani: The Making of a Martyr* (London: Marshal, Morgan & Scott, 1978), 35.

in London.²³ Five men, all Baganda (one of them a clergyman),²⁴ were arrested in connection with this assassination attempt. Relations between Obote's central government and Buganda remained sour until the military coup in January 1971 led by Idi Amin.

The Church and the Battle of Mengo

As already mentioned, the news of the battle of Mengo, and the flight to exile of Kabaka Mutesa II, brought shock and outrage in all Buganda society, including the Church. The identity of Protestant Christianity as the "established" religion of the Buganda meant that the Church, Christians and their leaders in Buganda were deeply affected.²⁵ Rev Lubwama, Archdeacon of Namirembe at the time, became hysterical at the sound of guns from the Lubiri on the morning of 24 May; he spent all the day in Namirembe Cathedral, pacing up and down its length, praying, murmuring, and crying.²⁶ Rev P. Kigozi, a provincial youth worker at the time, prayed passionately for the Kabaka, his safety and return to Buganda, but could not bring himself to utter the name "Obote," that it "was bitter" on his lips.²⁷

Church life was disrupted all over Buganda. During the early months of the state of emergency in Buganda several churches did not hold Sunday worship services, as there was fear of the security forces that had been

---

23. Ibid., 126.

24. *Uganda Argus*, April 2, 1970, 1. The name of the clergyman is Rev Erisa Sebalu-Kasasa.

25. The Roman Catholic Church leadership remained non-committal in its response to the battle and exile of the Kabaka. The Roman Catholic Church had been identified with the Democratic Party (DP), and its members harassed by some of the leadership in Buganda in the run up to independence. DP had been perceived as a party against the Kabaka. In a pastoral letter by the Archbishop Joseph Kiwanuka circulated in November 1961, he defended his flock in their right to choose their leaders, and indicated his bias towards party politics, a position that the Mengo establishment was opposed to. Kiwanuka in the same letter warned the Monarchy about the repercussions of involvement in politics and objected to the formation of the Kabaka Yekka party. It is as though the attack on the Lubiri confirmed his warning. Joseph, Kiwanuka, *Church and State: Guiding Principles, Pastoral Letter of Archbishop Joseph Kiwanuka*, Kampala, November 1961, Bishop Tucker Theological College (BTTC) Archives.

26. Lubwama, OI.

27. S. Peter Kigozi, OI, Kampala 9 January 1997.

dispatched all over Buganda. But wherever the Christians were they prayed for the safety and return of their Kabaka.[28]

Outside Buganda, there is little indication that the rest of the country was unduly disturbed by the events at Mengo. Bishop Silvanus Wani, then bishop of Northern Uganda (1964–69) and the Chaplain General of the Uganda army, held a meeting with Obote after these events, at which he told Obote: "By God's help you should forgive such people,"[29] referring to the Kabaka and his men in the palace. Although Wani referred to a Church delegation that went to see Obote and condemned the attack on the Lubiri, no such delegation is mentioned in the official records of the Church. There was no official position or statement of the Church on the whole incident.[30]

While the battle of Mengo was raging, Archbishop Sabiti, who had been in office for only five months (having succeeded Leslie Brown), was in Fort Portal, the headquarters of the diocese of which he was bishop. On hearing the news of the battle and the flight to exile of the Kabaka, he travelled to Kampala. Distressed at the arrest and detention of Nalinya and Nabageleka, the Kabaka's sister and wife respectively, he went to see Obote to plead for their release.[31] This incident, however, was reported in the Buganda press, as a show of solidarity with Obote and his government in subduing Buganda. It was believed by many in the Church in Buganda that Erica Sabiti agreed with those who attacked the Lubiri.[32] Erica Sabiti then issued a statement:

> As a Christian leader, and knowing that many of our leaders in the central government and in Buganda government are Christians of different denominations, the only way for peace is to come back to God and repent of hatred, jealousy, tribalism and revenge.

---

28. Ibid.; and Lubwama, OI.
29. Silvanus Wani, OI, Kyambogo, Kampala, 15 January 1997.
30. Yona Okoth, OI Tororo, 16 January 1997. He was then Provincial Secretary of the Church of Uganda, and residing on Namirembe Hill.
31. Kigozi, OI, Kampala, 9 January 1997, and Geraldine Sabiti, O I, Kinoni Mbarara, 18 December 1996.
32. Lubwama believed that Erica Sabiti was aware and condoned central government action in attacking the Lubiri. Lubwama, OI.

Jesus is known in the Bible as the Prince of Peace, and for the situation as it is in Uganda today, I call upon you, who are His people, to allow Him to come into this situation and take control.

I am praying for the President and the Central Government and His Highness Sir Edward Mutesa, wherever he may be, and also for the Government and the people of Buganda. Uganda is a Christian country and my prayer is that Christ may be allowed to control the hearts of our leaders so that He can bring His peace and calmness.[33]

Although Sabiti seems to have been "on the fence" on these events neither condoning nor condemning either party, his neutrality was not accepted. Only one position was acceptable to Buganda: outright condemnation. Any other position was judged as acquiescence. Sabiti was therefore perceived to be pro-Obote. This came out clearly in the wake of the overthrow of Obote and his government. Rowdy mobs came to the residences of Sabiti and Okoth, demanding that they follow Obote, their man, to Tanzania.[34]

Another incident was the occasion of the thanksgiving service early in 1971, for the release of five government ministers[35] who were detained in early 1966 by Obote's government for opposing the process towards a Republic. Dunstan Nsubuga, then bishop of Namirembe, had invited the Archbishop to preside and preach at the service, but a group of angry worshippers slammed the door in his face and locked him out of the service and the Cathedral.[36] So when the body of the Kabaka was returned

---

33. Reported in *Uganda Argus*, Saturday 28 May 1966.
34. Okoth OI. Okoth was then Provincial Secretary for the Church.
35. They were: Balaki Kirya, Dr Lumu, Mathias Ngobi, George Magezi, and Grace Ibingira. Mutibwa, *Uganda since Independence*, 37.
36. Bishop Yokana Mukasa, Can Daniel Lubwama and Bishop Yona Okoth narrated this incident to me. All three were present. Yokana Mukasa, then dean of the Cathedral presided over the service after the Archbishop was shut out; Can D. Lubwama was one of those leading the service and Yona Okoth as acting that day as Archbishop's Chaplain. Can Lubwama could even remember the person who slammed the door in Erica Sabiti's face, one Ted Nassozi. It is also narrated by John Sebalugga-Kalimi, "The Life and Contribution of Dunstan Nsubuga (Bishop of Namirembe 1964–85) to the Church of Uganda," Makerere University, unpublished dissertation for the Diploma in Theology, 1988, 50. John Bikangaga believes that this action was engineered by the Cathedral

from Britain for official burial, Erica Sabiti stayed away from the memorial service at Namirembe Cathedral for fear of more violent action against him, although he had been invited to lead the service by Bishop Nsubuga. Referring to this incident Lubwama wondered how one who had betrayed "our Kabaka together with Obote, could now come to honour him! It was unthinkable."[37] Nsubuga is reported to have said that just before fleeing, the Kabaka visited him secretly and told him, "*Ffe tugenda. Naye Obuganda mubukuume.*" (We are going. You should look after Buganda.)[38] The "you" (plural), Kevin Ward believes, was a reference to both Baganda bishops: Dunstan Nsubuga of the Protestant Namirembe Diocese and Emmanuel Nsubuga, the Catholic Archbishop of Kampala, at Rubaga.[39]

The issues that had led to the battle of Mengo between the political power players were thus latent in the Church. Erica Sabiti was the focus of the protest for the Church in Buganda. The roots and development of the conflict in the political arena will help put in perspective the developments in the Church.

Roots of the Battle of Mengo

Several authors have discussed the causal factors and events of the battle at Mengo.[40] The most significant events were: first, the referendum in the "lost counties" in 1964 and subsequent formal dissolution of the alliance between the Uganda People's Congress (UPC) and Kabaka Yekka (KY) in August 1964. Second, the parliamentary debate in late 1965 in which the Deputy Army Commander, Colonel Idi Amin, and the Prime Minister, Milton Obote, and a few of his close associates were accused of embezzling money, gold and ivory obtained from Uganda's involvement with the rebels

---

Mothers Union, the official women's organisation in the Church. John Bikangaga, OI, 17 January 1997.

37. D. Lubwama, OI.

38. This is reported in Sebalugga-Kalimi, "Life and Contribution of Dunstan Nsubuga,"

38. Kalimi interviewed Bishop Nsubuga on 20 April 1986.

39. Ward, "The Church of Uganda amidst Conflict," 76.

40. Among them are: Kabaka of Buganda, *The Desecration of My Kingdom*; Ingham, *Obote, a Political Biography*, 103–126; Karugire, *A Political History of Uganda*, 170–198; Karugire, *Roots of Instability in Uganda*; Low, *Buganda in Modern History*, 235–250; Mutibwa, *Uganda since Independence*, 42–77.

in Congo-Zaire in the early 1960s. The infighting surrounding the debate led to the arrest and detention in February 1966 of five cabinet ministers on the orders of Obote. Third, the suspension of the 1962 Independence constitution and the post of President that was one of its provisions, provoking a drastic response form the Buganda Lukiiko. It passed a resolution giving the central government an ultimatum to remove itself from Buganda soil by 30 May 1966, a move which immediately precipitated a confrontation by force of arms and led to the battle of Mengo.

However, all these events occurring between 1964–1966 were symptoms of the unresolved question of the status of Buganda in a united independent Uganda. Phares Mutibwa observed that "Obote's difficulties in the 1960s were the same as Cohen's in the 1950s – that is how to bring home to Buganda the needs of a united and independent Uganda."[41] This question deserves some further attention because it was the composite of factors and relations surrounding the place of Buganda within Uganda that led to the battle of Mengo in May 1966.[42] As the story of the Church around this period unfolds, the same issue lay at the heart of the self-understanding of the Church in Buganda leading to internal tensions and conflict with the national Church leadership.

The "Question of Buganda"

When the British and other foreigners came to Uganda, the kingdom of Buganda was the most dynamic and sophisticated, the largest and strongest, and also the most prosperous of all Ugandan societies of the period.[43] Consequently, the centrality of Buganda was of paramount importance in

---

41. Mutibwa, *Uganda since Independence*, 38.
42. Kabaka Mutesa has narrated the episode in his book *The Desecration of My Kingdom* on 9–26, and has also placed it within the context of the ongoing struggle to resolve the question of Buganda within Uganda beginning with Mutesa I and the imposition of British Colonial administration. He has clearly shown that the question was uppermost in the negotiations between Buganda and the Protectorate Government. It was a major constitutional question, and various arrangements were arrived at in the 1900 and 1955 agreements. Tension and conflict surrounding the same question led to the Kabaka Crisis of 1953–1955, which was the precursor to the 1966 crisis.
43. Karugire, *Roots of Instability*, 18.

the British conception of the Uganda Protectorate.[44] Not only were the other kingdoms and areas incidental to the Kingdom of Buganda, but the British decided to administer them along the centralized hierarchical model of Buganda. Buganda was pre-eminent in Uganda in the mind of the British administrators and missionaries.

It was expedient for the British to collaborate with Buganda and its structure in subduing, governing and Christianizing Uganda. This pre-eminence in British policy, though not stated explicitly, was implied in the various agreements with the British of 1892, 1893, 1894, 1900 and 1955.[45] The Kabaka and the kingdom administration were well aware of this superior and special historical standing of the kingdom, and constantly sought to assert and preserve it. This led to tension and confrontation with the colonial government in the period leading up to independence.

The first major confrontation was what has come to be known as the Kabaka crisis of 1953–1955.[46] The colonial governor, Sir Andrew Cohen, had vision for a unitary state. This was bound to cause a head-on collision between the protectorate government and the kingdom of Buganda, which was committed to a federal status.[47] So when Cohen demanded that the Kabaka agree to constitutional changes that would provide for a unitary state, Mutesa's mind was made up that "in a contest of loyalty, I owed an allegiance to my own people and not the British Government."[48] On the basis of the 1900 agreement, Andrew Cohen deported the Kabaka to exile. The 1955 agreement that delineated the conditions, under which the Kabaka could return to his kingdom, only half defused the bomb. By it the

---

44. For a full discussion, refer to: Karugire, *A Political History of Uganda*; Low, *Buganda in Modern History*.
45. D. Anthony Low, *The Mind of Buganda: Documents of the Modern History of an African Kingdom* (London: Heinemann, 1971); Low and Pratt, *Buganda and British Overrule*.
46. Paulo Kavuma, *Crisis in Buganda 1953–55* (London: Rex Collings, 1979), and a major section of Kabaka of Buganda, *The Desecration of My Kingdom*. Kevin Ward has done a study of the crisis from the perspective of the Church, in his essay, "The Church and the Exile of Kabaka Mutesa II of Buganda (1953–55), an unpublished seminar paper presented at the Centre for the Study of Christianity in the Non-Western World (CSCNWW), Edinburgh University, New College, October 1993.
47. Kabaka Mutesa II acknowledges this as the cause for his confrontation with Andrew Cohen, in *Desecration of My Kingdom*, 114, 119–122.
48. Ibid., 120.

Lukiiko agreed to participate fully in the legislature of the Protectorate in exchange for the return of the Kabaka to Buganda.

Political power structuring and organization in the period of the late 1950s and early 1960s prior to independence continued to be dominated by the question of status of Buganda at independence. Frustrated at the handling of the matter by the Protectorate government, the Buganda Lukiiko on the 8th of October 1960, signed a memorandum to Queen Elizabeth II, terminating British Protection over Buganda as provided for in the 1894 agreement, and published a document, *Buganda's Independence*, which articulated Buganda's historic conviction and stand. A paragraph that succinctly expresses this reads in part:

> It is that special position which Buganda enjoys now that she wants to maintain even after Uganda's independence. Baganda believe that they can safeguard their prestige only through the survival, in a living and functioning form of the Kabakaship and the Lukiiko. The Kabaka is the spirit and the motivating power of political, economic and social activities, and the Lukiiko is the legislative forum of the Baganda. That is why anything, either extrinsic or intrinsic, that tends to weaken our institutions is bound to be resisted in Buganda . . .[49]

However, as the time for independence approached, the other nationalities sought an equal status for all kingdoms and districts in an independent Uganda. Political structuring and organization by the non-Baganda revolved around containing and "cutting to size"[50] Buganda's superiority. Although the two most dominant factors in the alignment of political forces in the period immediately after the Kabaka Crisis (1953–55) and prior to independence were religion and the question of Buganda,[51] it is the place

---

49. The Kabaka's Government, *Buganda's Independence*, Mengo, 1960, 27–28.

50. Karugire uses this phrase and believes it was Obote's inspiration in the negotiations prior to independence and his attitude to Buganda after independence. Karugire, *Roots of Instability*, 73.

51. Roman Catholic marginalization from political power was the most significant inspiration for the formation of the Democratic Party (DP) (cf. Low, *Political Parties in Uganda*, 22–23; and Karugire, *A Political History of Uganda*, 158–162).

of Buganda in a united and independent Uganda that tipped the balance of power. As A. G. Gingyera Pinycwa observed:

> The reaction from outside of Buganda's political dominance was one of suspicion, fear, and even hatred in some quarters, resulting in political parties being formed in other parts of the country to face up to the challenge or "Question of Buganda."[52]

The merger of the Uganda People's Union (UPU) and a wing of the Uganda National Congress (UNC) to form the Uganda People's Congress (UPC) was a consolidation of the non-Buganda front.[53] It has been acknowledged that anti-Catholic sentiments were instrumental in the momentous alliance on the eve of independence, between the UPC, a party that one analyst described as "an anti-Buganda party right from its inception"[54], and the Kabaka Yekka (KY) (Kabaka alone). The strong Catholic base of the Democratic Party (DP) and its nationalist-republican policy did not endear it to the KY, a party that was born to fight for the preservation of the federal status of Buganda.[55] However the primary issue around which the alliance was negotiated was the federal status of Buganda in an independent Uganda. The primary concern for the KY was the continuance of a federal status for Buganda, a condition that the UPC accepted, since it was the only way to capture the Buganda vote, oust the DP, and control the central government. The KY saw the alliance as the only way to destroy the DP with its nationalist ideals. Low observes:

> On this occasion an alliance with the UPC presaged a major share in the central Government of Uganda upon the attainment of self-government; this might be by far the best way to secure the special interest of the Baganda in the future; it might allow them to resume their former role of *primus inter pares*; while the leading politicians would have some

---

52. Gingyera Pinycwa, "Is There a Northern Question?," 52.
53. Low, *Political Parties in Uganda*, 31–32, and Karugire, *A Political History of Uganda*, 165–168.
54. Karugire, *Roots of Instability*, 44.
55. Ibid., 186; and Low, *Political Parties in Uganda*, 54–57.

very greatly enlarged opportunities for the exercise of political power.[56]

The alliance was struck, and was later sealed by the election of the Kabaka as constitutional Head of State (President) in 1963. The alliance achieved a status for Buganda within Uganda, which they had failed to secure through agitation, threats and resolutions to secede.

Mutibwa is right in arguing that:

> The Independence Constitution of 1962 was a compromise document to meet political problems that had beset the country since the mid-1950s. Its complex nature was the natural result of the pre-eminent position Buganda enjoyed, *vis-à-vis* the country's other kingdoms and administrative units, in Uganda Protectorate since the turn of the century. This pre-eminence has been attributed both to the excessively pro-Buganda policy, pursued by the British colonial government and vigorously implemented by the local administration and to "its historical authority and structure."[57]

> [For] when the Independence Constitution came to be written, the superiority of Buganda over the other three kingdoms (Ankole, Bunyoro and Toro) and the remaining administrative units of the protectorate, was emphasised.[58]

One would have supposed that with the 1962 independence constitution that enshrined the principle of federalism and the subsequent election in 1963 of the Kabaka as the President, the Buganda question would have been settled. However, to the extent that the question of Buganda in Uganda tipped the balance of power towards independence, it remained a major issue in the brokering of political power in the years after independence. As Obote, the Prime Minister, and his UPC consolidated their

---

56. Low, *Political Parties in Uganda*, 54–56.
57. Mutibwa, *Uganda since Independence*, 25.
58. Ibid., 26.

power and position in the National Assembly,[59] the alliance increasingly became irrelevant.

By early 1964 the UPC had an overwhelming majority in parliament and therefore was confident enough to bring to parliament the issue of holding a referendum in the "lost counties" of Buyaga and Bugangaizi,[60] a matter that the Kabaka opposed.[61] In his determination to keep the land and in anticipation of the referendum, the Kabaka tried to influence the outcome by resettling large numbers of Baganda ex-servicemen in those counties. But this scenario was sabotaged by a High Court ruling that only people whose names appeared on the electoral register of 1961 and 1962 would be qualified to vote in the referendum. When the referendum was held in November 1964, the population of those counties voted overwhelmingly to be returned to Bunyoro, to the chagrin of the Kabaka and the Buganda Kingdom government. This marked the end of the alliance, and the beginning of the mounting of tension between the central and Buganda governments.

At the time, cracks had developed in the echelons of power within the UPC.[62] UPC became polarized into two main factions grouped around Obote, the Party President, and Ibingira, the Secretary General. With this cleavage, there were clearly three groups at the centre, vying for political power – what Akena Adoko has termed "imperialist," "feudalist" and

---

59. There were some DP Members of Parliament and several others of the KY who "crossed the floor to join UPC." See Karugire, *Roots of Instability*, 51.
60. "The lost counties" was the territory that the British passed on to the Buganda Kingdom in 1896, in appreciation for Buganda's role in subduing and conquering the kingdom of Bunyoro. The Buganda agreement of 1900 had entrenched the region as part of Buganda. Towards independence, the kingdom of Bunyoro increased its agitation for a return of this area, but the British did not find it expedient to resolve the conflict before independence. It was provided for in the independence constitution that the Uganda government would carry out a referendum in those two counties, in not less than two years after independence to ascertain the wishes of the inhabitants as to whether they wished to remain in Buganda, return to Bunyoro, or to be constituted in a separate district. For a thorough discussion on this dispute, see Karugire, *A Political History of Uganda*, 199–237.
61. The Kabaka of Buganda, *The Desecration of My Kingdom*, 168–170, and Karugire, *Roots of Instability*, 51–52.
62. For the development of the power wrangles in UPC, see Mutibwa, *Uganda since Independence*, 32–33.

"nationalist" forces, led by Ibingira, Kabaka Mutesa, and Obote, respectively.[63] With the dissolution of the UPC-KY alliance, a realignment of political forces led to another informal but none-the-less strong alliance between the Kabaka and Ibingira forces. The interest of the former was the survival of the federal status of Buganda while the latter was poised to challenge Obote's leadership and remove him and his faction of the UPC from power.

The contest was so sour that there are reports of an assassination and coup plots towards the end of 1965 and early 1966.[64] All the parties at this stage gravitated to a military solution: Obote promoted Colonel Amin, and demoted Brigadier Opolot for reportedly allying with Ibingira and the Kabaka. The Kabaka also sought military support from some foreign governments. To remove Ibingira and his faction, and the Kabaka from centre stage, Obote ordered the arrest of Ibingira and four other ministers, and suspended the 1962 constitution.[65] The contest was removed from Parliament to the military, culminating in the battle of Mengo.

The "Question of Buganda" in the Church of Uganda

The premier position of the Church in Buganda in the Native Anglican Church was taken for granted by the missionaries. However in the transition process from missionary to indigenous leadership, tensions began to emerge as the place of the Church in Buganda became crucial in the Church's self-definition as a Church of Uganda. The period 1964–1967 was a time of transition in the leadership of the Church of Uganda. On 28 January 1964, at the Provincial Assembly, Archbishop Leslie Brown, who was also bishop of Namirembe Diocese, the premier diocese of Buganda, announced his intention to retire and make way for "African leadership" of the Church.[66] In March 1964 he appointed Canon Dunstan Nsubuga,

---

63. Adoko, *From Obote to Obote*, 1.

64. Ibid., 12–14, 39–52. Akena Adoko believes that the coup plots were masterminded by a coalition of the Ibingira faction and the Mengo establishment.

65. Ibid., 47–75 and Mutibwa, *Uganda since Independence*, 35–39.

66. Leslie Brown, "Opening Address to the Assembly by His Grace, Provincial Assembly," Appendix "A" of the "Proceedings of the Provincial Assembly, September 1964."

then Dean of Namirembe Cathedral, as his assistant bishop, an act that was construed to be preparation of a successor for the See of Namirembe Diocese.[67] This raised expectations and questions about his successor as Archbishop. He had played a dual role, as bishop of Namirembe and Archbishop of Uganda. Would the bishop of Namirembe continue as Archbishop?

Was Archbishop Leslie Brown aware of the significance, in the mind of the Baganda, attached to the place of the Church in Buganda in Uganda? It seems that the events in Buganda at the time increasingly brought him to this awareness. In his opening address to the Provincial Assembly in September 1964, he called for "adjustment between Buganda and the rest of the Country" that was necessitated by the decision by Parliament to hold a referendum in Bugangaizi and Buyaga.[68]

Moreover, the memory of the events of the Kabaka crisis of 1953–55 and the perceived collaborative involvement of Bishop Brown was still fresh. The Baganda had accused him of connivance and conspiracy with the protectorate administrators.[69] The absence of a specific prayer for the Kabaka in the newly printed Luganda Prayer Book was seen as further evidence of the conspiracy against Buganda headed by Archbishop Brown.[70]

Provincial Assembly Papers, COU Archives.

67. Dunstan Nsubuga was consecrated bishop of Namirembe on 21 November 1965. *Uganda Argus* 22, November 1965, 3.

68. Brown, "Opening Address to the Assembly." Adjusting took a long time because the diocese of West Buganda was reluctant to surrender the churches in the two counties. In response to Brown's charge a team of clergy was commissioned that year to consider the question of the boundary between West Buganda and Rwenzori dioceses. At a PAE meeting on 30 March 1965 the Executive entrusted the pastoral care of the Christians in Buyaga and Bugangaizi to the Archbishop who requested the bishop of Rwenzori to act on his behalf. Although it was resolved at the meeting of the Provincial Assembly of 26 January 1966 that the proposed transfer of the churches in the two counties should take place as soon as the two dioceses agreed to, it was not yet effected by the next Assembly of January 1967. No Executive or Assembly resolution was passed to transfer these churches. There was only an admission by the bishop of West Buganda, at the Assembly of 1968, that these churches were already under the care of Rwenzori diocese and that his diocese had seen no reason to make a resolution to that effect. PAE minutes 22 October 1964, 30 March 1965; and Provincial Assembly minutes of 26 January 1966, and 4, 5, 6 January 1967 and October 1968.

69. Kevin Ward argues this point in his paper "The Church of Uganda," 9–12.

70. The matter was raised in Buganda when in the reprinted Luganda Prayer Book in 1963 the Kabaka was not mentioned. The matter was so serious that Archbishop Brown took pains to explain in a press conference that: "the current Prayer Book had omitted

However, it was the issue of a successor to Brown as Archbishop that heightened the tension. Understandably, the Baganda wanted the maintenance of the status quo – the bishop of Namirembe as Archbishop. In fact a lobby group of laymen in the church, that called itself the Namirembe Christian Organization,[71] accused Archbishop Brown of wanting to appoint a Munyankole instead of a Muganda to replace him. In a statement at a press conference on 15 November 1965, Brown responded that it was "entirely and completely wrong to suggest that I have chosen a new Archbishop … There has been a good deal of misrepresentation or misunderstanding…."[72] He clarified that the Namirembe Christian Organization was: "an association of certain Christians but it is not in any way official. It has no authority to speak for the Church. . . . It is (sic) the Diocesan Bishops of Uganda, Rwanda, Burundi to choose him."[73]

The Archbishop is further reported to have said that he had not received any letter from any government official, either central or Kabaka's, regarding the election. He dismissed the Namirembe Christian Organization as a small group, members of the Namirembe Cathedral congregation.

> The people in this association are all people who sometimes worship in Namirembe Cathedral. I say sometimes because except for their Chairman, I do not know any of them … The only way they can influence the Church of Uganda is through the Parish Councils. If the Parish Councils were to feel strongly enough about their proposals, they should put them to the Diocesan Church Council. Then something might be done … But no parochial Church council has brought this matter up at all. In my opinion these people who want a Muganda

---

out (sic) due to problems with the old plates (printery) of which making new ones would take five years to make. So a temporary one has been organised which cuts out prayers for rulers but in the one to be made at the end of 1967, they will be included. . . . There had been no intention however to show contempt to the Kabaka or in other ways to cut him out of the book." Reported in *Uganda Argus*, 16 November 1965.

71. Lockard, "Religion and Politics in Uganda," 189; Wani, OI, confirmed the existence of such an organization, but could not recall any further details such as its membership. *Uganda Argus*, 13 November 1965, named one Wamala to have been the chairman of the organization.

72. Reported in *Uganda Argus*, 16 November 1965.

73. Ibid.

Archbishop are doing their cause more harm than good because they are upsetting other Christians outside Buganda.[74]

Although Archbishop Brown dismissed the Namirembe Christian Organization as a group without credibility and legitimacy to speak on behalf of any section of the Church, their agitation manifested fears in the Church in Buganda, over the election of an Archbishop other than the bishop of Namirembe, and worse still a non-Muganda. To the Baganda, a non-Muganda succeeding Brown would be tantamount to failure by the Church to recognize the founding role of the Baganda in the growth and spreading of the Church beyond Buganda. It was also feared Namirembe would lose its pre-eminence, be relegated to the status of a diocese among others, and its Cathedral would lose its identity as the worship centre for Buganda.

In spite of agitation for a Muganda Archbishop, Bishop Erica Sabiti,[75] was elected in November 1965 to succeed Brown as the first African Archbishop. This confirmed the suspicion among the leaders in the Church in Buganda that Brown was bent on ensuring that a non-Muganda succeeded him.[76] Margaret Ford rightly observed:

> It had seemed to them a foregone conclusion that their own Dr Dunstan Nsubuga, now Bishop of Namirembe, should be elected as the new Archbishop. Instead they had to watch in disbelief as Erica Sabiti, to them an unknown Munyankole from south-western Uganda, was elected and installed as Archbishop in their own cathedral, St Paul's, Namirembe, in 1966.[77]

---

74. Ibid.
75. This is the same Erica Sabiti that was one of the leading figures among the Balokole leaders in the dispute between the Balokole and Bishop Stuart over the Mukono Crisis in Chapter Three. Erica Sabiti (1910–1988), was ordained deacon in 1932; priested in 1933; and was saved in 1939. He was Rural Dean of Bweranyangyi Deanery 1951–1960. He became bishop of Rwenzori Diocese in 1960, a position he retained until Kampala Diocese was created in 1972.
76. Bishop Yokana Mukasa, OI, Kampala, 28 April 1997; Lockard, "Religion and Political Development in Uganda," 191.
77. Ford, *Janani*, 34.

Bishop Wani explained that the House of Bishops "chose Erica Sabiti because of his love and humility. He was really a committed bishop amongst us; a true Mulokole, with a message for the whole country; a humble man of God, full of love. He was not so tribalistic."[78] Although Bishop Wani asserted that the choice of Sabiti was "unanimous,"[79] it has to be pointed out that the two bishops of the predominantly Baganda dioceses of West Buganda[80] and Namirembe,[81] did not cast their vote in his favour. Granted that he was more experienced as a bishop than Nsubuga, and respected for his spiritual depth and commitment as a Mulokole;[82] however, for the bishops from Buganda these were not the primary concerns. The fact that the others from Ankole-Kigezi,[83] Mbale,[84] Northern Uganda,[85] Soroti[86] and Rwanda-Urundi[87] cast their vote in his favour gives content to the tribal factor that Wani alluded to. The Church leadership was divided along Buganda / rest-of-Uganda lines. Sabiti's election had delineated the issue that was to dominate the entire period of his archiepiscopal leadership; the place of the Church in Buganda in the whole Church of Uganda.

---

78. Wani, OI. Wani was among the bishops who elected Sabiti.
79. Ibid.
80. The present districts of Kibale, Kiboga, Masaka, Mubende, and Rakai constituted the diocese of West Buganda.
81. The present districts Iganga, Jinja, Kampala, Kamuli, Luwero, Mpigi and Mukono constituted the diocese of Namirembe.
82. Wani, OI; and John Bikangaga, OI, Kampala, 17 January 1997.
83. The present districts of Bushenyi, Kabale, Kisoro, Mbarara, Ntungamo and Rukungiri constituted Ankole-Kigezi Diocese.
84. The present districts of Kapchorwa, Mbale, Pallisa and Tororo constituted Mbale Diocese.
85. The present districts of Acholi, Apac, Arua, Kitgum, Lira, Moyo and Nebbi constituted the Northern Uganda Diocese.
86. The present districts of Kotido, Kumi, Moroto, and Soroti constituted Soroti Diocese.
87. The two countries of Burundi and Rwanda constituted Rwanda-Urundi Doiocese.

Erica Sabiti and the Church in Buganda – Namirembe Crisis

Sabiti was bishop of Rwenzori Diocese[88] at the time of his election. Phares Mutibwa has expressed the sentiments of the Baganda in response to his election thus:

> The Baganda, perhaps in one of their rare parochial moments, were angered by the choice of Sabiti which, they claimed, had been influenced or even dictated by Obote. They felt, not without reason, that they were the churches' "natural" leaders and therefore natural successor to the English religious leaders who had brought the Englishman's religion to Uganda. Had it not been Kabaka Mutesa I of Buganda who invited the first British Protestant missionaries, and did Christianity not spread into the other parts of Uganda from Buganda? Thus the Baganda questioned and wagged their fingers at the non-Baganda Christians.[89]

The disposition of the Church in Buganda towards Sabiti was therefore negative right from the start. They did not have confidence in Brown or the process he presided over leading to Sabiti's election. There was suspicion that the election was fraught with political gerrymandering, a view likely to have been promoted by Bishop Nsubuga.[90] But the political climate at the time, the heightened tension between Obote's Central government and the Kabaka's Buganda Lukiiko government, could have led some to such a conclusion. Sabiti was perceived as a stooge of Leslie Brown and not a consensus choice of the House of Bishops.[91] It was thought, among the Baganda, that one of the reasons Brown retired at the time he did was to ensure that a Muganda did not succeed him.[92]

---

88. The present districts of Bundibugyo, Hoima, Kabarole, Kasese, Masindi and the Eastern Congo-Zaire (then known as Mboga) constituted Rwenzori Diocese.
89. Mutibwa, *Uganda since Independence*, 67.
90. Kigozi, OI; and Wani, OI.
91. Mukasa, OI.
92. Ibid.; Wilson Mande, "Anglicanism and Ethnic Identity in Uganda," Namirembe, Kampala, un-published paper, 17. Mukasa believed that Sabiti was politically naive.

Sabiti's charge, at his enthronement, is revealing of the kind of person he was and his disposition *vis-à-vis* the Buganda-Uganda problem that was the most critical national issue at the time. He did not make any direct reference to it but instead, in a typical revivalist fashion, pointed to the cross of Christ as the answer to all social and political evils in the land. He stated:

> All our unhappy divisions, political, denominational, tribal and racial, disappear at the foot of the cross, where we meet together as sinners before our Saviour. When we allow the Lord Jesus to rule our lives, then we grow together as a family, we are one in Him, we are called by God to serve all His children, of all tribes and races, in order to bring them to Christ and become living stones within his Church.[93]

As a statement of his vision for the Church in "this new era," he singled out the place of the youth, and "the situation of malaise in some sections of the Church."[94]

One year later, in a statement to the 1967 Assembly reviewing the work and ministry of the Church in his first year as Archbishop, he made no mention of the Mengo Crisis, and only pointed to the need of submitting to the Holy Spirit's work and the Cross of Christ. Archbishop Sabiti said:

> All this will be useless, worthless, without the power and the fire of the Holy Spirit, blessing and breaking and cleansing and renewing us day by day, calling us continually to spiritual renewal in our Lord, and to steadily deepening obedience to his will. Our Lord is calling us to walk in His Way, the way of costly obedience and sacrifice. It is the way of the cross. It is the way He is calling us all in His service.[95]

What he referred to as a "situation of malaise" turned sour. Three issues over which there was conflict during his leadership highlighted the tension

---

93. Erica Sabiti, "Archbishop's Charge: Enthronement of the Most Rev Erica Sabiti," St Paul's Cathedral, Namirembe, 25 January 1966, Archbishops' Papers, COU Archives.
94. Ibid. This is how he characterized the moment in the light of his ascendance to the See, as the first African Archbishop of Uganda.
95. Erica Sabiti, "Archbishop's Address to the Provincial Assembly," January 1967, Provincial Assembly Papers, COU Archives.

over the Church in Buganda in the Church of Uganda, that constituted what is referred to in this thesis as "the Namirembe Crisis": Namirembe Cathedral; Church land; and the place and role of the Archbishop, and their constitutional implications.

Namirembe Diocese and Cathedral

Namirembe Diocese lost its bid for pre-eminence in the Church of Uganda with the election of Erica Sabiti as Archbishop and subsequent enthronement in Namirembe Cathedral on 25 January 1966. The next struggle for the Church in Buganda was the retention of its independence in a kind of "federal status," with Namirembe Cathedral as its symbol.

The Church in Buganda had so far enjoyed pre-eminence in the whole province. It was historically prior to the churches in other areas in Uganda, and was instrumental in their planting. The first bishop of Uganda and the first archbishop of the Province of Uganda, Rwanda, Burundi and Boga-Zaire, both had Namirembe as their headquarters. Leslie Brown was both bishop of Namirembe and Archbishop. In fact, at his accession to the archiepiscopal throne, he did not find the need to open a provincial office. The office of the diocese of Namirembe also served as the office of the new province,[96] and in its cathedral was the throne of the bishop of Namirembe who was also archbishop. The two thrones, though present from the inception of the province, were not physically distinguishable. Therefore to have a non-Muganda sit on the primate's throne, and the bishop of Namirembe on the lower throne, was fraught with sinister symbolism in the mind of Buganda. Thus although it was provided for in the Provincial Constitution that the Namirembe would be both a diocesan and provincial Cathedral, *de facto* and in the mind of the Baganda it was Buganda's cathedral, an issue that they had hitherto taken for granted. What was at stake for the Baganda was the shift in the identity of the Cathedral that was implied in having a non-Muganda sit at the Archbishop's throne.

The kingdom of Buganda as a whole, not just the Church in Buganda, had undertaken the construction of the Cathedral. Kabaka Mwanga and

---

96. The discussion to establish a Provincial secretariat began when Erica Sabiti became Archbishop.

his successor Daudi Chwa, and their governments, in particular under Katikiro Apolo Kagwa, took a very active interest in the construction of the successive structures.[97] Of the current Cathedral building Karen Moon observed that its construction was for long primarily an effort of Buganda until it was belatedly realized that it belonged to the wider Diocese of Uganda:

> Contributions thus far [1916] had almost all been raised by the Baganda. It had been felt that, as the Uganda Diocese was composed of a number of races and the Cathedral was the Cathedral Church of the whole diocese, all should take their part and share in the contributions and the work. It was realised that a fundamental mistake had been made when the Baganda had started the building without consulting the surrounding countries (sic). The whole Cathedral project was regarded as a Baganda effort, and the Kabaka's name on the foundation stone taken as proof. In early 1917 this situation seems to have been resolved. At a meeting of the church, it was reported, an apology was made by the Baganda for their initial mistake by a unanimous show of hands.[98]

Indeed it was only partially resolved. The resolution was only on paper but not in the feelings of the Baganda Christians. It remained the Cathedral for Buganda.

When Protestant Christianity became the "religion" of Buganda, Namirembe Cathedral epitomized its establishment. It was considered the Kabaka's church.[99] This sentiment had earlier been expressed at the consecration of the first African bishop and a non-Muganda, Aberi Balya, at

---

97. The present structure is the fourth in a series of others destroyed by nature's tempests. For the full story, see Karen Moon, *St Paul's Cathedral Namirembe: A History and Guide* (Richmond, England: Karen Moon, 1994), which is an account of the history of the Cathedral.

98. Moon, *St Paul's Cathedral Namirembe*, 39.

99. Twice the coronation of the Kabaka of Buganda, of both Daudi Chwa and Mutesa II, done by the bishop of Uganda, had taken place in the Cathedral. On the return of Mutesa II from exile, the first stopover for thanksgiving was at Namirembe Cathedral, and the 35th birthday thanksgiving and celebration of the Kabaka Mutesa took place in Namirembe Cathedral. *New Day,* 4 December 1965, 6.

Namirembe Cathedral. In a letter of protest to Bishop Stuart in 1947, Stanley Musoga, "representing all Baganda," wrote:

> The Cathedral at Namirembe belongs to the King of Buganda, and to the Baganda and is not for the other nationalities. . . . You have shown yourself a bad ruler but we are not going to allow Balya to be consecrated unless you are looking for war in Buganda. We ask that a Muganda be consecrated because we were given power to rule ourselves and the 1900 [Agreement] does not allow people of other tribes to sit on our councils.[100]

It is noteworthy that Mengo as the headquarters of Buganda establishment included among other centres Namirembe. What the palace at Mengo was to the Kingdom of Buganda, Namirembe Cathedral was to the Church in Buganda. It was not possible therefore to separate Namirembe Cathedral from the Mengo political establishment.

These sentiments can be appreciated when put in the context of the history of the Cathedral itself. The Cathedral was a landmark in the history of the Church in Buganda and indeed in the Buganda kingdom itself. Namirembe, the hill, was one of the historic sites in pre-colonial Buganda. It has been suggested that the hill was nicknamed *Ninamirembe*,[101] meaning "I have peace," because Kintu, the first Kabaka of Buganda, set up his camp on it after defeating Bemba in the battle of Budo in the twelfth century.[102]

Kabaka Mwanga gave the site to the CMS Mission in 1889 after the defeat of the Muslims by the Christian factions. Moreover, all the subsequent Kabakas of Buganda after Mwanga "came of age" in the Cathedral. Services to celebrate Daudi Chwa's and Mutesa II's eighteenth birthdays, when they were recognized to have come of age to ascend the throne, all took place in the Cathedral.[103] No wonder Mutesa II could refer to it as the Kabaka's

---

100. Quoted in Ward, "The Church of Uganda," 7. Balya was consecrated, and there was no war in Buganda, but "war" there was to come when Erica Sabiti tried to enter Namirembe Cathedral, in 1971 after the overthrow of Obote's government.

101. Bikangaga, OI. Bikangaga recalled that in a note granting the hill to the CMS, by Kabaka Mwanga referred to it as *Ninamirembe*.

102. Ibid., 4.

103. Moon, *St Paul's Cathedral Namirembe*, 40; and Harold Ingrams, *Uganda: A Crisis of Nationhood* (London: Her Majesty's Stationery Office, 1960), 60.

church.[104] It was the supreme *Kiggwa*[105] (Luganda word for the headquarters of a divinity) of Buganda. Just as Christianity had replaced the cult of the *Balubaale* in Buganda's traditional religion, so Namirembe had become the supreme *Kiggwa* of their new religion. It was inconceivable for Baganda to let go of their *Kiggwa*, worse still to one, who as they perceived him, was identified with the forces that wanted to destroy Buganda.

When Sabiti was elected Archbishop he was bishop of Rwenzori Diocese, with its headquarters at Fort Portal, two hundred miles from the centre. The issue of whether future archbishops should always occupy the See of Namirembe was discussed before Bishop Leslie Brown relinquished his position as Archbishop. Without realizing the consequences it was decided and put in the constitution that a bishop elected to become the next archbishop should remain bishop of the diocese he occupied prior to his election.[106] However the difficulties of an archbishop residing two hundred miles away from the centre raised the need to either create a new and nearby diocese or free the Archbishop from any Diocesan responsibilities. In fact it was thought by some that when Sabiti moved residence from Fort Portal to Namirembe he had his eye, not only on the archiepiscopal throne, but the bishop's as well.[107] There was no way in which the Baganda were going to let this happen. The closing of the doors to Sabiti in 1971 has to be seen as an expression of this sentiment.

The Provincial Assembly Executive (PAE), the executive committee of the Provincial Assembly, "expressed its deep regret over the unfortunate occurrence on Sunday, 31 January 1971, when the Archbishop of Uganda, Rwanda and Burundi was barred from entering St Paul's Cathedral, Namirembe."[108] The House of Bishops expressed their "very great concern and regret at what happened," and reaffirmed their unity, solid support and

---

104. The Kabaka of Buganda, *The Desecration of My Kingdom*, 101.
105. Kigozi, OI. Kigozi informed me that the evidence of this is in the fact that the worship drums of *Lubale Kibuka*, one of the most revered Buganda divinities, were brought to the Cathedral and are there to this day.
106. "Constitution of the Church of Uganda, Rwanda and Burundi 1960," Article VII(a). "On the Appointment of the Archbishop of Uganda and Ruanda-Urundi," 4, House of Bishops Papers, COU Archives.
107. Can Lubwama was certain that Sabiti was scheming for this. Lubwama, OI.
108. Minute 12/71 of Provincial Assembly Executive (PAE) meeting of 2 February 1971, PAE Papers, COU archives.

confidence in Sabiti as archbishop.[109] It is not on record that Nsubuga as the bishop of Namirembe protested against the action, which was interpreted to mean that he condoned it[110]. Buganda had lost the archiepiscopal See to a *munamawanga*,[111] a foreigner. It was not ready to lose the Cathedral as well. Moreover, one of the options that had been considered by the *Survey on Administration and Finance of the Church of Uganda*[112] to deal with the tension arising from the new situation created by Sabiti's election, was that the archbishop also becomes the bishop of Namirembe.

Namirembe's pre-eminence was first of all in Buganda; it was precisely because Namirembe was pre-eminent in Buganda that it became pre-eminent in Uganda. However the Church leadership at the national Provincial level wanted the Church in Buganda to accept that Namirembe Cathedral belonged to both Namirembe Diocese and the Province of the Church of Uganda. The Archbishop had a constitutional right to enter and preside over a national event,[113] which the thanksgiving service was considered to be.

Under the 1961 Church Constitution, Namirembe was to be, for ordinary purposes, the cathedral of the diocese of Namirembe. For national occasions the Dean and cathedral chapter would make the cathedral available. Therefore, when the plans to shut Sabiti out were leaked to the Provincial leaders they urged him to go, because staying away would have defeated the principle of this dual identity, and served the exclusionist agenda of

---

109. Quoted in *Uganda Argus*, 12 February 1971, 3.
110. Bikangaga, OI.
111. Lubwama, OI; Kigozi, OI. *Munamawanga* is a luganda word meaning foreigner. *Munamawanga* is singular and *Banamawanga* prural. It is the same word used in translating the word *gentile* in the Bible. This is how Baganda referred to other nationalities. Both Lubwama and Kigozi used the same words in expressing why it was hard for the Baganda to let Erica occupy the archiepiscopal throne in the Cathedral. Both Okoth and Wani acknowledged that this is how they were often referred to, as non-Baganda
112. The Church of Uganda, Rwanda and Burundi, *Survey on Administration and Finance of the Church of Uganda* (Namirembe: Uganda Bookshop Press, 1969), 6. The other options were the creation of a Diocese of Kampala and making the post of Archbishop executive.
113. This was provided for in the Church Constitution of 1961, that "an Archiepiscopal throne shall be provided for him [Archbishop] in the Cathedral Church of St Paul, Namirembe."

the leadership of the Church in Buganda.[114] A clash was inevitable. The dual identity of Namirembe Cathedral remained a thorny issue until 1971 when a settlement was reached.[115]

Housing and Land

The election of an Archbishop who was not bishop of Namirembe, and who needed to travel so far to come to the centre, raised a series of challenges in the relationship between the Provincial structures and the Church in Buganda (the dioceses of West Buganda and Namirembe). How was Sabiti to manage affairs at the centre of the Church, Namirembe, from the periphery at Fort Portal? Sabiti was concerned about this right from the start. In his charge to the Provincial Assembly, the day after his enthronement, after referring to the issue of the conflicts in West Buganda diocese, he said:

> There is one other point I would like to bring before your attention. The fact that I am Bishop of the distant Diocese of Rwenzori, as well as Archbishop of this province is bound to create problems. It is not going to be easy working from Fort Portal with the Provincial Staff based here in Kampala. One suggestion is that I should continue to live at Fort Portal and spend one week each month, or two weeks together every two months in Kampala. This means, of course, spending almost all my time travelling on the road either touring my own Diocese, or travelling between here and Fort Portal. It will also mean keeping two residences going. It has already been agreed that I should have an assistant Bishop, but I should like you to take the whole matter to the Provincial Assembly executive and other committees concerned.[116]

---

114. Bikangaga, OI. Bikangaga was one of those who urged Sabiti to go and face any consequences, for the sake of reasserting the dual identity of the Cathedral.
115. When it was finally resolved in 1971, two thrones were provided; the most prominent throne is for the bishop of Namirembe. The one for the archbishop is tucked in the middle of the thrones of the other bishops in the Province, as though to symbolize that while in the Cathedral the archbishop is only one among his fellow bishops.
116. Erica Sabiti, "Opening Address by the Chairman," Provincial Assembly, 26 January 1966, Provincial Assembly Papers, COU Archives.

The PAE took this matter up at their first meeting in January 1966.[117] They were also faced with the challenge that hitherto no land had been demarcated for Provincial use. The land on Namirembe hill, it was claimed, belonged to Namirembe diocese. But all these concerns had constitutional implications. The relevant but ambiguous article in the circumstances read:

> There shall be an Archbishop of the Church of Uganda, Rwanda and Burundi who shall be a Diocesan Bishop of a Diocese in the Province and who, whilst normally residing in his Diocese, shall have a house at Namirembe, Kampala, provided for him where he shall reside at regular intervals together with such offices as may be necessary for his work as Archbishop. An Archiepiscopal throne shall be provided for him in the Cathedral Church of Saint Paul, Namirembe.[118]

While Leslie Brown was Archbishop and bishop of Namirembe, the questions of a designated Archbishop's house, a provincial secretariat, and land on which to erect these buildings and other facilities for the Province did not arise. He resided in a house at Namirembe in Kampala and had his throne in the Cathedral as bishop and Archbishop. But with Erica Sabiti's election, who was "normally" resident two hundred miles away from Namirembe, with no officially designated house and office for Archbishop, they became immediate concerns. Although these issues were not new on the agenda of the Provincial Assembly Executive,[119] they now became urgent. In fact when Erica Sabiti came from Fort Portal for his enthronement, there was no house to accommodate him. He camped in a retreat

---

117. PAE Minutes, 31 January 1966, PAE papers, COU Archives.
118. "Constitution of the Church of Uganda," Article VII (a).
119. A process had already begun to build a house for the Archbishop. The process of amending the 1960 Provincial constitution, began in 1963, was in its advanced stages. The Provincial Assembly Executive was initiated as an advisory Committee, which he would consult in between Provincial Assembly meetings. However by 1964, it was acknowledged that the committee had grown to become an executive organ of the Provincial Assembly. In recognition of this, the position description of the PAE was revised during the Provincial Assembly of January 1967. A new board to continue with the advisory role had been created. Provincial Assembly Minutes of 4, 5, 6 January 1967, 9–11, PA papers, COU Archives.

house in the backyard of Bishop Nsubuga's palace home, whose facilities were anything but satisfactory for a person of the status of Erica Sabiti.[120]

The Provincial Assembly therefore acted fast to find a permanent home by searching for an appropriate plot on Namirembe hill to build, having concluded that this matter did not require a constitutional amendment.[121] Namirembe Diocese had already earmarked the same plot for the Archdeacon of Namirembe that a provincial team had selected as suitable. When Bishop Nsubuga and Archdeacon Lubwama were contacted to negotiate, they indicated that the Namirembe Diocesan plan could not be changed.[122] Instead another plot, below the Bishop's residence, was given to the Province to build the Archbishop's residence.

The issue of building a house for the Archbishop raised the thorny issue of land. It put on the agenda the question of what land on Namirembe hill was available to the Province. Up to this point all the land on the hill belonged to Namirembe Diocese, as successor to the Uganda Diocese. Therefore the Provincial Assembly executive put to Namirembe Diocese a request to confirm that "the compounds already marked out, surrounding the present Provincial houses and offices, are available for provincial use and development."[123]

In reply, the bishop of Namirembe asserted that the Namirembe Diocese "has a right, through its land Board . . . to express how best the land can be utilised. This requires careful planning; and the land Board is looking into this."[124] This implied that all the land at Namirembe hill belonged to the Diocese of Namirembe, and the authority to allocate plots was the prerogative of its land Board. In terms of land at Namirembe hill, it was thus established that the Province was subordinate to Namirembe Diocese. But this was not to be the last word.

---

120. Geraldine Sabiti, OI. Not only was it a very small house, as his wife, Geraldine, told me, it had no internal plumbing. Sabiti and his wife lived in the guesthouse only one night, as they just could not bear it. Whenever they were in Kampala, they stayed either with children, or with Dr Roy Billington, the CMS representative.
121. PAE Minutes 31 January 1966, 5–6 PAE papers, COU Archives.
122. PAE Minutes 31 January 1965, 4–5, PAE Papers, COU Archives.
123. PAE Minutes 29 November 1966, Appendix headed "Provincial Housing at Namirembe," PAE Papers, COU Archives.
124. Ibid.

When the *Ten Year Plan* committee, established by the Provincial Assembly of January 1966, submitted its report at the Assembly of 1967, it included in its recommendations the setting up of Church Commissioners to be the trustees of all land and other assets of the Church. This, like the creation of a diocese for the Archbishop, was a constitutional matter.

Constitution Crisis

The first Constitution of the Province of the Church of Uganda and Ruanda-Urundi had been adopted by the two dioceses of Upper Nile and Uganda in September 1961, in preparation for the inauguration of the Province and the election and enthronement of the first Archbishop of the Church.[125] In 1963 a process began to amend sections of the constitution to reflect the growth of the Church. And by the time of the election and enthronement of Erica Sabiti, the process had matured.[126]

At the January 1966 Provincial Assembly, a day after Erica Sabiti was enthroned Archbishop, a vote was carried which approved all the amendments to the 1961 Constitution. However, at a subsequent meeting of the Provincial Assembly Executive, it was agreed that it was inadvisable to publish the amended constitution because of anticipated constitutional questions that Sabiti, as the replacement of Leslie Brown, was bound to raise. The matter was shelved, to be reviewed after the next Provincial Assembly[127] scheduled to sit in January 1967. In that Assembly meeting, however, "The Draft Constitution of the Church of Uganda 1967" was approved in spite of the inclusion of the yet unresolved contentious issues.[128] But even this was not published as the substantive document; it remained in a draft form.

---

125. *New Day*, 9 September 1960.
126. The proposed amendments had already been approved by the Provincial Assembly of 1964, sent to dioceses for review and acceptance, so that by the 1966 Provincial Assembly, all responses had been received, agreement and blessing sought and received from the Archbishop of Canterbury.
127. PAE Minutes of 13 May 1966, PAE Papers, COU Archives, 10.
128. Provincial Assembly Minutes of meeting of 4, 5, 6 January 1967, PA Papers, COU Archives, 5.

Two other significant steps in 1966 by the PAE that had constitutional implications were the establishment of a Provincial Secretariat[129] and the commissioning of a committee to work on a ten-year plan. In order to be functional, the Secretariat needed, as a minimum, office space and staff housing, thereby raising the question of land earmarked for provincial use. *The Ten Year Plan* reflected this need in its proposals, and even recommended radical approaches on the use of church land as a resource towards developing a self-supporting church.[130] All these plans had direct bearing on Namirembe diocese and could not be implemented fully before amending the Constitution. But the Provincial Assembly approved the Plan at its meeting of 1967,[131] causing concern to Namirembe diocesan leadership. The situation was made more incongruous by the uneasy relationship between Sabiti and Nsubuga.[132]

What fanned constitutional fires were the two major steps by the House of Bishops and the PAE. First was the appointment of the Commission on Canon Law and Constitution at the beginning of 1967, under the chairmanship of John Bikangaga, and composed of one member from each diocese and others appointed by the PAE. The task of the Commission was to make recommendations that would streamline and bring up-to-date the Canons and Constitution of the Church to reflect developments and plans under the new leadership.

The second was the commissioning of a survey on Church administration and finances in Uganda in January 1968, also to be headed by John Bikangaga, as an added function of the Commission on Canon Law and Constitution. This was seen as a sequel and vital part of *The Ten Year Plan* intended to examine and recommend financial and administrative

---

129. A proposal by an adhoc committee of the PAE proposed a comprehensive secretariat, covering among several issues, housing for the Archbishop and other Provincial staff, the question of land and office space, Ref.: "Report of Adhoc Committee on the Provincial Secretariat," 1966, PAE Papers, COU Archives.

130. The Church of Uganda, Rwanda and Burundi, *The Ten Year Plan* (Namirembe: Uganda Bookshop Press, 1967), 25–28.

131. Provincial Assembly minutes of 4, 5, 6 January 1967, 15.

132. My informants on this period spoke about this uneasiness in the relationship between the two: Bikangaga, Kigozi, Okoth, Wani, and Lubwama.

measures that would enable an implementation process of the plan.[133] The survey was to cover Uganda, seeking proposals from all the dioceses.

It was the proposal by George Oguli from Soroti diocese, to the Canon Law and Constitution Commission, "to amend the Constitution to provide for the creation of a diocese of Kampala,"[134] made in May 1968, that ignited the constitutional fires, initialling a constitutional battle within the Church. The matter of creating a diocese for the Archbishop was the major recommendation of the Commission's interim report, proposing "that the Constitution be amended to make possible the creation of a diocese of Kampala of which the Archbishop would then become the Bishop."[135] The report evoked a stern response for Namirembe diocese. In a letter to the Provincial Secretary, the diocese questioned the integrity of the process that the PAE had adopted and rejected the recommendations. In part it said:

> 2. It cannot be denied that the sole purpose of the proposed amendment to the Constitution is to enable the Provincial Assembly to alter the boundaries of the Diocese of Namirembe. Kampala is an integral part of the Diocese of Namirembe, and therefore to create the Diocese of Kampala as recommended by the Commission which you set up to consider Mr Oguli's proposal, would be, to say the least, a serious violation of Article 11(b) which your Commission itself appeared to regard as sacrosanct in these words: "No such Diocese of Kampala could be contemplated without the consent of the Namirembe Diocesan Synod as laid down in Article 11 (b) of the Provincial Constitution. The Commission registered its profound conviction that no attempt must be made to

---

133. The survey was commissioned after responses to *The Ten Year Plan* from the dioceses had been discussed at the December 1967 Provincial Assembly meeting. Each Diocese was to set up a survey team that would collate proposals and submit them to a central committee. John Bikangaga was given the responsibility and full authority to undertake the task and set up survey machinery. The Church of Uganda, *Survey on Administration and Finance*, i.
134. PAE minutes of the Meeting of 6, 7 February 1969, Appendix 1, 1, PAE Papers, COU Archives.
135. PAE Minutes of 6, 7 February. 1969, 4, PAE Papers COU Archives.

diminish this safeguard through the use of any other section of the constitution."

3. We wish to emphasise our contention that while the amendment to the Constitution is the prerogative of the Provincial Assembly, the alteration of the boundaries of a diocese is not.[136]

Thus the PAE and the Church in Buganda began a protracted constitutional wrangle. It was clear to Namirembe diocese that only after they elected, as a diocese, to change its borders would "the question of amending some provisions of the Constitution, if at all, be considered, but not otherwise."[137] The diocese did not want to conceive of anything that would so radically redefine its identity within the Church of Uganda and therefore proposed an alternative amendment:

> The present Constitution provides that the Archbishop should normally reside in his Diocese but should retain a lodge at Namirembe. This change, which presupposes that the Archbishop would always have an Assistant or Suffragan in the Diocese, might be a compromise solution.[138]

They concluded that "there will be no change in the present set up. Now that the Archbishop's house at Namirembe is ready, what is needed is for His Grace to stay more at Namirembe than in Fort Portal."[139] Just like in the question of land, Namirembe Diocese had sought to reassert its separate identity. Although the PAE responded to Namirembe Diocese detailing the developments of the Constitutional question and clarifying that its intention was dialogue and consultation with Namirembe Diocese,[140] it was clear to the latter that the prerogative of having a Diocese carved out of Namirembe was their own.

---

136. Letter from Namirembe Diocese to the PAE, dated 29 November 1968, PAE Papers, COU Archives.
137. Ibid.
138. Ibid.
139. Ibid.
140. Letter from PAE to Namirembe Diocesan Council dated 18 February 1969, PAE Papers.

In the meantime, during 1968 Bikangaga and the survey team were visiting all the dioceses in the country, evaluating the status of Church administration and finances. Their final report, submitted to the House of Bishops and the PAE, in April 1969, complicated further the constitutional puzzle.[141] It not only reiterated the same recommendation to curve a Kampala diocese out of Namirembe. It amplified the issue, first by reviewing other possible options that would make space for the Archbishop, and second, by proposing other measures to strengthen provincial structures and authority. The three options reviewed, to deal with the Sabiti situation, and "make it possible for future archbishops of Uganda, Rwanda and Burundi to reside in Kampala,"[142] were:

a) The creation of a Diocese of Kampala, for the purpose.
b) Providing in the constitution that the Archbishop should also become Bishop of Namirembe.
c) Making the post of Archbishop executive so that he is not also a Diocesan Bishop.[143]

All the three were considered unfavourable to Namirembe. There were two other recommendations in the *Survey on Administration and Finance of the Church in Uganda* that irked Namirembe diocese. The first was the recommendation to establish a Provincial Electoral College to vet nominations whenever a vacancy of a bishop needed to be filled, and, together with the House of Bishops, act as a translating body.[144] The second was the proposal to form the "Church Commissioners of Uganda," to "be given full responsibility to develop church lands by building and managing property, houses, shops, and other income-producing protects."[145] To effectively study and respond to the Bikangaga Report,[146] Namirembe Diocesan

---

141. The *Survey on Administration and Finance of the Church in Uganda* was published in April 1969 and circulated to all the dioceses for discussion. Each diocese was to submit their responses and proposals to the Canon Law and Constitution Committee to integrate them in the draft amendments to the Constitution, to be discussed and adopted at the 1970 Provincial Assembly.
142. The Church of Uganda, *Survey on Administration and Finance*, 6.
143. Ibid.
144. Ibid., 13.
145. Ibid., 32.
146. This is how the *Survey on Administration and Finance of the Church in Uganda* was referred to in subsequent references at committee and publications.

Council appointed a committee chaired by the then Dean of Namirembe Cathedral, Yokana Mukasa.[147] It was believed by many in Namirembe circles that the Bikangaga Report had been influenced by some in the political establishment in the central government, the "people who wanted to destroy Buganda."[148]

This time West Buganda diocese joined with Namirembe diocese, and in solidarity expressed their disapproval of the way the PAE was managing the process and rejected the amendment to create a Kampala diocese, and the recommendations to give more authority to the Archbishop and Provincial organs. Namirembe diocese, in another memorandum, went further and rejected the entire process as contrary to the letter and spirit of Anglicanism.[149] In spite of the protests from Buganda, the Canon Law and Constitution Committee collated the proposals from the other dioceses, and integrated the structural changes proposed by the survey report into the amendments to the Draft Constitution (1967). The Provincial Assembly Executive circulated the proposed amendments to all dioceses for review and approval or rejection. The PAE included the Commission's Report and discussion of the amendments to Constitution on the agenda of the Provincial Assembly of December 1970 for final discussion and adoption.

The two dioceses, West Buganda and Namirembe, in protest, refused to send their delegation to the Assembly because they did not want to be part of a body that would debate and vote on an amendment which, according to Namirembe diocese, had not gone through "prior consultation."[150] The Assembly persuaded both bishops to contact their delegates. The Namirembe Diocesan delegates agreed to "attend the Assembly on the proviso that no vote be taken at this session on these items: i) Creation of

---

147. Mukasa, OI; Also Minutes of the Namirembe Diocesan Council, 19 September 1969. Namirembe Diocese Archives. The other members of the Committee were: Canon D. Mukasa, Rev J. G. Seng'endo-Zake, E. P. Kibuka Musoke, G. Kabiswa, and C. M. S. Kisosonkole.
148. Mukasa, OI.
149. A Memorandum from the Diocesan Council Retreat at Mukono, dated 3 May 1970, PAE Papers, COU Archives.
150. Provincial Assembly Minutes, 9, 10, 11 December 1970, 3, PA Papers, COU Archives.

Kampala Diocese, ii) Provincial control of Church land, iii) Establishment of a Provincial Electoral College."[151] Both delegations were persuaded to come into the Assembly. But in spite of the pre-conditions stated by Namirembe and West Buganda Dioceses for participating in the Assembly, the Assembly proceeded with the agenda as planned, at which point the delegates of West Buganda walked out.

Sabiti had in his charge pleaded with the Assembly to put the constitutional debate into the broader and more significant context of the mission of the Church thus:

> The proposals are of great importance. Nevertheless, from the beginning I wish to make it clear that they are not the most important items that lie before us. *The decisions we are faced with go deeper than a Constitution. They go beyond rules and regulations. They strike at the very heart of our faith and Christian life together. The decisions we are faced with have to do with the mission of the Church.* The evangelisation of the nation, our service to the people, and the quality of our life in the Spirit are basic issues we face. The proposals, which come before us, are meant to serve the mission of the Church and help deepen our life in Christ. The amendment of the Constitution must be seen as an aid to these more important matters. Our basic aim must be the renewal of the Church. The amendment of the Constitution is one step we must take if we are to move ahead with what we have been called to do. If we view the debate, which lies ahead of us, in any other way we shall have missed the point of what we have come here to do.[152]

In his view the constitutional discussions were to serve the Church's essential being as one Church of Uganda, visibly serving in each area or locality in Uganda. He had argued:

> The Church has men, but how can we share them so that if someone in Kigezi is needed in Soroti, as someone from Fort

---

151. Ibid.
152. Erica Sabiti, "Archbishop's Charge to the Church of Uganda, Rwanda and Burundi," at the Provincial Assembly of December 1970, 2, PA papers, COU Archives (italics mine).

Portal is needed in Jinja, they can in fact go where they are needed? We must develop a church structure that makes it possible for each part of the Church to help each other. We must stop thinking simply of my tribe, or my diocese and think of the entire Church and Nation. God is challenging us to think of ourselves as a unified people and to live as a unified people. Our job is to find practical ways of doing that.[153]

The practical way for the Assembly was to proceed with the agenda with or without the two dioceses in Buganda. It proceeded without Buganda and made a resolution to "establish in Kampala a Diocese for the Archbishop of Uganda, Rwanda and Burundi, and that a committee be appointed by the Assembly to work out and determine boundaries, using Constitutional means, of the said new Diocese."[154] It was debated and put to a vote and passed by 103 to 1, with 12 abstentions, all from Namirembe diocese[155] Thus the Church of Uganda had taken a vote without the full participation of the Church in Buganda, as the delegation from West Buganda had walked out. The issue remained unresolved since the Church of Uganda needed the cooperation of the Church in Buganda for the determining of the boundaries of the new diocese, and the latter would not cooperate. Namirembe served the Province with an ultimatum. That it had been:

> Resolved that all communication between the Province and this Diocese is closed until there has been proper formal negotiations between the Namirembe Diocese and the Province, in accordance with the 1967 Draft Constitution of the Province.[156]

Two months later West Buganda Diocese passed a similar resolution:

> To close ALL COMMUNICATIONS (sic) between our Diocese and the Province, until the proper, formal negotiations, and clear apology be made by the Province to the Diocese deserving the mockery astion (sic) that was done by

---

153. Ibid., 6.
154. Ibid.
155. Provincial Assembly Minutes, 9, 10, 11 December 1970, 3.
156. Letter from Namirembe Diocese to the Provincial Secretary, dated 26 January 1971.

the members of the Province at Mukono, and in agreement with the draft Constitution of 1967.[157]

A deadlock was reached. The Church in Buganda sought to assert its separate identity apart from the Church of Uganda, and the Church of Uganda had reasserted its national identity that it could not realize without the Church in Buganda. It was Idi Amin who used the force of his position as President to bring the Church in Buganda and the rest of the Church of Uganda to a round table conference, and resolved the impasse.

Resolution of the Namirembe Crisis

Most of the accounts on Idi Amin[158] and his relationship with Christianity and the churches in Uganda have portrayed him only as an instrument of the "powers of darkness" who wanted to destroy Christianity and the churches through an aggressive Islamization project.[159] What these accounts have not duly recognized is the place and significance of his intervention in resolving the crisis that was tearing the Church apart, and therefore his role in enabling the Church to redefine her identity in Uganda. Idi Amin enabled the Church to arrive at a resolution that had eluded it for several years. He was characterized as the "the hand of God"[160] in the situation.

Idi Amin: The "Hand of God"?

When Idi Amin took the reins of power through a military coup in January 1971, the rift between Buganda and Uganda in the Church of Uganda was at its worst. A rift between two factions, the National Association for the Advancement of Muslims (NAAM), and the Uganda Muslim Community (UMC), also tore the Muslim community. Amin was determined to bring

---
157. Letter from West Buganda Diocese to the Provincial Secretary, dated 12 March 1971.
158. The rise of Idi Amin and his regime are discussed in the next chapter.
159. They include: Festo Kivengere, *I Love Idi Amin* (London: Marshal Morgan & Scott, 1977); Muhima, "The Fellowship of His Suffering"; Kefa Sempangi, *A Distant Grief* (Glendale, California: Regal Books, 1979); Dan Wooding and Ray Barnett, *Uganda Holocaust* (London: Pickering and Inglis, 1980).
160. Bikangaga, OI. This is how Bikangaga, the Chairman of the *Ten Year Plan* and the Drafting Committee of the "Church of Uganda, Rwanda, Burundi and Boga-Zaire Constitution 1970," characterised Idi Amin's role in the resolution of the conflict.

harmony in the religious sector of the country in a bid to assert his legitimacy and win popularity. The official government dossier reported:

> This state of affairs in the Church of Uganda and in the Islamic religion was a cause of concern to the President when he took over the running of Uganda Government. So he decided to clear up the confusion in the religious denominations once and for all.
>
> First he appointed a Secretary for Religious Affairs to work in his office. This senior officer was to be responsible for all the matters that affected religion in Uganda. Secondly, the President convened a Religious Leaders Conference in Kabale. The task of the Conference was to discuss the problems that confronted each and every religion in the country, and to recommend solutions to them.[161]

The Kabale Conference convened in May 1971 was inconclusive on the problems of the Church of Uganda (and the Islamic faith). The two dioceses of Buganda stood by their previous resolutions and rejected the recommendations of the Kabale meeting, arguing that their delegates to Kabale had no official mandate.[162] The President convened another conference one month later in Kampala under the chairmanship of his minister of Works, Communications and Housing, a committed layman in the Church, James M. Zikusoka and the sponsorship of the Department of Religious Affairs that he had created in his office. Again no significant progress was made.[163]

Sabiti, under pressure to resolve the impasse, called a meeting between the PAE and Delegates of Namirembe and West Buganda Diocese on 20 October 1971. But the delegates from the two dioceses restated their position thus:

---

161. *The First 366 Days* (Kampala: Ministry of Information and Broadcasting, 1972).
162. Mukasa, OI. Also Sebalugga-Kalimi, "Life and Contribution of Dunstan Nsubuga," 53.
163. At this conference the Uganda Moslem Supreme Council (UMSC), bringing together the rival factions, was created.

1. That our two respective synods did not give us the mandate to discuss the so-called 1970 Constitution, nor to conduct any discussions under the said Constitution;

2. That our mandate is to conduct discussion under the proper and legal Constitution of 1961 with all its approved amendments. This then requires that the so-called 1970 Constitution should be rescinded to facilitate fruitful discussions between PAE and the delegates of the two Synods.

3. We have also noted that the PAE has no mandate from the PA to hold any discussions outside the so-called 1970 Constitution.

4. In the present circumstances we cannot see any useful discussion being conducted as we do not have the mandate to discuss under the so-called 1970 Constitution nor does the PAE have the mandate to discuss outside the said so-called Constitution.

5. The suggested items for discussion made by Bishop Lyth, as Consultant to Archbishop [the 1970 Constitution and Bikangaga Report], can only be undertaken after proper authorisation by the bodies that sent us. We shall therefore report the same to our respective Synods.

6. We wish to refute categorically the allegations made by His Grace and others that the two dioceses have already planned to separate from the existing Province. It must be stated that our dioceses very strongly uphold the present Province as duly constituted by the 1961 Constitution. If anything, it is the Province that has been trying to separate from the original Province's Constituency by bulldozing the dioceses and introducing upon us a new Constitution which is very contrary to the accepted spirit of the Anglican Communion.[164]

---

164. Report of Meeting between PAE and delegates of Namirembe and West Buganda Dioceses, held on 20 October 1971, 3, PAE papers, COU Archives.

Although Namirembe and West Buganda rebutted the assertion that they had sought to secede, there was evidence to the contrary. They deliberately defaulted on their obligations to the Province.[165] The two dioceses were already considering forming a "Province of Namirembe" to consist in the "first instance the Dioceses of Namirembe and West Buganda."[166] This document was circulating among the Church leaders in Buganda.[167]

At this Idi Amin personally intervened, ordered all bishops of the Church and their diocesan councils to meet him with his cabinet on Friday 26 November 1971. He spoke to them at great length, warning them of the repercussions of their failure to resolve the wrangles in the Church. That "the government of the Second republic will not accept any constitution in the Church of Uganda, Rwanda and Burundi except that which is agreed upon by the whole Province or at least by the majority of the component bodies of it."[168] For over six hours that day they deliberated but no progress was made.

When this stalemate was reported to Amin, he met them again the next day and informed them that together with his cabinet, he had concluded that the cause of the problems in the Church were due to both the Provincial and Namirembe Diocese offices being on the same hill. The Cabinet was therefore proposing that Namirembe diocesan headquarters relocate to a new site in Mukono, twenty-five kilometres away from Kampala, while the Provincial offices remained at Namirembe. Further that a Judicial Commission of inquiry headed, by the Chief Justice, was to be appointed to look into all the issues of the conflict. At this point he dismissed the meeting, and asked that they return the next day with a response.

---

165. Namirembe had not paid in any money for the bishop's support or for the Theological College for over a year and West Buganda had not paid at all in 1971.
166. "The Interim Constitution of the Province of Namirembe, Church of Uganda: The Articles of the Constitution," November, 1970. The Yokana Mukasa committee that was set up to study the Bikangaga Report drafted this constitution. Mukasa, OI.
167. *Uganda Argus*, 27 November 1971. Idi Amin in his address to the Church leaders informed them that he was aware of the existence of this document and about its circulation. He told them that he had seen the document to his alarm. Also *Taifa Empya*, 18 November 1971.
168. *Uganda Argus*, 27 November 1971.

This sent shock waves into the entire leadership of the Church. The Buganda Church leadership had only two alternatives: either to accept the government decision and lose Namirembe; or accept the creation of Kampala Diocese. The former was inconceivable and the latter might just be acceptable. The two delegates of the Provincial Assembly Executive to the meeting, the Rev Janani Luwum, the Provincial Secretary, and John Bikangaga decided to consult with the Archbishop of Canterbury. After which they determined that it would be detrimental to the whole Church to "cause Buganda Christians to feel that they have been pushed out of the Cathedral."[169]

On Sunday 28 November, the meetings began with a Holy Communion Service at which Festo Kivengere preached on two texts: Romans 13:8 and Philippians 2. Later the PAE and the House of Bishops had separate meetings. The bishops in their meeting "shared together their own sense of failure, weakness and loss of love, their own responsibility for lack of unity between them. All recognized the need for repentance and going back to the Cross."[170]

In the plenary that afternoon they reported the results of "having been at the Cross" together. Bishop Nsubuga announced that the leaders and the Christians in the Church in Buganda had agreed that Kampala Diocese be carved out of Namirembe. Bishop Lyth, who chaired the session on behalf of Archbishop Sabiti, started with a public confession, reminiscent of the Revival-style testimony:

> We met together before lunch and He [the Spirit of God] worked amongst us, convicting each one of sin, against Him and against His Church, and helping us to repent to Him and to one another. And I want to tell you that God has restored

---

169. Bikangaga, OI. Canon Bikangaga was present in the Kampala meetings as delegate of the Provincial Assembly Executive and in his capacity as the one who had chaired the Drafting Committee of the Constitution, and the *Ten Year Plan*. He told me that in the middle of the deliberations on the second day, Idi Amin personally requested him to explain the origin and history of the conflict as one that had presided over the drafting of the relevant documents.

170. "Report on Conference of Bishops and Diocesan Councils, called by H. E. the President of Uganda, General Idi Amin Dada, – International Conference Centre, Kampala, 26–28 November 1971, and State House, Entebbe, 29 November, 1971," 2, Archbishop's Papers, COU Archives.

fellowship to us in a way that we have not known for many months. For myself I have had to ask God's forgiveness and the forgiveness of my brothers and the forgiveness of our Baganda brethren for many sinful thoughts – thoughts of impatience and anger, thoughts which have not been thoughts of love. I thank God that he has forgiven me and I ask for the forgiveness here of any whom I have wronged.[171]

Speaking on behalf of the House of Bishops, he added:

We Bishops take our share – and it is a big share – of the blame for what has happened in our Church. We are all thankful to the President for the concern he has shown for the affairs of our Church . . . but at the same time we have a great feeling of shame that it has been necessary for him to intervene. In history God has used many people and things to bring about his Will . . . sometimes not as we would choose perhaps. God has been using HE and his Govt. to help us.[172]

Lyth then delivered the recommendations of the House of Bishops, which focused on four aspects of the conflict: secession; land and property; the dual identity of Namirembe hill; and the creation of Kampala Diocese. The bishops from Buganda had withdrawn their threat to secede. All the bishops had accepted, in principle, the creation of the Church Commissioners, to operate as an advisory group in respect of land and property which belonged to individual Dioceses, and to act in an executive capacity in respect of land and property belonging to the Province as a whole. On the creation of Kampala diocese and the status of Namirembe Cathedral:

The proposal is that the hill of Namirembe shall stand by itself, with a carefully worked-out legal arrangement covering land, roads of access, buildings, the Cathedral. The Cathedral would continue to be the Cathedral of Namirembe Diocese and also the Provincial Cathedral. . . . It is our united proposal and agreement that there shall be a Diocese of Kampala, and

---

171. Ibid., 3.
172. Ibid.

that we should accept H. E.'s offer of help with the building of a Cathedral, or enlargement of a Church for a Cathedral in Kampala, which would be the Cathedral of the Archbishop as Diocesan Bishop.[173]

Archbishop Sabiti followed. After confirming that Lyth's report was indeed as all bishops agreed, he continued with his own confession:

> All of us have felt very much humbled and felt much pain over the situation in our Church. I am sorry if it is self-pity if I say that I have felt it more when the Govt. and H. E. the President, of their goodness, started getting concerned and started stepping into our affairs it hurt me very much. I thought it was failure, and I repent here that I share in that failure. Three things mainly contribute to my failure: self-pity, mistrust of my brothers, and fear. Self-pity: I thought it was too much burden for me. Mistrust: what was written in the papers and letters against me made me mistrust almost everybody, especially my two brothers here of Buganda, thinking perhaps they were misinterpreting me to their people. I am sorry I did that. This led to fear. I ran into my shell and instead of being a leader the first among my brother equals, I was in a shell. Where I would have helped Dunstan I did not help, where I would have helped Bishop Tomusange I could not; even other Christians in Uganda. I am sorry about these things. . . . I am sorry about my mistrust and my fear. As the first among brother equals I should keep sharing with them what is good for the good of the Church. Please forgive me.[174]

Bishop Nsubuga also took his turn. After acknowledging the significance of Idi Amin's intervention and thanking him "for calling us together and advising us to sit together to discuss our problems," he said:

> The way we are sitting before you now, to me and I think to you, creates a new atmosphere in our Church. Things have

---

173. Ibid.
174. Ibid., 4.

> gone so wrong in many ways, because we have been living in a small corner away from each other. It is very sad. . . . We are all very sorry because we are all given work to do in the Church of God on earth and we have not done our part. We came to the bad decision of seceding; we all know that it is very, very bad, and I want to assure you now that we are very, very sorry for that. Let us come together afresh and see things in a new way and follow the way God wants us to take.[175]

The bishop of West Buganda also committed himself to the unity of the Church.

> I am going to say that West Buganda is no longer going by itself, it will go along with other Dioceses. We would blame others without blaming ourselves. When we met this morning I had to repent of the feeling that when we come to Namirembe every Bishop has to find where to stay. . . . I repent of blaming others without telling them. I would like to ask you to forgive me and to forgive my Diocese also. We have been involved in a big fight; we need a lot of prayer.[176]

In revival fashion, each of the bishops took turns in public confession, owning up to his "sins," walking in the light with his "brethren," and asking for forgiveness from the Church. The laity absolved the bishops, and when, in the context of what was more of a revival fellowship meeting than a business forum, a vote was called by Lyth, all the bishops recommendations were carried unanimously.

At a reception hosted by Idi Amin at State House Entebbe on Monday 29 November, a report of the decisions arrived at were made and Sabiti again applauded the President for his meaningful and timely intervention. "By your advice and stimulation you enabled us to work out our problems."[177] According to Bikangaga, the leading proponent of the 1970 constitutional amendments, the only way to explain the success of Amin's intervention was the "hand of God." He explained: "We have to bring in

---

175. Ibid.
176. Ibid.
177. Ibid., 8.

the hand of God there, in the sense that he [God] has a way of using unlikely instruments to achieve his goals. And he used Amin to resolve that [crisis]. I can see nobody else who would have done it."[178]

One visible element in the resolution of the crisis is the Revival ethos. As observed earlier, the Conference of Bishops and Diocesan Councils became a kind of fellowship meeting at which each of the aggrieved parties took turns to confess their "sins." This shows how the Church was permeated by the Revival ethos.

Archbishop Sabiti was keen to ensure that all the resolutions were implemented during his term of service as Archbishop. The Diocese of Kampala was inaugurated, and Archbishop Sabiti enthroned as its bishop on 16 January 1972. The Constitution Committee chaired by Bikangaga resumed its work, revised the *Draft Constitution of 1970* to incorporate the November meeting resolutions, and submitted the *Draft Constitution 1972* which was adopted and signed on Saturday 16 September 1972 at a meeting between the House of Bishops and PAE.[179] The Judicial Commission into the Church land presented their report and recommendations to the Church in June 1974 and a final report and recommendations were submitted to the President.[180] The April 1975 Provincial Assembly appointed Church Commissioners, the official Trustees for all Church land and property.

Reflection

The agitation by the Buganda government at Mengo for a special status for Buganda in Uganda was mirrored in the continued desire by Church leadership in Buganda to safeguard the pre-eminence of Namirembe Diocese in the Church of Uganda, and its identity as a Church for Buganda. The leadership of the Church in Buganda feared that the efforts by the national

---

178. Bikangaga, OI.
179. Minutes of Meeting of Provincial Assembly executive, with the House of Bishops present, Sat 16 September 1972, PAE papers COU Archives.
180. Letter and Report to General Idi Amin, from Archbishop J. Luwum, on "The Commission of Enquiry into Land Possessed, Owned, Acquired or Otherwise Held by the Church of Uganda, or any Diocese thereof for Ecclesiastical Purposes: 1973," Archbishop's Papers. COU Archives.

Church leadership to incorporate the same symbols of their heritage as part of the corporate heritage and identity of the Province would rob the Church in Buganda of the pre-eminent status that it had enjoyed since the founding of the Church. With the election of Erica Sabiti, instead of Dunstan Nsubuga, as the first African Archbishop of the Province of the Church of Uganda, Rwanda, Burundi and Boga Zaire, the Church in Buganda was faced with the challenge of redefining its identity in the context of its diminishing centrist role.

Did the accusations levelled against Sabiti of colluding with Obote and the central government against Buganda have a basis? Was Erica Sabiti, like Obote, guilty of an anti-Buganda sentiment? Granted that Sabiti was well regarded by Obote, evidenced in Obote asking him to baptize his two children at his country home at Akokoro in Lango;[181] it is not ground enough to suggest that Sabiti shared Obote's sentiments against Buganda. Others would point to the fact that Obote's government furnished the Archbishop's residence, as further evidence of a friendship between the two. Notwithstanding this circumstantial evidence, there is no reason to suggest that by implication Sabiti was one with Obote in the anti-Buganda stance. Other factors point to the contrary. First, Sabiti was himself of an aristocratic background. He belonged to the ruling Bahima of Ankole, with a brother who was a senior chief in Ankole. This would have given him sympathy for Buganda's monarchy. Second, true to his spiritual heritage as one of the fathers of the East African Revival, he was apolitical. Ward makes the point that:

> The fact that he was "saved" (*omulokole*) and a "brother" (*ow'oluganda*) was for him the most significant fact of his life, and far outweighed all class, ethnic, political or even church loyalties. He was not interested in politics, nor did he have the skills of compromise and flexibility.[182]

The political arena was, according to revival spirituality, part of the prohibited world for a Christian, and not any less a Christian leader. For Sabiti, to issue a statement condemning the government over the attack of

---

181. *Uganda Argus*, Monday 22 January 1968, 1.
182. Ward, "The Church of Uganda," 74.

the Kabaka's palace would be to meddle in politics, which was not his calling, as he understood it.[183] The strengthening of the Church through the Revival was his highest priority.

The Church in Buganda faced two challenges. First, it was challenged to change its role, from a "mother" to a "sister" of the churches she had helped to plant. It seems that in the mind of the Buganda Church its pioneering role had accorded it a kind of special status. Second, it was challenged to distinguish itself as a Christian community, and therefore to transcend the socio-political boundaries that characterized the conflict surrounding the "question of Buganda." The challenge was to affirm the Church in Buganda as part of the Church of Uganda, without denying its identity as a church for the Baganda. The timing of the election and enthronement of Erica Sabiti, a *munamawanga*, at Namirembe, a Cathedral that was perceived to belong to the Kabaka and the Baganda, served to bring to the fore the contradictions and tensions in its historical-political *sitz im leben*.

Our account of the Church has shown that there are parallels and similarities with the situation in the political arena: Obote and his central government parallel Erica Sabiti and the PAE; the Kabaka and his Buganda Government parallel Nsubuga and the Namirembe Diocese; the Constitution Crisis of 1966–67 parallels the Church Constitution Crisis in 1967–71; and the resolution of the tensions was by force: on the one hand violent force of the military, while on the other, coercive force from Idi Amin. However there are two striking differences in the process toward a resolution. First, in the political arena, there was an immediate imposition of republicanism on Buganda, while in the Church the process was slow, filled with anguish and quest for compromise, a process that took the Church another four years to conclude after the political resolution. While in the political arena traditional authority had to give way to national centralized machinery, the resolution in the Church was such that both local and national roots were recognized and maintained in the one church identity.

Second, the forces that engendered resolution in the Church were a symbiosis of those from within and without, negotiations between the

---

183. Geraldine Sabiti, OI, 1996. Geraldine, Sabiti's wife explained to me that this is why her husband could not make a public statement of condemnation.

Dioceses of Namirembe and West Buganda and the PAE together with Idi Amin's intervention; while in the political arena it was through the utilisation of other political instruments. Clearly the turning point in the story is the intervention of Idi Amin, a Muslim military dictator. Idi Amin's intervention and subsequent resolution of the crisis in the Church of Uganda shows that the process of becoming church in a particular historical, social-political context, is not formed only by forces from within, but also from without. Internally the Church was captive to the forces of its historical-political *sitz im leben*, and was too frail to liberate and disentangle itself. It required forces from without to free it from the contradictions and inertia of its history and enable it to emerge with a renewed identity. It is the "world," that entity that does not consider itself to be "of the church," that enables the church to rediscover her being and identity.

Although some may argue that the primary issue at the centre of the crisis in the Church was tribal,[184] it is my contention that the critical issue was the social-political identity of the Church of Uganda, as a whole, *vis-à-vis* the Church in Buganda. It was not primarily an ethnic issue because firstly the Baganda are not as ethnocentric as they are sometimes portrayed. They have a strong culture of hospitality towards other ethnic groups. At the time of these conflicts there were as many as thirty-six other ethnic and racial groups within the borders of Buganda, most of them permanent residents.[185] Second, the unity of the Church in Buganda was not just ethnic. If it were so, the schism in West Buganda Diocese would not be a part of the story of the Church in Buganda when serious leadership wrangles over the location of the diocesan headquarters split it.[186]

---

184. Both Bishops Wani and Okoth saw the issues in the period under review as purely a result of Buganda's ethnocentrism

185. The thirty-six groups are listed in Mutebi, "Towards an Indigenous Understanding," 36.

186. When West Buganda was carved out of Uganda Diocese its headquarters were at Masaka with Festo Lutaya as bishop. In 1964 Bishop Lutaya decided to transfer the headquarters to his hometown of Mityana, sparking off protest from the Deanery of Masaka, and a rift in the diocese. The people of Masaka and Mityana are ethnically Baganda, but they were engaged in wrangles that tore their diocese apart. Erisa Sentogo has dealt with these conflicts in his study, "The Conflicts Surrounding the Creation and Development of an Anglican Diocese of West Buganda (Uganda), 1960–1976," Makerere University, unpublished Diploma in Theology dissertation, 1981.

Third, the "Baganda" were not just an ethnic category, but a *body politic*. In fact although they share a common culture and language, the history of the Buganda clans and that of the consolidation of power of the kingdom of Buganda indicates that they were of varied origins and backgrounds. Buganda was a geo-political entity that emerged over a period of years through a process of migrations and conquests.[187] Buganda's unity was based on a common social-political history centred on the Kabaka. It is for this reason that the attack on the Kabaka's palace ignited fires of protest in all sectors of Buganda life, including the Church. Erica Sabiti became the focus of protest in the Church, but also was the opportunity for the whole Church to redefine itself as a new social reality whose identity depended not on the people's historical social-political context, but the common heritage in Christ. The Church in Buganda needed to see itself as both local-indigenous and national-universal, belonging to Buganda and Uganda. The settlement that was arrived at the 28 November 1971 meeting provided for the continuity of the particular identity of Buganda within the corporate identity of the whole Church of Uganda.

---

187. This is the subject of Kiwanuka, *A History of Buganda*.

CHAPTER 5

The Church in the Amin Regime, 1971–1979

The story of the Church during the first decade of post-independence Uganda, revolved around the development of a corporate identity in an environment charged with a Buganda *versus* rest-of-Uganda divide, mirrored in the conflict between the leadership of the Church at the national level and in Buganda. The pivotal role of President Idi Amin in resolving the bitter conflict between the two Church leadership centres, the Province and Namirembe, was acclaimed. However, as the account in this chapter shows, it was the brutality of Idi Amin and his regime that thrust the Church into the most challenging era since the religious wars of the late 1880s. This had far reaching implications for the Church, its identity, ministry and mission. Therefore, although the story of the events leading to the capture of state power by Idi Amin and the tyranny of his regime has been told by many,[1] it is re-told briefly to put into context the developments in the Church during that period.

Idi Amin's regime was brutal from beginning to end. However, its brutality was not apportioned evenly throughout the period or even on all Ugandans, as the account in this chapter shows. The terror apparatus of

---

1. Some of the works that deal with the Idi Amin regime are: Ingram Grahame, *Amin and Uganda: A Personal Memoir* (London: Granada, 1980); David Gwyn, *Idi Amin: Death-Light of Africa* (Boston: Little, Brown and Co., 1977); Jan Jelmert Jorgensen, *Uganda: A Modern History* (London: Croom Helm, 1981), 267–330; Martin, *General Amin*; Ali Mazrui, *Soldiers and Kinsmen in Uganda: The Making of a Military Ethnocracy* (London: Sage Publications, 1975); Mutibwa, *Uganda since Independence*, 58–124; Judith Listowel, *Amin* (New York: IUP Books, 1973); Sempangi, *A Distant Grief*; George I. Smith, *Ghosts of Kampala* (London: Weidenfeld and Nicolson, 1980); Wooding and Barnett, *Uganda Holocaust* (London: Pickering & Inglis, 1980).

the regime was directed against those it perceived as enemies, real or potential, and was intended to consolidate its hold on power. Top on the list of Amin's enemies were the people from Lango[2] and Acholi, whether in the army or in the civilian populace, because of their association with Obote and the UPC.

Given the significance of Idi Amin and his military regime to the entire account of the Church, a section of the chapter examines the emergence of the military as a major player in the socio-political history of Uganda, and the place of the army in the ministry of the Church. Idi Amin's rise to power and the causal factors of the regime's tyranny are also considered.

Three elements emerge in the story of the Church in this new milieu. First, the crucial challenge that the regime presented to the hitherto quasi-established status of the Church in the light of the ascendance of Islam and the military. Second, the Church's re-contextualization of its mission and ministry in a hostile social-political environment and among a terrorized people. The story of the Church in Lango,[3] an area that bore the brunt of the regime's terror machine, highlights the significance of the pastoral dimension of mission and ministry in this context. The Church's identification with the people is visible in its ministry of prayer and the Word, and the subordination of its Protestant identity to a new relationship with the Catholic Church in Lango. The third issue was the murder of Janani Luwum, the Archbishop of the Church of Uganda, and its impact on the life of the Church and the country.

The issues surrounding the murder of Archbishop Janani Luwum and its significance for the Church's self-understanding is discussed in greater detail because Luwum represents a new paradigm in the life of the Church and his story highlights the inadequacy of the church-state analytical approach. The church-in-the-world paradigm puts his death in the context of his formative Revival heritage and the institutional narrative of the Church.

---

2. Note: the area is "Lango" and the people, plural "Langi" and singular, "Lango." In case of "Acholi," the same word "Acholi" is used for area and people – both singular and plural.

3. It was not possible to do research in Acholi due to the war that was going on between government troops and the rebels, the Lords Resistance Army (LRA), from 1991 to the present time.

The Coup and the Regime

At about 3:45 p.m. on Monday, 25 January 1971, a hesitant voice announced on Radio Uganda that the armed forces of Uganda had overthrown A. Milton Obote and his government. About half an hour later, the same voice returned to the air and announced that the armed forces had given power to their fellow-soldier, Major-General Idi Amin. The reader of the announcements was later identified as Warrant Officer (Class II) Samuel Aswa – fated to die three years later at the hands of Amin. But at that historic moment, when he was struggling through the text which listed the famous eighteen reasons why Obote had been toppled, Aswa must have shared the excitement of some of his countrymen at what was happening.[4]

With Samuel Aswa's announcement the reign of Idi Amin and his military dictatorship began. The announcement of the military coup[5] brought joy and celebration to many, particularly in Buganda, and mourning to others, especially in the heartland of UPC – the North, the East and large sections of populations in the West. The celebration and mourning was not because of Idi Amin and his supporters who had captured power, for they were hardly known to the Ugandan public. Rather it was the fall of Obote and his UPC government that evoked jubilation among those for whom Obote and UPC represented oppression and a gloomy future. For Buganda, Amin was a "saviour" from Obote, and his oppression; he also represented their hopes for the restoration of the kingdom of Buganda, a

---

4. Mutibwa, *Uganda since Independence*, 78; and also the Uganda Governement publication: *Uganda: The Case for the Second Republic* (Entebbe: Government Printer, 1971), for the historic eighteen points.
5. For a detailed account of the events leading to the coup: Ammi Omara-Otunnu, *Politics and the Military in Uganda 1890–1985* (London: Macmillan Press, 1987), 78–101; Smith, *Ghosts of Kampala*, 67–81; Mutibwa, *Uganda since Independence*, 71–77.

hope they expressed to him in August 1971.⁶ There were celebrations and memoranda of affirmation to Idi Amin from various sections of Buganda.⁷

Churches throughout Buganda, both in the Roman Catholic and the Church of Uganda congregations, held thanksgiving services. Retired Bishop Lutaaya of West Buganda diocese is reported to have hailed Amin as "our redeemer and light of God."⁸ The archdeacon of Namirembe, Canon Daniel Lubwama, referring to the take over, said: "God listened to the people of Uganda for what they prayed, and all that has happened in this country has been done by God."⁹ There was a big thanksgiving service organized by the bishop of Namirembe at Nakivubo Stadium, and another one by the Catholic Archbishop at Rubaga, which Amin attended.¹⁰

Others who rejoiced were those who considered Obote's declared socialist policies enshrined in his "Move to the Left" strategy with its constituent policy statements,¹¹ to be oppressive, notably the traders.

Buganda's jubilant mood contrasted sharply with the mood in the districts of Acholi and Lango,¹² the latter being the home district of deposed President Obote. "A dark shadow (that) hung over the Diocese of Northern Uganda."¹³ "All along the road out of Gulu were hundreds of people with bundles on their heads, fleeing into the bush."¹⁴ There was sadness, fear, and panic all over the two districts, as soldiers loyal to Idi Amin combed

---

6. *The First 366 Days*, 63, records a meeting in August 1971 between Amin and Buganda elders, at which they demanded the Kabakaship to be restored.

7. Mutibwa, *Uganda since Independence*, 88–89, has produced the praise showered on Amin from various leading Baganda. These include: Prince George Mawanda-Chwa, elder brother of Kabaka Mutesa II; Joshua Mayanja Nkangi, the last Katikiro of Buganda prior to the attack of the Lubiri; Abu Mayanja, leading politician and chief architect of the UPC-KY alliance; Amos Sempa, prominent politician in Buganda and formerly kingdom minister.

8. Ward, "The Church of Uganda," 79.

9. Rev Canon Daniel Lubwama, reported in *Uganda Argus*, 18 January 1971, 1.

10. John Bikangaga, OI, Kampala, 17 January 1997.

11. These include: the Common Man's Charter, October 1969; National Service published October 1969; Communication from the Chair of April 1970; the Nakivubo Pronouncement of May 1970; and the New Methods of Election of Representative of the People to Parliament, published August 1970.

12. Acholi district was constituted of the present day Gulu and Kitgum districts, and Lango, of the present day Apac and Lira districts.

13. Ford, *Janani*, 48.

14. Ibid.

the villages in search of those who were loyal to Obote.[15] The coup was greeted with sadness also in the areas where the support for Obote and UPC was strong such as Kigezi, Teso, and sections of Ankole.

Among the foreign countries that were reported to have endorsed and aided the overthrow of Obote and his government were Britain and Israeli.[16] Julius Nyerere and his government stood by Obote and worked with him to mobilize an anti-Amin regime campaign among several African nations, with some success.[17]

Given the divided reactions to Amin's accession to power, in effect facing him with a divided country, his policy of centralizing power in his own office and the military had a rationale that needs to be recognized. He created and perfected a military apparatus to achieve this end, consisting of the Public Safety Unit, State Research Bureau, Military Intelligence and the Military Police, with their headquarters at Naguru, Nakasero adjoining the State Lodge, Malire barracks at Lubiri, and Makindye barracks, respectively, dominated by the Nubi and his kinsmen from West Nile. With these four units Amin purged the army, and terrorized and brutalized his real, potential and imaginary enemies.

Although terror and tyranny spanned the entire eight years of Amin's rule, there were periods of intensity. The first period was the twelve months after the coup, when the terror machine was directed against the Acholi and Langi in the army.[18] For although the coup was announced as "one of the most peaceful *coups d'etat*, with only small-scale inter-army fighting on that night . . . confined to the barracks,"[19] the truth was revealed in the

---

15. Eyewitness accounts by Y. Opolo Apelo, OI, Lira, 27 September 1996; Bishop Melchisedek Otim, OI, Boroboro, 27 September 1996; Musa Odongo, Lira, 27 September 1996; Julius Peter Obonyo, Lira, 27 September 1996.

16. George I. Smith discusses the involvement of the British and Israeli governments in the process leading up to the coup in his book *Ghosts of Kampala*, 67–81. Britain's involvement was confirmed by its early recognition of Amin's government.

17. Kaunda and the Zambian government were natural allies to Obote, having been part of the "Mulungushi Club," a loose association of the post-independence party governments in Uganda, Tanzania, and Zambia. Those drawn in were: Somalia, Ethiopia, and Sudan. D. Martin, *General Amin*, 53–56.

18. Martin, *General Amin*, 130–157, for a detailed account. Also *Violation of Human Rights and the Rule of Law in Uganda* (Geneva: International Commission of Jurists, 1974), 26–45.

19. *The First 366 Days*, 1.

days and weeks after, as loyalist troops weeded the barracks of opposition, real or potential. The first targets were Langi and Acholi officers, and men who were presumed to be loyal to Obote, their kinsman. Langi and Acholi soldiers were massacred *en masse* in Jinja, Moroto and Mbarara barracks, at Mutukula prison on the Tanzania boarder and at Palabek in Acholi, near the Sudan boarder. David Martin has recorded that:

> Throughout February [1971] Amin's soldiers roamed through Lango district hunting down soldiers who had not reported back to their units. Many, along with their relatives, were killed. Women were raped by groups of soldiers and shops and houses ransacked.[20]

Hundreds who were arrested were butchered in the killing houses of Nakasero,[21] Makindye and Malire.

The second period of intense terror followed the rebel invasion in September 1972, this time directed more broadly against all those closely associated with Obote and the UPC, and key figures in Buganda like Benedicto Kiwanuka, leader of the DP and then Chief Justice.[22] Prominent leaders of UPC who were not killed fled into exile. Again Acholi and Lango districts bore the hardest brunt of the terror during this period. After this Amin's energies were directed to the "Economic war"[23] and creating a loyal Islamic community in Uganda.

Once he had purged the army of the dominance of Acholi and Langi, eliminated or forced into exile prominent Obote/UPC supporters, and effectively projected his pro-Islam posture, he could then use both the army and Islam in restructuring local administration and developing a social

---

20. Martin, *General Amin*, 137.
21. Wycliffe Kato, *An Escape from Kampala*, n.d., Centre for Basic Research Archives, has a graphic description of the Nakasero Prison cells where Luwum is believed to have been murdered.
22. *Violation of Human Rights*, 45–61.
23. Uganda Government Publications, *Uganda's Economic War* (Kampala: Ministry of Information and Broadcasting, January 1975), 1, explains that "Economic War" meant "having a black Ugandan at the control of every economic activity in the country." The booklet gives a detailed policy statement, justification and implementation of the program. The major component of this "war" was the expulsion of the Asian business community.

base. This preoccupied the Regime during the period between mid-1973 and 1976. Mamdani has observed that:

> No oppressive regime can survive for long unless it manages to win support from beyond the narrow confines of the class whose interest it serves. To do this, it may employ a series of methods ranging from nationalistic chauvinism and demagogy, to petty reforms and privileges for a section of the oppressed.[24]

In pursuance of the goal to "win the support from beyond the narrow confines of the class whose interest it [the Amin Regime] served," prominent positions in all sectors of public service went to either Muslims or those from his home area, West Nile.[25] Rutiba has observed that at this time:

> Amin also promoted Muslims to influential positions in all sectors of public service. Becoming a Muslim was a *sine qua non* for one to be a Provincial Governor, District Commissioner, and other heads of government departments.[26]

Over time, military officers and Muslims from the West Nile province progressively filled top posts in the civil service and parastatal organizations. As A. G. Gingyera-Pinycwa observed:

> Although he [Amin] started off initially with a broad based cabinet of highly educated men, he soon began to disband and replace them mainly by Nubians/Moslems and other people – his main criterion being that the candidate be either a Nubian/Muslim or from West Nile.[27]

The third peak of massacres spanned a longer period from 1976 to the downfall of the regime.[28] It was sparked off by: the Israeli raid to free hostages

---

24. Mahmood Mamdani, *Imperialism and Fascism in Uganda* (London: Heinemann Educational Books, 1983), 55.
25. Jorgensen, *Uganda*, 282.
26. Eustace G. Rutiba, "Religions in Uganda, 1960–1993," in *Uganda: Thirty Years of Independence, 1962–1992 – Assessments*, eds. Khiddu E. Makubuya, V. M. Mwaka, and P. G. Okoth (Makerere University: The Committee for the Workshop, 1994), 389.
27. Gingyera-Pinycwa, "Is There a Northern Question?," 52.
28. One leading churchman killed during this period was Bishop John Wasikye, then Bishop of Mbale. He was killed, on 17 April 1979 in Mbale, by troops loyal to Idi Amin

in 1976; fresh coup attempts leading to the death of the Archbishop and two ministers; and, the 1978–79 so-called liberation war led by a combined force of Tanzanian troops and Ugandan rebels. It was the Langi and Acholi again who suffered most because they dominated the ranks of the rebel army under the command of Tito Okello and Oyite Ojok, an Acholi and a Lango, respectively.

Three issues that the Amin regime brought to the fore, that created a challenge for the Church's self-definition in a new socio-political context are: the place of the military in civic-political leadership; state-sponsored violence, terror and tyranny; and, the ascendance of Islam as the "established" religion. To understand better the life of the Church in this milieu, it is necessary to examine the development of each and reflect on how the Church reformed and adapted in order to continue being church in this transformed context.

The Rise of the Military and Idi Amin

There is need to explain the rise of the military to dominating the socio-political scenery of Uganda during the Idi Amin Regime, why it became dominated by Nubi, and why the people who suffered most from its brutality were the people from Acholi and Lango. This will set the context for understanding the Church's life and work in the army and among the people of Lango.

Nubian troops were the backbone of the colonial army in Uganda.[29] Since the army, in pre-independence Uganda, was developed to fulfil the

---

as they were fleeing from the UNLA. *Uganda Times*, 4 July 1979.

29. The identity of the Nubi is a subject of contention. It is not being suggested in this account that all the Nubi were foreigners; the "Nubi" are not, strictly speaking, an ethnic category but a migrant community of people originally descended from Emin Pasha's Sudanese troops, and later infused with recruits from other sudanic ethnic groups, particularly from the West Nile region, such as the Kakwa, Madi, and Lugbara. Some works on the origins and identity of the Nubi of Uganda are: Omari H. Kokole, "Idi Amin, 'The Nubi' & Islam in Ugandan Politics 1971–1979," in *Religion & Politics in East Africa*, eds. H. B. Hansen and M. Twaddle (London: James Currey, 1995), 44–55; and H. B. Hansen, "Pre-colonial Immigrants and Colonial Servants. The Nubians in Uganda Revised," *Africa Affairs* 90, no. 361 (October 1991): 559–580. In the literature "Nubi" and "Nubian" are used to refer to the people. In this essay, "Nubi" refers to the people, and "Nubian" is the adjective, except when it a direct quotation.

colonial agenda of territorial conquest, pacification, and defending British colonial standards of law and order, it was expedient for the colonial administration to rely on "alien" troops. This also explains the massive recruitment from Acholi, after the first and second world wars, when there was increased demand to recruit from the more indigenous populations. The colonial three-fold principle of deploying troops that "a soldier should be of a different race, a different (and distant) geographical origin, and a different religious faith from the population area of posting,"[30] may have led them to recruit from Acholi, since the area of deployment was among the southern kingdoms of Buganda, Ankole and Toro.

Omara-Otunnu has advanced three other reasons for Acholi constituting the main recruiting ground for the colonial government. First, that the Acholi had offered least resistance to the establishment of British rule and were seen as friendly to the administration. Second, that the Acholi had a very loosely organized social structure, and territorially small political and military units, in contrast to the Southern Bantu kingdoms who were organized on a large scale. "The Acholi form of organisation rendered large-scale military mobilisation very difficult"[31] and therefore the Acholi were a relatively "safer group to deal with, from the colonial authorities' point of view, than those ethnic groups, which were well organised on a large scale."[32]

The third reason that Omara-Otunnu has advanced for the dominance of the Acholi in the army is that because the military profession was associated with the most lowly and uneducated, it did not attract those from Central Uganda, who were the more educated and therefore preferred white-collar jobs. In the other East African countries efforts were made to redress this mentality by recruiting educated people into the military, but this did not happen in Uganda.[33]

Although the Langi were perceived to be culturally similar to the Acholi, the colonial administration did not recruit troops from among them as it did from the Acholi for fear that the Langi may be a political liability. This

---

30. Omara-Otunnu, *Politics and the Military in Uganda*, 24.
31. Ibid., 32.
32. Ibid., 33.
33. Ibid., 46–47.

suspicion arose from their alliance with Kabalega during the war with the Bunyoro kingdom in the 1890s, when they granted him asylum. Later in the colonial period, however, these objections to recruiting men from Lango were dropped, and together with Acholi, the two districts became the main recruiting areas.[34]

Africans were restricted to the rank and file of the army, in which loyalty and obedience were required and from which there was hardly any opportunity to rise to the upper ranks of the military hierarchy where they could pose a challenge to colonial administration. At independence therefore, ill-equipped, uneducated men from northern Uganda, the majority of whom were Acholi and Langi with a small number of Nubi, dominated the Uganda Army, a force of about seven hundred men.[35] The only Islamic presence in the Army was the Nubi.

When Obote, a man from Lango, became Prime Minister at independence, redressing the imbalances in the army was not a priority, because he was preoccupied with the more urgent questions of balancing the political forces that had propelled him to power. The mutiny of 1964 provided an opportunity to redress the imbalances in the army as the sister independent governments of Kenya and Tanzania had done in response to mutinies in their armies[36], but even then he did not, because he needed the northern army as a back-up in the mounting political tug of war between him and the Kabaka of Buganda.[37] The military carried the day and instead were granted their demands for increased pay. The man he used to quell the mutiny was the Minister of Internal Affairs – Felix Onama – Idi Amin's kinsman.

An accelerated program in the africanization of the military command structure was undertaken and Majors Idi Amin and Shaban Opolot were appointed commanders of the only two battalions. Within months of the mutiny, the General Service Unit (GSU) whose most important role was

---

34. Ibid., 32.
35. Ibid., 47.
36. Ibid., 4864.
37. The Kabaka of Buganda was grieved by the fact that Obote took action without consulting him as Head of State. Kabaka of Buganda, *The Desecration of My Kingdom*, 178–179. Around this period the question of a referendum in the "lost counties" was gaining momentum.

counter-insurgency, was set up by the government as a paramilitary force, under the control of Akena Adoko, Obote's kinsman.[38] Thus the mutiny, rather than serve to redress the ethnic imbalance in the military, entrenched the dominance of Acholi and Langi in the military.

By handling the mutiny the way it did, the civilian government acquiesced in military might, and thereafter attempted to manipulate the military for political purposes. The turning point was the 1964–67 Mengo-Constitutional crisis, a period during which Amin rose to become the top commander in the army.

The Rise of Idi Amin

At independence there were only two officers who had been promoted to higher ranks, Shaban Opolot and Idi Amin, commissioned lieutenants in August 1961 a month after internal self-government had been granted, clearly on political rather than professional grounds, since neither had the stipulated educational qualification.[39]

Idi Amin had already distinguished himself as a loyal, capable, and ruthless soldier. The high point of his performance in the colonial army was his involvement in the subduing of the Mau Mau in 1955.[40] Smith has recorded Amin's brutal treatment of the rebels:

> He served again in Kenya during the Mau-Mau uprising. His method to make prisoners reveal where their spears and other weapons had been hidden was direct, simple and effective. Africans being interrogated by Amin were made to stand alongside a table. Each was ordered to place his penis on the table surface. Amin stood beside them, machete in hand, asking the question, "Where are the weapons?" and getting rapid responses.[41]

---

38. Omara-Otunnu, *Politics and the Military in Uganda*, 65.
39. Ibid., 43. In the context of the impending hand over of political power by the colonial administration, more were prepared for commissions. They included: Tito Okello Lutwa, Juma Musa, Pierino Yere Okoya, David Ogwang, A Karugaba and Suleman Hussein – two from Acholi, two of Nubi caste, one from Teso and one from Ankole. Ibid., 45–46.
40. Ibid., 30–35.
41. Smith, *Ghosts of Kampala*, 49.

A point at which Amin's excesses should have been dealt with was when in 1962, a few months before independence, it was reported that the platoon under his command had "tortured many in one village before killing suspects" in a mission in Turkana to disarm cattle rustlers. "They forced the victims' relatives to bury them. The Turkana people complained and the Kenya government, still under colonial rule, sent a protest."[42] The colonial government refrained from handling this matter, although the Governor admitted that the nature of the offences should have obliged the government to take criminal proceedings against Amin. The issue was handed to Prime Minister-designate Obote, who for fear of the implications of criminal proceedings and almost certain dismissal from the army of one of his only two senior officers, recommended only severe reprimand.[43]

The Amin-Opolot factor explains in part Idi Amin's rise in the post-independence period. There is no evidence that the two had any grievances against each other. However, rival political forces used them, as the military increasingly became a crucial player in the arbitration of political conflict. At the height of Mutesa-Obote strife in late 1965 and early 1966, the Kabaka of Buganda courted Opolot into his political faction. Obote took a move and gave more strategic responsibilities and authority to Idi Amin. On the day of the arrests of the five ministers in February 1966, Colonel Idi Amin was appointed Army and Air Force Chief of Staff, while Brigadier Opolot was made Commander of the Army, clearly stipulated as an advisory position.[44] Amin rose above Opolot in spite of having been implicated in the gold-ivory scandal in the Congo. To weaken further the Mutesa political camp, officers connected with Opolot or one of the five Ministers were demoted or transferred to less important units of the Army. Brigadier Opolot was later removed from the Army, and Idi Amin elevated to Commander of the Army.

No sooner had Amin risen to these heights than a rupture developed in his relationship with Obote and both made moves to groom loyalist troops and officers in the military.[45] In a bid to curb indiscipline in the

---

42. Ibid., 52.
43. Ibid., 52–53.
44. Ibid., 72–76.
45. Fully discussed by Omara-Otunnu, *Politics and the Military in Uganda*, 78–91.

army, a Military Police Force was created in January 1967, under the command of two of Amin's associates.[46] In the context of the growing uneasiness between Amin and Obote, Amin ensured that the military police was constituted predominantly by loyalist troops from West Nile.[47] When the Bamunanika Palace was turned into a barracks under the command of another Amin associate, a Nubi,[48] Amin took advantage of this and secretly recruited more troops from among the Nubian population.

It was the assassination attempt on Obote in December 1969 that precipitated the final showdown between Amin and Obote. Amin was suspected and accused of having been an accomplice with the assassins. Okoya, an Acholi, who Amin considered a rival, put this challenge forth.[49] One month later, Okoya and his wife were murdered at his home in Gulu. A commission of inquiry into Okoya's murder, appointed in January 1970, pointed to Amin as the chief architect. At this time Obote was looking for the least turbulent way of removing Amin from the army, where Amin was aggressively building his support. Amin's involvement with the Anya Nya in their rebellion against the Khartoum government, in violation of official policy, and the embezzlement of funds in the army, became a window of opportunity for Obote to remove him. But Amin, aware of these moves, took advantage of Obote's absence. So while Obote was at the Commonwealth summit in Singapore, he marshalled support from the loyalist troops, and with the help of his kinsman Onama and some foreign governments, ousted Obote.

The Church and the Military

Although the Protestant Church enjoyed the quasi-established status in the pre-independence period, as narrated in chapter 1, it had no role in the development of the military. There is no evidence that the religious wars in Buganda in the late 1880s and early 1890s had any impact on the

---

46. The two were Lt Mustafa Adrisi, and Second Lt E. Anguduru, both from West Nile.
47. Omara-Otunnu, *Politics and the Military in Uganda*, 79–83.
48. Smith, *Ghosts of Kampala*, 63, 74. The head was Lt Hussein Marella. After the coup he was put in charge of the Military Police.
49. Okoya was promoted to Brigadier the same day Amin was promoted to Major General, an act that Amin is said to have suspected signalled his removal.

subsequent development of the King's African Rifles. The military was not an essential element in the evangelization of Uganda, and did not emerge to become a significant target group for the Church's evangelization project. Although it is on record that Silvanus Wani was the chaplain of the army from the Second World War period,[50] and continued to be the only chaplain up to the time of Idi Amin, there is no evidence that he gave the military priority of service. He was first a teacher, then a full-time parish minister, later on Diocesan Secretary and Treasurer of Northern Uganda diocese, and then its bishop. There was no time after the Second World War when his primary assignment for ministry was the army.[51]

It was Amin's regime that dragged the Church into considering the military as a mission field. As part of his strategy to project a non-partisan approach to religion Amin pumped more effort and money into developing the chaplaincies in the barracks. In February 1972 Amin commissioned six officer-chaplains to serve in different battalions[52] and by the end of 1973 each battalion had a mosque as well as Roman Catholic and Church of Uganda chapels with their respective chaplains.[53] Festo Kivengere admitted consternation when he received an invitation from the army headquarters early in 1972 to conduct evangelistic missions in all the barracks. Kivengere wrote:

> A surprising invitation came to us from army headquarters to preach the love of God in all the army barracks around the country early in both 1972 and 1973. We were transported in military vehicles and accompanied by the chief army chaplain, Bishop Wani, and all personnel were commanded to attend.

---

50. Lloyd, *Wedge of Light*, 8.
51. S. Wani, OI, Kyambogo, Kampala, 15 January 1997.
52. *Uganda Argus*, 21 February 1972, 1.
53. Some of the Chaplains were: Rev Major Odeke, Senior chaplain; Rev Capt Baba, Masindi Artillary Regiment; Rev Lt Sam Lubogo, Fort Portal Battalion; Rev Lt Nekemiya Kyongyereire, Malire Regiment; Rev John Businge, Kifaru Mechanised battalion. For example an elegant church building was built by the Regime in Mbarara barracks and consecrated at the expense of the government. *The Dedication and Consecration of St Paul's Church of Simba Mechanised Regiment, Mbarara, Uganda Army on 25 June 1978*, printed by Ministry of Defence, Kampala. COU Archives, Archbishop's Papers.

On many occasions after that, we met soldiers who said they found Christ as Saviour during those visits.[54]

There is no record to suggest that this initiative from the army stimulated further requests by the Church to do more such preaching missions.

The Church had no historical precedent for its own involvement in mission and ministry to the military. The military was not part of its world. The Church's lack of interest in the military as a mission field is clear from the two crucial documents of the Church, developed in the 1960s, giving a thorough review of the status of the mission and the ministry of the Church and a comprehensive plan. They are *The Crisis in the Christian Ministry in Uganda*, published in August 1964[55] and *The Ten Year Plan*, published in March 1967.

In its summary of the present critical situation of recruitment to the ordained ministry, *The Crisis in the Christian Ministry in Uganda* identified areas in national life where there was "a critical lack of an adequate ministry of the Church."[56] The report identified "the whole range of government and business life; the complex work in urban areas and industry; chaplaincies and the teaching of religious knowledge in almost all senior educational institutions."[57] The document makes no mention at all of the need to develop specialized ministry to the military.

The Statement of Mission in *The Ten Year Plan* highlights the need for: "a new vision of the demand of our Lord upon us, His people, to reach out into the whole of life – into the cities and towns and villages; into the factories, the shops, the plantations, the trade unions; into the hospitals and the prisons."[58] No mention at all of the army barracks! The chapter on "Service to the Community" deals in detail the need to reach out in the fields of education, adult education, youth work, health and welfare, medical work, rural work, urban work, Mothers' Union and women's work, home and

---

54. Kivengere, *I Love Idi Amin*, 19–20.
55. This was a report of the Provincial Conference on Recruitment to the ordained Ministry, convened at Makerere University May 28–31, 1964, which brought together church leaders from the entire province. Provincial Assembly Papers, COU Archives.
56. The Church of Uganda Publications, *The Crisis in the Christian Ministry in Uganda* (Kampala: Uganda Bookshop Press, 1964), 1.
57. Ibid.
58. *The Ten Year Plan*, 6.

family life, social and economic development, literature, radio and TV[59] – a long list, without mention of the military. The military had never been in the Church's plan or strategy.

So the entrance of the military to centre stage in the social-political life of Uganda took the Church by surprise. The Church did not know how to relate to the new milieu except to reposition itself defensively as an institution.

The "Establishment" of Islam

The Church had hitherto enjoyed the benefits of being the quasi-established "religion" of Uganda, since its victory over the Roman Catholics in 1892. On the religious landscape of Uganda, the only significant "other" until the time of the Idi Amin regime was the Roman Catholic Church. Although Islam preceded Christianity in Uganda and was instrumental in forming an open environment for the acceptance of Christianity, it really never became a significant force for the Church to reckon with until this time. As the regime consolidated its hold on power through the use of the military and Islam, the Church of Uganda repositioned itself into a defensive posture in order to survive. The ascendance of Islam was a new element in its external relations, because the new regime not only deposed the Church from its "quasi-established" position but also groomed Islam to take over.

When Idi Amin, a professed Muslim, captured state power, the Muslim community celebrated in hope that Islam was once again to enjoy the benefits of established religion. Amin exploited this sentiment, and began to project a pro-Islamic posture. Idi Amin's project to "Islamize" Uganda has attracted a lot of discussion.[60] Its significance for our study lies in the fact

---

59. Ibid., 8–16.

60. Among those who have discussed the issue are: Hamidullah, "Islam in Uganda and its Contribution to National Development," in *The Role of Religious Organisations in Development of Uganda*, ed. A. H. Abidi Syed (Kampala: Foundation for African Development, 1991), 83–85; A. B. K. Kasozi, "Christian-Muslim Inputs into Public Policy Formulation in Kenya, Tanzania and Uganda," in *Religion & Politics in East Africa*, eds. Holger B. Hansen and Michael Twaddle (London: James Currey, 1995), 223–246; Kasozi, *The Spread of Islam in Uganda*, 116–120; Kokole, "Idi Amin, 'The Nubi'," 44–55; Muhima, "The Fellowship of Suffering," chapter 3 entitled "Amin's 'Moslemization' Plan";

that for the first time since the religious wars of the late 1880s, the Church awoke to the reality of Islam as significant part of its "world." However it was not a "world" to evangelize, but rather a socio-political force to contend with.

The argument has been put forward that Idi Amin's project to "establish" Islam was inspired primarily by political rather than religious ambitions.[61] This conjecture builds on the artificial dichotomy between religion and politics. In the history of Uganda, religion had a political dimension, and politics had a religious dimension. The two were intertwined, a fact that Amin must have been aware of. It is our contention that Amin's Islamization project had both religious and political motives. The two served one another.

Islam itself had once enjoyed the benefits of being the established religion in pre-colonial Buganda, in the 1870s during "her golden era,"[62] but lost it when the Islamic "party" was vanquished by a combined force of the Protestants and Roman Catholics in 1890.[63] And since then, further attempts were made for Islam to regain that position, with no success.[64] Although the Islamic community was a significant player in the political manoeuvres since the 1950s, it never succeeded in regaining control of the centre. During the late 1950s their significance was recognized for their vote in a political race that was essentially contested between the Roman Catholic DP, and the predominantly Protestant UPC. The importance that Obote attached to the Islamic vote motivated him to facilitate the

---

John A. Rowe, "Islam under Idi Amin: A Case of Deja Vu?," in *Uganda Now: Between Decay and Development*, eds. H. B. Hansen and M. Twaddle (London: James Currey, 1988), 267–279.

61. Most Islamic sources argue from this perspective. In fact some have suggested that the progress of Islam slowed down during the Amin era due to excessive interference from the regime. Kasozi, *The Spread of Islam in Uganda*, 109, 123. In my view the situation was more complex. Other factors show that Islam became stronger during the regime.

62. Kasozi, *The Spread of Islam in Uganda*, 20. This is how Kasozi characterizes the period 1862–1875 when Islam reached its highest peak in the country. John Rowe in his essay, "Islam under Idi Amin," has drawn parallels between this period and the period under Idi Amin and examined the continuity and similarities in both.

63. For a detailed history of Islam, Kasozi, *The Spread of Islam in Uganda*. Hamidullah's essay "Islam in Uganda" is a short but succinct review of the story of Islam in Uganda.

64. The Muslims sought to regain their control of Buganda in 1895 through another battle, but were summarily defeated, and effectively condemned to becoming a marginalized community in the socio-political development of Uganda.

formation of the National Association for the Advancement of Muslims (NAAM) in the 1960s to strengthen UPC's political standing.[65] However, as Hamidullah observed, "even after achieving the political support Obote needed from Muslims, there were neither reciprocal benefits nor any attempts to redress the unjust treatment suffered throughout the colonial and post-independence periods."[66] Therefore Amin needed to re-draw the religious map of Uganda, for the sake of Islam and also to create a constituency that would provide a political support base at home and abroad.

Omari Kokole has also argued that the Nubian factor was another two force that "shifted his regime towards a pro-Islamic posture."[67] The Nubi in the army were the key loyal force that enabled Amin to overthrow Obote and decimated Obote's loyal troops. Amin needed them to keep his hold on power. Therefore he had to service their interests, among which was building the Islamic faith. Kokole has made the point:

> It was the addition of the Nubi constituency to the historically related and overlapping Kakwa/West Nile base which tilted the balance more clearly in favour of Islam, the Nile Valley and the Arab world more broadly. On the whole, the Nubi overlapped with, and reinforced, the Kakwa and other Bari-speakers as ethnic groups. The Nubi factor also made Idi Amin's regime more ethnically mixed than otherwise it would have been. The two primary and defining characteristics of the Nubi – Islam and the Arabic language – cut across ethnic or "tribal" boundaries.[68]

The Nubi took centre stage in Idi Amin's Islamic project. They were the natural allies who would help him constitute a loyal Islamic constituency. If Idi Amin doubted the loyalty of a leader or a section of the Islamic community, he quickly removed and replaced them, invariably with a Nubi. This was the case among the Muslims in Lango. Amin could not trust them, being kinsmen of his archenemy Obote. Amin's pro-Islamic posture

---

65. NAAM was created as a rival to the Uganda Muslim Community (UMC) that was Buganda-based and therefore more inclined to supporting Kabaka Yekka.
66. Hamidullah, "Islam in Uganda," 78.
67. Kokole, "Idi Amin, 'The Nubi'," 48.
68. Ibid., 45–46.

of the early years of his rule gave the impression that all the Muslims were favoured, and so the Langi Muslims were shocked when in 1974 their entire leadership was arrested and detained.[69] The reason given for their arrest was that they were contributing money towards rebel activity based in Tanzania to overthrow the government.[70] A Nubi replaced the Langi district Khadi.

The creation of the Uganda Muslim Supreme Council (UMSC), in June 1971, and its subsequent inauguration in June 1972, was a cornerstone in setting the foundation for the ascendance of Islam. Hamidullah appraised the benefits of the UMSC to the Muslim community thus:

> Wishing to symbolise the achieved unity [resulting from the creation of the UMSC], Idi Amin donated the twelve acres on the historical Old Kampala Hill to the Uganda Muslim Supreme Council to be used for the construction of a national mosque and the headquarters of the UMSC pointing out that this was the *first piece of land officially given to the Muslims for religious purposes by the government as they had received no land as a religious organisation in the 1900 Uganda Agreement.* Again to make the whole exercise workable, Idi Amin launched a fund for the construction of the UMSC and the national mosque. On this occasion, the officials of the Supreme Council were inaugurated, Idi Amin appealed to all countries of the Muslim world to contribute towards the realisation of the noble venture pointing out that for years the *Muslims had had no external help as there had been for Christians.* In answer to this call, several Muslim countries poured millions into the newly created UMSC.[71]

---

69. Haj Musa Odongo, OI, Lira, 27 September 1996. Those arrested were: the District Khadi, Sheikh Adam Ayo; his brother, a county Sheikh, Mohammed Otim; the district UMSC chairman, Sheikh Ibrahim Agwa; and another Sheikh, Musa Opio. Ibrahim Agwa was killed shortly after his arrest. Odongo is the son of Sheikh Adam Ayo. He narrowly escaped arrest and for five years was in hiding in the remote villages of Lango, Palisa and Moroto. He carries scars of bullet wounds on his stomach and leg.

70. Ibid.

71. Hamidullah, "Islam in Uganda," 83 (italics mine).

With the expulsion of the Asian business community, Amin had wealth, which he would use to hold together the pro-Amin Islamic alliance. So a large percentage of the properties were allocated to Muslims, and the UMSC became "one of the largest collective landlords in the economic history of independent Uganda."[72]

The creation of an Islamic constituency at home enabled Amin to reconfigure Uganda's image abroad, with a view to obtaining new foreign benefactors. Kokole observed that Amin shifted towards a pro-Islamic posture to attract Arab financial support. He was given the cold shoulder when he visited Israel and Britain in July 1971 to buy arms and other military hardware which made him realize that they would not be reliable any longer in supporting him and his regime as they had done in overthrowing Obote. According to Smith the decisive moment was the meeting in Germany in February 1972 with some Libyan officials. Colonel Gaddafi extended an invitation to Amin to visit Tripoli on his return journey from Germany.[73] He must have given the impression to Gaddafi and the Libyan leaders that Uganda was predominantly Islamic. In a communiqué signed after the meeting Amin and Gaddafi agreed that "religion and nationalism create history and motivate the march of nations and peoples towards progress and revolution. Islam provides a good example."[74]

Two months later Amin expelled all the Israelis in the country accusing them of "milking" the economy, and declared solidarity with the Arab and Palestinian cause against Israel and their "Zionist expansionism." He then declared Uganda an Islamic state, and invited King Faisal and Gaddafi to visit in 1972 and 1974 respectively. Their visit strengthened further the Islamic cause at home. According to Hamidullah, "these two were the first missionaries for Islam in Uganda."[75] But it also bolstered Uganda's image as an Islamic state. Subsequently Uganda was admitted to full membership to the Organisation of Islamic Conference (OIC) at the Lahore Pakistan Conference of 1974, thus identifying Uganda, with a Muslim population of less than 10%, with a political as well as cultural network of

---

72. Kokole, "Idi Amin, 'The Nubi'," 53.
73. Smith, *Ghosts of Kampala*, 90–94.
74. Ibid., 93.
75. Hamidullah, "Islam in Uganda," 83.

states with predominantly Muslim populations. Uganda became an Islamic state on the principle that "the religion of the ruler is the official religion of the state."[76]

Amin also sought to weaken Christianity's hold on social power, and in particular Protestants who hitherto had enjoyed socio-political dominance and were therefore seen as allies with his archenemies, Obote and the UPC. Jorgensen has rightly observed that:

> Whereas the Obote regime had united Protestants and Muslims (as very junior partners) against the Catholic DP, the Amin regime attempted to forge a Muslim-Catholic alliance (with Catholics as the junior partner) against the Protestants. Even in West Nile the alliance proved shaky. Although Christians (mostly Catholic) outnumbered Muslims among the 17 West Nilers (sic) who served in Amin's cabinet, the Christian "majority" was an illusion. Christians simply experienced a higher turnover, whereas Muslims enjoyed staying power.[77]

To further curtail the hitherto dominant position of Christianity, Amin employed law and public policy reformulation through decrees, to further consolidate and entrench the pre-eminence of Islam over other faiths.[78] He banned all other Protestant Churches and organizations except the Church of Uganda, encouraged public conversions from Christianity to Islam, made Friday a day of rest in addition to Sunday, de-gazetted various Christian holidays and replaced them with a number of Islamic public holidays.[79]

The new ascendancy of Islam caused fear in the Church. Establishment of a religious denomination results in its leaders and adherents viewing it as a socio-political institution. The emergence of other religious groups is therefore viewed with suspicion, and fear of loss of socio-political power.

---

76. This is Ali A. Mazrui's argument in "Religious Strangers in Uganda," 21–38.
77. Jorgensen, *Uganda*, 306.
78. Kasozi makes this point as well in his essay, "Christian-Muslim Inputs," 238.
79. In 1976 Amin added Idd-el-Azhur; in 1977 he added the birth of Mohammed, and in 1978 he issued decree no. 10, the Public Holidays Act (Amendment) Decree, 1978, which formalized these additions as well as making Friday a day of rest. In the same decree he de-gazetted Good Friday, Easter Monday, and Boxing Day. Decree signed on 8 July 1978, *Public Holidays Act, Decree no. 10*, (Entebbe: Government Printers, 1978).

The emergence of the Islamic faith, propelled by state power, resulted in the Church repositioning itself defensively. The bishops expressed their unease over "one particular religious organisation . . . being favoured more than any other, so much so that in some parts of Uganda members of Islam who are in leading positions are using these positions to coerce Christians to become Muslims."[80] The challenge to the Church of Uganda was "to be church" without being the dominant church.

The Church in the Regime

The immediate reaction to the overthrow of Obote's regime in the Church of Uganda can be differentiated according to the Buganda *versus* rest-of-Uganda divide. In Buganda there was enthusiasm and affirmation for Idi Amin. In a message to him, Bishop Nsubuga of Namirembe diocese said: "We are all overwhelmed by your magnanimity and do hope and pray that God will bless your efforts in building a happy and prosperous united Uganda."[81] In the rest of Uganda, the Church was uncertain and defensive. To the extent that the regime did not attack a particular area or region, the Church in that particular region ignored what was happening in another region. So while the Church in Buganda paid glowing tribute to the regime as its "saviour," the Church in Acholi and Lango knew the regime as a tyrant. The official response of the Church, sent to Amin, was as follows:

> The Provincial Assembly Executive of the Church of Uganda, Rwanda and Burundi, meeting in Kampala on 2 February 1971, expressed gratitude to the Military Head of State Major-General Idi Amin Dada for consulting recently with Church leaders, including the Archbishop of Uganda, Rwanda and Burundi.
>
> The Executive noted with appreciation the General's call to the nation and armed forces to exercise restraint and refrain from molesting people, either in vengeance or in acts of looting. It supported the General's stand on this matter.

---

80. Letter to Idi Amin from the House of Bishops dated 5 February 1977, House of Bishops' Papers, COU Archives.

81. *Uganda Argus*, 5 April 1971, 5.

The Church, through preaching and encouragement, will continue to do everything possible to promote unity, peace and brotherhood of all men. The Church further prays and appeals to all people that more restraint on the part of the civilian population and the armed forces will be exercised in order to avoid any further damage to properties and unnecessary loss of life.[82]

The Provincial Assembly Executive minute does not express the jubilation of Buganda or the gloom of Acholi and Lango. It was a cautious response, because the Church was seeking to contain the different and contradictory perspectives within its fold. A national consensus was not possible given the regional disparities that arose from the disparities in their social-political development.

There was no reference to the atrocities of the regime in Northern Uganda in the first Provincial Assembly meeting since the Amin coup of January 1972. Instead a motion was moved:

That His Grace the chairman should write to His Excellency the President, expressing the thanks of the Church of the Province of Uganda, Rwanda and Burundi for his keen interest and help in the religious affairs of the nation, and for all that he has done to bring the Church through its difficulties.[83]

Again at its meeting of August 1972, no reference was made to the heinous crimes of Amin's regime so far, in spite of the presence of thirteen delegates from Northern Uganda. The minutes of this meeting indicate that most of the time was spent discussing the 1972 Draft Constitution. The only reference to the government was the resolution to acknowledge with "gratitude to the government for its generosity"[84] by giving the grant of one hundred thousand Uganda shillings[85] towards Kampala Diocese,

---

82. Minutes 13/71 of PAE Meeting of 2 February 1971.
83. Proceedings of the Third Meeting of the Second Provincial Assembly held at Bishop Tucker College Mukono, 10–13 January 1972. PA Papers, COU Archives, 6. Conspicuously a Muganda, the Rev Canon Yokana B Mukasa, moved the motion.
84. Proceedings of the Meeting of the Third Provincial Assembly held at Bishop Tucker College Mukono, August 1972. PA Papers, COU Archives, Min 20/72, 2.
85. This was equivalent to about US $12,000.

the Church of Uganda Namugongo Martyrs Site and for the setting up of a Trust Fund.

It was an advantage to Idi Amin to keep the Church grateful, defensive and uncertain. While he projected to the Islamic community at home and abroad that his regime was decidedly pro-Islam, he presented himself to the Christian community in Uganda as one who had the churches' interests at heart and that he was non-partisan in dealing with all faiths. In his first meeting with all the bishops of both churches and Muslim leaders, he told them that "whatever he did, he respected God and he was doing all in the name of God."[86] He created a department of Religious Affairs in the Office of the President, ensured that he attended all the important Church meetings and conferences,[87] made financial contributions to various causes and had regular meetings with the Church leaders. At such meetings he would use persuasive language to appear genuinely concerned for the Christian cause, and even claimed that "the Grace of God" had chosen him and the church leaders alike.[88]

Reference has already been made to the Conference of all Religious Leaders in Kabale of May 1971, in chapter 4. At another meeting after the notice of expulsion of the Asians, to which he called the leaders of the three faiths, he "revealed that he was appointed by God to lead this country and emancipate it from corruption, malpractices and economic bondage."[89] He also "directed ministers and permanent secretaries to see to it that public servants attend churches and mosques regularly."[90] He already had to his credit his involvement in the resolution of the Church of Uganda conflicts.

---

86. *Uganda Argus*, 1 February 1970, 2.

87. For example: He was at the inauguration of Kampala Diocese and enthronement of Sabiti as bishop in January1972 (reported in *Uganda Argus*, 17 January 1972, 1); he launched the appeal for the building of the church and office of the bishop of Kampala Diocese and pledged a contribution of US $1000 (reported in *Uganda Argus*, 21 February 1972, 1); he closed the Conference for Archbishops of the Anglican Provinces of Africa, in March 1972 (reported in *Uganda Argus*, 3 August 1972, 1); he opened the All Pastors Conference at Makerere, in September 1972 (reported in *Uganda Argus*, 13 September 1972, 1); and he opened the Provincial Assembly of April 1975 and donated 200,000 Uganda shillings (equivalent to about US $1000) "to assist in spreading the gospel and developing projects" (reported in *Uganda Argus*, 29 April 1975, 1).

88. Reported in *Uganda Argus*, 27 April 1971, 1.

89. Reported in *Uganda Argus*, 15 August 1972, 1.

90. *Uganda Argus* 4 February 1974, 3..

Some Church leaders believed him, particularly those from Buganda and West Nile, and went as far as referring to him as a "God-fearing man."[91] Amin had succeeded in dividing the Church's response, and in a sense kept the leadership guessing as to what he was about.

Amin learned that to attack the Church, as a whole, was counter-productive. The occasion arose when in March 1974 Amin was reported on national radio to have said that there was "only one Christian religion – Catholic – and one Muslim religion. It was disagreement that brought about the Protestant religion as the latter wanted bishops to marry while Catholics refused."[92] The bishops responded by preparing a hard-hitting memorandum in which, "as representatives of millions of our Church members in this country, [we] feel sad about this, and would therefore plead with your Excellency's reverence of God, and friendship,"[93] they asked him to recant his statements. They demanded that "in matters of our faith in Jesus Christ, we would appreciate it if His Excellency would consult us before making a national statement about our Church of Uganda."[94] Any open protest to the regime by any of the national organs of the Church was therefore kept to the periphery until the election of Luwum as Archbishop.

The Church in Lango

The people of Lango were bound to face the worst from Amin's regime because, first, it was the district home of Obote, and Lango was one of the heartlands of UPC. Second, a large proportion of the Uganda army had been Langi. Third, the secret service para-military organization, the General Service Unit (GSU) headed by Akena Adoko (a cousin of Obote), had also been dominated by Langi.[95] (See Map 2, Lango and Neighbouring Districts, p 204.)

---

91. Bishop Wani, reported in *Uganda Argus* 13 February 1973, 1.
92. Quoted in "An Open Statement by the Bishops of the Church of Uganda to his Excellence the President of the Republic of Uganda, Al-Hadji General Idi Amin Dada," House of Bishops' papers, COU Archives, herein referred to as "An Open Statement."
93. "An Open Statement."
94. Ibid.
95. Olal, "Church and Politics in Lango-Uganda," 27.

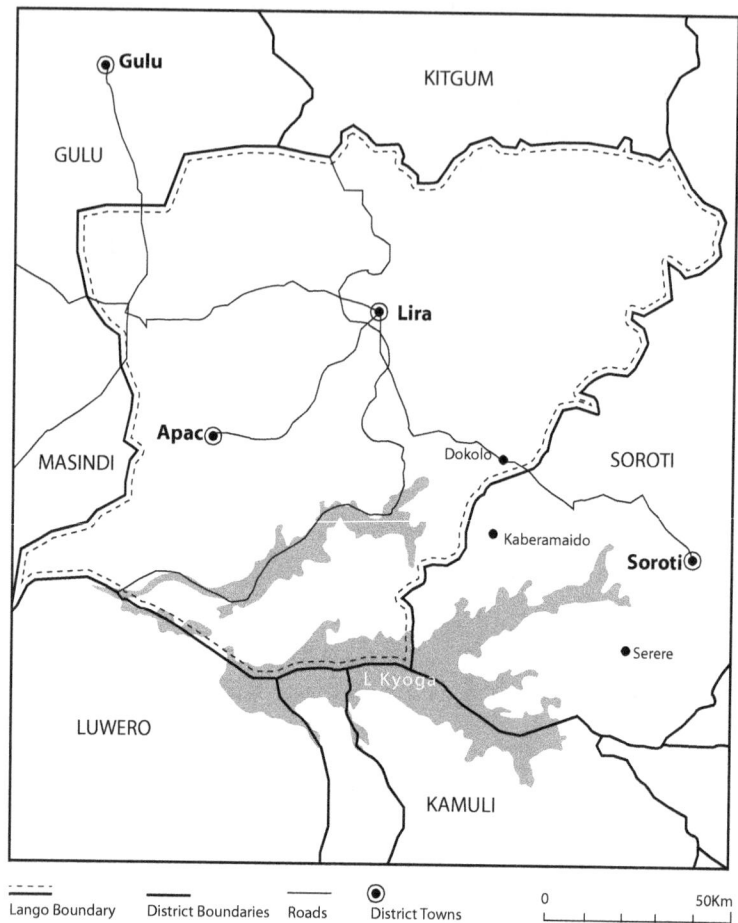

Map 2: Lango and Neighbouring Districts

The different religious communities in Lango initially responded differently to the Amin coup. The Church in Lango greeted the coup with anger, and fear, while the Catholic Church, which had all along been a bitter opponent of the Protestant church, greeted the occasion with some relief. The historic rivalry between the Protestants and Catholics in Uganda was particularly bitter in Lango. The Provincial Advisory Board had observed in

1968 that "there was much fear and bitterness against the Catholic Church in Northern Uganda."[96]

In some villages the Protestants would denigrate the Catholics as those who "eat dead animals, [are] drunkards and [are] poorly educated."[97] The Catholic Church had on many occasions accused the UPC government of favouring the Protestant church at the expense of the Catholics because the opposition party, the DP, was perceived in Lango as a Catholic party. So they voiced their support for the coup in anticipation that the military leaders were going to favour them. The leadership of Bishop Asili from West Nile as Roman Catholic bishop of Lango, did not help since he was perceived to be on the side of the regime, whose leadership was dominated by people from West Nile.[98]

But this soon changed when both Roman Catholics and Church of Uganda members alike received their dead from the different barracks all over the country during the first year of Amin's regime. For as early as

> the second week [after the coup] the wives and children of soldiers began to arrive in Lira from various army barracks in the country. They were dispatched in buses and army lorries escorted by armed soldiers. These women told sad stories of how Lango and Acholi soldiers were massacred by soldiers loyal to Idi Amin.[99]

At that point the Christians concluded that their enemies were Muslims since most of those killed were Christians and Amin was publicly showing his favour for Islam. According to one Church of Uganda clergyman from Lango, "one good result of the military regime was that the Catholics and Anglicans were united through common suffering. They formed a united front against the Muslims, their common enemy."[100] Like in the 1890s, Islam once again forced the Protestants and Catholics to unite against a

---

96. Report by Provincial Literature and Radio Board, Provincial Advisory Board, COU, 15 October 1968, 3, PAE papers, COU Archives.
97. Apelo, OI.
98. Olal, "Church and Politics in Lango-Uganda," 27; Bishop M. Otim, OI, Lira 27 September 1996; Levi Okodi, OI, Lira, 27 September 1996.
99. Olal, "Church and Politics in Lango-Uganda," 28.
100. Ibid., 37.

common threat. The recognition of the need to stand together against a common enemy led the Bishops of the Church of Uganda and the Roman Catholic dioceses to write a joint pastoral letter to their faithful to stop their historical quarrels forthwith.[101] This close relationship was demonstrated further when the service to mark one hundred years of Protestant Christianity in Uganda was organized jointly at Akii Bua Stadium in Lira on 30 June 1977. The preacher and guest of honour on the occasion was the Roman Catholic bishop of Lira.[102]

The Langi Muslims were guarded in their response to the overthrow of Obote and the rise to power by Amin, just like other Muslims in the heartlands of UPC. Like all other Muslims outside Buganda, the majority was sympathetic to UPC. The fact that a Muslim had taken over as president signalled hope of increasing their share of the political power. Two factors shifted their response to outright support of the government in the first three years: first, the perception among the Christians that their enemy was Amin and his fellow Muslims, although the Langi Muslims did not consider Langi Christians their enemies;[103] second, the declared pro-Islam posture of the regime. But this positive orientation towards the regime changed in 1974 when the core of the district Muslim leadership was arrested and detained.

By 1974 all the religiously based hopes and antagonisms among them diminished as arrests and killings became clearly indiscriminate. All the Langi realized that the enemies of the regime in Lango were not determined on the basis of religious affiliation, but that all Langi were "guilty."[104] All the people of Lango were terrorized and brutalized. The regime especially targeted the leaders of the community in civic and business life, regardless of religious or political affiliation.[105] Moreover, for the Langi populace in

---

101. Otim, OI.
102. Olal, "Church and Politics in Lango-Uganda," 28.
103. Odongo, OI.
104. Ibid. Odongo, a Moslem, told me that when Idi Amin took over, the Muslim community in Lango rejoiced, hoping that their day had come. But soon this changed.
105. Otim. A sample of those killed (list given by Julius Peter Obonyo, OI, Lira, 27 September 1996): Ben Otim – Secretary General of Lango District; George Olong – Administrative Secretary, Lango District; George Omolo – Prominent businessman in Lira town; William Oloma – as above; Otim Enyozi – as above; Otim Opul – as above; John Omule (RC) – Health officer, Lango District; Ongom Ajik – Asst. Secretary

general, the institutional conflicts between the Protestant, the Catholics and the Muslims became abstract and irrelevant. For example, several children from a Muslim background regularly attended the children's Sunday school programme at St Augustine Parish Centre; and many were even baptized.[106]

This shift in the perception of the Islamic community was manifested elsewhere in the country. At the national level there were joint actions and leadership consultative meetings between the leaders of the three faiths. During the Makerere incident of 1976, when the students went on strike and the strike was put down with brutality by the military, both Archbishop Luwum and the Catholic Cardinal drove up in their cars into the campus, boldly making inquiries and letting their presence and concern be felt.[107] The same year there was a consultation by leaders of the two churches at which they invited the Muslim leaders. At that meeting Luwum was elected to chair, and all leaders of the three faiths "passed resolutions deploring the killings, the harassment, the looting, and the excessive power given to intelligence officers to execute people."[108] Idi Amin sent an angry reprimand to Luwum for having organized a meeting without his permission.

As already pointed out, the first peak period of massacres was 1971–72, soon after the coup, when the largest number of those who were killed were soldiers. During the second peak period, 1977–79, it was the leaders of the Langi community and the adult males were the targets, for fear of their involvement in the rebel activity that was gaining momentum. The Church in Lango had its fair share of loss of its lay leadership and membership.[109] It

---

Manager, Lango Co-operative Union; Okuja – Headmaster of a Secondary School; Omara Ebek – Ass. Administrative Secretary, Lango District; Amobay – Proprietor of Northern Province Bus Co., the largest bus service in Northern Uganda; Ibrahim Agwa – leader in Islamic Faith and UPC; Mohammed Orech – as above. All of these were killed in the period 1971–74. During the period 1977–79: Ben Ongom Ogati – businessman; Abdulla Anyuru – Chairman of Public Service Commission.

106. Obonyo, OI. Obonyo was Sunday school teacher in the Parish throughout the Amin regime. When I asked for the Baptismal register to confirm this, I was told they were not available. The place was looted during the 1979 war.

107. Kivengere, *I Love Idi Amin*, 40.

108. Ibid., 42.

109. Otim, OI; Ameri Max-Olet in his study, "The impact of the wars on the Diocese of Lango, with specific reference to Lira Town Parish, Church of Uganda, between 1976–1989," Makerere University, Kampala, unpublished Diploma in Theology dissertation,

is estimated that by 1979, when the regime was overthrown, over 75 percent of the adult women in the Church were widows.[110]

The Church became a "sanctuary" of comfort and consolation. People are said to have even slept in church halls. Except for the early months of the regime and the period between 1977–79 when people did not attend church services for fear that Amin operatives would find them and massacre them, churches were full on Sundays. Lira Town parish, which had one congregation prior to 1971 had, by 1979, fourteen congregations. The Lira town congregation grew and the number of services offered each Sunday doubled from two to four.[111] Rev Y Opolo Apello, who served as vicar and archdeacon of Lira, recalled how the people were fervent in prayer, reading the Bible and singing locally composed choruses and hymns.[112] The message of those choruses tells us something of their indigenous spirituality during these times:

> 1) The greatest message, message of Jesus
> The greatest message, message of Jesus
> The great message, message of Jesus
> This message satisfies indeed.
> 2) The word of truth, the word of Jesus
> The sweet word, the word of Jesus
> The holy word, the word of Jesus
> The word of life, the word of Jesus.
> 3) The word of mercy, the word of Jesus

14, has recorded that in Lira Town Parish, lost the following lay leaders during the first and second peaks: Kezekia Oluma, Ben Omor, George Omolo, Micheal Onapa (daughter of the parish treasurer), Otim Ogune, John Otim, Ogwok, John Okuja (who was then headmaster of St Catherine Secondary School, Boroboro), P. Obote, Abraham Agwa, and Elyak.

110. Max-Olet, "The impact of the wars," 14.

111. Charles Odurukami, OI Kampala, 27 August 1996 (Odurukami served in Lira Town parish from 1976-82); Julius Peter Obonyo, OI Lira, 27 September 1996 (Obonyo was Chairman of the laity for the St Augustine Parish Church during the Amin years). Apelo, OI. Apelo was Vicar at the Lira Town Parish from 1971–76 and Archdeacon of Lira from 1977–79. He was arrested during the latter period, accused of participating in rebel activity and only too glad that he was not taken to the Lira barracks. He believes he would have been killed, because Rev Atim, a pastor from Akokoro, Obote's home village who was arrested the same time was killed in the barracks.

112. Apelo, OI.

The word of the kingdom, the word of Jesus
The word of salvation, the word of Jesus
The word of love, the word of Jesus.
4) The word (message) of reconciliation, the word of Jesus
With which Jesus reconciles the people
The word of reconciliation, the word of Jesus
This word satisfies me indeed.
5) The message (word) of help, the message of Jesus
Which Jesus helps with people, the message of Jesus
The message of healing, the message of Jesus
The message of care, the message of Jesus.
6) The message of knowledge, the message of Jesus
You will lead me to Jesus
You will lead me to Christ
On matters of this world
You defeat all of them.[113]

The focus in this song is on the wonder and impact of the word in its various forms, and its power in enabling those under stress to stand. It is also a prayer. The same message is found in the following hymn, but with an application to both the individual and the community.

1) Poverty won't disturb me
Poverty won't disturb me
Poverty won't disturb me in heaven with Jesus.
2) I will be with happiness
I will be with happiness
I will be with happiness in heaven with Jesus.
3) No death will affect (kill) me
4) There will be no hunger
5) There will be no crying
6) I will fear no darkness
7) I will have no enmity with anyone

---

113. *Kilega Par Jo Ducu, Wer Me Pako Lubanga*, (Lwo Prayer Book and Hymnal, Revised), (Kampala: Centenary Publishing House, 1979), no. 103, 448. Translation by Rev C. Odurukami.

8) We shall live forever
9) We shall love one another
10) We shall love our Lord Jesus
11) We shall praise Him joyfully
12) If I accept Him, He will accept me
13) If I reject Him, He will reject me
14) We love our Lord Jesus
We love our Lord Jesus
We love our Lord Jesus
Because he has loved us.[114]

The songs focus on the Christ narrative and its impact both on the individual and the community, as a source of encouragement to stand in faith whatever the circumstances. There is a strong emphasis on the hope of heaven, where there will be no more hunger, death, crying, darkness and enmity, but happiness, love, and life forever.

A major component of the ministry of the Church was pastoral visits and support to those traumatized by the regime because of the death of loved ones at the hands of the regime.[115] The story of Caroline Ongom, a parishioner at the Lira town parish church and widow to Ben Ongom,[116] and the significance for her of Rev Odurukami's pastoral ministry and fellowship with other Christians is a typical example.[117]

Ben Ongom was killed by firing squad in September 1977. Caroline was left a widow at twenty-eight years of age. Ongom was first arrested during the first peak of massacres that hit Acholi and Lango in March 1971. He spent four months in Makindye Barracks prison and was released July 1971. He was rearrested in September 1972 after the September foiled

---

114. Ibid., no. 112, 453–454.

115. When Bishop Melchisedek Otim fled into exile in 1977, Bishops Gereshom Ilukor of Soroti, Remelia Ringtho of West Nile, and Yustus Ruhindi of Bunyoro-Kitara took turns in providing Episcopal oversight over Lango diocese until the appointment in 1978 of William Okodi as Suffragan bishop of Lango Diocese. Max-Olet, "The impact of the wars," 14.

116. Caroline Ongom, OI Lira, 27 September 1996. Ben Ongom is the man who led the State Research Bureau officers to the late Janani Luwum's home at Namirembe, and then later to the home of Bishop Okoth in Tororo.

117. Apelo, OI. He told me of similar stories of his work, visiting, praying, and reading the Bible with them.

invasion by the rebels based in Tanzania. He spent nine months of torture in Makindye Barracks prison and was released in 1973. For the next two years he was in hiding, and his family did not know his whereabouts. During the year 1975 there was relative peace and calm in the country, so Ongom came out of hiding. Caroline and their four children joined him, and they lived together in Bukoto, a suburb of Kampala.

It was early February 1977, while Caroline was away with the children in Lira that Ongom was arrested again, together with Abdullah Anyuru, then Chairman of the Public Service Commission.[118] Caroline made several attempts to see her husband but with no success. It was when the court proceedings started that she was able to see him. She narrated the incident thus:

> I was eventually able to see my husband in court before he was killed. He told me that it was OK to die. They had burnt his fingers, all his toes, mouth and private parts. You could not recognise him. He said it was OK for him to die as he would not be useful if he lived. I had gone with my sister. This was the last time [I saw him]. Although I went to Kampala for the firing squad, I could not have courage to watch it.[119]

Each time Ongom was arrested, he was accused of supporting the former regime, Obote's rule, and of financing rebels. The last time he was arrested in February 1977, it was alleged that he was part of the racket of those who imported arms to overthrow the Amin regime.

Caroline narrated how the Rev Charles Odurukami, then serving at the St Augustine Parish centre, in Lira town Parish Church, was like a brother to her as he visited her family regularly to pray and read the Bible for them. The family of Chandy, a lay leader in the Church and head teacher of one of the schools in Lira was also very close to her family. "We would always sing songs of praise," Caroline recalled.

> So I have been close to the priests. I have been a sister to them. Rev Odurukami always read for me the book of Job [in

---

118. Ongom, OI. They were arrested in front of the Norman Cinema (present day Kampala Pentecostal Church Building) and taken to Makindye.
119. Ibid.

the Bible]. I know if it was not my fate, my husband would not have been killed. Job helped me to accept this as my fate . . . whenever I had a problem somebody from Church would come to me. The Church is my family.[120]

Mrs Ongom's statement, "the Church is my family" names her experience of the church as a social reality in her moment of need. As a member of the same Church, it is also a statement of self-definition. Within the Church context, fellowship and fellowship meetings were associated with only the saved ones, members of the Revival. Although Mrs Ongom did not classify herself as one of the Balokole, fellowship with believers is what sustained her. The Church had become part of her identity in a profound way. This was not only for Ongom but also for many in Lango. Home fellowship groups of this kind thrived all over Lango.[121]

Archbishop Luwum and the Regime

Janani Luwum[122] was elected in May 1974 to replace Archbishop Erica Sabiti who was retiring that year. Luwum could not be persuaded by superficial talk about being God-fearing because he knew the atrocities of the Idi Amin regime right from the beginning. He had once as bishop of Northern Uganda appealed to his brother bishops early in 1972 to protest to the regime for the senseless murders in its early months, but "after some hesitation they sought audience with the President."[123] His election as Archbishop effectively relocated the Church's voice of protest and resistance from the periphery to the centre.

The election of Janani Luwum may, on face value, suggest that it was a conscious step for the Church to move towards confrontation with the regime, by electing a man from the diocese of Northern Uganda, the

---

120. Ibid.
121. All my informants in Lira referred to such groups.
122. At the time of Luwum's election he was the bishop of Northern Uganda, covering Acholi and Lango – present day Gulu, Kitgum, Apac and Lira districts. Born in 1922 and saved in 1948, he was ordained deacon in 1953 and priested in 1956. He was Vice-Principal for Buwalasi Theological College 1962–1964, and then Principal 1965–1966. He was Provincial Secretary from September 1966 to 1969 when he became the bishop of Northern Uganda. Ford, *Janani*, is a short biography of Luwum.
123. Ford, *Janani*, 50.

heartland of Obote's support, and by extension, of Idi Amin's opposition. This was not the case. First, as Ward observed, "the bishops were not thinking in political terms. Luwum was elected because he was felt to be, spiritually and intellectually, the most competent person."[124] Second, at the time of his election, the Acholi and Langi were no longer the only target of the regime. Moreover, as it has already been pointed out, the period mid-1973 to 1976, during which he was elected was relatively quiet and calm.

While the Church did not elect him as an aggressive strategy, in Janani Luwum the Church had elected a man who was to prove most disagreeable to Amin. He was an Acholi, a Mulokole, and known by character to be courageous and bold. The earlier period of his leadership (1974–1976) was relatively calm. However, the government must have kept a close eye on him due to his association with the Acholi and the UPC,[125] the archenemies of the regime. And Luwum must have intervened on several occasions on behalf of many who "disappeared" at the hands of the military machine of the regime. However, there is no record of any confrontation with Amin or any of the agents of the regime prior to the cataclysmic events of February 1977, when he was killed.

Death of Archbishop Luwum

Luwum was accused of being part of a clandestine plan to overthrow the government by force of arms, together with Bishop Yona Okoth of Bukedi diocese; Ben Ongom, a businessman from Lango; Erinayo Oryema, an Acholi, who was then a government minister; and, Oboth Ofumbi, a Japadhola from Tororo. Oryema was then also a government minister. Ongom was the first to be arrested from his home in Kampala on 1 February 1977, with several cartons of ammunition.[126] Four days later, on 5 February, at about 1:30 a.m., Ongom led his captors to Janani Luwum's

---

124. Ward, "The Church of Uganda," 83.
125. Ibid. Ward has made the point that "in political terms Luwum was inevitably seen as 'UPC'" because of the way the UPC government in 1969 got involved in his enthronement as a bishop of Northern Uganda diocese.
126. Kivengere, *I Love Idi Amin*, 45–46.

home, the official residence of the Archbishop, at Namirembe,[127] having named Luwum as an accomplice in the acquisition of ammunition to use against the government. After a thorough and ruthless search, no arms were found and the men left with their captive. In the evening that day, the same group went to Bishop Okoth's residence in Tororo, thoroughly searched it, and arrested him.[128] Here too there were no combat arms, except for a shotgun and rifle for hunting purposes. Later the next day he was released. But in both incidents the government report said that arms had been found. Concerning Okoth:

> The President disclosed that some arms were captured near the home of Bishop Okoth of Tororo, who received them and transported them to Archbishop Luwum, because he was at the border where the arms from Dar es Salaam through Nairobi could easily be channelled. After the search of Bishop Okoth's house, he was also left intact but the arms were transported to Kampala.[129]

In a hard-hitting letter, the entire House of Bishops registered their "shock and protest at this kind of treatment to the top leaders of the Church of Uganda, Rwanda, Burundi and Boga-Zaire."[130] Idi Amin is reported to have telephoned Luwum on the evening of Sunday 13 February. The content of their telephone conversation is unknown,[131] except that the president is reported to have been in "a rage, and Janani had to listen to some terrible words and accusations from him."[132] And that "finally, Archbishop Luwum was able to speak to him from the heart, very firmly, but in love. The president banged the receiver down angrily."[133] The two had a meeting the next day, 14 February, at which it is reported that "the president and

---

127. A full report of the attack is in Muhima, "The Fellowship of His Suffering," 134–137.
128. Ibid., 140–142, for full report.
129. *Uganda Argus,* 12 February 1977, 1.
130. Letter to President from House of Bishops dated 10 February 1977. The full letter has been reproduced in Muhima, "The Fellowship of His Suffering," 1982, 143–148.
131. I made an attempt to interview Luwum's wife in January 1997, but she declined to give me audience.
132. Kivengere, *I Love Idi Amin,* 50.
133. Ibid.

the Archbishop had quite an exchange. The Archbishop put his case quite clearly, not contesting the search of his house but the manner in which it was done – at midnight by gunpoint."[134] In the government newspaper the next day it was reported:

> Field Marshal Amin disclosed to the Archbishop that 11 boxes containing hundreds of automatic Chinese arms and thousands of ammunition and grenades sent by Obote to Uganda for subversive activities sometime before the sixth anniversary of the military administration had been captured by Ugandan civilians. . . . The boxes had been intercepted by schoolchildren and some civilians. They found them near Archbishop's house and later reported to the security forces for action.[135]

Idi Amin then summoned all the religious leaders to a meeting on Wednesday 16 February at the International Conference Centre, Kampala. Present were all bishops of both the Roman Catholic Church and the Church of Uganda, leaders of the Islamic faith, diplomats, senior military officers, and the whole Cabinet.[136] There was a display of guns in the grounds of the Conference Centre.

At that meeting the bishops presented another memorandum to Idi Amin, protesting against his accusations against Luwum and demanding that he instead concentrate on bringing under control his intelligence officers "who not only go out to investigate and arrest, but carry out death sentences and executions without trial."[137] It was at this gathering that Luwum was arrested, together with Oryema and Ofumbi, allegedly "for involvement in subversive activities."[138] They were subsequently murdered.[139]

---

134. Ibid., 51. It should be noted that Festo Kivengere was not present at this meeting. He must have got the report of the meeting from Luwum.
135. *Voice of Uganda*, Kampala, Tuesday 15 February 1977, 1.
136. *Voice of Uganda*, Kampala, Thursday 17 February 1977, 1.
137. Prepared response of the House of Bishops of the COU, to His Excellency on Wednesday 16 February 1977, House of Bishops' Papers, COU Archives.
138. *Voice of Uganda*, Thursday 17 February 1977, 1.
139. For a full eyewitness account, see Kivengere, *I Love Idi Amin*, 51–55. Although the *Voice of Uganda* claimed that the three died in a car accident, it is widely acknowledged that they were shot.

The general view about Luwum is that he was an innocent Christian martyr,[140] who was a victim of "the persistent force of ethnicity in Uganda life."[141] However, the reality was more complicated. Several factors point to Luwum's awareness of a plan to overthrow the Idi Amin regime by force of arms. His relationship with those with whom he was implicated point to this. Luwum knew Ben Ongom,[142] the man in whose home were found boxes of arms. Luwum had several meetings with him at his home prior to the February events.[143] Luwum and Oryema were old friends from before their high school days.[144] And Luwum and Okoth were long time colleagues and friends in the Church of Uganda. Oboth-Ofumbi hailed from the same small ethnic group in Tororo, the Japadhola, as Okoth. The African proverb that "there is no smoke without fire" may be applied here.

As bishop of Northern Uganda, Luwum had met in every part of the diocese "wailing Langi and Acholi mourning their dead. He comforted those who mourned, encouraged the fainthearted, and urged us all to forgive as Christ forgave his enemies who hung upon the cross."[145] He had, as a leader of the Acholi and Langi, bled in his heart over the massacres of 1971–1972. The story of Ben Ocan's wife is a tale of thousands of wives in Amin's Uganda. Dorothy Ocan, pleading with the Uganda High Commission in London for news about her husband, who had disappeared, wrote:

> I cannot look at the faces of my children. To see our only son aged nine years; to wake and find my sensitive gentle

---

140. This is the view held by L. Pirouet in her article "Religion Uganda under Amin," *Journal of Religion in Africa* 11, no. 1 (1980): 22–23; and Muhima in his study; "The Fellowship of His Suffering," 105–109; and Ward in his essay, "The Church in Uganda," 84–85.

141. Ward, "The Church in Uganda," 85.

142. "Report of a very serious incident at the Archbishops house in the early hours of Saturday 5 Feb 1977," in Muhima, "The Fellowship of His Suffering," 134.

143. A very close relative who saw Luwum at the home of Ben Ongom on several evenings, meeting and talking privately with Ongom gave this information to me. This relative confirmed the government report of the cartons of arms and ammunition to have indeed been in Ongom's possession, and that Ongom was in regular contact with Obote in Tanzania. Luwum was also in contact with Obote. Name of informant withheld on request.

144. Ford, *Janani*, 37. Oryema is the one who chaired the committee for Luwum's enthronement in January 1969.

145. Ibid., 50. Luwum was highly acclaimed for his pastoral heart and actions.

twelve-year-old daughter sobbing in the night. I have not been strong enough to tell the older, Angom, our fourteen-year-old who is away at school, or our little Dongo. . . . Ben held her the moment after birth and laughed and danced with her. Please send us any scrap of news you can get; I have reached a dead end in my inquiries. I beg you, please, to let me know however terrible the news. These are violent times, I understand.[146]

Such were the pastoral concerns in Luwum's ministry. He must have known of the massacre at Karuma Bridge when Acholi and Langi soldiers were "bayoneted and their bodies thrown into the falls" in February 1971. All this, Luwum had to bear, as bishop of northern Uganda. Five years on, Idi Amin's heart had not changed, but only become more callous. It is possible that after Luwum's several pleas and protests to Idi Amin over the merciless and senseless murders of several innocent people, he had come to the conclusion that Amin's removal by force of arms was justified as a last option.

Bishop Okoth himself came to this conclusion:

> When Archbishop was murdered, and I went to exile, I started praying that he [Amin] may be overthrown. I worked closely to support the armed struggle. I gave up the idea [of not using guns]. Amin came by gun and I knew he would go by the gun. I would support the people using the gun. . . . I was committed that he be removed by any means. I personally did not know how to hold the gun, but there are people who God called to hold a gun and could do it. So I was actively supporting the liberation forces.[147]

Although Okoth admitted that he changed his mind after the February 1977 events, it is plausible to suggest that that change of mind began prior to his exile years given his relationship and association with Obote[148] and

---

146. Dorothy Ocan, Quoted in Martin, *General Amin*, 217.
147. Yona Okoth, OI, Tororo, 16 January 1997.
148. Okoth's relationship with Obote dates back to their high school days at Gulu Secondary School, Okoth, OI.

those implicated in the plan to overthrow Amin. It is more likely that Luwum, like Okoth, may have changed his mind and sought to support those "God had called to hold the gun." Amin had lost his moral legitimacy as the president of Uganda, and therefore had to be removed by force as the last resort.

Certainly Amin's intelligence network would have tracked down all the associations and communication within this network of relations.[149] On every count, from Amin's perspective, Luwum was guilty: an Acholi; a member and leader of the Church of Uganda, Obote's Church; one who had chaired several sessions that sent memoranda of protest; and to confirm it all for Amin, intelligence reports connected him to rebel activity. Janani Luwum was judged to be a subversive agent, and a criminal, one who deserved the treatment that Idi Amin gave to all those whom he so judged – murder in cold blood.

In a meeting between Luwum and Amin in the presence of Luwum's wife on 14 February 1977, Amin accused Luwum "of collaborating with Obote to create chaos, and using the centenary celebrations to cover up his political activities."[150] Luwum was aware of the consequences of his confrontation with Amin. On the eve of that fateful day of his death, his wife Mary pleaded with him to get out of Uganda, but Janani refused because "he had no guilty conscience over those accusations, [and therefore] he would not run away."[151] And on the day of his death, Mary pleaded again and told him that if he went for the meeting at the International Conference Centre, he would not return, to which Luwum replied, "If I die, my blood will save Uganda."[152]

About two hours before his death, as Luwum and all the bishops listened to the charges against him, Luwum turned to Bishop Festo Kivengere and

---

149. Amin's intelligence network was renowned for its sophistication and ruthlessness. Bikangaga believes that each time Amin's Intelligence made an accusation against an individual, 90% of the time there was a grain of truth. Bikangaga, OI.
150. A "first-hand" report recorded by Henry Okullu, in "The Role of a Church Leader in Society Today," unpublished Janani Luwum Memorial Lecture, Kampala, 16 February 1985.
151. Ibid., 4.
152. Ibid.

whispered: "They are going to kill me. I am not afraid."[153] Luwum embraced his death. He knew Amin's verdict: guilty. He knew that from the perspective of his calling, his mission and ministry, he was not guilty. He was only fulfilling his calling as a minister of the gospel, and so was *not afraid* to face the consequences. When the last orders were given to Luwum to see the President, he turned and smiled to his brother bishops and said, "I can see the hand of the Lord in this."[154]

It is significant that Luwum considered his imminent death as a "ransom" for Uganda, and not just the Church of Uganda. His preoccupation was not with the institutional Church, but for the people of Uganda. To understand Luwum's death only in terms of Church-State confrontation[155] misses the paradigm shift that Luwum's death represents in understanding the Church. Luwum in seeing his death as "for Uganda," affirms the existence of the Church as not for itself but for Uganda. Luwum saw himself as a minister in the Church for the world. This also sheds light on his understanding of ministry.

The premonition that his death would "save Uganda" attaches vicarious significance to it. The "vicarious factor" in Luwum's perspective to his suffering is what distinguishes his death from others. The significance of Luwum's death is not just in how he died, but more importantly, that even when he was aware of the potential danger of his actions and those with whom he was associated, he chose to stay and whatever the consequences. He linked what he was going through with his calling as the pastoral-leader of the Church, and the implied responsibility for Uganda.

This is not to downgrade the importance of how he died. He died a criminal's death, according to Amin and his functionaries. The death was brutal. An eyewitness account of the damage on his body is graphic:

> 1. There was a hole in his throat below his adam's apple through to the back of his neck.

---

153. Quoted in Ford, *Janani*, 86.
154. Ibid., 87.
155. Hansen's perspective is that Janani Luwum was "a victim of the tension between Church and State" in Hansen, "Religion and Politics in Independent Uganda," 13.

2. Deep wounds on both armpits. It appeared as though his chest had been shot in the armpit, and the chest was bandaged.

3. There was a hole on his left lower stomach going through his back. It could be a wound inflicted by something like a sword.

4. His back had been broken by cutting it with a sharp instrument.

5. Lastly his loins had been cut off, and around the lower area was all bandaged. There was no other wound apart from a few bruises on the left leg.[156]

As the account has shown, Luwum was not the first to suffer such bestiality at the hands of Amin's butcher machine. Luwum was to be numbered among the thousands who "disappeared,"[157] the thousands that were never accorded a decent burial.[158] Luwum died like them and indeed with them.

During the week after Luwum's death, four bishops fled the country for exile: Festo Kivengere of Kigezi;[159] Melkisedek Otim of Lango; Yona Okoth of Bukedi;[160] Benon Ogwal of Acholi,[161] leaving nine bishops who acted quickly to stabilize the Church. The first significant step was the election of Silvanus Wani to replace Luwum.

---

156. Okullu, The Role of a Church Leader," 6–7. Bishop Okullu was a close friend to the Luwum family. In fact after Luwum's death, his family moved to live with the Okullu's in Kisumu, until Amin was overthrown.

157. Those who were picked by the State Research Bureau or Public Safety and killed, were said to have "disappeared."

158. The government did not release Luwum's body for official burial at Namirembe on 20 February 1977. Soldiers carried the body to his village home, Mucwini, and an Archdeacon assisted by 3 priests buried him at Mucwini Church. Prior to the burial, Luwum's mother, 3 priests and 2 laymen viewed it, one of whom told Bishop Okullu the state of the body as it was found. "The body was that of Archbishop Luwum; it was completely naked; wrapped in a blanket; his Episcopal ring was on his finger; and red socks on his feet. His purple cassock, soaked in blood, lay beside his body in the coffin." Okullu, "The Role of a Church Leader," 6. Also, Ford, *Janani*, 89–93, for the empty grave at Namirembe.

159. Kivengere, *I Love Idi Amin*, recounts the story of his flight.

160. I interviewed both Okoth and Otim who acknowledged the support of the wider Christian community. Okoth dressed as a Muslim as he crossed the Uganda-Kenya border.

161. Benon Ogwal went into exile again during the NRM regime.

Silvanus Wani, Successor to Janani Luwum

The accession to the Archiepiscopal See by Silvanus Wani,[162] a kinsman of Idi Amin, on 18 March 1977, one month after Luwum was killed, was interpreted by some to having been an imposition by Amin.[163] But it was a well considered choice by the House of Bishops[164] recognizing Wani to be a "Mulokole," a godly and spiritual man, and a "father" figure with high integrity and respect among his brother Bishops.[165] As a kinsman and an "uncle"[166] to Idi Amin, it was hoped that he would prevail over Idi Amin and check his excesses. The election was in keeping with the defensive position the Church had maintained throughout the regime.

Wani did not expect his election, nor did Idi Amin. In fact Amin sent an envoy to ask him to resign.[167] Evidently Idi Amin was not happy with the choice, as he was aware that Wani knew him very well and could speak to him about anything. And speak and challenge, Wani did:

> I had audience with Amin from time to time, challenging him to stop killing people. He became more worried about me, as I asked him constantly about people who had disappeared. . . . Some of our people were forced to chew centenary badges.

---

162. Silvanus Wani (c1915–) was saved in 1937, ordained a Deacon in 1943 and to the priesthood in 1944. He became Chaplain in the Army in 1943, a role he continued to play until the downfall of Idi Amin's Regime. He was Diocesan Secretary/Treasurer for Northern Uganda Diocese 1960–1964, and then bishop of the same diocese 1964–1969. He became first bishop of Madi/West Nile Diocese 1969–1977; Dean of the Province, 1973–1977; and become Archbishop in 1977. Silvanus Wani, OI; Wani, "How to Make Christ Relevant," 2; and Lloyd, *Wedge of Light*.

163. Bishop Yustus Ruhindi, OI, Kampala, 2 March 1994. Bishop Silvanus Wani, OI, Kampala, 15 January 1997.

164. Bishop Y. Ruhindi was asked to consider becoming Archbishop, but declined. Advice was sought from Erica Sabiti, who recommended Wani. Ruhindi, OI; Wani, OI; and Wilson Baganizi, OI, Namirembe, 16 January 1997. Canon Baganizi, in whose house the House of Bishops sat to elect the Archbishop, was Provincial Secretary for the Church. He was present in the meeting. He confirmed that both Y. Ruhindi and Amos Betungura were asked to consider candidacy for the post, but declined. Dunstan Nsubuga was not asked, because though younger and known to have been willing, he was not as "spiritual."

165. Ruhindi, OI.

166. Not a real blood uncle, but the fact that they were of the same tribe, Kakwa, and Wani was an elder, he would rightly be referred to as an uncle to Amin. Some, however, took this to mean a "blood uncle."

167. Wani, OI.

> . . . Later he did not want to see me again. . . . He stopped his agents as well from following me up.[168]

The letter to Idi Amin, introducing Silvanus Wani as the new Archbishop, written one month after the death of Luwum, reflects the dilemma the bishops were in and how afraid they were of any further confrontation. In a sense, they declared a "ceasefire."

> The Bishops of the Church of Uganda, Rwanda, Burundi and Zaire wish to thank Your Excellency for the audience you gave us on 17 March 1977 in which you assured us of Your Excellency's and Your Government's support for the Church, and particularly over your assurances and support for the centenary celebrations due to take place in June this year. We thank Your Excellency for your most useful and fatherly advice, not only on that occasion but also for the most needed help Your Excellency and Your Government have given to the Church in the past.
>
> The House of Bishops met on the 18 March 1977 to elect a new Archbishop and unanimously elected Bishop Silvanus G. Wani, who was then Dean of the Province, as the new Archbishop. Although Bishop S. G. Wani was reluctant to stand and personally preferred a younger Bishop to become the next Archbishop, he had the support and encouragement of the other Bishops and because of the trust they had in him, he was duly elected the new Archbishop at the election chaired by the Provincial Chancellor, and Bishop Wani accepted the appointment to the office of the Archbishop because of the trust and confidence of his colleagues as a call from God.[169]

In that meeting of 17 March 1977, one month after the murder of Luwum, Idi Amin "was extremely happy to receive the Church leaders, whom he described as the true sons of Uganda and leaders of the Church of

---

168. Ibid.
169. Letter to His Excellency, Life President of Uganda, signed by the Rt Rev Dr D. Nsubuga, Dean of the Province, dated 23 March 1977, House of Bishops Papers, COU Archives.

Uganda, who were dedicated to preach the word of God to their followers as well as people of Uganda in general."[170] He assured the bishops that " he personally, the Defence Council and the government were not in any way against the Church of Uganda in particular."[171]

In addition to the Dean's letter, the Archbishop-Elect wrote to Amin thanking him "personally for giving (us) the House of Bishops, an audience on 17 March 1977." He continued:

> I and the House of Bishops felt most happy to have been assured by Your Excellency over the centenary celebrations of the Church, allowing for the sale of badges, T-shirts, and other items as proceeds towards the centenary and your full support for the Church. However as there is *need for more assurance* [italics mine for emphasis] and there is need to give as much publicity to our remotest churches as possible, we intend to write to all our Christians in order to *dispel any lingering fears among our people*. We are happy to note, that Governors and DC's are co-operating in this exercise of spreading the assurances. In this connection, I wish to request that if possible Your Excellency confirm the declaration of a Public Holiday along with the full support for the centenary celebrations in a letter before we give out publicity.[172]

Assurances were given and 30 June 1977 declared a public holiday for the celebration of the Church's centenary, and the celebrations took place all over the Province without any incident.

Amin continued to project an image of "not-against-the-Church." He continued to give support to Church causes. When the Archbishop requested assistance towards enabling Bishops to attend the Lambeth Conference in 1978, Idi Amin chartered a plane for them, and gave them some security to accompany them![173] Having been warned by "uncle Wani," that "if

---

170. *Voice of Uganda*, 18 March 1977, 1.
171. Ibid.
172. Letter to His Excellency, Life President of Uganda, signed by the Archbishop Elect, dated 24 March 1977. Archbishop's Papers, COU Archives.
173. Ruhindi, OI. The agents are said to have attended the meeting, causing a spectacle at Lambeth.

you refuse the whole world will curse you," to which Idi Amin replied, "*Tafadhali, watakwenda*" (Swahili, meaning "Please, they will go"),[174] once he had ascertained that Lambeth Conference was not intended to plan against his regime.[175]

Reflection

The institutional model of the church serves the interests of a church which has some social-political leverage and whose geographical boundaries are coterminous with the geo-political boundaries of the state. The category church-state becomes useful as an analytical model. Within the context of establishment, the church-state relationship remains one of partnership, as long as both institutions serve each other's interests. However, once the state perceives the church as having ceased to serve its interests, the church becomes part of the opposition, and this will lead to confrontation. On the other hand, once the church perceives the state as no longer serving its interests, it repositions itself either into a defensive posture and strives for survival, or into fresh confrontation.

During the pre-independence and Obote eras, the Church of Uganda was more or less the partner to the state and the Roman Catholic Church in the opposition. However, with the "dis-establishment" process engendered by the Amin regime, both the Church of Uganda and the Roman Catholic Church, being large institutions with social-political weight, were partners in the opposition. This realignment of social-political forces led to a paradigm shift in the Church's self-definition, no longer as the "Protestant" Church but *a* church of Uganda. It is significant that in the records and writings referring to the Church after the incidents of 1977, there is hardly any reference to the Church as Protestant but rather as Church of Uganda

---

174. Ibid.

175. Baganizi, OI. Baganizi was then Provincial Secretary. He told me the story how Amin "locked" up the bishops at Lweza Training Centre (a Church property seven km away from the capital). Then having ascertained what Lambeth was about, he chartered a plane, half loaded it with coffee, with bishops and security agents in the other half. The agents who were Muslim were given Christian names, and on return reported that the Bishops had discussed homosexuality, which caused consternation to Amin. Amin announced that COU Bishops had accepted homosexuality. The record was put right when Wani submitted to him the official Lambeth report.

or Anglican. Although it is possible to infer from this that the Church was rediscovering its Anglican heritage, my contention is that it is not "Anglicanism" being rediscovered, but a new identity at two levels. First, as a national church, catholic in its extent, and second in its relation with the Catholic Church, no longer Protestant.

The "catholicity" of the Church of Uganda was most expressed during the Amin regime, where the term catholic is used as "expressing the unconditional priority of the church community above communities of race, speech, culture, state, and class."[176] Unlike previous times when the church's response to socio-political violence caused by State machinery was variegated and differentiated regionally, as was the case over the question of Buganda, this time the entire national Church was together, protesting, pleading and applauding. Luwum's leadership and death was instrumental in bringing the Church to this point.

The Protestant identity of the Church receded because rivalry with the Catholic Church became irrelevant in the light of the more immediate threat to the Church's being – the tyranny of the Amin regime. The rediscovery of the "self" of the Church was simultaneous with the rediscovery of the "other," the Roman Catholic Church, no longer as rival, but as partner. The account of the Church in Lango showed that the common experience of suffering refocused the energies of the leadership and membership of these two historically rival churches to solidarity in the face of the common threat, the Idi Amin regime. This is an extremely significant development in the relationship of the two Churches given their historical animosity in Lango. It is also instructive that similar solidarity was reported elsewhere in the country.[177] This demonstrates how the corporate identity of the church is not static but rather formed in context.

However, the apparent grassroots solidarity between the two churches was not reflected at the national level in the same proportions. Kevin Ward has observed that during the Idi Amin era the two churches seemed to

---

176. Karl Barth, *Theology and the Church* (London: SCM Press, 1962), 277.
177. The shift in the relationship between the two churches in Lango from opponents to partners was not limited to Lango. It was reported in other parts of the country, for example in Kigezi. See Kivengere, *I Love Idi Amin*, 37, 41. Kivengere refers to a time when the two churches conducted services and missions together in Kabale, Mbarara and at Makerere University and were keen to publicise this new image of their relationship.

pursue a policy of dis-engagement, so that although the more fundamental tension between the Catholic and Protestant churches abated, "there was no corresponding coming together for common action."[178] It is noteworthy that there was no joint memorandum presented to Idi Amin during the events of February 1977.

While the church-state perspective limits the consideration of Luwum's death to church-state confrontation, the "church in the world" paradigm takes us beyond the institutional confrontation, to relating it to the individual dimension in the conflict. The "church in the world" takes cognisance of the fact that Luwum was an Acholi, a *Mulokole*, and the Archbishop of a church that was associated with Obote's regime. The significance of Luwum's conjecture that if he died "his blood would save Uganda," and not just "the Church of Uganda," points to Luwum's awareness of his service not just in relation to the Church, but to Uganda. It was not only the Church that was suffering at the hands of the brutal dictator; it was all Uganda. It is precisely because his mission was not the protection of the Church but rescuing the people of Uganda from the brutal dictator, that he could have considered supporting those "called to handle the gun," to rid Uganda of the tyrant. This would not be the case of the church versus the state in armed conflict, but a people against the forces of darkness that Amin's regime was serving.

In my view the "ceasefire" correspondence with Amin from the "remnant" of the House of Bishops arose from perceiving Luwum's death only from the church-state perspective; thus their need for assurances by the state for another institutional function, the celebration of the Church centenary.

Louise Pirouet, Kevin Ward and Edward Muhima have discussed the question of whether Janani Luwum died as a political martyr or a Christian martyr. Pirouet, for her part, believes that Amin falsely accused Luwum of being involved in an armed plot. To quote her:

> The only weapon the religious leaders used was words (in spite of Luwum being falsely accused by Amin of being involved in an armed plot), though we shall later find the Roman Catholic

---

178. Kevin Ward, "Catholic-Protestant Relations in Uganda: An Historical Perspective," *Africa Journal of Theology* 13, no. 3 (1984): 182.

Church in Kenya turning to educating clergy and laity in human rights. The Ugandan religious leaders' minuted decision, to "fight evil and violence" in their country was misunderstood: bishops and clergy were accused of preaching sermons, which incited violence when they preached sermons about the fight against evil.[179]

Pirouet is essentially arguing that Idi Amin fabricated and concocted evidence against Luwum. She has suggested that Luwum was killed as a result of Amin's perception that Luwum was leading the Church in a rebellion against the government, especially given the magnitude to the plans then for celebrating the Church centenary.[180] She exonerates Luwum and all the bishops and clergy from responsibility of any violent protest against the Idi Amin regime.

However, as the account has demonstrated, Idi Amin's enemies were not only those who were violent. The sermons against violence and evil were enough to implicate any as an enemy since they were interpreted to be targeting the regime, as indeed they were. In fact Muhima has referred to what was evidently a subversive "anti-government sermon. The preacher emphasised that time had come when the government should be told to stop buying Russian Mig-jets and buy commodities such as sugar and salt, which would benefit Ugandans more."[181] This account, however, has gone further to considering the plausibility of some association of Luwum with violence.

Kevin Ward has argued that Luwum was killed primarily "because he was an Acholi rather than because he was a Christian."[182] Although Ward admits later that Luwum also died because of his Christian convictions, he relegates it to a secondary place.

> Luwum died as a representative leader of the Acholi, who (with other Lwo groups), as a people, were blamed for opposing

---

179. Louise Pirouet, "The Church and Human Rights in Kenya & Uganda," in *Religion and Politics in East Africa*, eds. Holger B. Hansen and Michael Twaddle (London: James Currey, 1995), 251.
180. Pirouet, "Religion Uganda under Amin," 22.
181. Muhima, "The Fellowship of His Suffering," 47.
182. Ward, "The Church in Uganda," 84.

Amin. But the impact of the bishop's letter and the "Christian" opposition to Amin should not be discounted. Amin was no doubt extremely angry at this forthright exposure of the nature of his regime and its production, with Luwum's signature at the head, may have sealed his fate.[183]

He adds:

> In emphasising the ethnic element in Janani Luwum's death, I want in no way to detract from the idea that he died as a Christian martyr. Certainly he died as a witness to the truth for the sake of Christ and a defender of the rights of the Uganda people as a whole. The 16th of February is widely remembered as Janani Luwum's Day – he is already in the Church of Uganda's calendar of saints, along with Bishop Hannington and the Uganda martyrs of 1886. But Luwum was and is the victim of the persistent force of ethnicity in Uganda life.[184]

The crux of Ward's argument is the ethnic factor in Uganda's political history, an argument that is tenable if Luwum's death is seen only from the perspective of the Idi Amin regime. The demerit of arguing that Luwum died primarily as an Acholi, and not as a Christian, is in limiting the consideration of his death to the perspective of the regime, and therefore separating his Acholi and Christian identities. However if his death is considered also from Luwum's perspective, his unitary identity is preserved – an Acholi-Christian-leader. One can not consider him to be a Christian without being Acholi, or an Acholi without being a Christian.

Muhima has argued that it is the composite of factors, events and relations around Janani Luwum that led to his death, "not as a criminal, although he was treated as if he had been one, but as a Christian martyr who stood for what he believed was right."[185] Muhima has followed the sequence of events in the showdown between Luwum and Amin, climaxing in the search of the Archbishop's residence, which evoked a stern protest from the House of Bishops. Muhima concluded:

---

183. Ibid., 85.
184. Ibid.
185. Muhima, "The Fellowship of His Suffering," 109.

It was probably because of this opposition that Amin ordered his men to arrest the Archbishop and the two ministers. They were arrested on February 17, 1977 (sic) and killed on that same day. A few days later four bishops were forced to flee for their lives.

Some Ugandans whom I interviewed in April and May, 1980 also felt that it was probably the bishop's open letter which provoked Amin to take the action that he did. But *knowing how forthright Archbishop Luwum was, and taking into account that he was an Acholi in a most prominent position and knowing how much Amin resented him, I reckon that Amin would have sought some way of liquidating him even if the bishops had not sent their letter* [italics mine].[186]

Muhima recognised that it was the total identity of Luwum that led to his death, and therefore concluded that he was a Christian martyr. But Muhima, like Pirouet exonerates Luwum of any subversive political activity except for his avowed boldness to stand for the truth, because "he could not involve himself in matters that were of a political nature."[187] My contention is that it was precisely because of Luwum's faith and leadership concerns that he may have considered supporting the use of force to stay Idi Amin's carnage.

It is not necessary to rehearse the argument that locates Luwum's death to his Acholi roots, particularly given his prominence as the Archbishop of the Church of Uganda. Kevin Ward has made the case for this eloquently.[188] The contention here is that a discussion of Luwum's death should also consider it from Luwum's perspective. It emerges that a crucial factor is his Revival heritage, with its Cross-inspired sense of mission, openness and courage. This courage is what prevented him from fleeing, in spite of his wife's bidding and therefore led him to his violent death. Luwum brought the values of Revival beyond the fields of personal piety to the arena of state-sponsored tyranny and violence. In a sense Revival ethos led

---

186. Ibid., 108.
187. Ibid., 107.
188. Ward, "The Church in Uganda," 83–87.

him beyond itself, to considering involvement in a "political" act, in the spirit and power of the Cross.

A relevant digression to the story of Dietrich Bonhoeffer in Germany, during the Hitler regime in the 1930s and early 1940s, will shed some light on what might have inspired Luwum to support clandestine activity against Amin's regime.[189] Although the historical contexts of both men are very different, there are cords of similarity in their progression from a pacifist, non-resisting posture to one of outright opposition.

The carnage and injustice against the Jewish people inspired Bonhoeffer's mission of mobilizing the confessing church as a resistance movement against the German State. He believed that there is a point where a church needs to consider the option of resistance, in a situation where the state had lost its legitimacy. As early as April 1933, after it became clear to him that Hitler was developing a program to oppress the Jews, he expressed this conviction on "the Church and the Jewish Question":

> The state, which endangers the Christian proclamation, negates itself. That opens up three possibilities for action by the church against the state: first . . . asking the state whether its actions are legitimate . . . Secondly, helping the victims of state action . . . The third possibility is not to tie the victim to the wheel but actually to destroy the spokes of the wheel. Such a course would involve the church in direct political action.[190]

Bonhoeffer was convinced that it was the responsibility of the church to act in defence of the defenceless, failure of which demanded repentance. When in 1938 it was evident to him that the regime was not relenting in its brutality and its project to exterminate the Jewish population, Bonhoeffer decided to work under cover to overthrow the regime. To do anything less would have been tantamount to conniving with evil. When plans were advanced to overthrow the government in 1940, Bonhoeffer wrote:

---

189. When Amin broke off diplomatic relations with Israel and embarked on a diplomatic crusade among African nations to isolate Israel, he likened his mission that he considered as heroic to Hitler's crusade to exterminate the Jews. Reference to this is made in the portion of the "Telegram from Idi Amin Dada to Dr Kurt Waldheim, Secretary General of the United Nations," 11 September 1972, in W. Kato, *Escape from Kampala*, 87.
190. Dietrich Bonhoeffer, quoted in Eberhard Bethge et al., eds., *Dietrich Bonhoeffer: A Life in Pictures* (London: SCM Press, 1986), 106.

> The church confesses that she has witnessed the lawless application of brutal force, the physical and spiritual suffering of countless innocent people, oppression, hatred and murder, and that she has not raised her voice on behalf of the victims and has not found ways to hasten to their aid. She is guilty of the deaths of the weakest and most defenceless brothers of Jesus Christ.[191]

His involvement in clandestine activity to assassinate Hitler and overthrow the regime was his way of raising his "voice on behalf of the victims." It is noteworthy that this was the same Bonhoeffer who in 1936 had, after much agonizing, come to the conclusion that "Christian pacifism dawned on me as being a matter of course, though shortly beforehand I had passionately fought against it."[192] My contention is that Luwum, like Bonhoeffer, had come to the conclusion that Amin's regime had forfeited any moral legitimacy and therefore had to be removed.

Granted that in Idi Amin's eyes, Luwum was guilty as a political criminal, and therefore condemned to a criminal's death "Amin-style." In that sense Luwum should be numbered among the hundreds of thousands of political martyrs who perished, having been judged by Amin and his terror apparatus as criminals. Luwum himself was not a politician by vocation, nor did he consider himself one; but his words and actions had serious political implications. Thus Mamdani could credit Luwum's death not to devout Christianity, but rather to ardent nationalism.[193] It is in the same vein that Ward's ethnic argument helps in understanding Luwum's death from the standpoint of the Amin regime. However from the perspective of Luwum, credit must be given to the sum total of his Acholi-Christian-leader identity. From this perspective there is no need to dichotomize Christianity and nationalism as Mamdani does, but rather in recognition that Luwum's Acholi-Christian heritage is what explains his nationalism.

---

191. Ibid., 184.
192. Ibid., 84.
193. Mamdani Mahmood, *Imperialism and Fascism in Uganda* (Nairobi: Heinemann, 1983), 56.

One other point to note about Luwum's criminal death: it authenticated his ministry. He shared in "the suffering of his flock."[194] In seeking to serve those under his care, he suffered what they suffered. Effective ministry is exercised in "sharing." The critical preposition that defines ministry is not "over" or "to," but "with," for the minister "stands with," "walks with," "prays with," "mourns with," "suffers with" and "dies with" the flock.

But ministry must go beyond authenticity to efficacy in order for it to be accorded the credit of being Christian; that is, beyond solidarity and identification to suffering service. Identification is not a mark of Christian faith, but an affirmation of the common and shared experience of the church community with those outside it, those "of the world." If Luwum's death were only about identification, it would be counted as one of many – neither the first nor the last – at the hands of the brutal regime. It is Luwum's sense and consciousness of mission, expressed in the phrase "save Uganda," that accords him a place on the roll of the martyrs of the Christian faith.

---

194. Okoth, OI. Okoth believed that this is one of the reasons for the significance of Luwum's death in the Church of Uganda.

CHAPTER 6

The Church in the Obote II Regime, 1981–1985

One of the enduring lessons from the story of the Church of Uganda is that the narrative of any church is incomplete without the account of the historical context in which the church is being formed. Hence, the tensions within the Church during the late 1960s lessened in the 1970s, giving way to a new sense of unity, as a result of the suffering experienced in the whole Church during the Idi Amin regime. However when a combined military force of Tanzanian troops and Ugandan rebel forces overthrew Idi Amin's regime in April 1979, the socio-political scene was radically transformed. The period of political instability that followed resurrected old cleavages in Ugandan society and gave rise to new ones. The Church reconfigured in this new milieu. This chapter focuses on the story of the Church in the post-Amin era, during the Obote-UPC regime, from 1980 to 1985.[1]

---

1. Between April 1979 and December 1980 there were three governments under the banner of Uganda National Liberation Front (UNLF) until the general elections in December 1980. Y. Lule led the first government. He was the Chairman of UNLF elected at the Moshi Conference in March 1979. His government lasted 68 days. G. Binaisa who lasted less than a year succeeded Lule. The military commission under the leadership of Paul Muwanga, which organised the 1980 elections, led the third government. For an account of these UNLF governments: Karugire, *Roots of Instability*, 85–88; Mutibwa, *Uganda since Independence*, 125–147; Omara-Otunnu, *Politics and the Military*, 145–156. The 1980 elections ushered in what has come to be known as the Obote II regime. During the same period what was termed the "liberation war" was continuing in the Eastern and Northern parts of the country. As expected, the greatest resistance to the liberation forces after the fall of Kampala, was in the West Nile region, Amin's home, and home to most of his loyal troops. The Acholi and Langi in the liberation forces extensively destroyed life and property in Arua, avenging themselves for the atrocities against them and their people during the Amin regime. The most severe massacre was in October 1980. It was not possible to do research in West Nile, due to insecurity and rebel war in the

233

During this period an anti-government armed rebellion emerged, based in much of Buganda. The insurgency and counter-insurgency measures created a displaced and traumatized population in an area of Buganda that became known as "Luwero Triangle."[2] Following the declaration of Obote and UPC as winners of the December 1980 elections, an insurgency broke out. Obote's assumption of government leadership was, for the people of Buganda, for whom the memory of the ruthless deposition of their Kabaka and the demise of their kingdom was still fresh, a "bad dream"[3] becoming reality. Buganda became a base for an anti-Obote campaign, led by Yoweri Museveni.[4]

As the story unfolds, three issues will be identified that are key to understanding the nature of the turbulence in the Obote II regime. First, the dissension that surrounded the person of Obote in the alignment of political forces at the time, and the resurgence of the "northern question." Second, the strategic role of Buganda in the anti-Obote campaign. Third, the dislocation and traumatization of an entire rural population in the Luwero Triangle. These factors are also central in shaping the story of the Church during this period,[5] as reflected in the life of the Church at both national

---

region at the time of field research 1993–96. For some detailed discussion on this period, see: Gingyera-Pinycwa, "Is There a Northern Question?," 54–55; Mutibwa, *Uganda since Independence*, 137–138.

2. The area where the war was mostly concentrated was called "triangle" because its three boundaries formed a triangular shape. The boundaries were: Kampala-Luwero-Gulu road, Kampala-Mityana-Mubende road and River Kafu (see Map 3, Luwero Triangle and Neighbouring Districts, p 237).

3. This is how historian P. Mutibwa described it in *Uganda since Independence*, 149.

4. Although there were two other rebel groups based in Buganda, the Uganda Freedom Movement (UFM) led by Andrew Kayira and the Federal Democratic Movement (FEDEMU) led by Nkwanga, the National Resistance Movement (NRM) and its military arm the National Resistance Army (NRA) emerged as the strongest and most organised group. The NRM was formed out of a merger in June 1981 between the Popular Resistance Army (PRA) led by Y Museveni and the Uganda Freedom Fighters (UFF) led by the first post-Amin President Yusuf Lule. The Uganda National Rescue Front (UNRF) led by Moses Ali operated from West Nile and across the Sudan border. Yoweri K. Museveni, *Sowing the Mustard Seed: The Struggle for Freedom and Democracy in Uganda* (London: Macmillan Publishers, 1997), 140–143.

5. The major sources for this are: Bishop Misaeri Kawuma, OI, Nsangi, Kampala, 20 April 1997; Amunoni Salongo Mujabi, Kiwoko, Luwero 20 September 1995; Bishop Yokana Mukasa, OI, Kampala, 24 April, 1997. Daudi Serubidde "The Pastor's Experience," Kampala, unpublished manuscript, 1992. This is an important source, because Serubidde was Archdeacon of Luwero, the most senior Church leader based in the area through most

and regional levels. At the national level, the election of Yona Okoth, a long time associate of Obote, as Archbishop of the Church of Uganda in 1984, focuses on the Obote factor in the Church. At the regional level, the solidarity that developed between the Church in Buganda and the Roman Catholic Church, set against the absence of such a relationship between the Church in Buganda and the rest of the Church, indicating a lack of a national consciousness in the Church as a whole. The initiatives by the bishops of Namirembe and Lango dioceses towards reconciliation reflect the continuing search of a national consciousness of a church in a Uganda torn apart by conflicting social-political agendas.

The story of the Church in Luwero during the war highlights the significant role played by catechists and the priority of the pastoral dimension of ministry over priesthood in the indigenization of the worship, mission and ministry of the Church in a turbulent context.

The chapter concludes with some reflection on the ecclesiological issues that emerge during the period, which include: turbulence as an element in redefining the Church's self-consciousness and identity; the "catechist" as "pastor" *de facto*; the subordination of the canonical ministerial order of bishop-priest-deacon to pastor-ship; and, the notion of "sacrament" in a turbulent context.

The "Bandits" War in the Luwero Triangle

On 6 February 1981 a rebel platoon of twenty-seven soldiers under the command of Yoweri Museveni attacked Kabamba School of Infantry. They overran the barracks, captured a few guns and vehicles, and sped with their loot into the bush. With this attack, Museveni with his platoon launched a military resistance and campaign against the elected government of Milton Obote that had been sworn in only two months before.[6] Henceforth, until

---

of the war period. "The Pastor's Experience" is an autobiography, and has a large section focusing on his experience and that of the Church during the war.

6. Two authoritative sources of the Luwero Triangle war are: (1) National Resistance Movement, *Mission to Freedom: The Story of NRM-NRA* (Kampala: NRM Secretariat, 1990). This is a compendium of *The Uganda Resistance News* from 1981-1985. The Uganda Resistance News was the official newsletter of NRM-NRA, edited, printed and circulated clandestinely, except in foreign capitals and in the bush where NRA was in control. (2) Museveni, *Sowing the Mustard Seed*. This is the autobiography of

the overthrow of Obote and his government in 1985, the government referred to Museveni and his National Resistance Army (NRA) as bandits and the NRA also referred to the government troops as bandits.[7]

From the small beginning of the Kabamba attack, the areas of conflict expanded and by the beginning of 1983, the whole of Luwero, Mubende and Mpigi districts and as well as parts of Mukono, were engulfed in war;[8] an area later referred to as the Luwero Triangle. (See Map 3, The Luwero Triangle and Neighbouring Districts, p. 237.) By the beginning of 1985 the rebel force had grown from its small platoon of twenty-seven at the Kabamba attack with only twenty-seven rifles, to a full army of six battalions with 1,800 guns.[9] Throughout that period rebel forces continued with their offensive, except for a brief period in 1981 to allow for the Tanzanian troops to withdraw from Uganda. But the government troops made four major offensives: one in 1981 with some support from the Tanzanian troops; two others in 1982 and 1983 led by Oyite Ojok;[10] and the fourth led by Ogole, an Iteso, which started late in 1984 through to mid-1985. This last one was the largest offensive, but it occurred at a time when there were rifts in the army command structure among the Acholi and Langi.

Yoweri K. Museveni, the one who led the campaign and resistance against the Obote/UPC government.

7. *Uganda Times,* 1 April 1981; *Uganda Times,* 24 October 1981; *Uganda Times,* 6 February1982; *Uganda Times,* 2 March 1982; National Resistance Movement, *Mission to Freedom,* 12, 75, 147–149. Rebels also referred to the government troops as "Oboteist soldiers" or just "Obote's soldiers," Museveni, *Sowing the Mustard Seed* 154–155.

8. Museveni, *Sowing the Mustard Seed,* 136–173. Museveni chronicles the growth and expansion of his forces, and the geographical area under their control.

9. Ibid., 163.

10. Oyite Ojok who was the Army Chief of Staff and the closest to Obote of all the commanders died during this offensive in December 1983. The rebel forces claimed they had brought down his helicopter. National Resistance Movement, *Mission to Freedom,* 196–199.

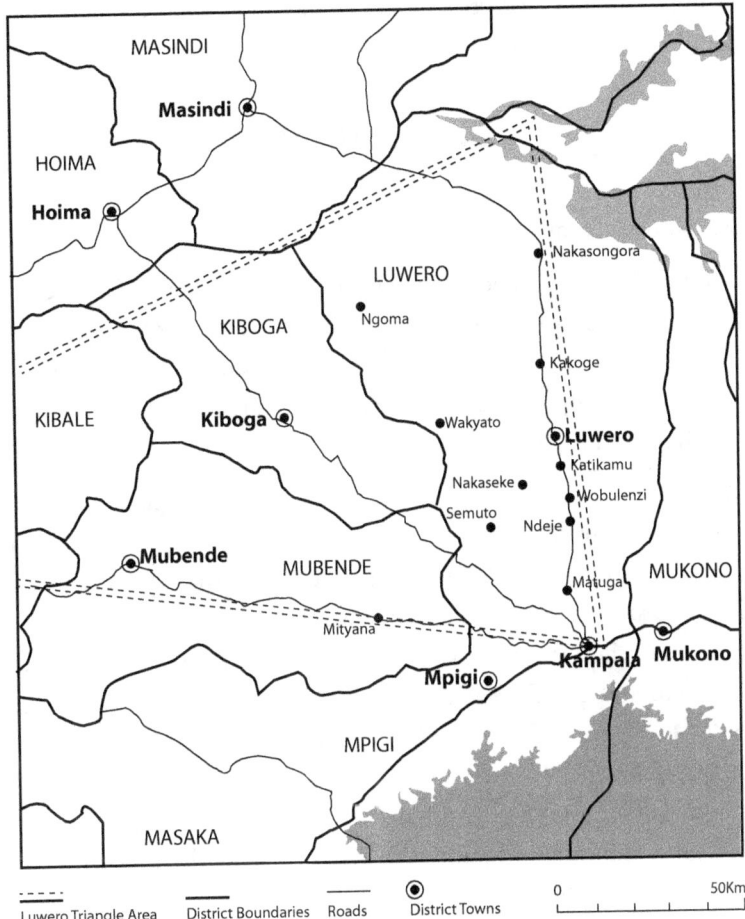

Map 3: The Luwero Triangle and Neighbouring Districts

For those five years, based in the Luwero Triangle, Museveni and his rebel army waged a "protracted people's war," a three-phased strategy aimed at the removal of Obote: "guerrilla warfare, mobile warfare and finally conventional warfare."[11] The turbulence caused by this war was manifested in the anarchy and tension in Kampala, massive people movements and displacements in the Luwero Triangle and neighbouring districts into camps,

---

11. National Resistance Movement, *Mission to Freedom*, 9.

with the accompanying destruction of all social institutions in the area, and thousands of deaths, particularly in the Luwero Triangle.

Roots of the War

The reasons for taking up arms against the government were given by Museveni, then commander of rebel forces:

> Obote and his henchmen rigged the December 1980 elections. UPC came into power by fraud. We believed the elections would be free and fair, but this was not the case. So we had to take up arms against Obote and start a struggle against Obote and his government.[12]

Although Museveni and his group put forward the rigging of the 1980 elections as the primary reason for going to the bush,[13] the controversial election results only detonated a time bomb that had been planted in the process of amalgamating all the anti-Amin forces. All the major contestants of the December 1980 elections, that is, Obote and the UPC; Ssemogerere and the DP; and Museveni and his newly formed Uganda People's Movement (UPM),[14] had a predetermined result arising from contradicting analyses of Uganda's political landscape.

Obote and the UPC considered and prided themselves as the major Ugandan military and political force leading to the overthrow of the Amin regime, and therefore saw the winning of the elections as a deserved reward for their liberation efforts. During the political campaigns leading to the December 1980 elections, one of the arguments that Obote put forward was that none of his opponents could boast of a significant

---

12. Museveni in *Mission to Freedom*, 63.

13. This was the most popularly held view at the time and was also put forward by some authors, notably Mutibwa, *Uganda since Independence*, 51. My considered view is that the issue was the Obote factor in the post-independence political developments in Uganda, an argument developed in the next section, thereby laying ground for the developments in the Church, in particular the election of Y. Okoth as Archbishop, and the Church during the Teso-based rebellion.

14. Obote, Ssemwogerere and Museveni were the leaders of UPC, DP and UPM, respectively, contesting for post of President of Uganda, in their capacities as leaders of parties. The other contestant was Mayanja-Nkangi, and his Conservative Party (CP) that was in many ways a minor, with its historic base as the Kabaka Yekka.

military contribution to the liberation struggle. He would always chide Ssemogerere, then leader of the DP, and his party, to display their army.[15] Similarly he would challenge Museveni, who was known to have contributed to the liberation forces, to display his commanders.[16] Moreover, although Tanzania had provided ammunition and troops that constituted the largest component of the liberation forces, Obote and his group were convinced that the support had been rendered on Obote's ticket.

The Democratic Party counted on the Catholic and Buganda vote and predetermined that on the basis of sheer numbers, they would win the election. The Catholic Church commanded a following of about 40 percent of the population, and Buganda is the largest region of the four: Western, Northern, Eastern and Buganda. Museveni and his Uganda Patriotic Movement also held this view, but they were sceptical about DP's capacity to retain power because they felt that DP's leadership had ideological limitations.[17] In Museveni's words:

> It was clear that two scenarios were emerging. One was that the UPC would rig the elections and claim victory. They would be in a position to sustain that claim with the support of the armed groups under their influence. The other possibility was that the DP, reinforced by the many people who had been disenchanted with the UPC over the years, would win the elections, but they would have to contend with the real possibility of a military coup.[18]

According to Museveni, the UPM and the DP, the only way UPC could win the elections was by fraud. In keeping with his analysis, Museveni was against holding the elections because "the political problems the country faced could not be solved merely by the exercise of holding an election."[19]

The two causal factors, for the bush war were Obote and the military, and these two were hand in glove. In the period running up to the overthrow of

---

15. Mutibwa, *Uganda since Independence*, 150.
16. Adoko, *From Obote to Obote*, 302.
17. Museveni, *Sowing the Mustard Seed*, 117.
18. Ibid.
19. Ibid., 118.

the Idi Amin regime, political and military organization revolved around the person of Obote. On the one hand was Obote's return to Uganda and the pro-Obote troops in the liberation forces; and on the other, the two groups that constituted the Uganda National Liberation Army (UNLA) were built on a pro-Obote, anti-Obote basis. The pro-Obote force, the Kikoosi Maalum (KM), was built from the remnants of the pro-Obote/UPC troops in the first UPC government, 1962–1971. Acholi and Langi predominantly constituted this faction of the UNLA, and were led by Tito Okello. Museveni led the anti-Obote faction of the Front for National Salvation (FRONASA).[20] Obote became a critical factor in the political and military equation at the time. He was kept out of the Moshi Unity Conference in March 1979 for fear that he would be a divisive factor.[21]

The Obote-factor determined to a large extent the alignment and re-alignment of political forces in the immediate post-Amin administrations.[22] His shadow seemed to haunt Lule, the first post-Amin President. Museveni, an insider then, as Minister of Defence, believes that one of Lule's problems was "his morbid fear of and ignorance about Obote in particular, and the northerners in general."[23] Among other reasons for the deposition of Binaisa from presidency was his attempt to block Obote's return to power as President, by seeking to outlaw political parties.[24] But he could not implement his agenda because he had no military support. Omara-Otunnu expresses the point succinctly:

> The crucial point is that, in the struggle for power, no single group could prevail unless it had the backing, even if only tacit, of the military. The military had become the final arbiter of power. This became very clear in the events surrounding

---

20. Museveni admits that it is those who were not ready to work with Obote that formed FRONASA. Ibid., 54.
21. Ibid., 104.
22. D. Mudoola makes this point in his essay "Political Transitions since Idi Amin: A Study in Political Pathology," in *Uganda Now: Between Decay and Development*, eds. Holger B. Hansen, and Michael Twaddle (London: James Currey, 1988), 280–298.
23. Museveni, *Sowing the Mustard Seed*, 110.
24. Mutibwa, *Uganda since Independence*, 134–136.

The Church in the Obote II Regime, 1981–1985

the removal of Lule and the installation of Binaisa as his replacement.[25]

Obote's return from exile therefore in May 1980 focused and heightened the anti- and pro-Obote contest. The climax was the December 1980 elections.

Obote and the pro-Obote dominated command structure of the UNLA were the reason for the discredited elections as fraudulent. As already indicated, Museveni could not believe any results that declared Obote as winner. In his view Obote was one of the causes for pitfalls in the political formation of Uganda[26] and therefore it was hoped that the elections would send Obote to political oblivion through a decisive vote against him. Museveni believed that it was not only him who wanted to fight Obote, but that:

> The Ugandan people had hoped to defeat Obote through the ballot box and formed a great anti-Obote coalition involving the original members of the DP, mostly Catholics, those who belonged to Kabaka Yekka, those who had deserted the UPC, and those who had no political affiliation. All these factions chose the DP as the easiest political defence against the threat of Obote's return to power.[27]

However these hopes were frustrated because, as Museveni later admitted, the Military Commission that organized the elections was predominantly pro-Obote. Museveni observed that:

> Two clear forces now emerged on the Military Commission. Numerically we were in a minority on the Commission because I was the only active anti-Obote member. Paul Muwanga, Oyite Ojok and William Omaria were pro-Obote. The other two, Tito Okello and Col Zed Maruru, while not

---

25. Omara-Otunnu, *Politics and the Military*, 148.
26. Museveni's aversion for Obote dates as far back as 1966 and this was what motivated him to acquire the necessary military skills to break his monopoly. Museveni, *Sowing the Mustard Seed*, 32.
27. Ibid., 115.

necessarily pro-Obote, were not actively against him either. So I was left alone to hold the line against Obote.[28]

When Obote was declared the winner of the elections, by the pro-Obote Military Commission – a verdict deemed by the Commonwealth Observer Group to be the result of "a valid electoral exercise which should broadly reflect the freely expressed choice of the people of Uganda,"[29] Museveni moved the contest to the bush, to wage an "anti-Obote struggle."[30] The most logical base for such a struggle was Buganda, Obote's archenemy territory, a fertile ground for an anti-Obote campaign because of the events of mid-1960s that saw the deposition of the Kabaka, and the destruction of an institution that defined Buganda's identity. Mutibwa has rightly observed that Obote and the UPC government

> did not have the support of those who mattered, particularly in Central Uganda which was the heart of the nation containing the capital. It soon became clear that, like in the late 1960s, Obote's regime operated from within an enemy's camp, surrounded by hostile Baganda with whom he had now established a relationship of intense mutual suspicion and hatred.[31]

It was hatred for Obote that defined the character of the rebellion. It was the obsession "to remove this evil man, root and branch, from the political life of Uganda, for good"[32] that inspired the merger of Museveni's Popular Resistance Army and Lule's Uganda Freedom Fighters to form the National Resistance Movement.

Conversely, it was commitment to Obote that would determine the success or failure of ending the rebellion. Obote and his government

---

28. Ibid.
29. The Commonwealth Observer Group, *Uganda Elections, December 1980: The Report of the Commonwealth Observer Group* (London: Commonwealth Secretariat, 1980), 4. Archbishop Silvanus Wani is reported to have congratulated Obote on his victory after the "free and fair elections." *Uganda Times*, 12 June 1981.
30. Museveni, *Sowing the Mustard Seed*, 112. The three chapters in his *Sowing the Mustard Seed*, in which Museveni discusses the Luwero war, are headed "Fighting Obote," a clear indication what the war was about. Ibid., 121–173.
31. Mutibwa, *Uganda since Independence*, 149.
32. Lule in his letter to the Commonwealth Prime Ministers and Heads of Government reproduced in *Mission to Freedom*, 31.

therefore needed a loyal military force, which he embarked on building. The most logical place to turn to was Teso, to build on his Acholi and Langi based army.

First of all, Teso was one of the areas in Uganda where Obote and the UPC already enjoyed most popular support. Second, the Iteso were in a state of despair over the Karimajong cattle rustlers from the north, who were now more effective thanks to the firearms that they had looted from Moroto barracks when Idi Amin took over in 1971.[33] The Iteso were therefore eager to acquire the skills and instruments of violence to counteract these Karimajong rustlers. So they joined the military in large numbers and Obote used them in particular to build the Special Force, a specially trained police force to deal with the insurgency and rebellion in Luwero Triangle.

Obote's government also built a para-military organization, the National Security Service (NASA), a counter-intelligence force to weed out of the civilian population any rebel supporters and to look out for disaffection in the army. It is not a wonder that the demise of the Obote regime was sparked off by a crack in the loyalty of the troops, a cleavage along Acholi-Langi lines sparked off by the death in a helicopter crash of his most trusted commander, Oyite Ojok a Langi. His replacement by another Langi, Smith Opon-Ocak, caused disaffection among top Acholi commanders, leading to the military coup of August 1985 led by the two top Acholi commanders, Tito Okello and Bajilio Okello.[34]

It is difficult to ascertain to what extent the "northern question"[35] was in play in the emergence of the bush war. What is evident is that it was part

---

33. Charles Ocan discusses this in his paper "The Political Situation in Teso" presented at the Seminar on the Political and Economic Situation in Uganda, at the Commonwealth Institute, London, June 1992, 2. CBR Archives, PF 320.9 OCA (1992) 1. We shall return to this subject in the next chapter when we look at the Teso-based rebellion against the NRM/A regime of Y. Museveni.
34. Mutibwa, *Uganda since Independence*, 160–165; also Omara-Otunnu, *Politics and the Military*, 160–165.
35. The "northern question" like the "Buganda question" is about the special role of northern Uganda, covering the areas of Acholi, Lango and West Nile, in the socio-political history of Uganda. It is discussed in detailed by A. G. Gingyera-Pinycwa in his two works: "Is there a Northern Question?," and *Northern Uganda in National Politics*. The "northern question" is very complex, because unlike the "Buganda question" that arose from the central role played by the kingdom of Buganda, the area described as "north," that is West Nile, Acholi and Gulu, has never had a homogenous socio-political structure.

of Museveni's analysis of Obote's dominance of Uganda's post-independence politics. Museveni's motivation to develop FRONASA was partly to provide "balance" in the UNLA against the northern dominated KM. Museveni was convinced that:

> Obote was unable to come to terms with the idea of a non-northern army because his tenure of power had been based on manipulating that factor. He had based his rule on an Acholi-Langi army with a scattering of other northern peoples. They had monopolised all access to the instruments of force and thus ensured his undemocratic hold on power.[36]

Among the Baganda as well, there was a northern-southern consciousness in their perception of the war. In Singo, for example, Mukibi observed an anti-northern mentality, that:

> Because the UNLA soldiers were mostly drawn from the northern part of the country, the people, because of the intense anger, generalised that all the Northern people were bad. The blame of all inhuman acts has been put not only to those who committed them but even their fellow tribesmen. So sentiments of hate and desire to revenge have been directed to all, and not those who are responsible.[37]

Some authors have argued that the Luwero war showed a north-south ethnic divide in Uganda, or Bantu versus Lwo.[38] In my view the real rift was between Buganda and the north and not a general north-south divide because there was a substantial Bantu leadership that opposed the Museveni rebellion.[39] The war recreated the question of the existence of a

---

36. Museveni, *Sowing the Mustard Seed*, 103.
37. Paul Mukibi, "The Impact of the Guerrilla War (1981–5) and the Challenge of Rehabilitation for the Church in Kiboga Area Singo Uganda," Makerere University, Kampala, DipTh dissertation, 1987, 28.
38. Among them are Mutibwa, *Uganda since Independence*, 16–163, and Omara-Otunnu, *Politics and the Military*, 176.
39. The NASA was led by a fellow Munyankole, C. Rwakasisi, and was dominated by Banyankole.

distinct northern Uganda from a southern Uganda, which became a causal factor in subsequent rebellions.[40]

The Impact of the War

In the capital Kampala, fear and tension gripped the population as the war was going on in the bush. NASA, the government security agency, under the directorship of Chris Rwakasisi,[41] was active in arresting and detaining any suspected to be collaborators with the rebels. Nile Mansions, the 4-star hotel adjoining the International Conference Centre in Kampala, became one of the interrogation and torture centres.[42] The barracks at Mbuya, Lubiri, Makindye and Kireka were the major detention centres. Operations were set up at random to search for guns in an area, and hundreds of arrests made, usually on a tip that there were rebels in an area. Insecurity in the city rose with several armed robberies and deaths. Roadblocks were set up all over the city and countryside to arrest "bandits," but these became places of torture. At the slight suspicion that one may have some connection with Museveni or the rebels, he or she was picked up and taken away, some never to be seen again.

Throughout the war period the people in the area were constantly on the move. This led to displacement and depopulation of entire villages, and the establishment of "refugee" camps. In the first half of the period of the war, 1981 to mid-1983, people just fled for their lives, escaping from either the rebels or the government troops. On the one hand there were those who were not supportive of the rebels, who therefore became targets of their fury. On the other were those who supported the rebellion, and either joined the rebel front or supported it from the sidelines. This was the

---

40. Gingyera-Pinycwa, in his book *Northern Uganda in National Politics*, has argued that the distinction northern-southern originated in the colonial period, and was entrenched in people's minds by the dominant role played by northerners in the political and military leadership of the country. He has located the cause for the emergence of the armed rebellions against the NRA/M government that developed after 1986 to this divide.
41. Chris Rwakasisi was a Minister of State in the Office of the President in charge of security.
42. National Resistance Movement, *Mission to Freedom*, 99, 215. Other interrogation centres were at Afro Motors, Milton Obote Foundation offices in Industrial area, Uganda House, Argentina House, and the State Security Centre at Nakasero.

majority. As Baganda, they were natural allies with the rebels because of the grudge they still held against Obote over the deposition of their Kabaka in 1966. Part of the reason for their enthusiastic support for Museveni was the hope that once he brought down Obote's rule he would restore the Kingdom of Buganda.[43] Kyakulagira, from his research in Luwero, observed that:

> Since the Baganda had had a long hatred for Obote, it was not difficult to be convinced and take action. On getting convinced, the teachers [in schools] extended the same to secondary school students. This resulted into many schools loosing teachers and students to the guerrillas in the bush. The elderly peasants who could not join actively gave their support through providing food and information. This promoted guerrilla activity greatly and steadily.[44]

There were many in the Church in Luwero who were convinced that the Museveni rebellion had God's stamp of approval, and therefore worked to support it. One such was Yedediya Kayima, a Mulokole and resident of Matuga, one of the operational areas in Luwero triangle. When Museveni, with a group of about forty other rebels, came to Kayima's home,[45] Kayima felt obliged to provide for their needs, having been convinced that their mission was a worthy cause for peace. He had first carefully weighed the options before him: he could report them to the authorities, which would be detrimental for them; or he could have declined giving them any help and they would go away hungry. Kayima's judgement was that neither of these options was worthy of consideration by a man of his standing as a Mulokole. So after Museveni outlined to him the nature of their mission, he was convinced that their cause was worthy of his support and blessing of as "a man of God."[46] Kayima and his wife cooked for the group and prayed

---

43. Daudi Serubidde, OI, Namirembe, Kampala, 17 January 1995; and Yedediya Kayima, OI, Mengo, Kampala, 29 April 1997.
44. S. K. Kyakulagira, "The Work of the Church in Luwero C.O.U. Archdeaconry, Uganda during the Guerrilla War 1981–1986," Makerere University Kampala, unpublished Diploma dissertation, 1988, 12.
45. Kayima, OI.
46. Museveni, *Sowing the Mustard Seed*, 132. Museveni acknowledges that Kayima was a keen supporter of the rebellion.

for them that God might bless their mission. The basis of Kayima's support to Museveni and his group was his judgement that Museveni's mission was identifiable with the will of God.

This kind of support was crucial for the rebels but endangered the population. In outlining the strategy of the protracted people's war, Museveni clearly stated that one of the objectives of the NRM was "to enlist the participation of the citizenry in the conduct of the war."[47] From the government perspective it was not possible to distinguish a "bandit" from a regular civilian, since the rebel army had the support of the civilian population. Therefore government troops targeted both the rebel army and citizenry because both were perceived as enemies to the Obote regime. The experience was often bitter and entire populations had to abandon their villages, fleeing from an army that was unleashed against them. Their first stop was either a religious centre or the urban areas, where there was better security, food and medicinal provisions.[48]

During 1983 most of the rural populations were moved to live in camps. Ironically, both the government troops and the rebels were keen that the people should evacuate their villages. The idea of camps as a scheme by government had two purposes. First, it would isolate rebels from the civilian population, since by the very act of evacuating villages, it was implied that anyone who stayed there was part of the rebel group. Second, by herding the entire civilian population into camps, they curtailed any involvement or support by the civilian population for the rebel army. In June and July 1983 government troops forcibly evacuated people to camps.

As government troops were forcibly evacuating the villages, the rebels too were evacuating people in the areas under their control. For the rebel army it was expedient for strategic reasons to retain in the war areas only those who were active in the war as combatants. As outlined by Museveni:

> Firstly, it would allow us to concentrate our forces for offensive operations against the enemy, instead of being forced to scatter our few rifles to try and protect the population, which

---

47. National Resistance Movement, *Mission to Freedom*, 255.
48. Elias L. Kizito, "The Church of Uganda's Role towards the Displaced Christians in Mityana Diocese 1980–1984," Makerere University, Kampala, unpublished Diploma in Theology dissertation, 1984, 13–14; and Kyakulagira, "The Work of the Church," 18–21.

we would not be able to do effectively because we could not stop the UNLA from penetrating the Luwero Triangle. . . .

Secondly, a depopulated Luwero Triangle would starve the enemy of information. Although the people supported us, and were reluctant to give information about us to the enemy, Obote's thugs could always extract it through torture.

Finally, a less populated operational zone would reduce the need for the supply of food and medicines.[49]

By the end of the year most of rural Luwero Triangle was depopulated. People were herded in refugee camps scattered all over the Triangle.[50]

Life in these camps was anything but bearable. Serubidde and Kyakulagira, both of whom had a first hand knowledge of their condition, have called them "concentration camps,"[51] reminiscent of the Nazi Germany during the Second World War, because of the suffering of the people. According to Serubidde the government army administration "regarded the detainees (sic) in the camps either as guerrillas (*abayeekera*) or at least suspected them of being guerrilla sympathisers."[52] Therefore the "concentration camps" became synonymous with "detention" camps, guarded heavily by troops. It was as though the civilian population that was always held suspect of supporting the rebels was now held as prisoners of war. Women of all ages were raped.[53] The people were kept hungry deliberately with hundred starving to death. The sheer numbers turned the camps into

---

49. Museveni, *Sowing the Mustard Seed*, 152.
50. Kizito, "The Church of Uganda's Role," 25; Kyakulagira, "The Work of the Church," 28; and Serubidde, "The Pastor's Experience," 76–93. There were camps at: Wabusana, Nakaseke, Katooke, Kibisi, Ndejje, Kikyusa, Kapeeka, Semuto, Kalega, Bakijjulula, Nakkazi, Luwero town, Kakooge in Luwero; Bukoomero, Sinde, Lwamata, Kiboga, Kikandwa, Busunju, Mityana Hospital, Kabulamuliro, Kakiinzi, Temanakali, Namigavu, Kateera, Kanziira, and Kigwanya in Mubende. In Mubende District the Probation officer's estimates of the numbers of people in the camps put them at about a quarter of a million, 65% of the population of the district. Kizito, "The Church of Uganda's Role," 22–25.
51. Serubidde, OI, Namirembe Kampala, 12 September 1995; Kyakulagira, "The Work of the Church," 28.
52. Serubidde, "The Pastor's Experience," 79.
53. Kyakulagira tells of one incident when several soldiers raped a mother, and a daughter of 18 years, in the presence of the latter's two younger brothers. Kyakulagira, "The Work of the Church," 15–16.

health hazards. Those who were lucky escaped to neighbouring peaceful districts where they lived as refugees.

The fact that Acholi and Langi dominated the UNLA, which was perceived to be primarily responsible for the suffering and misery of the Baganda in Luwero triangle, added to the traditional anti-Obote sentiment and hostility and bitterness towards the Langi and Acholi among the Baganda.[54] The war, however, extended the borders of their hatred for Obote to include all the people who hailed from the northern region of Uganda. The perception of the Baganda was that their suffering and misery, since the war at Mengo in 1966, was inflicted on them by "northerners," a reference to the people from the areas of West Nile, Acholi, and Lango. The Baganda held the "northerners" responsible for the attack on the Lubiri in 1966, because of the roles played by Obote and Amin, both from the north. The dominant role of the Nubi and Kakwa, also categorized as northerners among some sections of Buganda, in the Idi Amin regime, was judged to be the cause of carnage of the regime.[55] Consequently, the "northerners" were stereotyped as cruel and anti-Baganda among the Baganda, breeding feelings of bitterness and revenge.[56]

The "Skulls of Luwero"[57]

It is estimated that hundreds of thousands perished in Luwero triangle during the war. Some have put the estimates as high as three hundred thousand.[58] Although the National Resistance Movement government wanted the world to believe that the Obote regime and government troops were to blame for each one of the "Luwero skulls" as they displayed them in the

---

54. Kawuma, OI.
55. Ibid.
56. Ibid.
57. During the early years of the NRM regime, 1986–90 thousands of skulls were displayed by the government to show the extent of the atrocities of the Obote regime against the people of Luwero. The reference "the Skulls of Luwero" was adopted as reference to those who died in the Luwero Triangle war. Mutibwa, *Uganda since Independence*, 160; and Peter Otai, "Uganda: The Skulls of Luwero and the Legacy of Terror," October 1988, Unpublished document, available in CBR Archives PF 320.9 OTA (1992), 1.
58. Mutibwa, *Uganda since Independence*, 159.

months following their victory in 1986, it is not possible to apportion fully who was responsible. However, five factors account for the deaths. First there are those who died in the detention camps at the hands of brutal government soldiers. In one incident, the soldiers killed a man they suspected to be a rebel supporter and asked his children to suck his blood![59]

Second there are thousands who died as a result of horrid conditions in the camps especially the elderly and children. Serubidde describes one such camp at Ndejje, which he visited in May 1983:

> First it was very huge. It consisted of over four hundred huts. Secondly, the people showed all the worst signs of having been exposed to the natural elements for some two years. The adults were in rags. Almost all the children were naked. Thirdly, no one was free to leave the camp. Soldiers were a law unto themselves. Fourthly, of course there were many deaths. Lastly, when I first visited the camp, as with all the camps I was to visit in due course, the in-mates were very glad to see a pastor (*omwawule*). They kept asking me, "*Oyise wa?*" ("How have you managed to reach us?").[60]

Third, there were many civilians whose crime was to have been in the combat area. These were shot or hacked to death while in their homes by ruthless government troops. Each time the rebel army ambushed government troops, it would be followed by massive combing by government troops of the villages surrounding the areas of the ambush, shooting at sight "anything that moves," looting, raping and killing.[61] The UNLA soldiers killed any as long as they were found in an "operational" area, even in a church building; for example the massacre in Katiiti Church in Kalasa parish Church of Uganda in January 1982, where government soldiers shot the catechist and five worshippers right in the churchyard.[62]

---

59. This is an eyewitness account by Rev Blasio Sajjabi, OI, Semuto Luwero, 20 September 1995.
60. Serubidde, "The Pastor's Experience," 78.
61. National Resistance Movement, *Mission to Freedom*, 175, 187–191; Amunoni Salongo Mujabi, OI, Kiwoko, Luwero, 20 September 1995. Mujabi told me that three of his sister's children were taken away from him and shot as he watched.
62. Serubidde, "The Pastor's Experience," 106; Kyakulagira, "The Work of the Church," 22; and National Resistance Movement, *Mission to Freedom*, 105. The rebels

Fourth, there are the hundreds of soldiers on either side who died in combat or in rebel ambushes. There were thousands of government troops that died at the hands of the rebels through ambushes and attacks on military stations and camps.[63]

And fifthly, there were hundreds killed by the rebel forces, having been judged to be collaborators with the government troops. They included any civilians who resisted incorporation into the rebel ranks and any suspected to have been informers of the government troops. Members of the UPC and local chiefs loyal to the government were especially targeted.[64] Bukenya, a rebel then, later wrote: "The Batongole, Miruka, and Gombolola chiefs had either to flee at the rise of the people's power or change for the people. There was no one with differing ideas to be tolerated. You were either for the revolution or an enemy."[65] The Rev Shem Ndyabahiika, then parish priest of Kambugu was killed by the rebels on suspicion that he was a UPC functionary and an informer of the UNLA in the area."[66]

The Luwero war claimed the lives of thousands of people and has been christened by the Luwero people as *Olutalo dekabusa*, meaning "the war that left nothing."[67]

---

had encamped temporarily in Kalasa, a village fifty kilometres north of Kampala. As government troops combed the area in search of the rebels, they found a church service in session at Katiiti Church of Uganda and the catechist preaching. They took the catechist from the pulpit, and shot him together with the five worshippers right there in the churchyard as the rest of the congregation dispersed in fear. The troops turned the Church building into a temporary barracks.

Mujabi also recalled a time during the war when Kiwoko COU was occupied by liberation forces, Amunoni Mujabi, OI, and Kyakulagira has recorded several other such incidents, in Kyakulagira, "The Work of the Church," 12–14.

63. National Resistance Movement, *Mission to Freedom*, 33–36, 59–60, 77–80, 111–116.

64. The following referred to such incidents and concur; Alex B. Bukenya, *Inside Luwero Triangle* (Kampala: Kitaka Publishing and Trading Co. Ltd. 1992), 2, 72; Kyakulagira, "The Work of the Church," 8; Henry Kampujja, OI, Nakaseke, Luwero, 20 September 1995; Amunoni Mujabi, OI; and Mukasa, OI.

65. Bukenya, *Inside Luwero Triangle*, 14–15.

66. Mukibi, "The Impact of the Guerrilla War," 38. Also Mukasa, OI.

67. Amunoni Mujabi, "*Ebyafaayo by'Olutalo Dekabusa*," Memoirs of the Luwero Triangle War, unpublished manuscript, Kiwoki, 1996 (copy in my possession); and Mujabi, OI.

"Desecration" of Ecclesial Centres

Neither the rebels nor the government troops considered clerics and ecclesial centres "too holy"[68] for their political-military adventures. On one level, it is as though the rebels took advantage of their canonical "holy" status, hoping that if they used them, the government troops would be afraid of ransacking them because of their "holiness." But the UNLA commanders soon discovered that the rebels were using them and could no longer interpret canonical holiness as neutrality in the conflict. While the rebels always hoped that the perceived neutrality and innocence of clerics and ecclesial grounds would provide "cover" for their clandestine political-military program, the government troops had long said farewell to such innocence, and were determined to do anything to uncover the rebel's clandestine activities.[69] Two incidents[70] that reflect this scenario are the "desecration of Rubaga Cathedral" and the desecration of the "Holy Shrine" at Namugongo in February 1982 and May 1984 respectively.[71]

On another level, it seems that to the clerics, the rebels and the ordinary people, the use of ecclesial centres for the promotion of the "liberation" war did not contradict canonical holiness.

In the early hours of 23 February 1982, rebel forces shelled Lubiri barracks from positions in Rubaga Cathedral grounds.[72] The government troops responded the next day by invading the Cathedral grounds. Cardinal Nsubuga recounted what followed:

---

68. "Holy" is used here to connote the notion of "separated or dedicated for religious service."

69. In reporting such incidents of government troops desecrating ecclesial centres, the NRA/M chronicler of the war, *Mission to Freedom*, gives this impression. Examples: *Mission to Freedom*, 89–93, and 206–207.

70. Kyakulagira in his dissertation, "The Work of the Church in Luwero COU Archdeaconry, Uganda during the Guerrilla War, 1981–1986," has documented five other incidents, four of which were at Catholic Church Centres or with Roman Catholic clerics, 21–23.

71. National Resistance Movement, *Mission to Freedom*, 89–93, and 206–207. This is how the two incidents were reported by the *Resistance News* of NRA.

72. *Uganda Times*, 2 March 1982. Also admitted in Cardinal Nsubuga's Press Release to a press conference on 1 March 1982, reproduced in National Resistance Movement, *Mission to Freedom*, 89–93. Also Adoko, *From Obote to Obote*, 315–319.

As is customary, there were three Holy Masses celebrated on Ash Wednesday morning in the Cathedral, one at 6:30 a.m. the second one at 7:00 a.m. and the third at 8:15 a.m.

The 8:15 Holy Mass began as usual, with three priests celebrating at the High Altar. Being mainly a children's mass, about 1,500 or 2,000 were present, mostly of primary level, with about 100 adults. After the homily, before the blessing and distribution of ashes, a group of soldiers entered the cathedral by the main door. All were armed with guns. Some began ordering the congregation to leave the Cathedral . . .

The soldiers, each pointing a gun at a priest, forced the priests to leave the altar, shouting "OUT." . . . Following this, a thorough search was made of all the offices on the compound; that of the Priest in charge of relief work in the Archdiocese, the Chancellor's private office, the building that houses the Diocesan Archives; my own personal residence.[73]

In this operation sixty-seven people were reported killed. The NRA reported "people arrested from prayers under the pretext that they were guerrillas and they have never been seen alive again"[74]; Akena Adoko, a member of the UPC and close to the Obote II regime, claimed that "67 attackers were counted dead."[75] The sixty-seven had a dual identity, "worshippers" and "attackers."

In a strong worded statement Cardinal Nsubuga protested. In part he said:

(a) I hereby protest in the strongest terms against the godless and sacrilegious act of some members of the Uganda Army in violating my Cathedral and using military force in expelling the congregation, which was attending a religious function.

---

73. National Resistance Movement, *Mission to Freedom*, 90.
74. Ibid., 207.
75. Adoko, *From Obote to Obote*, 316.

(b) I protest and remonstrate energetically against the action of the military in forcing people at gunpoint, especially children, to leave the cathedral.

(c) I protest before God, as firmly as I am able against the use of military force in obliging three priests to leave the High Altar in their vestments during a solemn act of Divine Worship.[76]

The government mouthpiece, *The Times*, in its editorial of 3 March 1982 sneered at Cardinal Nsubuga's protest, wondering, "why should a whole Cardinal keep mute when a vehicle carrying patients, nurses and doctors is blown up by land mines but is quick to point out how sacrilegious it was for the security forces to search his Cathedral?"[77] Akena Adoko took the harsh criticism of Nsubuga's protest further by questioning the legitimacy of the use of the term "sacrilegious" in *The Times* editorial. He argued that in its use of the term sacrilegious, "*The Times* [had] failed to see why the search for the Cathedral by the security forces should be more sacrilegious than the use of the Cathedral compound by terrorists for savage acts."[78]

Although Nsubuga and *The Times* editorial viewed the incident at the Cathedral from two opposing sides, their arguments were based on the traditional interpretation of "holy" space, as space set apart for purely ecclesiastical services, based on the distinction and separation of the sacred and the secular. On this basis the conclusion that both rebels and government troops had "desecrated" holy grounds is justified. But there is another standard that goes beyond what we have referred to as canonical holiness; it is the holiness that is inclusive of other services, other than ecclesiastical, that may be justified on other legitimate grounds. This reinterpretation of holiness rejects the category holy space and its premise, the sacred-secular dichotomy, because in this sense all space becomes holy depending on the whether the purpose can be justified as serving the peoples' cause. From this perspective there is therefore no contradiction in the dual identity of

---

76. National Resistance Movement, *Mission to Freedom*, 90.
77. *The Times*, 3 March 1982.
78. Adoko, *From Obote to Obote*, 318.

"attacker" and "worshipper." The worshipper can at the same time be the attacker and vice versa.

The Namugongo Martyrs shrine borders Namanve Forest Reserve, which was used as a hideout by the rebels in 1984.[79] On the evening of 22 May 1984, government troops surrounded the Church of Uganda Seminary grounds that is part of the shrine complex and started an operation, "reprisals against the civilian population which in their eyes were acting as 'intelligence' for the 'bandits' of NRA and their sympathisers."[80] Some of the village residents had fled their homes into the seminary grounds, hoping that the soldiers would be dissuaded from attacking it because it was "holy" ground. However the soldiers pursued them, shooting and looting, and occupied the Seminary. They apprehended Rev Godfrey Bazira, the seminary principal, tortured him and his wife, demanding to know the whereabouts of the rebels. Bazira was then dragged away from his house and killed, and his body damped in a banana plantation nearby.[81]

The NRA mouthpiece, *Resistance News*, reported the incidence thus:

> The Obote government reached the peak of its shame when its murderous soldiers last May attacked Uganda' holiest shrines at Namugongo, killing hundreds of people including the Principal of the Church of Uganda martyrs Seminary, Rev Godfrey Bazira, savagely assaulting many others and destroying property worth millions of shillings.
>
> In their characteristic style, of course, the soldiers had gone to Namugongo to "flush out bandits' but instead turned their guns and knives to the innocent civilians after committing sacrilegious acts in the places of worship of all the three main religions in the country: Moslem, Catholic and Church of Uganda.[82]

Bishops Nsubuga and Kawuma went to see the then Minister of Defence, Paul Muwanga, to protest against the action of the soldiers,

---

79. Kawuma, OI. Kawuma believes there were rebels encamped in the forest.
80. National Resistance Movement, *Mission to Freedom*, 213.
81. Kawuma, OI.
82. National Resistance Movement, *Mission to Freedom*, 206.

and demanded an explanation for the death of the Principal. Kawuma recalls that Muwanga told them: "I am sorry if he is dead but I think my soldiers were very good. They did it very well. I think if I was one of them I wouldn't have left anybody alive there because they have been very naughty."[83] Muwanga's retort suggested that intelligence reports had implicated some people in the college, and most probably the Principal, in aiding the rebels in some way, particularly with food.[84] So, as in the Rubaga incident, both rebel and government troops had used the "sacred" people and places for "unholy" purposes, and this time going beyond denominational and religious divisions. The people's decision to use all space irrespective of religious labels implies further that for the people, not only was the sacred-secular categorization irrelevant but that denominational distinctions are a luxury. The basis of choice in the moment of crisis was the people and the fulfilment of their aspirations.

The Church and the "Bandit" War

The turbulence of the Luwero triangle was treated as a problem for the Church in Buganda and not as a national concern. Looking at the records of the Provincial Assembly, the House of Bishops and other provincial bodies of the Church during that period, there was no extensive discussion and debate over the issue. There was no official position adopted either in protest to the government, or in an effort to mediate and seek for reconciliation between the warring parties or even in condemning the atrocities of the army and the rebels in Luwero.[85] It was the bishops of the Church in Buganda who often protested to the government over the management of the insurgency.[86] In fact this regional Buganda identity superseded even

---

83. Kawuma, OI.

84. Bishop Kawuma also concurred with this view. Bazira was "isolated from the college community taken away and killed. His wife was also tortured. The only other member of the college community that was killed was a porter – a groundsman." Kawuma, OI.

85. I searched through the minutes of the House of Bishops, Provincial Assembly, and Provincial Standing Committee meetings during the period. Bishops Gonahasa, Kawuma, and Mukasa, who I interviewed, could not recall any such discussions in the House of Bishops.

86. Mukasa, OI; and Kawuma, OI. Mukasa was bishop of Mityana diocese and Kawuma assistant to Nsubuga in Namirembe diocese.

the traditional denominational Protestant-Catholic divide, as Kawuma asserted: "I think that Bugandaship with Cardinal Nsubuga and Bishop Nsubuga, was higher than the Roman Catholic thing. . . . It was stronger than just the Catholic and Anglican divide."[87] Kawuma affirmed the supremacy of the identity of Buganda in defining group consciousness in the turbulence in the Obote regime, over religious factors. From his perspective, the solidarity between the two Nsubugas – Emmanuel Cardinal Nsubuga, Archbishop of the Catholic Archdiocese of Kampala, at Rubaga; and Dunstan Nsubuga, bishop of Namirembe Diocese, at Namirembe – was greater than that between Nsubuga and his brother bishops in the Church of Uganda.

In fact it was not just the Catholic-Protestant barrier that was overridden; the voice of protest to the government was inclusive of all religious leaders in Buganda. As early as 1981 when the war in Luwero had broken out, and the vengeful actions of the army against the people of West Nile had reached alarming proportions, Bishop Nsubuga of Namirembe and Cardinal Nsubuga of Rubaga, together with the Muslim Chief Khadi, Kassim Mulumba (another Muganda); the Orthodox bishop Theopheodos Nankyama (also a Muganda); and Archbishop Silvanus Wani, who hailed from West Nile, another of the affected areas, protested jointly to Obote. In a long memorandum signed by the five, they pointed out how the country was slipping into anarchy as a result of the army being out of hand. In part they said:

> The security situation has gone from bad to worse. The groaning, tears, sighs and the pains of the people of Uganda, especially Arua and around Kampala, have forced us to seek an appointment with you, to bring to your notice our own experience, to discuss with you and to suggest ways and means of solving the problem.
>
> The Uganda you lead is bleeding to death. It needs a good Samaritan to give it first aid and treatment and healing. The tears that people around Kampala especially at Kapeeka, Semuto, Wakiso, Kakiri, Matuga, Namanve, Luwero and

---

87. Kawuma, OI.

Wobulenzi are shedding, have reached a quantity that should force those who lead to stop, listen to God, and examine their principles and have more compassion over those that are suffering and many that have lost their lives.[88]

Referring to the anarchy in the capital, they pointed out:

What the people around Kampala are going through is very much like what is going on in West Nile. For within three weeks, a total of over a hundred innocent citizens of Uganda, men, women, children and old people have been murdered mainly by the gun and by people who are there to protect and defend the citizens of Uganda.

We have no objections to operations made by the army to search for guns if they have enough evidence but we strongly object to the way it is done. Once they are sent in an area, they start shooting innocent people without discrimination. Property is looted, women and girls are raped, and many civilians desert their homes to save their lives. Thus the reputation of the army has been greatly damaged among the people. They can no longer trust them. As soon as they appear on site they run away.[89]

What really united the clerics was "the groaning, tears, sighs and the pains of the people of Uganda, *especially* Arua and around Kampala."[90] The clerics' solidarity was centred on the common experience of war and trauma caused by historical political allegiances. The instability in the West Nile region was a result of its association with the Idi Amin regime, and the Luwero Triangle war was linked with the historic animosity between the Baganda and Obote since the Mengo crisis in 1966. This explains the relegation of the Luwero Triangle problem to a purely regional issue, for Buganda, and not a national concern for the entire Church of Uganda,

---

88. "Religious Leaders Petition to Obote," in *Mission to Freedom*, 27–28.
89. Ibid., 28. Although the religious leaders pointed out government responsibility for what was happening in Kampala, Luwero and West Nile, no mention is made to seek for mediation between government and the rebels. Obote and his government were held solely responsible for the Kampala, Luwero and West Nile atrocities.
90. Ibid.

because even in the Church, it was perceived to be primarily political in nature and not about social justice. With the election of Yona Okoth, a long time associate of Obote, to succeed Silvanus Wani, this perception was entrenched deeper in the psyche of the Church.

Yona Okoth, an Obote-UPC Archbishop?

In September 1983, Yona Okoth[91] was elected Archbishop to replace Silvanus Wani[92] who was due to retire in January 1984. Of this election, Anne Coomes, the official biographer of Festo Kivengere, wrote, "it was not altogether a happy election, as many suspected there was some 'party politics' going on behind the scenes."[93] Festo Kivengere was the other candidate in the final round of contest for the See. One would have expected Kivengere, St Augustine's Cross award winner – "an award given only ever at the discretion of the Archbishop of Canterbury, for outstanding work on behalf of the Anglican communion world wide"[94] – and world-class evangelist, to be an obvious choice, but he was not to be. The story of Okoth's election points to his links and relationship with Obote and UPC as factors that tilted the balance in his favour.

When trying to outline the human factors that tilted the balance in favour of Yona Okoth, Kawuma argued that:

> Bishops, including Christians, are human beings, and they live in a human world. We are different in that we believe in God's power, but God's power works through people and the circumstances they are in. The circumstances in which the election of my brother Yona Okoth took place, were a

---

91. Yon Okoth (1927–) was saved in 1947 and ordained a deacon 1953. He was ordained to the Priesthood in 1955; became Diocesan Treasurer of Upper Nile Diocese 1958–61 and then of Mbale Diocese 1961–1963; Provincial Treasurer 1964–1965, and then Provincial Secretary 1965–1966 and also 1969–1972. During the two and a half-year gap, he was pursuing further studies in Canada, and Luwum became Provincial Secretary in his place. He was the first bishop of Bukedi Diocese, 1972–1983.
92. I owe most of the information on this section to Bishops Kawuma, Gonahasa, and Mukasa, all of whom were members of the House of Bishops that elected Yona Okoth. Okoth declined to be interviewed on this period of his service.
93. Anne Coomes, *Festo Kivengere* (Eastbourne: Monarch, 1990), 426.
94. Ibid., 412.

period largely and greatly influenced by UPC and so Bishops being what they are, it could have been that the majority of our House of Bishops had interest and concern, and they saw Yona Okoth as the man who could answer not only the political problems . . . [but also] social, economic, ethnical (sic) at the time . . . The majority feeling was that a man in Yona's standing and relationship will lead Uganda better in the circumstances in which we were.[95]

Kawuma also admitted that it was not only the freewill and judgement of the Bishops at work, but some "quiet influence on the Bishops"[96] from the political powers. Gonahasa was not as non-committal as Kawuma, in stating the case for Okoth as an Obote-UPC sponsored Archbishop. According to him, "Okoth was a UPC,"[97] and was therefore the preferred candidate to Festo Kivengere who had shown his disquiet with the Obote regime over its handling of the Rwandan refugees problem in southwest Uganda.[98]

The burden of this discussion is not primarily to prove that the Obote-UPC government gerrymandered Okoth's election, but rather to acknowledge that the political sentiments were present in the Church and that they

---

95. Kawuma, OI.

96. Ibid. This was the expression used by Bishop Misaeri Kawuma to describe the politicians' influence on the process. Bishops Yokana Mukasa and Lucas Gonahasa concurred that there was such an influence. Gonahasa in fact claimed that it was one of the bishops, known to be an Obote-UPC sympathizer, who was the mediator of a message from Presidents Office that may have influenced the second round vote the next day. Gonahasa recalled that after the indecisive rounds, some people came from President's Office and took the un-named bishop away that evening. Gonahasa also believes that the government donation of a Mercedes Benz to Bishop D. Nsubuga, presented to him by Muwanga a few months before the election, was part of the "quiet influence" in preparation for the elections.

97. Lucas Gonahasa, OI, Kadama Pallisa, 22 April 1997. According to Gonahasa, Okoth's allegiance to UPC came out when in 1979 he organised celebrations in his home village, Kisoko, Tororo, to celebrate the overthrow of the Amin regime. At the helm of the celebrations were the UPC stalwarts: Muwanga, Oyite Ojok and Rurangaranga. It is useful to put Gonahasa's information in the context of his admission that he and Okoth never worked well together throughout their service in the Church.

98. Coomes, *Festo Kivengere*, 419–423. There had been a scuffle between two local communities, those who considered themselves indigenous and refugee population, over cattle, which led to the eviction of the refugee population from their abode, apparently with the support of UPC functionaries. Bishop Kivengere sharply criticised the government for taking sides in the conflict.

influenced the process of Okoth's election as Archbishop. Okoth was a man whose political sympathies were not hidden. His association and relationship with Obote dated back to their school days at Gulu High School,[99] and while in exile he had openly identified himself with the Obote-UPC liberation initiatives, attended the Moshi Unity Conference on this ticket, and returned in 1979 as part of the liberation force.[100] The heavy deployment of security personnel at Okoth's enthronement in January 1984 was therefore interpreted by critics as further confirmation of the political influence in his election,[101] as a show of government's favour. The government's action of granting Okoth two armed policemen to guard him and his residence throughout the Obote II regime[102] was seen as evidence of Okoth's political links with the regime.

The plight of the Luwero Triangle residents did not receive the attention of the national structures of the Church during the leadership of Okoth. This was evident at the countrywide Partners in Mission Consultation held in February 1985, where the external partners observed the silence by the national church leadership over the issue of Luwero Triangle. The external partners mildly rebuked the Church for its lack of "prophetic voice" and drew the Church's attention to the matter of human rights.[103] They "pressed for some significant mention of the human rights violations going on around"[104] in the final report with no success. They called on the Church to defend these rights as mandated by its constitution, "to continue to speak in God's name, and to do so both publicly and privately, to the Government and the people of Uganda" and to challenge Ugandans "to renounce violence as the solution to their many problems."[105]

---

99. Okoth, OI. When Okoth was still bishop of Bukedi, he baptised one of Obote's children, a further indication that they were more than professional acquaintances. Obote's home Diocese was Northern Uganda during the time and one would have expected the bishop of Northern Uganda, S. Wani then, to perform the baptism.
100. Okoth, OI.
101. Coomes, *Festo Kivengere*, 433.
102. Mukasa, OI.
103. The Church of Uganda, *Evangelism and Development, 1985 PIM Consultation Report* (Namirembe: Mission Department, 1985), 84.
104. Coomes, *Festo Kivengere*, 434.
105. The Church of Uganda, *Evangelism and Development*, 84.

Out of a sense of isolation from the other dioceses, none of the dioceses of Mukono, Namirembe or Mityana, which were part of the Luwero Triangle, spoke of the "human rights violations going on around" in their submissions to the Consultation.[106] In fact of the three, only Mityana directly referred to violence:

> Instability (that) started in 1982 causing loss of many lives. Since then, 9 parishes (a third of the Diocese) have been abandoned, and buildings, property and farmland destroyed. This instability has had a negative impact on the Diocesan development efforts and call for prayer and support from the Partners. The Partners had this to state on the Mityana situation: "People from all walks of life were suffering innocently. The whole Church of Uganda must tackle this issue with utmost seriousness. Respect for people, as individuals, is at the heart of the Christian Gospel."[107]

The Namirembe Diocese only referred to the existence of orphanages "as a result of a decade of violence and turmoil," a "foreign idea to traditional Africa, which has valued so highly the 'extended family.'"[108] It is not that these dioceses were oblivious of the suffering of their people, but rather that they were aware that the rest of the Church did not share the same consciousness over the human tragedy that had befallen them, and were therefore uncertain about securing a national consensus over it.[109] What is also certain is that these dioceses did not think of their plight in terms of human rights. The external partners strove to get the Church to address the issue from the perspective of human rights violation with no success precisely because the Church did not see the Luwero Triangle problem in human rights terms. They could not name their experience in categories "alien" to them, but rather saw their plight from the perspective of their historical animosity between Buganda and Obote. So even for the leadership of the dioceses covered by the Luwero Triangle, the issue was not

---

106. Bishops Mukasa and Kawuma explained that the silence of their dioceses was due to this sense of abandonment from the other Dioceses. Mukasa, OI; and Kawuma, OI.
107. The Church of Uganda, *Evangelism and Development*, 35–36.
108. Ibid., 40.
109. Mukasa, OI; and Kawuma, OI.

perceived as an abrogation of social justice and human rights but rather as a result of the historic Buganda-Obote conflict.

The "Displaced" Church in Luwero

At the time the war broke out, Luwero district[110] was divided into two archdeaconries, Ndejje and Luwero. When the population was displaced and dispersed into camps and others fled the area, Yokana Baddokwaya who was Archdeacon at Ndejje fled the area in April 1982. A decision was taken in 1982 by the diocesan authorities in Namirembe to merge them into one archdeaconry, based at Luwero town under the pastoral oversight of Daudi Serubidde.[111] Serubidde's story is a vital part of the story of the Church in Luwero.[112]

Rev Daudi Serubidde was appointed Archdeacon of Luwero at the height of the war, towards the end of 1981. After a brief study tour in Britain during which a church helped him raise money to buy a Land Rover vehicle,[113] Serubidde moved with his family in March 1982 to his base in Luwero town. The town was one of the largest centres for displaced people in the Triangle and had a huge refugee camp. He described it thus:

> All the big waves of displaced persons arriving in Luwero took up refuge wherever they could obtain an empty building around town. The Luwero Senior Secondary School premises attracted quite a big crowd but were soon filled to capacity. People started to put up huts (*obusiisira*) and in the vicinity of the Secondary School I counted close to one hundred and eighty huts. School and Church latrines were all filled in ten days. The sanitary situation was deteriorating very fast, as a

---

110. In order to focus our study of the life of the Church in the war area, our research was in one part of the Luwero Triangle. Paul Mukibi's study, "The Impact of the Guerrilla War (1981–5) and the Challenge of Rehabilitation for the Church in Kiboga area Singo Uganda," Makerere University, Kampala, unpublished Diploma dissertation, 1987; and the interview with Bishop Yokana Mukasa, both of Mityana diocese, Mubende district, indicated to us that the essential elements of the life of the Church were the same throughout the area.
111. Daudi Serubidde, OI, Namirembe, Kampala, 12 September 1995.
112. Also acknowledged by Kyakulagira, "The Work of the Church," 28.
113. This was later to prove invaluable in his ministry to the people of Luwero.

result all sorts of epidemics were breaking out. At the time we reached Luwero, an average of eight people, mostly children, were dying every day in the Luwero camp.[114]

Five weeks after the Serubidde's arrival at Luwero, one of their children died as a result of a measles epidemic. Three months later, Serubidde had to move his family to Buzzibwera, a parish east of Kampala-Luwero-Gulu road that was thought to be more peaceful at the time,[115] because the situation was becoming more and more dangerous west of the road. A month later, even Buzzibwera became insecure, so that the family fled to live at Namirembe Hill in Kampala. What connected Serubidde with his "flock" while at Namirembe was prayer,[116] and his continuing pastoral work among Luwero refugees at Namirembe. The turning point came in April 1983. The Bishop had returned from a pastoral visit at the Ndejje camp and had been deeply moved by the desperate condition in which the people lived. While at a service in the Cathedral, the bishop asked Serubidde to return to Luwero. He told him:

> I have had a vision that we cannot keep away from the Luwero people anymore. With immediate effect, Serubidde, you have to serve the people. The Luwero people are your people. In peace and in trouble, they are your people. Serubidde, you must go to your people. Serubidde that is what it means to be a people's pastor. I hope Jesus will protect you. In any eventuality, you must stand beside your people. If you cannot stand beside your people at their difficult time, how will you claim to be their pastor when they settled down? And one day they will. Whatever is going on in Luwero, and whatever will come next, God says, Serubidde, go to your people. Go to your people!![117]

---

114. Serubidde, "The Pastor's Experience," 66–67.
115. His colleague Rev Matovu provided refuge. Matovu was the parish minister at Buzzibwera. Serubidde, "The Pastor's Experience," 72.
116. He met every Wednesday with Bishop Nsubuga to pray for Luwero. Serubidde, "The Pastor's Experience," 74.
117. Quoted in Serubidde, "The Pastor's Experience," 76.

After further prayer together, they made arrangements for him to leave for Luwero the next day. When he told Damallie, his wife, his encounter with Bishop Nsubuga, and the plan to return to Luwero, it was clear to her as well that the only way to be of service to the people of God was to be with them. Serubidde recalled Damallie's words: "If that is what God says, we cannot do otherwise. Let us have all our trust in God. God will protect you. Let us serve our flock."[118] For the next three years Serubidde split his weeks into two: one half in Luwero visiting camps, preaching, baptising, distributing relief, celebrating communion, and operating an "ambulance service" with his Land Rover;[119] and the other half with his family in Namirembe. Serubidde described his routine visits to the camps thus:

> First, I would greet them [people in camp, gathered] in the name of the Lord Jesus and then convey to them greetings from the Bishop and all the people in Kampala. After that we would pray and then I would give a short sermon. Irrespective of denomination, everyone in attendance would be very attentive to me. Lastly, any relief items from the Diocesan Headquarters would be distributed. The Diocesan relief distributed in May and June 1983 was extremely important to the inmates since this was before the Red Cross and other charitable organisations had started their operations in their various camps in the area. The relief items consisted mainly of salt, soap, milk, beans and maize flour.[120]

These three: prayer, preaching and relief distribution, were the core of his ministry during the period. He was Archdeacon of Luwero through the war period.[121] He headed a small team of clergy, among whom were: Lubwama in Singo, Gizamba at Bombo, Canon Sajjabi in Semuto; Johnson Kakiga in Luwero town; Yonasani Wandera in Ndejje; John Kisekka at Katikamu;

---

118. Ibid.
119. Ibid., 76–110. This is the full story of his work and ministry, his trials and tribulations and those of his colleagues and the people of Luwero.
120. Ibid., 78–79.
121. He moved from Luwero at the end of March 1990, having been transferred to become the Archdeacon of Entebbe. Serubidde, "The Pastor's Experience," 181.

G Kalyowa in Timuna; and Kalimukiza in Ngoma.[122] Kalimukiza's story is worth a paragraph as it shows how these men suffered with the community they served.

Yoweri Kalimukiza was parish pastor at Ngoma when the war broke out in 1981. There were several people who ran to his home for refuge as the rebel troops took control of the area. When the rebels withdrew, government troops moved in and found several people at Kalimukiza's house. It was usually the case that the local people took refuge at the home of a pastor, feeling more secure in the hope that the security agents would respect him and not attack his residence. However, the government troops had no such respect because they considered anybody in an area where the rebels were operating an enemy. He with several others were arrested and taken prisoners to the army barracks at Bombo. Serubidde picks up the story:

> Though at the time Reverend Kalimukiza was thrown into jail many prisoners were dying of hunger, Reverend Kalimukiza stayed alive for a long time before he died (and indeed before we ever knew he was in Bombo barracks). In the barracks there was a house-boy of a very senior officer who happened to have been born and raised up in Ngoma. The boy knew Kalimukiza. He used all sorts of strategies to keep the Reverend supplied with food at least once a day.[123]

The authorities in the barracks discovered this, arrested the boy and starved Kalimukiza to death. Damallie's remarks, recorded by her husband at the death of their second son, reflects something of the awareness of these servants of God of the nature of their mission and their commitment to it. She remarked, "Who are we not to share in what our flock is undergoing?"[124] Kalimukiza and the Serubidde's were indeed sharing in what their flock was undergoing.[125]

---

122. Ibid., 85, 91, 99–101.
123. Ibid., 101.
124. Quoted in Serubidde, "The Pastor's Experience," 68.
125. Another couple, whose service in Luwero cost them their lives, was William Nagambye of Ndejje, with his wife. They were killed early in 1982. Kyakulagira, "The Work of the Church," 24.

Sharing in the sufferings of the people often meant taking risks to serve. For Serubidde this often involved some clandestine work, as part of his ministry. He shuttled from camp to camp, helping to reunite family members that had been scattered in the process of fleeing. He had to do it skilfully, steering a middle course, trying hard not to be seen to be antagonizing either side of the conflict because his shuttles took him to areas controlled by both antagonistic armies.

The fact that the leaders of the Church suffered with the rest of the community made the Church more credible, because it authenticated their ministry. It also indicates that what distinguished the church from other communities was not its insulation from the struggles and pains inflicted by the world, but rather faith amidst the struggles and pains, manifested in its service. The Church as a human community suffered as the rest of the community, but as a faith community, it focused beyond its sufferings to the sufferings of all the people, irrespective of religious affiliation.

Catechists in Luwero

Catechists were the locus of this combination of suffering-service. They too had their share of suffering like all the people. For example:

> There was a man who had been serving as a catechist of Matuga at the time a Uganda National Liberation Army tank was burnt there. In the turmoil that followed that incident, the catechist, his wife with their baby had run to the bush in fear for their lives. One day when the husband had gone to look for food (*okusaka*), some soldiers met the wife (sic) and the baby and carried them off to one of the detachments where one of the commanders forced her to become his wife. Later, when the commander was posted to Kapeeka, he went with that woman and her baby.[126]

The commander lived with the catechist's wife for close to one year. On a tip by some of the people that escaped from the Kapeeka camp, Serubidde organized her safe escape to Kampala, at the risk of being discovered by the

---

126. Serubidde, "The Pastor's Experience," 88.

army officer and facing the consequences. Fortunately for Serubidde the commander never got to know![127]

The public expression of faith of the displaced communities revolved around the catechists or those who played that role, as they led the people in worship and prayers, preached, buried their dead and distributed relief. In camps where there were no trained or any people designated as catechists, Christians who had served as leaders in their congregations during the peaceful times took the responsibility and acted as catechists.[128] They rendered their services to the communities irrespective of religious affiliation.[129] In some instances these catechists were recognised as the camp community leaders.[130]

The itinerant work of Daudi Serubidde and a small team of clergy supported these catechists. Worship, prayers and preaching went together, depending on the amount of time they had and the location. There was no specific day set apart for worship, as all the days were the same. To them there were no "Mondays," "Tuesdays," "Wednesdays," or "Sundays"; they were just days, with the routine of night and day, with only one concern, survival. "All the time was either for looking for food or hiding."[131]

In the camps in the rebel-held territory, sometimes as they began the time of prayer together they would be warned of impending attack by the government troops at which they would immediately run. Among the cherished goods that a few people carried were the Bibles and the Hymnal/

---

127. Ibid., 87–89, for the full story.
128. Archdeacon Serubidde recalls how he was always amazed, during his visits to the various camps at finding catechists that he had never known before, only to be told that they were ordinary Christians who were acting as catechists. Often where such were not available he would appoint some leading and willing Christians to become the camp catechist.
129. Serubidde, OI, Kampala, 12 September 1995; Kampujja, OI; Mujabi, OI, and "*Ebyafaayo by'Olutalo Dekabusa.*" These four: worship, prayers, preaching, and burying the dead were the primary "offices" of the catechists in the camps. Mujabi was in charge of two camps in Singo that were four kilometres apart. There were Muslims, Roman Catholics, Church of Uganda, Pentecostals, and traditional religionists in the camps. Apparently the most active were the Catechists of the Church of Uganda.
130. Serubidde, OI, Kampala, 12 September 1995; Kampujja, OI. Kampujja was recognized as the leader of the Kapeeka camp of about 8,000 people.
131. Serubidde, OI, Kampala, 12 September 1995.

Prayer book.[132] Singing was always in hushed voices, for fear of inviting the fury of government soldiers, and it was mostly from memory, since many did not carry their hymnals with them. All who were present at the camp would participate in the worship and prayers irrespective of religious denomination.[133]

Worship and Sacrament during the War

Prayer, both public and private, was central to refugee spirituality. They prayed from anywhere: under trees, in school buildings, in houses, by the roadside, at the spring as people were queuing to fetch water, any place where there were people. As Serubidde puts it, "wherever we found people we prayed."[134] Catechist Mujjabi expressed it well: *Twasabanga buli kiseera, kubanga buli kiseera kyalinga kya kabi eri abantu* (we prayed all the time because each moment brought with it danger for the people).[135] Some prayers became part of the "war litany." The prayer that was said for protection was:

> *Ai Yesu Owekisa, tukwetaga oziyize akabi konna k'unyumba enno, nekuzabalala bona. Amina.*
>
> O Merciful and gracious Jesus, we need you to prevent all danger from this home and other homes as well. Amen.[136]

A quick prayer that would be said when suddenly attacked or in flight: *Mukama waffe tuyambe,* Our Lord God, help us.[137]

---

132. Amunoni Mujabi, "*Ebyafaayo by'Olutalo Dekabusa*," Notes. The Luganda Prayer book has a hymnal section, all bound together. In addition to the bible and prayer/hymnal book, Mujabi was always dressed in his cassock to mark him out as a church minister.

133. Kampujja, OI; Mujabi, "*Ebyafaayo by'Olutalo Dekabusa*"; Serubidde, OI, Luwero, 20 September 1995. There was no Muslim or Roman Catholic cleric that visited the camps regularly as did Serubidde who regularly visited all the camps.

134. Serubidde, OI, Luwero, 20 September 1995.

135. Mujabi, "*Ebyafaayo by'Olutalo Dekabusa*," Notes.

136. Ibid.

137. Ibid. When Serubidde gave a report of his work in Luwero to the Namirembe Diocese Council in May 1983, a resolution was passed enjoining all Christians in the diocese, in solidarity with those in Luwero, "from then until further notice to end our Lord's prayer with the words, 'O God the concord of peace . . .' or in Luganda, '*Ai Katonda aleeta emirembe . . .*'" Serubidde, "The Pastor's Experience," 78.

A vital aspect of the ministry of the catechists was the burying of the dead. The Baganda have elaborate burial rituals.[138] It was often impossible, given the conditions of life in the war, and the scale of the tragedy, for people to bury their dead, let alone follow these rituals. The added trauma of having just to throw away to the vultures their dead was abated by catechists, and in limited situations the clergy, organising simple funeral services for the people irrespective of denominational affiliation.[139]

Preaching was always central in the work of all those who served in the camps. In the context of war and death it was considered urgent to present the gospel of salvation, as preparation for eternity. Even those who would not have classified themselves as saved preached the necessity of the crisis conversion experience. The responsiveness of these captive audiences was phenomenal.[140] Some of the pastors and catechists are said to have been killed by the government troops because of their open preaching.[141]

Occasionally Serubidde and some clergy would in their visits celebrate communion. They did not ask of the communicants to first announce their religious affiliation or ritual preparedness, judging that these issues would receive their due attention after the war was over. After all it was not possible for the bishops to travel freely in the area to conduct confirmations. In the entire war period of five years, it was only in June 1983 that the three bishops of Namirembe Diocese, Dunstan Nsubuga, Misaeri Kawuma and

---

138. Kyewalyanga, *Traditional Religion*, 77–97. Kyewalyanga has a detailed description of the rituals from the time one is feared near death to the *kwabya olumbe* festivities three months after burial. *Kwabya olumbe* is the rite ending the period of mourning when an heir to the deceased is installed (the last funeral rites).

139. Kampujja, OI; Mujabi, OI; Serubidde, OI Namirembe Kampala, 12 September 1995.

140. Kampujja, OI. Kampujja said he was not a Mulokole at the time, but in his preaching he always challenged people to "get saved." He recalls that at least 36 people got saved through his preaching in the refugee camps then. He got saved in 1985, while at Namugongo Theological Seminary.

141. Mujabi, "*Ebyafaayo by'Olutalo Dekabusa.*" Mujabi remembered the following as having been killed because of their open preaching: Erisa Mukasa of Wakatama COU and Moses Sengendo of Lusanja COU, both catechists; Eria Kesi of Kiwoko COU, Eria Kawesa, William Ntege, William Musoke, all lay leaders from Lusanja COU. Other Catechists killed in the course of their ministry were; Wilson Kizito, Alfred Kabengwa, Samuel Kasule, and Zefaniya Mukalazi. Kyakulagira, "The Work of the Church," 26.

Livingstone Nkoyoyo conducted confirmation services.[142] The unavailability of the regular elements of bread and wine gave rise to some innovations. Boiled cassava or roasted *gonja* (plantain) were used as "bread," and PepsiCola, water sweetened with sugar, or banana juice concentrate were used as "wine."[143] The most important thing was the consecration of the elements. For the celebrants, the Eucharist was not a "sacrifice" or a "memorial of Christ's death" but a blessing, a protection from the brutal killers, and preparation for death.[144] This is a significant shift in the understanding of the functional value of the Eucharist on the part the clergy who administered it, but fits well in the pastoral orientation of the whole ministry of the Church. The functional value of the Eucharist was perceived in pastoral rather than priestly-sacrificial-memorial terms.

There were also several marriages conducted in the camps. Most of these were not newlyweds, but rather those couples who were already married according to traditional custom but wanted their marriages solemnized and blessed by the Church. In the Kapeeka camp Serubidde wedded sixteen couples.[145]

Thousands were baptized in the camps during the war. The issues of candidate preparation and following the Baptismal Order were considered to be of secondary value. All who wanted were baptized without asking their religious affiliation. The fact that they wanted to be baptized was enough, provided they accepted to be baptized in the name of the Father, Son and Holy Spirit.[146] It was the responsibility of the catechists to ensure that candidates for baptism accepted this basic premise. Moreover there was not enough time to go through the entire baptismal rubric, given that there were only six to seven working hours in a day because of a curfew that was imposed by the government army from 4:00 p.m. to 9:00 am. Yet the clergy had to travel distances within this same time and conduct a service. Hundreds were baptized, including some from Islamic and Roman

---

142. Serubidde, "The Pastor's Experience," 79. The confirmations were conducted at Ndejje, Katikamu, Luwero, Kakooge, Nakasongola, Kisenyi, and Nabiswera.
143. Serubidde, OI, Luwero, 20 September 1995; Sajjabi, OI.
144. Ibid.
145. Kyakulagira, "The Work of the Church," 134.
146. Sajjabi, OI; and Serubidde, OI, Luwero, 20 September 1995.

Catholic backgrounds.[147] Serubidde narrates how they coped with these large numbers:

> We had to find a way of baptising so many people in a very short time. What we did was to ask the baptism candidates to line up in four queues, facing the front. The four people at the front and/or their godfathers (if they happened to have them) would mention their names at a go. Then the pastor would say, "Brother in the name mentioned, I baptise you in the name of the Father . . ." after the mentioning the words "the Father," the pastor would also sprinkle water on the four heads at a go. The pastor would do the same at mentioning the words "the Son" and the words "and the Holy Spirit." The exercise would continue in the manner until the end.[148]

Twice Serubidde baptized one hundred and fifty people in a service, which had to last no longer than forty-five minutes.[149] Catechists also baptized in emergencies, when there was much danger and it was not hoped that a clergyman was expected. This was especially so in instances when some were on the point of death.[150]

One salient feature of the story that recurs in the accounts of the religious devotion of the people in the Triangle is the loss of confidence in the traditional cult of the *Balubaale* during the latter period of the war, as contrasted with the an increased devotion to Christianity.[151] In the earlier period of the war, before the dislocation of the population, it was possible for the traditional practitioners to engage in some ritual. Museveni has acknowledged that some of them invited him to their ritual ceremonies:

> They would say: *Omukulu, kilabika olutalo luno telugenda mumaso bulungi kubanga tetunaba kukola byakinansi,* meaning

---

147. Kyakulagira, "The Work of the Church," 21, 31. Rev Sajjabi is on record to have baptized 2,000 people in the camp at Semuto.
148. Serubidde, "The Pastor's Experience," 79–81.
149. Ibid., 81.
150. Sajjabi, OI; Mujabi, "*Ebyafaayo by'Olutalo Dekabusa*"; and Serubidde, "The Pastor's Experience." Sajjabi recalled baptizing about 700 children in one year during the war; Mujabi baptized 10 people who were at the point of death.
151. Kyakulagira, "The Work of the Church," 20.

that the war was not going very well because we had not performed traditional ceremonies. So they would take me with them, slaughter a goat, then we would jump over it, and they would say we would have to eat all the meat at once because if any of it remained, the ceremony would not have been completed . . . They would then say: *Nga kati bwokoze omukolo, nebwogenda nemundu emu, owamba Kampala*, meaning, "Now that you have performed the ceremony, even if you go with one gun, you can capture Kampala." They would reason that this was now possible *kubanga emisambwa gya bajjajja ffe kati gyenyigidde mulutalo* – that since the spirits of our ancestors had been mobilised and were now part of the war effort, we did not have to worry about the actual scientific preparation for waging a war.[152]

However, as the people were displaced from their villages, the traditional cult could not cope with the new social environment of a completely displaced and destroyed society, together with all the pillars of ritual practice. The sacred places were inaccessible; clan elders were displaced and could not play their traditional roles; there was no access to the ancestral grounds; and the distinction between priests and people had been diminished by the common dehumanizing and humiliating experiences in the camps.

With the end of the war in Luwero, early in 1985 when the rebel forces took complete control of the Luwero triangle, energies in the Church was turned towards relief and rehabilitation, aimed at healing the wounds inflicted by the war. Efforts were directed towards resettling the returnees from "exile" and rebuilding the social and economic fabric of society that had been destroyed by the war. This was done through Luwero-wide evangelistic missions, relief and community development projects supported by: the COU Provincial department of Planning, Development and Rehabilitation, and several international non-governmental organizations.[153]

---

152. President Yoweri K. Museveni in his "Address to Makerere University students and Staff at Freedom Square," Makerere University, Kampala. June 1991" in *What is Africa's Problem?*, ed. Yoweri K. Museveni (Kampala: NRM Publications, 1992), 116.
153. The pace was very fast and it culminated in the granting of Luwero a diocesan status, and the installation of the first bishop of Luwero Diocese in December 1991. Full story of

A component of this healing was experienced in the efforts to heal the ethnic bitterness between the Baganda and the Langi, in the dioceses of Namirembe and Lango, Luwero's mother diocese and Obote's home diocese, respectively.

Namirembe-Lango "Reconciliation"

The anti-northern sentiment was also present in the Church in Buganda.[154] The turning point for Bishop Misaeri Kawuma and, according to him, for the Namirembe Diocese was the Diocesan Mission of 1988, during which the central theme was reconciliation.[155] As a symbolic gesture, Bishop Kawuma had invited the Bishop of Lango, Melchisedek Otim, to be the main speaker at the climax services at Namirembe Cathedral. But that which was intended to be only symbolic turned out to be a transforming experience for Kawuma, and according to him, for the entire diocese, in changing their attitudes to the "northerners." In Bishop Kawuma's words:

> When he [Melchisedek Otim] came, God had convicted many of us about the hatred we had against anybody from the north, simply because they were the leaders. I mean, Obote was a northerner, and most of the soldiers were northerners. So in short it was the northerners who were killing our people, who had led Uganda to backwardness; . . . we had a wholesale hatred for anything they did. . . . But God spoke to me about this and said this is a wrong assertion. "You cannot blame people like that wholesale . . ." So when Melchisedek was coming, I said, "I cannot look at him just as somebody from the north, when we've been together, we are both bishops and brethren." And God said, "You are a brother and he is a brother," and then God showed me that what many northerners did is not restricted to them. . . . It is the sinful nature that we all share. . . . So it was not a tribe; it was not an ethnic sin. It was a human problem. And I said that since I could not

---

the rehabilitation program, Serubidde, "The Pastor's Experience," 110–181.
154. Kawuma, OI.
155. Ibid.

call all the Baganda, I said [to Melchisedek] on behalf of the Baganda who live in Namirembe Diocese, "I just want to say sorry about the things the Baganda did for the northerners."[156]

The two bishops embraced one another before the mammoth congregation in the Cathedral, and Otim also repented on behalf of Obote and the Langi for the ills against the Baganda.[157] Referring to the impact of this moment on his attitude towards the northerners, Kawuma commented:

> It is amazing. I have never looked at northerners after repentance in the same way I did before repentance (sic). When I meet them, they are my brethren. They can be bad people just like there are bad Baganda; but not just because they are northerners.[158]

Otim invited Kawuma one year later for a return visit to his diocese. Kawuma was so impressed as he visited the diocese, how the Langi were like the Baganda in many ways, like in their cultural courtesy and respect for their leaders. Kawuma recalls,

> That is when I took up their greeting. . . . I began to greet in Lwo whenever I went to my people in the diocese. I greeted them in the Acholi/Langi language, in Sunday schools, congregations . . . It is a Ugandan language and I hope that way we can show that we can jump barriers.[159]

To further foster the spirit of reconciliation, Bishop Kawuma invited Otim to be the preacher at the inauguration service of Luwero Diocese, and the consecration of Bishop Methuselah Bugimbi as the first Diocesan bishop of Luwero in January 1992.[160] Kawuma was now convinced that while there may be enemies in politics, "there were no enemies in God's camp" since "we are all children of God."[161]

---

156. Ibid.
157. Sam Mfitumukiza, OI Kampala, 1 May 1997. Mfitumukiza was present in the congregation.
158. Kawuma, OI.
159. Ibid.
160. Ibid.
161. Ibid.

Reflection

The fact that the "bandit" war was largely confined within the borders of Buganda reawakened the issue of the identity of Buganda *vis-à-vis* Uganda, an issue that had been laid to rest during the Amin regime. The issue at stake was not primarily ethnic but rather the old quest of restoring a separate social-political regional identity for Buganda within the whole of Uganda, by the restoration of their kingdom and Kabaka. The fact that the Baganda were supporting a rebellion led by a non-Muganda suggests that the basis of their support was not just ethnic considerations. The convergence of the old quest of retaining a separate identity of Buganda, with turbulence within its borders, heightened what Bishop Kawuma termed "Bugandaship." This quest was mirrored in the Church's diminishing consciousness of its Protestant identity and a refocusing on its "Bugandaship" manifested in the close cooperation between its leaders with those of other "religions"[162] and in particular the Catholic Church.

The desire by Bishop Kawuma, on his accession of the Namirembe See in 1985, to emphasize the Church's Anglican identity over its implied "quasi-established" status as a Church *of* Uganda, by including the label "Anglican" on the official letterheads, is further evidence of the demise of the consciousness of the Protestant identity of the Church of Uganda in Buganda.[163] The bracketed "Anglican" was an implicit acknowledgement that the Church in Buganda had surrendered its "established" status as the church *of* Uganda and had equal standing in society as other religions, and in particular the Catholic Church, within the context of what Kawuma termed "Bugandaship."

However, this solidarity of the Church's identity with "Bugandaship" is only a part of the story. The initiatives towards reconciliation with the "northerner" Diocese of Lango, the perceived political enemies of "Bugandaship," marks out the Church as a faith-community, and not just a socio-political entity; for if the Church were to affirm its "Bugandaship"

---

162. "Religion" is used in its indigenous Uganda sense, referring to Roman Catholic Church, the Church of Uganda and Islam as different religions.

163. Prior to Kawuma's change, the letterheads read, "Diocese of Namirembe, Church of Uganda"; but with his change they now read, "Diocese of Namirembe Church of Uganda (Anglican)." Diocesan Secretary's Files, Namirembe Diocese Archives.

only, it would no longer deserve to be called a church distinct from any other social-political organisation. The roots of this initiative towards reconciliation are in the Revival ethos. First the context was at a Revival-style Mission at Namirembe; and second the key players, Bishops Kawuma and Otim were *Balokole*.[164]

The Kawuma-Otim initiative was a witness to the faith of the Church. Kawuma's confession that, "I cannot look at him [Otim] just as somebody from the north, when we've been together, we are both bishops and brethren," was a confession of faith. Faith was the basis of his consciousness of being "brother to brother"; no longer just Baganda or "northerners" but people with a common heritage, "the sinful nature" and a common identity, as "brothers." Kawuma was enabled by his revival heritage to name the "northerners" as *aboluganda* (brethren).

In the Luwero Triangle context of war, displacement and camps, where the defining element of sociality of the community was "threat to life," and the entire community was fugitive, the distinction between "mission to the world" and "ministry in the church" was diminished. There was no opportunity when the Church could gather as a separate community, because the entire community was always gathered together in the camps or dispersed in the bushes. What distinguished the Church as a faith community from the "others" was its leadership, who became leaders not of the faith community alone but of the entire community. It is here that the vital "order" of catechist as a minister became crucial, for the catechist was always with all the people, not just to perform ecclesiastical liturgical functions, but to extend the grace of Christ to all the people, for "God so loved the world."[165]

The canonical Episcopalian three-fold order of ministry – bishop, priest and deacon – was not reflected in the experience of the Church in Luwero, in two respects: the office of the priest, and the role of the catechists in the nurture of the Church. The most significant functions of the priests were not priestly but rather pastoral. It was the visiting the faithful, praying with and for them, preaching and doing anything that would bring social and physical relief to them that constituted the ministry of the priests. Not

---

164. Kawuma, OI; and Melchisedek Otim, OI, Boroboro, Lira, 27 September 1996.
165. John 3:16.

once in "The Pastor's Experience"[166] does Serubidde refer to himself as a priest but always as a pastor. Although he recognized his priestly function of the administration of the sacraments, the value of the sacraments lay in their pastoral efficacy of blessing, protection and preparation for death.

The ministerial functions of the clergy were essentially pastoral, the same as those of the catechist. The difference was in ecclesiastical recognition, in that the catechist is not recognized in his right as a pastor, but always appended to the clergy as an assistant.[167] For although Serubidde expresses gratitude to "catechists like Mr Henry Kampujja (late in 1985 he was ordained) in Kapeeka camp, Miss Catherine Nakawuka in Ndejje camp, Mr Amunoni Mujabi in Kiwoko camp, Mzee Mrs Sendagala in the Semuto camp," it is their assistant roles of "gathering those to be baptised and those to be married in Church, and in giving them proper religious instruction," that he acclaimed them for.[168] The distinction between "clergy" and "catechist" was theoretical, because the catechists fulfilled the same essential functions as the clergy, and even more effectively because the catechists were present all the time with the people, while the ordained were among them as a "visitors."

Serubidde's work was essentially pastoral, like the catechists, but Serubidde was not as available as the catechists were because he visited the camps in the entire Luwero Archdeaconry four days a week from his residence at Namirembe. Part of the explanation for this is the small number of ordained ministers, which justifies further the assertion that catechists were central to the life and mission of the Church. They were present among the people all the time.

The *de facto* order is one: pastor, whereby bishops, clergy and catechists are all pastors. The bishop becomes the senior pastor or pastoral ruler, the elder among pastors, and the priests are pastors, working with the catechists,

---

166. "The Pastor's Experience" is an unpublished manuscript in which Daudi Serubidde chronicles his service and ministry. The largest section of it covers his service in Luwero during the war.

167. This appending of the catechist is seen for example in Serubidde's commendation for the work of Ssajjabi and Lubwama, both clergymen. He stated: "The work of the two Reverends, *assisted by the catechists*, should not go unrecorded" (emphasis added). Serubidde, "The Pastor's Experience," 91.

168. Ibid., 81.

who are regarded not as assistants but fellow pastors. This contrasts with the *de jure* order of bishop-priest-deacon, which in the Luwero context was a theoretical categorization without concrete expression. The central role of the catechists in the pastoral work in Luwero mirrors their crucial place in the planting of Christianity in Uganda, a fact acknowledged in chapter 1. It is also well documented by Louise Pirouet in *Black Evangelists* and Tom Tuma in *Building a Ugandan Church: African Participation in Church Growth and Expansion in Busoga 1891–1940*.

The way Serubidde and his team of pastors administered the sacraments could be judged as unorthodox if examined on the basis of the prescribed order of these services in the *Book of Common Prayer*.[169] However the issue for Serubidde, his team and the people was not orthodoxy but contextual efficacy. In the context of turbulence in which the Church had to continue its worship the sacraments were contextualized: in continuity with the traditional religious functional value and efficacy of material use in worship. "Water" in Baptism, and "wine" and bread in Communion are the equivalent to *mayembe* and *nsiriba*,[170] in the traditional cult of *Balubaale* among the Baganda. *Mayembe* and *nsiriba*, which were cult objects, "made out of cattle, buffalo or rhinoceros horns or out of leather; in some cases they were made out of gourds."[171] These objects were believed to "have supernatural powers of averting evil and bringing good fortune to their possessor."[172]

> The fetishes (*mayembe*) were worn around the neck and loins for curative and protective purposes. Each fetish (*jjembe*) had its function, for example a safeguard against diseases, snakes, sorcery, and wild animals. Some were used as protection on journeys, and some Baganda women wore them as medicines for fecundity. In some clans, the fetishes were credited with personality and invested with supernatural power. It was believed that a fetish (*jjembe*) could do anything demanded by

---

169. For example the baptism of adults, according to the *Book of Common Prayer*, requires a period of instruction and more rigorous scrutiny of the candidates. "The ministration of Baptism to such as are of riper years, and are able to answer for themselves," in *The Book of Common Prayer of 1662*, (London: Collin Publishers, 1968 edition).
170. Kyewalyanga, *Traditional Religion*, 128–130.
171. Ibid., 128.
172. Ibid.

its owner. Some even thought that a fetish was able to speak a language, which its owner understood.[173]

The cult objects were believed to mediate, transmit and ensure blessing, healing, protection, progress and prosperity, and to provide other such immediate individual and community needs. This is the same perspective implied in the way Serubidde and his colleagues approached the sacraments of Baptism and Holy Communion. The elements of "bread" and "wine" were to be received as "blessing" and Baptism was considered to be preparation for death. It was better for one to die baptized, than not. In this sense the Church became "sacrament" to the people through its various works of prayer, preaching, relief distribution and funeral services.

---

173. Ibid., 129.

CHAPTER 7

The Church in the Museveni-NRA/M Regime, 1986–1992

The account of the Church of Uganda in turbulent post-independence Uganda raises the question of what a church becomes in the context of armed rebellion and violence, particularly when the membership of the church are sympathetic to the causes of the rebellion. In the context of the Luwero Triangle war, the Church distinguished itself as the church of the people, through its identification with them in their suffering at the grassroots level. The manifestation of this identification was in the clergy and catechists, who embodied the Church's presence among people. However at the institutional-national level, the election of Yona Okoth as the Archbishop of the Church, who was sympathetic to the Obote-UPC government then in armed conflict with rebel forces of the NRA based in the Luwero Triangle, localized the experience of the "people's church" at the grassroots. Thus, at the institutional-national level, at least in the person of Okoth, the Church identified itself with the forces opposite to the feelings and aspirations of the Church at the grassroots.

The account of the Church in the Museveni-National Resistance Army/Movement (NRA/M) regime, which is the subject of this chapter, gives a different scenario, with both the archbishop and the grassroots identifying with the rebel movement. At the institutional-national level was Yona Okoth, an archbishop associated with the deposed Obote II regime and therefore viewed by the NRA/M government with suspicion; and at the grassroots was the Church in Teso that was sympathetic to the armed rebellion against the Museveni-NRA/M regime. As in the account of the Church in the Obote II period, the reaction in the Church is diverse and differentiated according to the social-political aspirations at the different centres of church life.

This chapter narrates the story of the Church during the first six years of the Museveni-NRA/M government, 1986–1992, during which there was an anti-government rebellion in the northern and eastern parts of the Uganda. Attention is given to the developments in the Church at the two levels: institutional-national, embodied in the Church's episcopal leadership; and at the grassroots, in Teso where the Church had to contend with an insurgency that reflected the grievances of the people against the government of NRA/M.

At the episcopal leadership level, Archbishop Yona Okoth's links with the vanquished Obote-UPC forces presents a "rebel archbishop" scenario and a "divided" House of Bishops. The issues that this scenario presented to the House of Bishops as it considered the development of a ministry of social concern are considered.

The Teso-based conflict and resultant turbulence is a natural sequel to the Luwero Triangle account because both accounts have the one common denominator, the Obote-UPC causal factor. In the Luwero Triangle account the rebellion was based on the historic anti-Obote/UPC sentiment; and in Teso, the counter-insurgency government measures were geared to routing out pro-Obote/UPC forces that were perceived to be the catalysts of the rebellion.

However the Teso account is different from Luwero in that it was not only the issues of political power that escalated the conflict, but also the cultural, socio-economic question of cattle, a defining feature of Teso identity. Cattle raiding that had hitherto been a socio-cultural phenomenon gained political capital due to the real and perceived involvement of government troops and agents. Due attention is given to this and other related factors that led to the insurgency, its impact on the Church, and the role of the Church in peacemaking, under the leadership of Gershom Ilukor, the bishop of Soroti diocese during that period.

Unlike the two accounts, of the Church during the Amin and Obote II regime, where there are several "grassroots" stories, the Teso account gives prominence to Bishop Gershom Ilukor. The dominance of Bishop Ilukor in the Teso account reflects the unfolding of the story as it was researched.

In the initial stages of my research in Teso, a lot of effort was made to find grassroots stories that were significant for understanding the developments in the Church, and several informants kept referring to the pivotal role of Ilukor in defining the response of the Church to the turbulence. Hence, space given in this chapter to discuss the role of Bishop Ilukor in shaping the Church's life and work during the turbulence.

The chapter concludes by reflecting on the questions that Okoth's leadership raises; the connection between indigeneity and ministry in a turbulent context; the Church's role in peace making; the presence of the Revival ethos in the Church in Teso; and the Church's pastoral-parental ministry.

Archbishop Yona Okoth: A Rebel?

As chronicled in the previous chapter, the primary object of the NRA bush war was to overthrow the Obote II regime. However, it was not the NRA that overthrew the regime, but mutinous Acholi-led troops in the UNLA, under the command of Brigadier Bajilio Okello. The latter constituted a Military Council government, with General Tito Okello as Head of State in July 1985. But Museveni and his National Resistance Army (NRA) continued their fight to overthrow the Military Council Regime, which they did on 25 January 1986. With the overthrow of the Military Council regime, the NRA/M had to contend with two vanquished forces: those still loyal to the Obote II regime, who were still on the run; and the remnant of the troops that remained loyal to the Okellos, especially from Acholi.

Both post-Obote II regimes found at the helm of the Church's leadership Yona Okoth, whose loyalty was perceived to have continued with the vanquished Obote-UPC powers because of his historic connections with them. The story of Yona Okoth, and his service as Archbishop in the Church at this time is significant, because of the implications of his relationship with the Obote II regime for his relationship with the new governments, and for his leadership of the Church. His leadership was marred by suspicion and accusation by NRA/M agents, that he was collaborating with the rebel forces that were still loyal to the fallen Obote II regime. Okoth had to contend with the suspicion that his association with the fallen government meant that he was opposed to the succeeding governments.

This suspicion was evident soon after the Obote-UPC government fell. His absence at the swearing in ceremonies of the new leaders: head of State, Gen Tito Okello; and Executive Prime Minister, Paul Muwanga, was interpreted by some of his critics as confirmation that he was loyal to the fallen regime, and disdainful of the new government.[1] The extent of this was manifested in the newspaper reports calling him and pleading with him to "forget him [Obote] and send a message of congratulations to recognise the new government."[2] Another incident that took place immediately after the fall of the Obote II government that clearly showed this disposition of suspicion of Okoth by the new political masters was the attack on his residence in July 1985 by NRA operatives.

To exonerate himself from these suspicions before the House of Bishops, Okoth called an extraordinary meeting of the House in August 1985. Okoth was at pains to explain to the House of Bishops that his absence at both ceremonies was not because he had fled the country; nor had he absented himself from the functions deliberately in scorn. His absence, he explained, was due first, to his ill health and second, he had "taken the body of my brother who died in Bugiri Hospital, home."[3] He had therefore delegated the responsibility to Bishop Misaeri Kawuma to represent him and the Church at the ceremonies. Concerning the attack on his house he reported that:

> On the 28th July [1985], Kampala was very hot, with shooting and looting. Some soldiers came to my residence and came right up to my bedroom where I was lying in bed and demanded for a key for any car.
>
> I asked them whose key, and they answered, "We have just come from the bush, we do not know. But we want any key." I tried to resist, but they were cocking their guns so the children

---

1. Absence at these two functions had been interpreted by some Mukono theological students as indicators of his continuing loyalty to the fallen regime and his reluctance to recognise the Military Council government, as Okoth himself reported to the house of bishops in August 1985. Yona Okoth, "Communication from the Chair at the House of Bishop's Special Meeting on 23 August 1985," House of Bishops Papers, COU Archives, 1.

2. Reported by Okoth, "Communication from the Chair."

3. Ibid.

gave them the key of the car belonging to the Archdeacon of Kitgum which was brought to my residence by Gen Tito Okello, about a week before the take-over.[4]

As though to prove to the House that the accusations against him were baseless, he pointed out that the homes of bishops of Busoga, Mbale and West Ankole had been attacked in the same month.[5] In Okoth's view it was not just the four Bishops, but the entire church that was associated with the fallen government. Okoth expressed his fears for the Church:

> I also have fear that if things go on in the way they are going now, our Church will be crippled a second time. This is because whether we like it or not, churches have been identified with particular political parties.[6]

However, it is noteworthy that the three other bishops who were attacked – Bamwoze of Busoga, Wesonga of Mbale and Bamunoba of West Ankole – were all suspected to be sympathetic to the Obote-UPC government that had been overthrown.[7]

This suspicion of Okoth's continuing loyalty to Obote-UPC spilled into the new Museveni NRA/M regime. Shortly after Museveni and his NRA/M took over government, Okoth was accused of being a member of a clandestine organization, Force Obote Back Again (FOBA). He was accused of attending several FOBA meetings in Tororo early 1986[8] that were purportedly planning the overthrow of the government by force of arms, and was named later as a defence witness in a treason trial of four FOBA operatives.[9] In Okoth's view these accusations against him were motivated by partisan and religious malice. In his address to the House of Bishops at their meeting in May 1986, he reported that he had brought these issues to the awareness of the President, ministers and people in Tororo over specific individuals and by name. He had pointed out:

---

4. Ibid., 1.
5. Ibid.
6. Ibid.
7. Bishop Gonahasa, OI.
8. Letter from Archbishop Y. Okoth to His Excellency the President, dated 30 December 1986, Archbishop's Papers, COU Archives.
9. *The New Vision*, 7, 19 July 1989.

> [The] specific individuals, and by name, all being members of the Roman Catholic Church in the areas and DP members who had been engaged in these sinister activities of spreading rumours about prominent Protestant and UPC supporters and sympathisers. These rumourmongers wanted the Protestant leaders, including myself to be eliminated by all possible pretences, hence the present tense situation in the area. The goal as they envisaged it was to come to power through [the] bloodshed of innocent people, mainly the Protestants.[10]

Okoth pursued this argument that since the accusations against him emanated from Catholic circles bent on the Church's downfall, what had happened to him could happen to any of the Bishops.

> It is possible that the Church of Uganda has become an escape goat (sic) for some institutions in the nation. Those who brand Protestants and the Church of Uganda's leadership as sponsors of FOBA must be carefully watched. Diligence on our part is essential. Unity is needed among us. Furthermore, it is our responsibility to educate our members to become adequately aware of the danger of those who lie about us.[11]

However Okoth's endeavour to project a Protestant-Catholic rift as the basis of the accusations against him did not succeed. About one year later, in May 1987, he was interrogated at his home over a similar association, as he reported to the President that:

> [In May 1987] two vehicles arrived at my residence. From the vehicles appeared army personnel who introduced themselves as officials from President's office. These three gentlemen told me that they were commanders and wanted to discuss some urgent matters with me . . .[12]

---

10. Archbishop Yona Okoth, "The present situation after the NRA took over the government on January 25, 1986," 4, Archbishop's papers, COU Archives.
11. Ibid.
12. Archbishop Yona Okoth's letter to His Excellency the President dated 2 June 1987, Archbishop's Papers, COU Archives.

The "urgent matters" were a meeting that he had with his three sons.[13] One of Okoth's sons had been named as a FOBA operative, a matter that, according to Okoth, was no secret to the President as his correspondence reveals:

> Your excellency, as you may recall, I had discussed with you my concern about my elder son, Sam Okoth, and you requested me to advise him to return to Uganda. This I did when I met him in Kenya at this time. I conveyed your message to him in the hope that he would see the reasons given.[14]

Religious factionalism was not the primary basis of the accusations against Bishop Okoth, but his individual historical association with Obote and the UPC. Since there were rebel movements that were associated with Obote, based in eastern Uganda and particularly in Okoth's home area, Tororo; and since was implicated as a "rebel," Yona Okoth was suspected to be party to the rebel initiatives.

A Divided House of Bishops?

The House of Bishops took up the matter of the accusations against Okoth as an individual matter. In a letter in June 1987 to President Museveni, protesting the manner in which the security forces "visited" the Archbishop, they said:

> Further Your Excellency, we have been greatly alarmed when, as House of Bishops, we have learnt that the Archbishop of Uganda, the Most Rev Yona Okoth, was without prior warning, visited on Sunday 31 May, 1987 at about 2:30 p.m., by three NRA Commanders accompanied by armed soldiers; and these Commanders demanded for an explanation from the Archbishop, to explain about people who had visited the Archbishop while in a Hotel in Nairobi on his way back from a Church meeting in West Germany.

---

13. Ibid.
14. Ibid.

> This surprise visit to the head of a Church without due notice was humiliating, intimidating and embarrassing. We would propose that it would be better if His Excellency wants any information from the Archbishop, could either ask him to come and meet his Excellency or his Excellency would send one of his government ministers to meet the Archbishop.[15]

In the meantime as Okoth was having to exonerate himself from any links with rebel groups, he also led the House of Bishops in demanding that government follow peaceful steps in dealing with rebellion that had now proliferated in many parts of the country. At the House of Bishops meeting on 23 April 1987, to which they invited the President, they pleaded:

> We have noted that insecurity exists in some areas in Uganda in Kasese, Karamoja, Northern Uganda and some Eastern parts of Uganda, where houses are set on fire, property looted, cattle taken, people tortured, and lives destroyed. This leaves many people displaced and has invited a lot of confusion both from within the country and outside. In some cases food distribution to displaced persons has not been possible. Reports reveal that these atrocities are committed by uniformed persons with arms. This is creating insecurity and famine in the Nation.
>
> It is our plea and prayer that all the opinion leaders of this nation should be invited by government to share in the creation of peace, security and development in our nation.[16]

However, in spite of these appeals, battles between government troops and rebels continued in the northern and eastern parts of the country and other Bishops were "visited" by security forces. Bishop Ilukor of Soroti was forcibly taken from his residence for interrogation; the same thing happened to Bishop Okille of Bukedi and the Assistant Bishop of Northern Uganda, Gideon Oboma, was attacked three times early in 1987.

---

15. Letter to His Excellency, from House of Bishops, dated 4 June 1987, House of Bishops Papers, COU Archives.
16. Memorandum of the House of Bishops of COU, presented to His Excellency Y. K. Museveni, Kampala 23 April 1987, 2, House of Bishops Papers, COU Archives. The President was present in the House of Bishops, sitting at Namirembe, Hannington Chapel, at the time when this memorandum was presented.

It is instructive that all these Bishops, who were assaulted by security personnel of the NRA/M government, hailed from the eastern and northern Uganda, areas known for their historic allegiance to Obote-UPC. This is an indication that the regime connected them with the rebel movements that emanated from this region. The bishops seemed to have made this connection. In a follow up letter dated 4 June 1987, demanding explanation on the harassment, by the Tororo NRM administration and NRA Commanders, of Okille, the bishop of Bukedi, the bishops challenged the government to face up to the implications of the continued use of violence to resolving the problem of rebellion:

> We have sadly learnt that in the Eastern and Northern Uganda Region, cattle raiding is increasing and continuing, and that through this dangerous exercise many families have been left poor and many displaced, and some killed during the cattle raiding exercise.[17]

On 24 September 1987 the Archbishop decided to write to the President again, since it had "become more and more difficult to get audience" with him[18], following the 4 June letter of the House of Bishops, demanding again explanation of the harassment of the bishop of Bukedi. Bishop Okille had been "searched on the accusation that he was harbouring FOBA people."[19] However in February 1989, while Okoth was away in the USA, accompanying the President on an official visit in response to the President's invitation, security officers forcibly entered Okoth's Tororo residence and thoroughly searched it. He was still suspected to be aiding, in some way, those fighting to overthrow the regime.

In a four-page memorandum in February 1989, the bishops raised these issues to the President. The memorandum dealt with several national issues ranging from grassroots elections to barter trade, and towards the end they pointed out to him:

---

17. Letter to His Excellency, Y. K. Museveni, from the House of Bishops, dated 4 June 1987, 1, House of Bishops papers, COU Archives.
18. Letter to His Excellency, from Archbishop Yona Okoth, Re: "Insecurity Surrounding Some Church of Uganda Leadership," dated 24 September 1987, Archbishops Papers, COU Archives.
19. Ibid.

> 1. Archbishop Yona Okoth's house in Tororo was entered and searched, by security officials; while he was accompanying Your Excellency on your American visit.
>
> 2. Bishop Nicodemus Okille of Bukedi was subjected to a body search at a public function in his Diocese.
>
> 3. Bishop Geresom Ilukor of Soroti was recently ordered out of bed, by security men, in the middle of the night; and made to walk 12 miles, before he was finally brought back.
>
> 4. The site being prepared for building a Cathedral in Lira was taken over by the Army and occupied. So far all efforts to have it handed back to us for the necessary development have been futile.
>
> Such humiliation, we feel is unjustified and should be checked. *Let us hasten to add that we don't believe such treatment of Church leaders is representative of Government attitude towards us and what we represent.* Your love and respect for your Bishops was admirably demonstrated by your care and assistance, in the burial arrangements, of our beloved Bishops Dunstan Nsubuga, Erica Sabiti and Festo Kivengere.[20]

Clearly, the House of Bishops did not want to generalize that the attacks on the other bishops were the rule but rather the exception. They still preferred to treat them as individual and isolated cases. In the same memorandum however they appealed again to government to seek peaceful ways of ending the conflict and war in northern and eastern Uganda:

> In some parts of Gulu, Soroti and Karamoja, where there is still insecurity, we appeal to the government to continue on the road of seeking a lasting solution by peaceful means, as "violence breeds violence." To this end if we as Church leaders can be of use in enabling the parties in conflict to talk peace,

---

20. "Memorandum to His Excellency the President of Uganda Yoweri Kaguta Museveni at State House on 23 February 1989," 3 (Italics mine), House of Bishops Papers, COU Archives.

we humbly offer ourselves. We advise that as peace and stability returns to affected areas of Northern and Eastern Uganda, every effort should be made to accelerate the rate of development projects in those areas.[21]

The February 1989 memorandum has two messages in one. On the one hand there is commendation, while on the other there is condemnation. It would be rash to conclude that the House of Bishops was therefore divided on the basis of the apparent contradictions in the memorandum. They all came from contradictory political climates: peace and war; rebellion against government and solidarity with government; and some were embattled bishops and others pampered.[22] The House mirrored the situation in the country: the peaceful areas of the South and West, and the turbulent North and East.

This is the reality of the church in the world, that the church reflects the socio-political context; if there are contradictory perspectives in society they will be mirrored in the church. The difference with the church is that they ought to co-exist together, allowing each to manifest without swallowing the other. So in the same House of Bishops there were two messages. On the one hand the Bishops were calling and challenging government to live up to its accountability to the people, thereby keeping its distance.[23] And on the other hand acknowledging "the love and concern for *your* Bishops," advising and encouraging the government to continue its work of development in which "we are workers *together* under God in the service of his people of Uganda"[24] and thus identifying with government.

The Church and Social Concern

Unlike during the entire Obote II era, when the Luwero Triangle war was treated as a regional problem, for Buganda, the discussion thus far has

---

21. "Memorandum to His Excellency the President of Uganda Yoweri Kaguta Museveni at State House Entebbe on 23 February 1989," 1, House of Bishops Papers, COU Archives.
22. Bishop Kawuma mentioned that he had a pastoral relationship with the President. Misaeri Kawuma, OI, Nsangi, Kampala, 20 April 1997.
23. Letter to His Excellency, Y. K. Museveni, from the House of Bishops, dated 4 June 1987, 1, House of Bishops papers, COU Archives.
24. Ibid., 3.

shown that the House of Bishops attempted to give corporate attention to the issues and challenges of civil and political strife in the early years of the NRA/M regime. In fact as early in the NRA/M regime as August 1986, the Provincial Assembly directed that a structure be created in the Church that would continue to research and reflect on social concern issues in Uganda. The Assembly:

> Noted with great concern the problems of insecurity, acts of lawlessness and other related issues of injustice and social concern in the country at the time, and directed the Provincial Standing Committee to appoint a Social Concern Committee as a measure to deal with these issues.[25]

The Social Concern and Refugee Committee, chaired by the bishop of Lango, M. Otim, was set up by the Provincial Standing Committee[26] and charged with:

> One: To study the given situations of social concern in the Province of the Church of Uganda and inform the Church.

> Two: To advise the Church on the kind of appropriate actions to be taken in such situations.[27]

It was clearly stipulated in the terms of reference of the committee that it was not part of its mandate to "discuss issues of social concern with the government or inform it of the Church's stand on such issues; and that, relationship with the government should be left to the Archbishop or the House of Bishops."[28]

It should be recalled that the Archbishop at the time, Yona Okoth, was elected after some influence from the Obote-UPC regime and held suspect by the NRA/M regime. A situation therefore existed where the Church set itself to develop a social concern mission at a time when its leader was by default not favourable to the regime of the time.

---

25. Rt Rev M. Otim, in his "Address to the Members of House of Bishops at Lweza Training and Conference Centre," 1, House of Bishops Papers, COU Archives.
26. The Provincial Standing Committee is the successor to the PAE.
27. M. Otim, "Address to House of Bishops," 2.
28. Ibid.

In its first submission to the House of Bishops, the committee, through its chair, Bishop Otim of Lango, brought to the House's attention the need to deal with the matter of proliferation of "voices" from the same Church over the same issues, which, in their view, contradicted the office of a bishop.

> A bishop is a church (sic), a representative of Christ on earth. He is a father of all or should be so. When he speaks, he does not speak only for his diocese, his tribe or for a particular area; he speaks for the whole church. When he falls, the whole church falls; when he errs, the whole church bears the blame. That is why the unity of the Church and the solidarity of the Bishops are very important.[29]

The quote from the Social Concern Committee's submission above highlights a problem in the self-understanding of the Bishops *vis-à-vis* the nature of the church, and locates the initiatives for social-action in the office of a bishop. This perception in part explains the dilemma that the Committee pointed out, of the lack of a unanimous voice on socio-political issues. For if each bishop saw himself as the church, his personal point of view become the church's view and in a multifaceted socio-political environment this posture hinders corporate view. It is, in my view, the source of what the Committee called "generalising a local situation."[30]

The problematic issue in the Church's episcopal leadership, which the committee called "generalising a local situation," is what had militated against solidarity, unity and cooperation on issues of social concern in the country. Otim submitted that:

> There is also a problem of *generalising a local situation*. When there is peace in one area of the country, some individual Bishops from those areas go on shouting peace, peace, in and outside the country, not knowing that there is no peace in other parts of the country. That had been the case with the then Dean of the Province, while leading quiet time to open the Provincial Assembly at Mukono in August 1986, who

---

29. Ibid.
30. Ibid.

talked of peace prevailing in Uganda, when at that very time there was fighting in Northern Uganda. The bishop spoke in total ignorance of what was happening in the rest of Uganda. He travelled from Hoima to Kabale for a convention, and from Kabale to Mukono for the Assembly. There was peace in those areas, but he was wrong to generalise a local situation. That brought protests and disagreements in both the House of Laity and the House of Clergy. The way the Dean spoke gave a poor picture of and lack of concern for the suffering of people within the same province.

Likewise, when there is peace in one area and problems in another, some bishops go on talking about the problems, problems and problems only, not thanking God for the peace prevailing in other parts of the Province; that one also shows a poor knowledge of and a lack of concern for some people within the same Province. We must realise that peace in Uganda has all along been partial. When one part of the country is peaceful, another part is suffering. Bishops as fathers of all, must show in their words and works that they do know what is happening in the Province and are concerned about them all.[31]

This plea, to the episcopal leadership of the Church, to intentionally focus on regional or local problems as issues of national concern was a new way for the Church. The issue at stake was the question of nationalizing local or regional problems without losing the particularity of the local. The call by the Social Concern Committee focuses on one endemic feature of the Church's episcopate, as it has re-acted in turbulence; the way local or regional identity has superseded national identity. It was yet to be seen whether this call would be heeded in dealing with the turbulent situation in Teso.

---

31. Ibid.

Cattle Rustling, Rebellion and War in Teso

There are three phenomena that led to turbulence in Teso during the Museveni-NRA/M regime: the extended problem of the Karimajong cattle raiders; the perception by the NRA/M administration of Teso as "enemy" territory due to Iteso[32] historic association with Obote and the UPC; and third, the subsequent emergence of a rebel movement, and violent confrontation with the NRA.

Cattle raiding, among the Karimajong, was part and parcel of their traditional way of life. Like their neighbours the Pokot and Turkana of Kenya, one of the traditional ways of increasing their cattle herds is by "collecting" from their neighbours. The weapons of this trade were traditional spears, bows and arrows, with a few homemade rifles. The Karimajong, Turkana and Pokot raided among themselves and only occasionally, would go beyond to the non-raiding peoples of Teso, Acholi and Lango, particularly in the dry season. In Teso it was the two counties in the northeast, Amuria and Usuk, bordering Karamoja, that were frequently attacked by cattle rustlers and developed coping community mechanisms to defend their kraals. (See Map 4: Teso and Neighbouring Districts, p 296.)

However the acquisition of automatic weapons transformed the nature and exercise of this hitherto "acceptable" practice, and increased the magnitude of the destruction associated with it. It was after the overthrow of the Idi Amin regime in 1979 that the Karimajong first acquired large numbers of guns from Moroto barracks when soldiers fled and deserted it.[33] Some of the guns were sold to the Karimajong. With these guns, cattle rustling took on higher degrees of ruthlessness involving killing, looting other livestock and burning of houses.[34] To combat this recklessness, during Obote II regime, the government developed and trained a people's militia force in

---

32. The region is Teso, the people *Iteso* plural, singular male is *Etesot*, and singular female is *Atesot*, and the language is *Ateso*.

33. Michael E. Okwii, "The Economic Revolution in Teso and its Effects on the Life and Mission of the Church during the 1980s with particular Reference to Serere Parish," Makerere University, unpublished Diploma in Theology dissertation 1990, 37. Here after cited as "The Economic Revolution in Teso."

34. Thomas E. Irigei, "The Social Change and its Effects on the Morals of Iteso with Specific Reference to Ngora, COU Archdeaconry Soroti Diocese," Makerere University, unpublished Diploma in Theology dissertation 1990, 44.

Usuk and Amuria, a para-military force, and armed them to defend Teso from Karimajong cattle rustlers.

Map 4: Teso and Neighbouring Districts

But the gains made during the Obote II regime were reversed by the massive recruitment of Karimajong into the army and the support and involvement of government troops in cattle rustling during the short-lived Okello regime. Cattle rustling escalated. For the Karimajong, their incorporation in the UNLA meant more ammunition for cattle rustling, with which it turned into a lucrative business, since in addition to raiding cattle they looted "property like saucepans, plates, clothes, foods such as groundnuts, chicken, turkeys and ducks. There was also much raping of women, murder and burning of people's houses and food granaries."[35]

The support by the Okello-government troops of the Karimajong raiders is associated with Teso's historical political support of Obote and UPC. Teso was bound to suffer reprisals and subjugation by Okello Military Council regime as a heartland of support for Obote and UPC. The regime had found ready allies in the Karimajong warriors and raiders, who were keen on increasing their herds. The Okello-government forces therefore supported the Karimajong raiders by providing weapons and using a helicopter gunship. It is alleged that the helicopter was used for distributing ammunition to different raiding groups in Teso[36] and also for surveillance, locating herds so that the ground forces could loot them.[37]

After the NRA captured power in Kampala, some of the defeated UNLA-Okello regime troops surrendered, and others, particularly from Acholi, fled the capital, retreating towards the north, through the eastern route.[38] As they fled, they looted and killed indiscriminately, particularly in the major towns of Jinja, Tororo, Mbale and Soroti. The areas that took the heaviest toll of their vengeful actions were those that were strongholds of support for Obote-UPC government, and therefore Teso was bound to take its share of suffering. It was with relief that the people of Teso received the NRA soldiers, who were pursuing some of the dissident Acholi troops. Their relief was not only associated with "liberation" from the wrath of fleeing Acholi soldiers, but also from the entire Tito Okello rule during which "Teso had been afflicted by marauding bands of savage and ruthless raiders and cattle rustlers set loose by a decadent and short-lived military regime of the Okellos."[39] But this brief honeymoon with the NRA came to an end

---

35. Ibid., 46.
36. Ibid., 44–45.
37. Yoweri K. Museveni, in his speech at the First Anniversary of NRM, reproduced in Y. K. Museveni, *What Is Africa's Problem?* (Kampala, NRM Publications, 1992), 41.
38. Peter Otai, "Political and Security Situation in North and Eastern Uganda," a paper presented at the Seminar on the Political, Economic and Security situation in Uganda at the Commonwealth Institute, London, June 1992, in CBR Archives, PF 320.9 OTA (1992) 2, 5. This route was the only exit open.
39. D. M. Ochyengh, "Proposals on the Restoration of Stability, Peace and Progress to Teso (15 December 1991)" to the Chairman Presidential Commission of Teso. Document at CBR Archives PF 3209.9 (1992) 1, 4–5.

soon after NRA had established an administration over Teso, in both Kumi and Soroti districts.

The NRA could not trust the Iteso who had been a major part of the force that had fought them during the Luwero Triangle war, led by what was then known as the Special Branch, a para-military force that was predominantly composed of Iteso.[40] The NRA administration perceived itself to be in enemy territory and therefore set itself to diffuse a possible rebellion. Its obsession with potential rebellion in Teso, heartland for Obote-UPC support, arose from its historical mission as outlined in the previous chapter, "to remove this evil man [Obote], root and branch, from the political life of Uganda, for good."[41] The UPC, right from its pre-independence formative years, dominated the political landscape of Teso. Membership to the UPC cut across ethnic and religious lines.[42] The NRA therefore expected resistance and took measures, which in their view would pre-empt it.

According to the Iteso, the NRA/M administration sought to build a local political support base by suppressing pro-Obote/UPC leadership and allying with Democratic Party stalwarts and Iteso leaders who were on the UPC fringes.[43] This was confirmed in their minds by the arrest and detention of several prominent Iteso elders during the months of December 1986, and January and February 1987,[44] who were accused of being

---

40. Among the top commanders was one John Eregu, an Etesot. Gershom Ilukor, OI, Soroti Diocese office, Soroti, 19 March 1996.

41. Lule in his letter to the Commonwealth Prime Ministers and Heads of Government reproduced in National Resistance Movement, *Mission to Freedom*, 31.

42. Charles Ocan, "The Political Situation in Teso," a paper delivered at the Seminar on Political and Economic Situation in Uganda" at the Commonwealth Institute, London, 1992, 2. CBR Archives, PF 320.9 OCA (1992) 1. Although the population of Catholics by far out-numbered that of Protestants and Teso had various large ethnic groups, DP remained a minority party. The major ethnic groups in Teso are: the Bakenyi, a Bantu group, on the shores of Lake Kyoga; the Kumam, "cousins" to the Langi, living in Kumi; and the Iteso, the largest of them, living in both districts of Kumi and Teso.

43. Charles Ocan, "The Political Situation in Teso," 3. Ocan gives the example of Mr Okuraja, murdered by UPA rebels, as one of the DP Stalwarts, and Okurut, whose "UPC history in Teso was obviously in doubt." Ibid.

44. George Oguli, OI, Soroti 18 March 1996; among them George Oguli, Oduc and Etonu. G. Oguli had been Chairman of the Electoral Commission during Obote II regime. Oguli was arrested on a Sunday, as he was coming out of church, and was taken to Kotido in Karamoja where, with other Iteso, he was detained for one year. "May be it was the providence of God," Oguli said as he recalled that in February 1988 the President visited Kotido and on recognizing him, ordered his together with several others.

members of a rebel group, Force Obote Back Again (FOBA).[45] This gave the impression to the Iteso that NRA/M administration was against mainstream Teso. However, since many of the Iteso had resigned themselves to the fact that UPC had been vanquished by the overthrow of the Obote II regime, this did not embitter them as much as the disarming of the peoples' militia, and the arrest of some ex-service men.[46]

As part of the process of establishing an NRA/M administration in Teso, NRA disarmed the people's militia, and demanded that all ex-servicemen, who had served in the defeated and now defunct forces of UNLA and Special Force, report to the NRA/M administration centres.[47] Disarming the militia resulted in north Teso becoming vulnerable to the Karimajong cattle raiders, who immediately took advantage of a defenceless border between Karamoja and Teso and plundered cattle kraals beginning in Usuk. In the meantime, the ex-servicemen who surrendered were detained, and many of them reportedly killed.

According to Michael Okwii, an Etesot, the Karimajong rustlers looted, raided and killed under the watchful eye of the NRA troops who were stationed at all local administration centres in the two districts of Kumi and Soroti in Teso.[48] In some cases, it was reported, some of the NRA soldiers raided with the Karimajong.[49] Like their predecessors the Military Council, the NRA are said to have provided air-cover for the ground troops and raiders by using a helicopter gunship for surveillance, for whenever it was "sighted patrolling a certain area, the people of that area would be assured of raiders coming."[50] The proportions and extent of cattle rustling reached during the Museveni I regime were not known in the history of Teso.[51] In the words of Michael Okwii, an Etesot himself:

---

45. Oguli, OI.
46. Charles Obaikol, OI, Serere, 2 March 1996.
47. Ocan, "The Political Situation in Teso," 3.
48. Okwii, "The Economic Revolution in Teso," 40–41.
49. Oguli OI; Ilukor, OI. Both of these informants said they were aware of some NRA/M leaders that ferried cattle in wagons to unknown destinations, but were believed to be going to the slaughterhouses in Kampala. Obaikol said that when he started his work in Serere in 1990, it was only the NRA soldiers that grazed cattle. Obaikol, OI.
50. Okwii, "The Economic Revolution in Teso," 39. Also corroborated by Ilukor, OI.
51. Ibid.

> So such circumstances surrounding rustling activity forced people to associate rustlers with the government. So under such frustrating atmosphere many people were desperate, and others were forced to join the rebel movement, which sprang up in Usuk in 1987 as their only source of hope of redemption.[52]

For the Iteso therefore their hostility and rebellion was provoked by the apparent collaboration of the NRA with their archenemies, the Karimajong cattle rustlers.[53] One grasps the enormity of the bitterness and hostility generated by the way the NRA managed the transition when put in the context of the central place that livestock in general and cattle in particular played in the life of the Iteso: economic, social, and religious. Lawrence, one of the colonial administrators, observed in the early 50s:

> In all the religious and social ceremonies of Teso life, livestock plays a most important part. In the initiation of *asapan*, when the youth takes on his new manhood name, he must suck the udder of a cow to indicate approval. The entrails of the sacrificial ox or goat will tell the future, and the sacrifice of a goat with special markings will help to cure sickness; its stomach contents must be smeared on the patient. If a woman has failed to observe her clan taboos, sickness will befall her and her children; a bull must be suffocated and the woman must wear the skin of the dewlap and tie pieces of meat round the necks of her children. Cattle are an essential part of bride price; a bull must be slaughtered at burial ceremonies.[54]

Cattle were essential in sustaining agriculture, because the ox-plough was the dominant tool for tilling the land since its introduction by

---

52. Ibid., 40. In Serere county about 98% of the cattle population was looted during the raids of 1987. Ibid., 37–38. All the people who I interviewed that owned cattle before the escalation of rustling (it was only one without!) lost them. For example: Rev Osuret lost 48; Mr Olupot lost 51; and Rev Yeku Angois, lost 107 belonging to the wider family.

53. This was the unanimous opinion of all those interviewed in Teso, including the group of leaders meeting at Odudui Parish, Soroti Archdeaconary, composed of Rev Yeku Angois, Steven Ariko (catechist), Nelson Omaje, and Justine Ojuri.

54. Lawrence, *The Iteso*, 144.

missionaries in 1909. Okwii affirmed the continuing central role of cattle in the life of the Iteso.

> Cattle keeping has been the nucleus of the economy of Iteso; oxen boosted agriculture. Traditionally cattle . . . were more for prestige, marriage, buying land, food, paying debts, etc. than for cash. The Iteso never valued the monetary worth of a cow. Ownership of many herds of cattle was the most important thing. Even the educated people "banked" their money in cattle; they valued to see their animals increase in number [rather] than an interest in the bank.[55]

The value attached to cattle was also reflected in attitudes about giving in the Church, to the extent that one could be judged to be more committed as a Christian if he or she made an offering of a cow in the church.

> Even in the Church the biggest offering one could give was a cow or a bull and he would be called a good Christian and considered more important than a person who offered money. However, only Christians of rare qualities did the offering of a cow or bull to the Church.[56]

Given a situation where the people's livelihood and identity depended on ownership of cattle, the perception that the new government of NRA/M was collaborating with those plundering this base led to a collision and rebellion. Okwii, has summarized what led to rebellion in Teso against the Museveni regime thus:

> With the increase of cattle raids and the NRA/NRM government caring less about them, coupled with arbitrary arrests and tortures of the ex-government officials by the NRA soldiers, the "wananchi" were very much provoked and so the ex-soldiers of UA [Uganda Army], UNLA, Special Police Force and People's Militia Force mobilised themselves to wage a war against what they termed as the persistent social injustices inflicted upon the people of Teso, sanctioned by the NRM

---

55. Okwii, "The Economic Revolution in Teso," 13, 14.
56. Ibid., 15.

government as a punishment to the Iteso, Obote's staunch supporters.[57]

In Bishop Ilukor's view, the problem was compounded by the fact that those at the helm of NRA/M leadership in Teso were young, inexperienced men, oblivious to Teso recent history. Therefore, on one hand was an NRA/M administration that considered itself in a hostile environment, while on the other hand the people of Teso considered the NRA/M administration was antagonistic to them and determined to decimate them with their resources.

War in Teso

The ex-servicemen who did not report to the NRM, and the disarmed People's Militia, regrouped towards the end of 1987, to protect themselves from any further onslaught from Karimajong raiders, and to repulse any attempts by NRA to use force against them. At this stage there was no overt political mission to overthrow the NRM regime. Different groups of militia and ex-servicemen organized themselves under different commanders, based in different areas.[58]

It is the politically defranchised Iteso, who had been part of the Obote II regime and most of whom at this time were living in exile, who on realizing that a climate of rebellion had developed in Teso, took advantage and put a political dimension to it. Among them was Peter Otai who had been Minister of State for Defence in the Obote II government. Otai formed a rebel organisation, Uganda People's Front (UPF) and tried to organize these disjointed rebel groups into the Uganda People's Army (UPA), but in reality had no control over them in the field.[59] Otai stated the mission of UPF/A thus:

---

57. Ibid., 39.
58. Othniel Okalebo, OI, Ngora, 18 March 1996. In Katakwi, to the north, under the command of Charles Ojirot, alias Jesus Ojirot; in Soroti under the command of John Eregu alias Hitler; in Serere under the command of Omeda; and in Ngora under the command of Alpha.
59. Ilukor, OI; Ocan, "The Political Situation in Teso," 3.

> The struggle waged by the Uganda Peoples Front and Army (UPF/A) in Uganda is primarily political: it is a struggle to liberate the people from the grip of totalitarianism in which power is concentrated in Lt Gen Museveni. . . .
>
> The military component UPA has always been used as a complement (sic) to protect the people subjected to torture, murder, and rape. The UPA was formed to help people protect their property and food crops being destroyed by the NRA under the pretext that it is necessary to destroy the food crops in granaries and fields in order to deny it to the guerrillas. The UPA military activities can be de-escalated in direct proportion to the NRA de-escalation of rape, murder and torture of the people.[60]

With the formation of UPF/A and their declared political mission "to liberate the people from the grip of totalitarianism in which power is concentrated in Lt Gen Museveni,"[61] what were hitherto acts of self-protection by the peoples militia and ex-servicemen, turned into a war of political rebellion with the goal to overthrow the NRA/M regime. By the end of 1988 all Teso was under the control of rebels. The people in Teso supported the rebels, because of their perception that the NRA was collaborating with the Karimajong cattle raiders.

NRA/M administration was also determined wipe out the rebellion. Their five-year rebel war in Luwero Triangle had given their insight into rebel strategies and tactics. In order to eliminate rebels from rebel held areas, "there was a policy to destroy food stocks that were assisting the rebels."[62] Aware that the rebels could "buy cattle or cassava or both from the peasants in the areas"[63] it seemed not to matter to the NRA/M that the Karimajong raiders were plundering the cattle population in Teso. Consequently everyone in Teso who owned cattle lost them either to the Karimajong, or to the

---

60. Otai, , "Political and Security Situation," 4.
61. Ibid.
62. Museveni quoted in *The New Vision*, 27 June 1989.
63. Museveni, in his paper given to NRA officers at Bombo Military Academy, August 1990, "How to Fight a Counter-Revolutionary Insurgency," reproduced in Museveni, *What Is Africa's Problem?*, 153.

NRA, or to the rebels.[64] In July 1989 the NRA commanders outlawed all fishing activity in Serere County, "claiming that rebels benefit from fish."[65]

The other policy employed by NRA was to evacuate rural populations from villages into camps.[66] The idea was to move the entire district populations into camps, so as to isolate the rebels and curtail population involvement with the rebels, as was the case in Luwero triangle. In Kumi there were over ten camps, with the largest one at Ngora County headquarters.[67] Although there were no camps set up in Soroti district, there were displaced people all over the district, the majority living in towns.[68]

The "Skulls of Teso"

Reminiscent of "the skulls of Luwero," Okwii has described the impact of the war on Teso thus:

> The area which was one of the richest parts of the country [Uganda], provided other areas with cassava, millet, cattle, goats, poultry, etc., [was] reduced to a wasteland, unable to sufficiently feed its own people and scattered with bones and *skulls of people* that have been brutally murdered by NRA, cattle rustlers and rebels.[69]

Okwii has apportioned blame for the "skulls of Teso" to three parties: NRA, cattle rustlers and rebels. Bishop Ilukor concurred:

> The army were killing people; the rebels were killing people; the rebels were fighting with the army; the army were dying;

---

64. Ilukor, OI.
65. Okwii, "The Economic Revolution in Teso," 47.
66. Museveni, quoted in *The New Vision*, 27 June 1989.
67. Letter from the Office of the Deputy Minister, Ministry of Relief and Social Rehabilitation, to Donor Agencies, dated 3 July 1990. AEE Archives, Kampala; Bishop G Ilukor, OI. The other camps were at Mukura, Kapir, Okwakela, Olimai, Aukot, Kelim, Atutur, Kanyumu, Mukongoro, Bukedeya, Nyero, Kachumbala and Kidongore. African Evangelistic Enterprise, Kumi Displaced Peoples' Project Report, dated 30 June 1990. AEE Archives, Kampala. African Evangelistic Enterprise was one of the organizations active in supporting Soroti Diocese with relief supplies.
68. African Evangelistic Enterprise Staff reported 250,000 people in Soroti "with no help at all," in December 1990.
69. Okwii, "The Economic Revolution in Teso," 46 (emphasis added).

> [and] the rebels were dying . . . If the army heard that rebels had passed near your home; if the rebels heard that the army had passed near your home they would come and kill you.[70]

Some have put the total of those who died during the war to 100,000.[71] Thousands died at the hands of NRA in its several operations to wipe out the rebels.

> When the NRA launched a new offensive against the rebels, it involved severe abuse against civilians. They brutalised and massacred many of them, destroyed and burnt their houses, looted foodstuffs and destroyed those they could not carry; even crops in gardens.[72]

The NRA employed "cordon and search operations"[73] in which all able-bodied men were rounded up for the purpose of identifying and isolating rebels from among them. In one such incident in Ngora county in July 1989 about three hundred men were detained in a disused railway wagon at Mukura, and about seventy were killed. Some were shot, and others suffocated to death.[74]

Thousands died in the camps, especially the elderly and children, due to hunger, malnutrition and appalling hygienic conditions as a result of overcrowding. In the camp at Ngora, the largest of all the camps in Kumi, at which a population of two sub-counties were herded, at least twenty-four people were said to be dying each day, and by the time the camp dispersed towards the end of 1990, graves covered an area of two and a half acres.[75] It has been estimated that up to 4,000 people died in this camp.[76]

---

70. Ilukor, OI.
71. Otai, "Political and Security Situation," 6.
72. Albina Oguti, quoted by Okwii, "The Economic Revolution in Teso," 45.
73. *The New Vision*, 24 July 1989. "Cordon and search" was an expression used, referring to the screening operations that were mounted all over Teso, in June and July 1989, to identify rebels.
74. *The New Vision*, 24 July 1989; also *The New Vision*, 28 August 1989.
75. Thomas Adupu, Rev Naboth Hannington Arutu, and Rev Charles Obaikol, OI, Serere, 2 March 1996; and Archdeacon Charles Okwii, OI, Ngora, 2 March 1996.
76. Ilukor, OI.

The rebels killed anyone they suspected not to be supporting their cause. For example one of the areas that suffered heavily at the hands of rebels was Serere area because:

> When the idea of rebel movement arrived in Serere most Bantu [Bakenyi] never welcomed the idea, so they reported the matter to the NRA training wing in Serere. Consequently most supporters and sympathisers of the rebel activity were rounded up and beaten, others killed and some put in prison.[77]

The rebels avenged themselves against the Bakenyi, plundered Serere and massacred many.[78] The rebels also killed several chiefs and local Resistance Council (RC) officials because by default, their serving with the NRA/M government was considered subversive to conduct of war, and the rebel cause.[79]

A "Rebel" Church in Teso

The entire region of Teso was engulfed in war because the critical issue of cattle and cattle rustling affected all Teso. Consequently the rebellion enjoyed the sympathy of most of the population, including those in the churches. As one of the catechists admitted: "The way I understand it, during that time when we had this problem, almost everybody was involved in the rebel activity, because you could actually give assistance directly or indirectly, trying to protect your life."[80] But it was not only for self-protection that the Iteso supported the rebels; it was also because the rebels initially seemed to represent the people's interests, the protection of their cows from what they perceived to be an alliance between the Karimajong and the NRA to plunder them.

The NRA experience as rebels in Luwero Triangle shaped its attitude and conduct of war in Teso. They had used Christians, clerics and church

---

77. Okwii, "The Economic Revolution in Teso," 40–41.
78. Lucas Gonahasa, OI, Kadama, Pallisa, 22 April 1997; and Okwii, "The Economic Revolution in Teso," 41.
79. Oguli, OI. The Resistance Council officials were locally elected at village levels, a system that was initiated by the NRA/M during the Luwero Triangle days.
80. John Steven Ariko, OI, Odudui parish, Soroti, 1 March 1996.

property for clandestine activity, and therefore held suspect Teso clerics and churches as rebels and rebel ground respectively. The local populace were not aware that this was so in the early period of the war, 1986–87. Whenever there was an attack by NRA in an area, they would flee to take refuge in church buildings, convinced that the army would fear to desecrate such "holy" places. The exact opposite happened. In one incident in Soroti Archdeaconry, villagers ran into a church building, and the NRA pursued them, and killed some as others fled.[81] The populace therefore realized that church premises could no longer be places of refuge.

Clerics too were treated as rebel suspects. Rev Canon Yesero Okare, during one of his pastoral visits to Kaberamaido was told that wearing the collar did not imply he could not be a rebel. After all, during the Luwero Triangle war they, too, would put on collars so as to go through government armed road checks.[82] Just like other leaders and people in Teso, several clergy were detained: towards the end of 1987, in a town-wide NRA sweep in search of rebels, Bishop G. Ilukor, together with Canon Yesero Okare, were among those detained overnight at a military post in Soroti;[83] the Rev Job Osuret was detained for three months in 1987;[84] in 1988 when three government ministers on a peace mission were abducted by rebels in Kumi, Rev Okalebo who had led them to the rebel enclave in Ngora, was later arrested and detained for months, allegedly for conspiring with the rebels.[85] While in prison Okalebo was whipped on the back in five instances, each time he was given thirty-nine strokes. One pastor, Rev Odeke, is said to have been killed by NRA in Bukedea 1988. When Bukedea was taken over

---

81. Rev Canon Yesero Okare, Soroti, OI, 1 March 1996. Rev Okare was archdeacon of Soroti at the time.
82. Ibid.
83. Ilukor, OI; Okare, OI. Ilukor was taken from his house at night dressed in pyjamas.
84. Rev Job Osuret, OI, Kumi, 19 March 1996; Joash O. Olupot, OI, Kumi, 19 March 1996. Rev Osuret was priest in Ngora from 1983–1990, then became Archdeacon of Kumi from 1990. He was Archdeacon of Kumi at the time of the interview. Olupot was headmaster of Ngora High School from 1982 through the period of the war in Teso; was detained four times by the NRM on suspicion for being a rebel; lost 51 cows – 45 to the Karamajong and the rest to the rebels. One of the four times, he was detained with Rev Osuret.
85. Okalebo, OI.

by the rebels, Odeke chose to stay with the people, and were among many killed by NRA as rebels.[86]

Ministry in Turbulent Teso

There were different patterns of ministry in the churches and among the people depending on whether people were still located in their villages or were living in camps. For most of the period of turbulence, and for most of Teso, people remained in the villages under the control of the rebels except in Kumi District in 1990 when the NRA/M administration evacuated people from their villages and put them into camps.

In the rebel held areas, one would characterize the population as living in constant fear of either the rebels or NRA. Sunday worship services, when they occurred, were packed to capacity.[87] What often disrupted them and got the congregations fleeing for their lives was the appearance of NRA soldiers. In one church in Soroti Archdeaconry, NRA soldiers appeared as the service was beginning. The entire congregation ran away and left the two clergy alone in the church, in spite their bidding to "be firm, do not run, stay and be killed with us here."[88] The people could not stay because they believed that if they did the NRA soldiers would harass them and even kill some.[89] It was the commitment of these clergy and catechists to "stay with" and "be killed with" the people that stands out.

Although the reason given for not fleeing the region was that they were not in conflict with either the rebels or the government soldiers, certainly these church leaders were more committed to their Iteso "flock" than they were to the government soldiers. Engwau expressed his sentiment thus: "I have no problem with soldiers or rebels. I am a father and mother to them. I pray for the soldiers and for the rebels."[90] This image of a parent, and specifically a mother, that Engwau had come to cherish as an appropriate description of the character of the church's ministry, must have been used

---

86. Ibid.
87. Okare, OI.
88. This was covering Soroti County, in which Soroti town is located, and was all under the control of the rebels, except a 1-mile radius of downtown Soroti. Ilukor, OI.
89. Okare, OI.
90. Enos Engwau, OI, Serere, 2 March 1996.

in reference to the rebel Iteso rather than the NRA. Engwau reiteration that "whether the child is bad or good, you don't send the child away"[91] furthers the argument that the leaders' primary commitment was to the Iteso sons in the rebel ranks.

However it is significant that Engwau perceived his leadership responsibility and commitment in parental terms. Rev Okwii also subscribed to the image of the church as a mother, one who "nurses, cooks, sacrifices and can easily know the pain of her children."[92] For Bishop Ilukor, the mother image is the most appropriate description of the reality and experience of the church among the people because "people regarded the church as the mother which . . . fed, treated, wanted them to be alive. All this is what it means to be a mother."[93] The Church was among the Iteso rebels as a mother is to her children.

Another feature of the life of the Church in Teso during the war was the growth in cooperation between the clergy of the Catholic Church and those of the Church of Uganda. But it should be noted that the Protestant-Catholic relations in Teso were generally cordial. The historical rivalry between the Protestants and the Roman Catholics that was characteristic of relationship of the two churches in most areas of Uganda was diminished in Teso by the political developments on the eve of independence. The development of political party affiliation in Teso towards independence was not on the basis of religious affiliation. The majority of the Iteso, Protestants, and Catholics, associated with the Uganda Peoples Congress. As Rev Naphtali Opwata put it: "It is the only [political] party people knew."[94] The wartime added to this cordiality the dimension of cooperation, engendered by the common experience of suffering. In some parishes it is the Catholic Church that supplied elements for Holy Communion to the Church of Uganda pastors throughout the war period.[95] On several occasions leaders from the two sister churches met "to find solutions for

---

91. Ibid.
92. Okwii, OI.
93. Ilukor, OI.
94. Naphtali Opwata, OI, Soroti, 1 March 1996.
95. Esero, OI.

the war."⁹⁶ Bishop Ilukor referred to several times when he met with his counterpart of the Catholic Church, and worked on some peace missions with the Father in charge of the Catholic parish Church in Soroti town, Fr Cochran.⁹⁷

As in the Luwero Church narrative the significance of the "order" of catechist was evident in Teso during the war.⁹⁸ As in Luwero Triangle, the secret of their service was the fact that they were with the people in all the diversity of their experiences: fleeing, in the camps, depleted of their cattle and mourning of their dead. They were with the people, praying, preaching and distributing relief when it was available, and in many cases talking to rebels to lay down their weapons.⁹⁹

Unlike the Luwero account, there were no mass baptisms during the war.¹⁰⁰ Holy Communion services were seldom held. In Serere Parish where there was a resident priest throughout the war period, there was not even one Holy Communion service from 1986–1990.¹⁰¹ The absence of many baptisms could be explained by the fact that the period in the camps in Kumi was not as long as that in the Luwero Triangle. The life span of the Kumi camps was about one year, a period not long enough to do the work of preparing baptism candidates. The absence of Holy Communion services however cannot be due to time constraints. Although the Teso clergy gave the scarcity of elements to use as the reason,¹⁰² the more plausible explanation is that while the Luwero churches had a longer Eucharist tradition prior to the war, this was not the case with Teso. Holy Communion was not that central to the worship life of the Church in Teso even prior to the insurgency. So the Teso pastors could give the unavailability of

---

96. Okwii, OI.
97. Ilukor, OI.
98. All the clergy interviewed emphasised their role in the camps and running churches.
99. Osuret, OI.
100. Okwii, OI. Okwii was in charge of the largest of all the camps, at Ngora, and said that the "baptisms in the camp was not so much."
101. Okwii, OI. 62. There were two pastors, E. Engwau 1986–1989, C. Obaikol 1990–present. E. Engwau, OI.
102. Engwau, OI.

the elements as the ground for not administering communion while the Luwero pastors[103] were quick to adapt to the scarcities by using alternative elements.

It was prayer and the ministry of the Word in various forms that brought courage, comfort and strength in the midst of those life-threatening conditions, in the camps, on the run in the bush, or in prison. Prayer and the Word of God were the most important foci of the clergy in their service and ministry.[104] The clergy and catechists centred their ministry to the people in camps on preaching and Bible study.[105] In Ngora camp Rev Charles Okwii organized Bible reading groups and was amazed at the positive response and the amount of singing, in spite of the suffering. Some of the popular choruses sang in those meetings are:

> *Ijo bon Yesu, ijo bon Yesu* (3 times)
> *Katoma ocan ka ijo bon Yesu . . .*
> Number one Jesus, number one Jesus . . .
>
> *Emamei ibone ikaruni Edeke . . .* Hallelluyah (3 times)
> Nothing will be impossible before God
>
> *Emamei bobo lokiyuuni isio kilema*
> *Edeke ediope* (3 times)
> There is no other God that will deliver us apart from you
>
> *Ejokuna Edeke, Hallelluia, Ejokuna Edeke*
> *Ejokuna Edeke Ejokuna*
> *Ekadeke* (4 times)
> God is so good, He is so good to me.[106]

The Enos Engwau, who was archdeacon of Serere during the peak period of the war 1987–1989, was once attacked by a group of seven rebels at night.

> When the rebels asked me to open, I *prayed*, asked God what to do. I then opened the door and they came in. There were

---

103. Can Blassio Sajjabi, OI, Semuto, Luwero, 20 September 1995.
104. Engwau, OI; Okwii, OI.
105. Obaikol, OI; and Okwii, OI.
106. Text and translation given to me by Charles Okwii, OI.

seven . . . God gave me courage. They had come to kill me. Then I *preached* to them . . . After that we made a circle and I *prayed for them*, and then they went away.[107]

Okalebo, during the six months in detention found prayer to be the most important spiritual discipline; so did Osuret and Olupot. In fact both Okalebo and Osuret led prayer services while in detention.[108] George Oguli during the one year in prison in Kotido, found that his Bible and *Daily Power*, were his "most valuable property" and it was "nothing other than reading the Bible"[109] that encouraged him to have hope.

In recognition of the importance of prayer, Bishop Ilukor initiated a program of prayer with all-day fasting in Soroti cathedral, every Saturday. These prayer meetings began at the time cattle raiding escalated in proportions, in late 1986, and continued through to the end of 1989.[110] Ilukor believes that the Ministerial Peace Mission of late 1988 and the declaration by government of an amnesty to surrendering rebels was a change of heart by government, resulting from the concerted prayers of the people. The change of heart is debatable. The government must have realized that ending the war through military confrontation was going to be a hard and arduous journey and therefore changed tactics. However, whether the government had a change of heart or not is hard to tell, and is inconsequential to this account. It is Ilukor's interpretation of the government measures as a manifestation of change in its attitude to the Iteso that is significant, because it is an indicator of change in Ilukor's perception of the government. It is even more significant that Ilukor credited the perceived change to prayer. No one can provide a scientific proof that certain events have been wrought by prayer because prayer does not belong to the realm of science. That prayer is credited to be responsible for certain happenings is a statement, not so much about the events, as it is of the interpreter. It is the one who prays that will appreciate prayer and its results; prayer is a "work"

---

107. Engwau, OI (emphasis added).
108. Okalebo, OI; Osuret, OI; and Olupot, OI.
109. Oguli, OI. Oguli was using the devotional guide *Daily Power* brought to him in prison by his wife.
110. Ilukor, OI; Okare, OI.

of faith. The recourse to prayer in the rank and file of the Teso Church is a manifestation of faith.

The other critical aspect of service was relief and medical work, in the camps and villages.[111] The diocese of Soroti linked up with relief agencies and was actively involved in food distribution, provision of clothing, immunization of children and provision of agricultural inputs.[112] However it was the Church's leading role in the restoration of peace that reflects the significance of its presence in Teso during the war period.

The Church as a Peacemaker

Following the discussions in the House of Bishops at the beginning of the NRA/M era, that considered developing a social concern ministry through which the whole Church would seek to be an advocate for peace, one would expect that the civil strife in Teso would be given due attention by the Provincial organs of the Church, such as the Provincial Assembly, the House of Bishops or the Provincial Standing committee. On the contrary, one is struck by very general references to "some parts of Gulu, Soroti and Karamoja, where there is still insecurity" and general appeals "to the government to continue on the road of seeking a lasting solution by peaceful means, as 'violence breeds violence.'"[113] The issue in fact disappears from the agendas of these meetings after the second half of 1989.[114] The question of peace for the people of Teso became localized; it was the responsibility of the Church in Teso.

There were four major initiatives for the restoration of peace: two by the Museveni I and II regimes; one by the Church; and the other by Iteso elders. But the most significant of these was the one played by the church, through its leaders, clergy and lay.

---

111. Okwii, OI.
112. The partnership of the Church with African Evangelistic Enterprise in providing relief services was particularly acclaimed. Ilukor, OI; and Okwii, OI.
113. "Memorandum to His Excellency the President of Uganda Yoweri Kaguta Museveni at State House Entebbe on 23 February 1989," 1, House of Bishops Papers, COU Archives.
114. Both Bishops M. Kawuma and G. Ilukor, in personal interviews corroborated this. Kawuma believed that it was a local problem, and Ilukor confessed feeling abandoned by the House of Bishops.

The first initiative by Museveni I regime was a Ministerial team in 1988 composed of some Iteso ministers in the government, with a mission to "reach the rebels"[115] and talk them into cessation of hostilities with government. When these ministers contacted Ilukor to share his "views about the war in Teso" and propose a way toward ending violence, Ilukor invited some clergy and elders in Soroti to a meeting with them. A strategy was put in place to send pastors and elders to the rebel leaders in the villages all over Soroti District to collect the views of the rebels. As Bishop Ilukor put it, "I sent clergy to go to the villages to come with messages from the rebels."[116]

In Kumi District the government ministers elected to contact and talk to the rebel leaders directly, according to Ilukor, defying his advice "never to try and go out of Kumi, never to try and go out of Soroti until I say it is safe."[117] Although two clergymen, Othniel Okalebo who was then Headmaster of Ngora Girls Secondary School, and a CMS missionary Tim Britton, who drove them in his car to the rebel enclave in Serere, assisted the ministers,[118] it was against Ilukor's advice. In the process, the ministers were abducted and taken hostage by the rebels. On hearing of the failure of the mission and abduction of the ministers, Bishop Ilukor travelled to Serere, sought out the rebel leaders and the ministers:

> I tried to see the ministers and the rebels but I couldn't. I only saw a few of the leaders of the rebels. When the rebels heard I was at Serere, they transferred the ministers nearer to Soroti; then I followed them up to near Soroti. They transferred the ministers further north; and then they took them back to Serere. "We shall bring them back to you," the rebels told me. "We want them to see the atrocities, which their government had done." But I was telling them, "Don't waste time. You write the things and let them take them to the government."

---

115. Okalebo, OI. They are: Aporu-Okol, Ekinu and Okurut. Okurut was Minister of Labour; Aporu-Okol, Deputy Minister of Animal industry; and Ekinu an MP.
116. Ilukor, OI.
117. Ibid.
118. Okalebo, OI.

They did not want; and Otai was then strong. He said they would never release them.[119]

However, Stanslus Okurut was released. In a combat effort to free Aporu Okol and Ekenu from captivity, Ekenu was killed. Aporu Okol was freed, and the peace mission ended with further violence.

There were also attempts by Iteso elders to persuade both "our children"[120] and the government to lay down arms. Although Bishop Ilukor perceived this as a purely non-church initiative, Archdeacon Charles Okwii of Ngora believed it was an initiative of "elders in the church," and named Gideon Orena, Epaphras Aisu, Bethuel Opio and Naphtali Eteni as elders in the church who spearheaded this initiative in Kumi[121]. Rev Job Osuret went to the village of Kanyum and held a meeting with village elders and young men as part of the effort to restore peace in the area. The message was one: while acknowledging that their cows were lost and that the government had some responsibility for it, war would not restore the cows to the people, and therefore the urgent thing to do was to give up violence.[122]

The Presidential Commission for Teso was another initiative by the government for the restoration of peace in Teso. President Museveni appointed it at the end of 1990, and its purpose was to restore peace to the region, and build confidence in the people of the government. A look at the membership of the Commission shows the church's presence. The Chairman of the Commission, Professor Epelu Opio, was an active member of the Protestant/Anglican University Chapel of St. Francis, Makerere; the Secretary, Grace Akello, a member of the Church of Uganda; Stephen Akabway, a Mulokole of long standing from his student days in the 1960s; member, George Oguli[123] was a commissioned Lay Reader, and a prominent member of Soroti Cathedral congregation. Oguli, an uncle to Peter Otai, was the only member of the commission residing in Teso and in

---

119. Ilukor, OI. Bishop Ilukor stayed in Serere for two weeks trying to secure release of the ministers. Okare, OI.
120. Okwii, OI. This is how he referred to the rebels.
121. Ibid.
122. Osuret, OI. Kanyum was one of the rebel's strongholds. Okwii, OI. The other strongholds in Kumi were Ngora, Amuria, Serere, Nyero.
123. This is the same Oguli who proposed the creation of the Kampala Diocese in Chapter Four. Usher Wilson commissioned him a Lay Reader, in the 1960s. Oguli, OI.

charge of co-ordinating contacts with rebels. As one who spent one year in prison, detained for being suspected to collaborate with rebels, his motivation was for peace in Teso, and the service of God. Reflecting on the success of his mission in persuading many rebels to stop violence, he said: "I have my reward in heaven; I don't want to take credit."[124]

In speaking to the rebels, he would concur with their justified cause of their grievance, but argue that violence had added more misery because not only were the cows gone, but Iteso were dying in the conflict:

> I would always talk in reference to the Bible in everything . . . My message was that of the prodigal son in Luke. I would always start the meetings with prayers. I was actually preaching most of the time.[125]

Re-echoing the co-operative relationship between Protestants and Catholics in Teso, he acknowledged the support and assistance of one of the Catholic priests who served in Soroti throughout the war period, Fr Cochran.

> I went to Father Cochran to give me a lift [in his car], to see one of the rebel leaders. He agreed and we went together to see this rebel commander. We travelled 4 km. Then when we were about to reach I went alone . . . The man appeared with a dagger, pistol and a gun with long hair, as a mad man. I did not know the man but he knew me well . . . God was straight to me. He told me to tell him I had come to take them. That is what I told him and he agreed. They came out with their guns and everything. I asked him to come with the bodyguards.[126]

According to Oguli, prayer was the source of his courage. "When I pray, I don't fear . . . the secret of my life is prayer."[127]

The contribution of Bishop Ilukor in restoring peace to Teso, as leader of the Church, is unmistakable. For although suspected by the Museveni's regime to be a rebel sympathizer, he was undeterred in his crusade to

---

124. Ibid.
125. Ibid.
126. Ibid. The name of the rebel commander was Patrick Akum.
127. Ibid.

restore peace to Teso, until the cessation of hostilities and the end of the insurgency in 1991.¹²⁸

Bishop Gershom Ilukor: A "Rebel" and Peacemaker

In the two years immediately after Museveni and the NRA/M assumed power, a vacuum of leadership was created in Teso. Several were detained and others ran into hiding or in exile. Ochyengh observed:

> During that time [1986–1989] political and opinion leaders like Oduc, Oguli, Etonu, etc., had unfortunately been arrested and put away. Many others like Omaria, Anyoti, Otai, etc. had earlier fled from the area; while some of those who had remained in the area like Mzee Anyoti, Awenu, Eswau, etc. had been intimidated and gone into hiding. Many intellectuals and useful sons and daughters of Teso had got scattered and absconded from their birthplace.¹²⁹

It is in this context of "total absence of leadership of any kind – socio-political, administrative or otherwise"¹³⁰ in Teso, that Bishop Ilukor emerged to be the leader of the moment and a peace broker.

Gershom Ilukor, bishop of Soroti diocese Church of Uganda,¹³¹ covering both districts of Soroti and Kumi, was aware that he too was suspected by the Museveni regime of being sympathetic to the rebels, just like his fellow Iteso clerics and "flock." On the basis of the criteria that the NRA/M seemed to judge any of the Iteso to be a rebel or rebel sympathiser, Bishop Ilukor qualified. He too could be perceived as an Obote-UPC man.¹³² He was an Etesot, who knew Obote personally and was therefore suspected to

---

128. All the informants on the Teso insurgency spoke with commendation of the pivotal role that Ilukor played in the end of the insurgency. They were all unanimous that without Ilukor, it is possible that the war would have been prolonged.
129. Ochyengh, "Proposals on the Restoration of Stability," 3.
130. Ibid.
131. Gershom Ilukor (1935–) started his church ministry as a catechist in 1956 at Kumi. After eight years as a catechist he was ordained a deacon in 1964 and later as a priest in 1966. He became Diocesan Secretary/Treasurer of Soroti Diocese in 1972 until 1975. When Rt Rev A. Maraka, who was then the bishop of Soroti Diocese died in October 1975, Ilukor was elected to replace him and consecrated in January 1976.
132. Bishop M. Kawuma, OI, Nsangi, Kampala, 20 April 1997.

be anti-Museveni I regime. He had paid a friendly visit to Obote at State House early in 1985, during the last months of his ailing regime.[133]

However, Ilukor never saw war as the solution to the problem. He was convinced that war would not restore to the Iteso their cattle and their dignity. So he mounted a crusade for the cessation of violence and war.

> I used to go to the villages to tell the rebels to tell the people that *we* should stop fighting; it will never bring *us* any good thing. And also here [in Soroti], I used to preach that fighting will never, never, bring peace. The army should stop killing people. Those things will never help us.[134]

First of all he stayed in Teso throughout the period of war. Even when it seemed as though his life was in danger, especially when he was taken from his home late in the night in 1987, dressed in pyjamas, and taken for interrogation at the NRA command post in Soroti town, he did not flee afterwards. In fact Ilukor was detained five times during the entire war period.[135]

Second, against all odds, he paid pastoral visits to all areas of Teso, encouraging the people, and in the latter period after all Teso cattle had been plundered, urging them to give up fighting. At the end of 1987, when the whole of Teso was in the hands of rebels, Ilukor wrote a pastoral letter urging his "flock" to intensify prayer and seek for peaceful ways of bringing the Museveni I regime's attention to their plight and grievances. He urged the people to "sit down and talk; write down your points as to why you are fighting and let us present them to government"[136], instead of continuing with violence. Bishop Ilukor recognized the influential role of women in the villages and urged them to speak to their husbands and sons who were rebels. In addition to encouraging them to bring their young children for immunization, he asked them to tell them the older ones to quit violence.

He followed this up with conferences throughout the Diocese, at Archdeaconry centres and at the Diocesan headquarters in Soroti.[137] The

---

133. Ilukor, OI.
134. Ibid., (emphasis added).
135. Ibid.
136. Ibid.
137. The Soroti conferences were held in 1988, 1989 and 1990.

purpose of these conferences was to encourage and strengthen the people; to talk together about the causes of the war and how to end it. At these conferences he also invited government leaders to participate and interact with church leadership and the people.[138] However, in addition to encouraging the people to talk to the government, Ilukor put in place a process of talking to those who had taken up arms against the government. The good relationship that the two main churches enjoyed became an asset, because the rebel leaders were members of their churches. Hitler Eregu was a Roman Catholic, Sam Otai, who was said to be second in command to Eregu, was a member of the COU. Erasmus Wandera, bishop of the Catholic diocese of Soroti, Fr Cochran and Bishop Ilukor teamed together on the peace mission to the rebel commanders.[139]

Bishop Ilukor felt that his efforts for peace were not welcomed in the early years of the conflict, 1987–89: "I had opposition from both sides; from the government side, they wanted to fight and from the rebel side, they wanted to fight."[140] But this opposition did not deter him in his crusade for peace. Early in 1990 some of the rebels began to surrender, and government became more eager to seek for a peaceful resolution of the conflict through the appointment of the Presidential Commission for Teso later that year. By the end of 1991 most of Teso had returned to peace, though without cattle.

The faith-motive in Bishop Ilukor's work is evident. As in the case of the "change of heart" by the government, so it was with his initiatives; they were all a work of God, according to him. Referring to his plea for the cessation of violence, he acknowledged that: "Mine was a small voice . . . I wouldn't say I had anything to do with the change . . . but the Lord himself talked to those people."[141] And while he identified with the grievances of the Iteso against the government, he neither took sides with the Museveni I regime, in its crusade to wipe out insurgence by force; nor with the rebels to, "take up arms in order to coerce the NRA"[142] to the negotiating table.

---

138. Ilukor, OI.
139. Ibid. Fr Cochran and Bishop Ilukor talked with Eregu.
140. Ilukor, OI; Okwii, OI.
141. Ilukor, OI.
142. Otai, "Political and Security Situation," 4.

He took sides with peace. It was not for the gain of political power that he worked for reconciliation.

However there is another element of Bishop Ilukor's boldness – his personality. Granted that he was sympathetic to the Teso rebellion and had faith in God; he was also known to be a courageous man. He had manifested the same quality when early in 1985 he visited Milton Obote together with Bishop Wesonga of Mbale, and warned him. He recalled:

> We told him, "You will be overthrown again because you have left things to drift to a bad level . . . people in the villages are poor! You have wasted time with other things, but you have not cared for the people in the villages and corruption is too much."[143]

During Obote's last visit to Teso, at Ngora, Bishop Ilukor in his sermon further challenged him: "God chose us but we have to be responsible to his people and responsible to Him; and if we are not, he will not overrate [us], whether I am a Bishop or what."[144] What he did with his "friend" Obote, pointing him to his accountability to God and his people, he now did even more to the NRA/M administration, while preaching in Soroti Cathedral, pleading with the army to "stop killing people." Ilukor took the same plea to the rebels and convinced many to "stop killing people,"[145] and to his credit by the end of 1991 Teso had returned to calm. According to the Iteso, they had paid the ultimate price of their association with Obote-UPC.

Reflection

Was Yona Okoth a rebel against the government of the NRM? One thing, for a certainty, he was not an enthusiast of the government and he could not be. First, his historical Obote-UPC connections did not endear the government to him. And second, he hailed from an area, Tororo, which was not enjoying quiet under the NRM regime. From the perspective of the government, he was suspected to be collaborating with rebel forces

---

143. Ilukor, OI.
144. Ibid.
145. Oguli, OI; Okare, OI.

for precisely the same reason: his Obote-UPC connections and the emergence of the FOBA rebel group with bases in Tororo. Moreover his son was known to be part of one of the rebel groups. It is also possible that the memory of the NRM operatives that were part of the so-called liberation army that overthrew the Idi Amin regime could recall that Okoth had been one with them in military struggle against the regime.[146] The NRA/M security machinery must have suspected that he could do the same for a regime that was opposed to his Obote-UPC heritage. He was therefore treated as one who colluded with the rebel cause.

Okoth, also, could not have confidence in a regime that had inflicted trauma to him through the numerous security searches. There seemed not to be reason enough for him to shift his political allegiance from his historic links with Obote-UPC to the NRA/M political agenda. The very least that can be concluded is that Okoth was sympathetic to the rebel political cause.

The issue that Okoth's rebel connection raises is to what extent a church leader can be involved in socio-political action without being seen to side with individuals and their governments, instead of human dignity and social justice. Having allied himself too closely to the Obote-UPC political agenda, he found himself in a quagmire once that agenda was overthrown. His entire service during the NRA/M regime was therefore characterized by defence; on the one hand seeking to exonerate himself from his past political allegiances, and on the other, seeking to legitimatize his plea on behalf of the politically and socially dispossessed. He did not succeed in either one because each attempt was interpreted in the light of his past associations, and besides, a section of the House of Bishops he presided over also suspected that his political loyalties lay with the vanquished Obote-UPC political forces.

Dan M. Ochyengh, an Etesot and a critic of Museveni I regime, described the condition of Teso at the end of the war in 1991 as "totally devastated, . . . a case of spilled milk."[147] Why would a devastated people turn

---

146. Okoth, OI. Okoth actively participated in raising money for buying weapons to overthrow the Amin regime.

147. Dan M. Ochyengh in his "Proposals on the Restoration of Stability, Peace and Progress to Teso (15 December 1991)" to the Chairman, Presidential Commission of

to the church the way the Iteso did? Okwii, an Etesot clergy, reflecting on the Teso turbulence, observed that:

> People look at God as their only source of security; so they go to Church to pour their anguish to their protector and it is also in Church that they can hear words of comfort and encouragement, where they are treated as human beings, whereas the government sees the local people as either rebels or agents of rebels. In the Church they are also given material support – clothes, hoes, etc. It is therefore natural that people flock to where they are cared for.[148]

Okwii suggests that the credibility and integrity of the Church was authenticated by its distinctive treatment of the Iteso "as human beings" and not as "either rebels or agents of rebels." The only way the Church was able to recognize "the human" in "the rebel" was because the Church herself was "rebel." It is this identification of the Church with the people, embodied in its leadership, which commended the Church to the Iteso. The fact that throughout the turbulence the leadership of the Church in Teso reacted in ways that resonated with the feelings and aspirations of the Iteso conferred upon it the identity of a church for the people.

Bishop Ilukor, who stands as the prime peacebroker on account of his bold, courageous and selfless service, was accepted as a credible advocate for the people precisely because he was one among them, perceived to support the rebel cause and therefore one with the rebel population. In other words, Ilukor's "rebel" experience authenticated his ministry. He was not only *one among* them, but also *for* them. Indigeneity not only authenticates ministry but also the prior condition of authentic ministry.

Archbishop Okoth's leadership illustrates this principle further. During Obote II, Okoth was associated with the ruling government, and could therefore not speak credibly on behalf of those in Luwero who were suffering. However, in the Museveni-NRA/M regime his association with the North and East qualified him to speak, and to lead the Church in the new social-concern consciousness, bringing local-regional issues to a national

---

Teso, 1. Document at CBR Archives PF 3209.9 (1992), 1.
148. Okwii, "The Economic Revolution in Teso," 55.

platform. Okoth's perceived solidarity with some rebel activity in eastern Uganda, and his knowledge of the local situation, enabled him, in one sense, to "universalize" locality. In another sense this led to a tendency for him to deny the distinctiveness of another "locality" whose experience was not identical to that of his own.

This leads us to consider what in my view was an abortive attempt to institute an effective ministry for advocacy. The social concern project initiated by the Provincial Assembly in 1986 did not take off due the failure in the House of Bishops to balance the "universalizing" and "localizing" forces. This failure, I believe originated from the perception that "a bishop is a church, a representative of Christ on earth. He is a father of all or should be so. When he speaks, he does not speak only for his diocese, his tribe or for a particular area; he speaks for the whole church."[149] This elevated view of the office of a bishop hindered the development of collegiality in the House of Bishops. The fact that there were several bishops experiencing the impact of rebellion in their dioceses and through personal attacks, and that there were several others whose dioceses enjoyed peace and security, seems to have made consensus even more problematic.

The idea of the church as sacrament among the people, which we observed in the Luwero account, is also visible in Teso. Although the liturgical innovations were not at the scale of the Church in Luwero, it is the leadership that modelled this sacramental element of the Church's presence. The work of Bishop Ilukor was acclaimed and respected, because he embodied the blessing that the Church was perceived to mediate.

The perception that the leadership of the Church in Teso embodied "blessing" seems to be an extrapolation of the idea that religion should mediate blessings to society. This is a possible way of understanding the view by Peter Otai, chairman of the main rebel organization in Teso, that in order to restore peace and democracy in Uganda, political leadership should be handed over to religious leaders as an interim measure. He proposed that:

---

149. Rt Rev M. Otim, in his "Address to the Members of House of Bishops at Lweza Training and Conference Centre," 1, COU Archives, House of Bishops Papers.

A National Convention or forum be convened in a neutral country to enable representatives of the government, representatives of all opposition groups, representatives of all political parties and representatives of Churches in Uganda to attend so as to agree on:

The establishment of a caretaker government headed by a troika of the *main religious leaders* of Uganda, i.e. Head of the Roman Catholic Church (Bishop), Head of the Anglican Church (i.e. Church of Uganda) and the Muslim Chief Khadi, who should constitute a joint Presidency.[150]

Otai's view was that religious leadership was the remaining credible cadre of leaders. Of course Otai's proposal could also be dismissed as a political ploy. In my view however, his proposal for a "government headed by a troika of the main religious leaders of Uganda" illustrates the perception that religion mediates blessing in society.

One other feature in the Teso account, which is in the Luwero story as well, is the influence of Revival ethos. In spite of the aversion to the Trumpeters' version of revival that came to Teso in the late 1950s and early 1960s, Revival ethos was evident in the life of the Church in Teso.[151] Indeed there were some in the church for whom getting saved was sectarian, likened to "religious prostitution,"[152] because in their view it was "enough to be baptised in the name of Christ."[153] Yet there were many in the church in Teso, not least among them the clergy, who said they were saved, without being associated with the Trumpeters.[154] The emphasis given to preaching

---

150. Otai, "Political and Security Situation," 11.

151. Ilukor, OI; Oguli, OI. The version of Revival that reached Teso in the late 1950s and early 1960s was that of the Trumpeters. The church leadership at the time rejected it, and in some cases the Trumpeters were beaten by some clergy and Christians protesting their aggressive evangelistic methods as they attempted to preach to congregations leaving Sunday worship services, as was their custom. Bishop Usher Wilson rejected the group and never welcomed it in the church, and so did Bishops Tomusange and Maraka after him.

152. Oguli used this term explaining why he did not want to get saved. Oguli, OI.

153. Oguli, OI.

154. Among the clergy interviewed were: Bishop Ilukor, O. Okalebo, C. Okwii, C. Obaikol; and so were some lay Christian leaders like Kenan Egadu, OI, Soroti, 2 March 1996.

during the war owes its roots to this ethos. In a rather expressive way Okwii, Archdeacon of Ngora, emphasized: "Me, I was saved. I was using my personal experience."[155]

Bishop G. Ilukor referred to 1983 as "the turning point in my life" at a Revival-style convention, hosted by Soroti diocese and conducted by, among others, Bishop Festo Kivengere. Ilukor's testimony, though not in strict revivalist language is certainly revivalist in orientation:

> I came to know the Lord when I was in primary school. People like Kigata came and talked to us. I was in Kumi then. I started realising that it is better to know the Lord *better*, rather than knowing him in an *ordinary* way. Then in 1956, the Archdeacon of Ngora, who was from Australia, talked about salvation and challenged us to serve the church . . . It is then I left drinking. Then in 1983 we had a convention here and in that convention someone talked about fear; that fear which was preventing me from declaring and coming openly in Jesus' name; I also had fears about the convention that it would not succeed and I was thinking of myself as an important person . . . then I publicly confessed [Christ].[156]

The distinction that Ilukor makes between the "ordinary" and "better" way of knowing the Lord is the Revivalist distinction between a "nominal" Christian and a "real" Christian, or between *Omukristayo* and a *Mulokole*, which became a reality in his life in 1983. But that Ilukor's testimony lacks the punch lines of traditional revivalist style is a sign that Ilukor expressed his revival experience in a "local" idiom.

A major feature of the story of the Church in Teso is the centrality of the pastoral dimension to the work of the leaders in the Church. Bishop Ilukor distinguished himself as the elder pastor, seeking out any and all the "flock," and working for their safety and peace. The parental image of Engwau, and Ilukor's characterization of the church as a "mother" suggests that it is not only the ministers in the church that have a pastoral

---

155. Okwii, OI.
156. Ilukor, OI. Rev Othniel Okalebo who had already been ordained in 1983, said he got saved during the convention. Okalebo, OI.

function, but that the corporate identity of the church is pastoral-parental. The corporate image of the church as parent is visible when its leaders fulfil their pastoral responsibilities. For when the leaders are among the people identifying with them and serving them, then the church will be said to be for the people; but when the leaders are overbearing and demanding, then a different image of the church emerges, of an institution that lays burdens on its members.

CHAPTER 8

The Church in the World: Toward an Ecclesiology

Archbishop Erica Sabiti's reflections on the story of the Church of Uganda, in his "Charge to the Church of Uganda, Rwanda and Burundi" in the December 1970 Provincial Assembly, serve as a point of departure for concluding this account of the Church of Uganda. He summarized the story of the Church of Uganda thus: "Service to the suffering; unity of the people; the knowledge of God. These are the great themes of our history . . ."[1] Expanding on the theme of service, Archbishop Sabiti explained:

> If we look at our history, it is clear that our Church has made gifts of the highest value to the life of the people of Uganda, Rwanda and Burundi. . . . The first gift we have given is practical service to the poor, the weak and the sick. Poverty, ignorance and disease have for centuries broken the will and taken our people. In response to these needs we have built a school system that reaches into every community of our land, we have built hospitals, introduced cash crops, helped farmers and worked to improve community services.[2]

Reflecting on the theme of the unity of the people, he asserted:

---

1. "The Proceedings of the Second Meeting of the Second Provincial Assembly held at Bishop Tucker College, Mukono, December 9, 10, and 11 1970; Appendix 'B': The Archbishop's Charge to the Church of Uganda, Rwanda and Burundi, December 1970." Provincial Assembly Papers, COU Archives, 4.
2. Ibid., 2.

> If we look at our history, we see that we have been and must remain men of unity. Our history is one that shows a continuing struggle to break down the walls that divide men; a struggle to transcend the divisions of tribe, clan, language, culture and race, which have for too many years held us back and even weaken us and too frequently prevent us from doing what God has given us to do.[3]

On the knowledge of God, Sabiti amplified:

> If we look at our history, we also find that our Church is an Evangelical Church. I do not mean Evangelical as a Church party, but Evangelical in the only true sense of that word. We have stood for the fact that the most important issue in life is the relation we have with God. . . . We have sought in many practical ways to improve the life of the people of Uganda. But from the beginning we have known that the greatest gift we have to offer is Christ himself.[4]

Archbishop Sabiti was attempting to define the ecclesiological identity of the Church of Uganda in its historical-socio-cultural context.[5] In his view, the Church's historical mission is service to the world; its identity, unity in a context of socio-cultural diversity; and its *raison d'être*, the evangelical gospel leading to a faith-relation with God.

Following the precedent set by Sabiti in 1970, this chapter attempts to decipher the salient features and themes of the story of the Church of Uganda in such a way that will help define the Church's ecclesiological identity.

The first section of the chapter summarizes the story by identifying the shifts in the Church's image and identity through the historical epochs of pre- and post-independence Uganda. The underlying argument is that two forces shaped the Church: the historical religio-cultural socio-political

---

3. Ibid., 3.
4. Ibid.
5. It is important to note that the historical moment in which Sabiti's made these remarks was the December 1970 Provincial Assembly which debated *Survey on Administration and Finance of the Church in Uganda*, otherwise known as the Bikangaga Report. This is the time discussed in chapter 4 of this book.

context, and the demands of its faith-relation with the Christ-event. The Church was therefore constantly readjusting itself to realities in each epoch.

In the second section, the chapter takes further the narrative-descriptive methodological framework of "the church in the world" and recasts it as a hermeneutic-theological model for developing an ecclesiology. After elucidating the process of indigenization as the starting point for developing a "church in the world" ecclesiology, it focuses on the Revival notion of testimony as a descriptive-interpretative paradigm for being and becoming church, an organizing principle for reflecting on the narrative of the Church of Uganda.

The third section of the chapter identifies and discusses four motifs that provide a framework for constructing an ecclesiology for the Church of Uganda. They are: authenticity and its implications for corporate faith; identity and its implications for ministry; the church's mission as a sacrament for the world; and the church as a mystery in the world. The chapter concludes with a brief statement of the issues that may warrant further research in the study of the Church of Uganda. It commends the "church in the world" methodological approach for the study of African Church history and ecclesiology.

The Changing Image of the Church

The "church in the world" methodological approach to the historical study of the Church of Uganda is based on the assumption that there is a symbiotic relationship between "the church" and "the world." H. Richard Niebuhr has observed that:

> The Church lives and defines itself in action vis-à-vis the world. World, however, is not object of the Church as God is. World, rather, is companion of the Church, a community, something like itself with which it lives before God. The world is sometimes enemy, sometimes partner of Church, often antagonist, always one to be befriended; now it is co-knower,

now the one that does not know what Church knows, now the knower of what the Church does not know.⁶

The Church of Uganda continually redefined itself *vis-à-vis* the historical, religio-cultural and socio-political "world" of Uganda, sometimes seeking to pattern itself to it, at others reacting antagonistically.

The Church in the Pre-Independence Period

In the genesis period, in the first two decades of the founding of the Church in the context of the centralized kingdom of Buganda, intense rivalry with Islam and the Roman Catholic Church determined the Church's corporate identity as Protestant. The victory of what had become a "Protestant party" against the Catholics in 1892 further entrenched its Protestant identity, becoming the "religion" of the rulers of the kingdom, taking the place of traditional religion, with Namirembe as the supreme *Kiggwa* (headquarters of a divinity) of Buganda. Having won the allegiance of the Kabaka, the Protestant Church became the "established" on the basis of the principle of *cuius regio eius religio*, "whosoever reigns shall determine the religion of his territory."

As the Church spread beyond Buganda, it carried along its quasi-established image. The rivalry between the Protestant and Roman Catholic missions in Buganda was also perpetuated throughout the process of planting churches in the rest of Uganda. Thus, although the CMS believed they were planting an Anglican Church, and christened it "the Native Anglican Church," in its own consciousness the Church was Protestant. This Protestant-Catholic rivalry was so ingrained in the psyche of the Church that it shaped the socio-political development of the country, to the extent that on the eve of independence political organizations were built along that divide.

As the Church grew and spread it attracted a large membership, resulting from the combination of its quasi-established status, the Protestant-Catholic rivalry and the introduction of formal education as a tool for evangelization. It was a social imperative to belong to a particular church.

---

6. Niebuhr, *The Purpose of the Church*, 26.

But the attraction of a large number of adherents also resulted from the process of adapting Christianity into traditional-cultural-religious thought patterns. Religion among the people of Uganda was a way of life. Since Christianity was being integrated into the total life of Ugandan societies, membership to the Church was expressed in similar ways to membership to traditional religion. The CMS missionaries were disturbed that the tremendous response to baptism was not matched by commitment to the Church and a change in the moral lives of the adherents as they expected – a phenomenon they regarded as "nominalism." To the missionaries "nominalism" was a negative phenomenon, but to the indigenous people, a large "nominal" membership was the evidence that Christianity had become their "religion" and a way of life.

The emergence of the Revival movement in the 1920s and 1930s introduced new criteria for defining and distinguishing "real" Christianity from "nominal" or "ordinary" Christianity. Although the impact of the Revival and its incorporation in the Church was varied, it nonetheless introduced a new paradigm in being church, with its emphasis on the cross of Christ, "fellowship" or "new clan-family" and the notion of "testimony" as that which authenticates individual and community faith. This is what distinguished "real" from "nominal" Christianity. The Revival doctrine of separation from the world, that meant being "in the world but not of the world," was another way of making the distinction. The "real" Christian being the one who is "in the world but not of the world" because of the experience of the Cross of Christ; and the "worldly" whose life style is based on values emanating from created world and the world of lust, greed, hatred, drunkenness – in short – of sin. This implied that the institutional church "must not be confused with the true church. The former entails membership cards, and being written down on baptismal registers."[7] The identity of the true church, according to the Revival, was "in the world but not of the world," "the "hidden remnant," the "inner circle," the "true fellowship," "an organism rather than an organization."[8]

---

7. Church, *Every Man a Bible Student*, 117.
8. Ibid.

At the time of independence, in 1962, all the above features were present in the Church. It was Protestant, quasi-established, "nominal" and revivalist, in differing degree in the different areas of Uganda. It was in the Church in Buganda that all four could be said to be present in competing degrees. It should also be noted that the pre-eminent position accorded to Buganda in the pre-independence period created a Buganda *versus* the-rest-of-Uganda divide, in both the political arena and the Church.

The Church in the Post-Independence Period

On the eve of independence and during the period following, in the context of the struggle for control of the centre between Buganda and the central government, the leadership of the Church were awakened to the reality of the Buganda *versus* the-rest-of-Uganda divide in the Church. The Church refocused its energies on its internal self-hood, its identity and mission as a church for Buganda *and* Uganda. The protracted tug of war between the leadership of the Church in Buganda and the Provincial organs, narrated in chapter 4, was essentially a search for the corporate identity of the Church. Although Sabiti, in his charge to the Provincial Assembly in 1970, asserted that unity had all along been a historic mark of the Church's identity, it was more true to say that the Church's history had shown "a continuing struggle to break down the walls that divide men; a struggle to transcend the divisions of tribe, clan, language, culture and race."[9]

This struggle remained a characteristic feature of the Church, as each political era highlighted the "dividing walls" in Uganda's history. They include the Christianity-Islam divide and the historic Protestant-Catholic rivalry. As the story of the Church during the Idi Amin regime showed, the Protestant-Catholic division was significantly surmounted in the process of the Church's response to the regime's carnage. In the context of an "established" Islam, the Protestant-Catholic divide receded in significance and the Church repositioned itself for survival. At the grass roots, this repositioning resulted in some forms of cooperation between the Church of Uganda and the Catholic Church, as was narrated in the Lango account.

---

9. Sabiti, in Church of Uganda, *Survey on Administration and Finance*, 3.

The Church in the World: Toward an Ecclesiology

In the context of civil wars and insurgence during the Obote II and Museveni regimes, the Church was faced with a different kind of violence. While the violence of the Idi Amin regime engendered a united response in the Church, it was not the case with the civil wars in the Obote II and Museveni eras. The problem in the latter two eras was the fact that the civil wars struck chords of sympathy within the Church. In the case of the Obote II period, the people of the Luwero Triangle, including members of the Church of Uganda, were generally sympathetic and supportive of the Museveni/NRA rebellion, while some in the leadership of the Church at the national level, notably Archbishop Yona Okoth, was more inclined to the Obote-UPC government agenda. The scenario changed during the Museveni-NRA/M regime, because there was a "rebel"[10] Church in Teso and a "rebel" Archbishop Okoth, presiding over a House of Bishops of divided sympathies. At the institutional level, therefore, the Church during both eras was characterized by indecision and lack of unanimity in its response to violence. The Church was struggling with the "walls" of regionalism that divided Uganda arising from the imbalances and particularities in the socio-political development of Uganda.

At the grass roots, however, the Church identified itself as a church of the people, as the Luwero and Teso case studies showed. In these contexts the Church's mission and ministry was defined, not according to ecclesiastical precept and order, but rather the suffering communities of which the Church was a part. Erica Sabiti's reflections on the story of the Church in 1970, emphasizing the priority of the Church's mission and ministry of pastoral service to the world, were prophetic.

Thus, the account of the Church of Uganda is the story of a church that is always in the process of "becoming church" as it encountered new contexts and adapted in the process of history. The image and identity of the Church is not static, but dynamic, as Niebuhr has asserted, "the church lives and defines itself in action vis-à-vis the world." In the changing religio-cultural-socio-political historical "world" of Uganda, the Church of

---

10. The word "rebel" is used to "connote sympathy to the agenda of the rebels or insurgents."

Uganda kept pace; "now it is co-knower, now the one that does not know what Church knows, now the knower of what the Church does not know."[11]

The Church in the World: An Ecclesiology

The paradigm of the "church in the world" has three components: the first is the world; the second is the church; and the third is the preposition "in" which denotes the relation between the first two. The burden of the discussion is not the creation of either the church or the world. In fact the notion "church in the world" presupposes the historical priority of the world to the church; the world preceded the church, and therefore the church is historically contingent upon the world. The ecclesiology of the Church of Uganda is about the nature of the church as it continually defined itself and worked out its mission and ministry "in" the historical cultural-socio-political "world" of Uganda, and particularly, in turbulent post-independence Uganda.

An Indigenous Church

The Church of Uganda is an indigenous church. A superficial view of the Church of Uganda might suggest that it is not yet truly an indigenous church because many of its faith forms, for example, the liturgy, hymnody and liturgical paraphernalia, were not born in Ugandan religio-cultural context.[12] This thesis has shown, however, that the story of the Church is an account of a process of indigenization at all levels. It was due to indigenous concerns that Kabaka Mutesa invited missionaries to come to his kingdom. Once accepted as the religion of Buganda, Christianity was integrated into Kiganda society. Even the forms that were transmitted as alien, such as *The Book of Common Prayer*, were appropriated on the basis of indigenous cognitive structures, thereby adapting them to indigenous

---

11. Niebuhr, *The Purpose of the Church*, 26.

12. It is this perception that inspired John Mbiti's call to the Church of Uganda to "Africanise Christianity, that is, give it an indelible African character," in *The Crisis in Mission in Africa*, 2. John Poulton in his article "Like Father, Like Son: Some Reflections on the Church of Uganda," *International Review of Mission* 50 (1961): 297–307, argues that the Church of Uganda did not advance beyond the nineteenth century expression of evangelical missionary faith.

forms. Kiganda traditional custom and religion, as with other Ugandan nationalities, was very strong on ritual,[13] one of the features of *The Book of Common Prayer*. Philip Turner has expressed this well:

> All influences from Europe have been filtered through a grid of more traditional ideas and assumptions. The character of the various churches in Africa cannot be traced to a single line of back to mission influence. To make this assumption is to adopt, consciously or unconsciously, the picture of the passive black man; the favourite opinion of the paternalist. Now as always Africa implacably hoards her integrity. She has made Christianity her own and she has done it in her own way.[14]

The point here is that every encounter, apprehension and incorporation of "the other than us" is always on "our" terms, in "our" idiom. Therefore the appropriation of "the other than us" takes the shape given by "us" and therefore reflects to a greater or lesser degree "our" concrete historical, religio-cultural and social-political *sitz im leben*.[15] Lamin Sanneh has made the point:

> Missionaries may be one step ahead in the historical transmission of Christianity with Africans serving as secondary agents, but in the process of local assimilation Africans were to the fore, with missionaries now in a reverse position, overwhelmingly inferior in the local adaptation of a religion they helped to introduce.[16]

This is indigenization proper, a reactive process to "the other than us," or "the other than ours." It occurs both by adapting the new to fit into the old, and by the old renewing and restructuring itself to accommodate the

---

13. Both Mutebi's and Kyewalyanga's works, "Towards an Indigenous Understanding," and *Traditional Religion, Custom and Christianity*, respectively, show this.
14. Philip Turner, "The Wisdom of the Fathers and the Gospel of Christ," *Journal of Religion in Africa* 4, no. 1 (1972): 46.
15. In the field of hermeneutics, this could be referred to as "receptor-hermeneutics" as distinguished from the "transmitter hermeneutics." René Padilla in his essay, "The Contextualisation of the Gospel," *Journal of Theology for Southern Africa* 24 (1978): 12–30, has shown how this precedes all other objective reflective hermeneutic attempts.
16. Lamin Sanneh, "The Horizontal and Vertical in Mission: An African Perspective," *International Bulletin of Missionary Research* 7, no. 4 (1983): 166.

new. It is a feature of community formation in a particular place and at a particular time.

By implication indigeneity is not static. To define "indigenous" as that "belong naturally,"[17] is misleading because indigeneity is dynamic, resulting from the dynamic process of indigenization.

Each of the images of the Church of Uganda identified above resulted from the process of indigenization. "Nominalism" resulted from indigenizing the Christianity that was transmitted by the CMS missionaries into traditional religio-cultural understanding of religious commitment. Revival spirituality, elucidated in chapter 3, was embodied in indigenous forms of expression, such as the fellowship meeting, a similar motif to the traditional clan-community meetings in traditional custom. As the Church encountered new situations it renewed its old-self to fit the new, as in the diminished significance of the Protestant image in the context of quasi-established Islam in the Idi Amin regime.

Indigenization, as thus described, does not refer to the theological task of inculturation, or the process of engineering and producing a type of church which, in the words of Mbiti, "will bear the imprint MADE IN AFRICA, and which will not be a cheap imitation of the type of Christianity found elsewhere or at periods in the past."[18] It does not describe the proactive task that "involves africanizing church structures, personnel, theology, planning, commitment, worship, transaction of its mission, and financial independence."[19] While not denying the necessity of this task for validating the role of the church in a particular socio-cultural context, indigenization is first and foremost *reactive*, before it is *proactive*.

An Indigenous Faith

The story of the Church of Uganda is also a story of indigenous faith. This is evident right from the origins of the Church in Buganda and throughout the pre-independence period. It is faith, which according to Sabiti is "the

---

17. This is how *The Concise Oxford Dictionary*, ninth edition (London: Oxford University Press, 1996), defines "indigenous."
18. Mbiti, *The Crisis of Mission in Africa*, 2; B. Idowu makes a similar call in his book, *Towards an Indigenous Church*, 9–14.
19. Mbiti, *The Crisis of Mission in Africa*, 2.

most important issue in life . . . the relation we have with God,"[20] that marked the history of the Church. The pages in Kabaka's court and capital died for their faith; it was indigenous agents from Buganda who pioneered the work of evangelism beyond Buganda; and the Revival was an indigenous faith movement.

The story of the Church in the post-independence turbulent context is full of evidences of the triumph of faith in suffering. Archdeacon Lubwama's recourse to prayer, as the battle raged in the Lubiri, was an act of faith; Archbishop Luwum's fearless encounter with Idi Amin, can only be explained by faith; Serubidde and the catechists in Luwero were inspired by faith in their pastoral service; and it was in faith that Bishop Ilukor could credit his crusade for peace and reconciliation as ". . . the Lord himself talked to those people."[21]

The faith *of* the community will always be visible in indigenous form because faith is an existential reality. The challenge is determining, in the account of the Church of Uganda, how to distinguish one act as originating from faith, from another that may be inspired by other concerns. This requires identifying the marks of faith, which will distinguish acts of faith from those that are not. The way to identify the marks of faith is by determining the point at which faith is manifested in the process of indigenization. An examination of the response of the Church to a particular situation when contrasted with the response of "the world" to the same situation will delineate faith actions from other actions that may be originated by other causes.

Consider Kayima's experience in Luwero.[22] When Museveni with a group of rebels, sought his support, Kayima's initial reaction was to go ahead. But then he began to wonder whether it was the will of God for him to support the rebels. Kayima's search for a mark or stamp of God's approval for him to support Museveni's rebellion is what distinguishes his decision as a faith-choice. It is crucial to note that Kayima's Christian identity is not authenticated by the content of his choice but rather the process

---

20. Sabiti, in Church of Uganda, *Survey on Administration and Finance*, 3.
21. G. Ilukor, quoted on p. 319 in this book.
22. See pp. 246–247 in chapter 5.

by which he arrived at the choice. After all, most Baganda had made the same choice to support the rebellion without recourse to the will of God.

Kayima's anecdote illustrates a two-dimensional process of response visible in the entire account of the Church. First, there is first "natural" reaction that arises from indigenous concerns shared by the community of which the church is a part. This is accommodation, whereby the sociality[23] of the church is indistinguishable from that of society. Thus for Kayima, as for most of the people in Luwero, the most "natural" thing to do was to support the insurgents. It was apparent that the Obote II government was antagonistic to the social-political aspirations of the Baganda irrespective of religious affiliation.

The second dimension of the reactive process arises from the church's second nature – faith. It is faith concerns that caused Kayima to inquire as to whether the NRA rebellion was in the will of God. Kayima's decision to support the rebellion thereafter was based on his conclusion that the rebellion had the stamp of God's approval. There will be many other Luwero residents who decided to support the rebellion on the basis of diverse considerations other than faith. Kayima's support for the rebellion is a faith-act because of the process by which he made the choice and not its content – he decided to support the rebellion after an assessment of the situation on the basis of his faith-relation with Christ.

Two other stories in the Church that demonstrate the two-dimensional process in faith-response: the first is the story of the Church in Buganda soon after independence, and the second is the Church in Teso during the insurgency of 1986–1992.

One of the pillars of Kiganda society, a mark of its indigeneity and identity, was the place and role of the Kabaka and the kingdom. In the period running up to the independence of Uganda and after, the restructuring of social-political relations between the colonial central government and Buganda revolved around this issue, which what has been called "the question of Buganda." As discussed in chapter 4, the question of Buganda was the root of the Mengo crisis in 1966–67. It was the same issue that was at the centre of the Church's internal conflicts, during the transition

---

23. "Sociality" of community refers to the dynamics and characteristic features of the internal relations of a community.

of leadership from Archbishop Leslie Brown to that of Erica Sabiti. The struggle by the two dioceses of Namirembe and West Buganda to retain the symbols of Buganda's national heritage, and the Provincial Assembly Executive's efforts to integrate them into the Church's national identity, affirm the Church's indigenous identity. The Church shared the same social-political reality as the rest of the society in Buganda and Uganda.

If this were the end of the Church's story, the church would not be different to the world, unless faith was manifested in the process of response. The election of Eric Sabiti, a non-Muganda, as Archbishop of Uganda, instead of Buganda's favourite, Bishop Dunstun Nsubuga, was an effective test of the nature of the Church in Buganda. Would the Church in Buganda accept Sabiti as one of them on the basis of the common participation in the Christ narrative? Sabiti's words at his enthronement, pointing the Church to the Christ-event as the basis of faith identity, are worth quoting again. He stated:

> All our unhappy divisions, political, denominational, tribal and racial, disappear at the foot of the cross, where we meet together as sinners before our Saviour. When we allow the Lord Jesus to rule our lives, then we grow together as a family, we are one in Him, we are called by God to serve all His children, of all tribes and races, in order to bring them to Christ and become living stones within his Church.[24]

Sabiti here points to a common heritage as sinners for whom Christ came. It is inherent in the logic of Sabiti's argument that sin distorts indigeneity – the different denominations, tribes and races – because it distorts true humanity, which is only rediscovered by submitting to the Lordship of Christ. Under the rule of Christ indigeneity is not destroyed but redeemed because the narrative of Christ has capacity to contain the plurality of culture, language and race, into one new indigenous identity, the family of Christ. Sabiti's call implies that faith in Christ reconfigures indigeneity. The family of Christ, accordingly, is the faith-family, the new clan-community in Christ.

---

24. Sabiti, "Archbishop's Charge."

In the Teso account, the decimation of the cattle population and the consequent war during the first era of the National Resistance Army/Movement (NRA/M, 1986–1992) affected all the Iteso, "churched" or "un-churched," because it touched the essence of being an indigenous Etesot. Cattle were the symbol of Iteso dignity and identity. They played the central place in "all religious and social ceremonies of Teso life"[25] and were "the nucleus of the economy."[26] So when, according to the Iteso, it was beyond doubt that the NRA/M functionaries were collaborating with the cattle raiders, the ensuing rebellion against the government was an expression of indigenous revolt, a natural response, seeking to defend and protect their indigenous heritage. It should therefore not cause consternation that the immediate reaction for the Church in Teso was involvement and support for the rebellion, affirming that the church as a community is rooted in the concrete reality of life and its turbulence in the world.

However, rebellion was not the last word of the response in the Church. When all the cows had been plundered, people displaced into camps and the whole of Teso under a cloud of despair, its faith identity was manifested in the Church's recourse to prayer with fasting. It is significant that Bishop Ilukor perceived the success of his peace missions to have resulted from prayer. This is what makes the Church's initiatives in reconciliation a faith-choice, because they arrived at it from an assessment of the situation in prayer and consultation, as narrated in chapter 7.

Discussion of the indigenization of the Church and the evidence of faith in the Church implies that ecclesiological study is an exploration of the process of indigenization, an inquiry into the process of becoming a faith-community. Ecclesiological study entails a three-pronged approach: first, identifying the constitutive elements and factors in the church and the world; second, describing features of change in the world and their attendant consequences in the church; and third, examining the processes of reaction in both church and society, so as to recognize the indicators of the faith identity of the church. Ecclesiological identity will be determined by recognizing the marks of faith.

---

25. Lawrence, *The Iteso*, 144.
26. Okwii, "The Economic Revolution in Teso," 13.

It is here that the Revival and its notion of testimony provide a descriptive-interpretative paradigm of being and becoming church in Uganda.

"Testimony," an Ecclesiological Paradigm

In the Revival narrative, the notion of testimony was both the life and narrative of faith; of the relation with Christ at individual and corporate levels, spanning the whole life in its temporal dimensions of past, present and future. Although there were tendencies to limit the notion of testimony to only the oral version, both life-action and speech were what constituted an authentic Revival testimony. The point of the oral version was to describe the faith-decision in the past, and in the present perpetual moment of crisis that is engendered by the paradoxical nature of faith-life, to be *in* the world but not *of* the world. True to the quality of a veritable narrative, "testimony" was both portrait and description.

There are two directions that the witness simultaneously faces: toward Christ, a reference and acknowledgement of the Christ-event as the ground of faith; and toward the world, to live out that faith and summon the world to turn to Christ and be saved. This two-dimensional posture is what defines the identity of the witness and therefore gives content to his or her testimony. It is an affirmation of one's continuing quest for identity in the Christ narrative, as implied in the phrase, "all of us who are saved," and in the summons to "let us preach" to the world, as depicted in one of their hymns:

> All you brethren Let us preach and pray
> All of us who are saved That our kinsfolk may be saved
> Let us think So that Jesus may be glorified
> Of what should be done For salvation
>   Beloved of Jesus Beloved of Jesus . . .
>   As He saved us
>   We too must preach.[27]

---

27. *Ebyeshongoro Eby'Okujunwa*, Hymn No. 47 (Words original; tune from Budo).

Note the usage of the subjective: "we," "us" and "ours" in referring to their relation with Christ and the world, an affirmation of a two-dimensional identity that was the essence of "testimony." The only way the testifier maintains this identity is by keeping the focus on both the Christ-event and the world; the former is the ground of faith, and the latter is the locus of faith praxis and the object of the message of salvation.

For the Balokole, their life in the world was justified by the mandate from God, engendered by their status in Jesus, to call the world to salvation in Christ. They saw life in testimony terms, contrasted with those of the world who "seek the pleasures of this world" and are bound by Satan, as in this portion of a Revival hymn:

All the people of the world	Satan has bound them
Mostly seek	And made them stupid
The pleasures of this world	So that they may not understand
And fame	Salvation (matters of salvation)
All we who are saved	All we . . .[28]
Let us preach to them	

What distinguished the "saved" from the "worldly," the *Abalokole* (saved ones) from the *Abakristayo* ("ordinary" Christians), the "real" Christian from the "nominal" Christian, was their disposition toward the world, resulting in a distinct lifestyle. The testimony was what showed this difference. The Balokole believed that an appropriate life response to the cross of Christ led to a life "separated from the world." The Balokole believed that the use of the "world" in this sense is similar to Jesus in his characterization of the relationship between the faith-community he was creating and the world[29], when Jesus said:

> I remain in the world no longer, but they are still in the world and I am coming to you . . . I have given them your word and the world has hated them, for they are not of the world any more than I am of the world. My prayer is not that you take

---

28. Ibid., part of Hymn No. 48, verses 1 and 2. (Words original; tune from Luganda chorus).
29. Ibid.

them out of the world but that you protect them from the evil one. They are not of the world, even as I am not of it. . . . As you sent me into the world, I have sent them to the world.[30]

Testimony was therefore always a narrative of the "in-between," enacting and describing the faith-life of the Balokole, at both individual and community levels, "in the world and not of the world." It is crucial to note that in Revival spirituality the individual's testimony found its identity within the context of the community.

The testimony-theme in Revival spirituality has the same usage as the witness-theme in the scriptures. H. Strathman, in his word study, has actually shown that the two English words, "testimony" and "witness," are interchangeable in their biblical Greek usage because they have the same etymology.[31] He has further observed that "*martyria* is (thus) initially always action; but it can take on the sense of *martyrion*, evidence, as content of the statement made, whereas the latter can never have the sense of an action."[32] A. A. Trites has also shown that the word *martyria* in the New Testament denotes both the verbal and life bearing witness, attesting to the truth that is to be presented, represented and defended.[33] Witness refers to the identity of a person who witnesses and the act of witnessing. In fact in Pauline usage, "it can no longer be a matter of a document, or a piece of evidence, recollection, giving encouragement or warning; the word is used in the sense of the gospel, the proclaimed message of salvation in Christ."[34] Testimony therefore also denotes the Christ-narrative. When applied to the historical process of being and becoming church, "testimony" is the action of the church in the world and the content of its verbal witness.

---

30. John 17:11, 14–16, 18.
31. H. Strathman in *New International Dictionary of New Testament Theology*, Vol 3:Pri-Z, ed. Colin Brown (Exeter: The Paternoster Press, 1978), 1039. *Martyria* refers to testimony; *martyreo*, to bear witness; *martyrion*, the testimony or evidence or proof; and *martys*, a witness.
32. Ibid.
33. A. A. Trites, "Witness, Testimony," in *International Dictionary of New Testament Theology*, Vol. 3:Pri-Z, ed. Colin Brown (Exeter: The Paternoster Press, 1978), 1049–1051.
34. Ibid., 1043.

"Testimony" gives content and form to the "in" in the "church *in* the world" paradigm.

There are two possible dispositions of a community to the world, and therefore two kinds of lifestyle in the world; worldliness and what the Balokole called "separateness" that is called "churchliness"[35] in this book. "Worldliness," as the disposition and lifestyle of the community shaped only by worldly values and standards, is contrasted with "churchliness," a disposition engendered by the faith-relation with the Christ-event, resulting in a lifestyle that is consistent with the values and standards that faith dictates. This is the disposition of faith, which determines the community's relation to the world of which it is part. The Revival notion of "testimony" functions as a means of distinguishing between the two.

The fact of an institution called the church does not tell us anything about its disposition to the Christ-event or the world. In fact it is possible for a community to be called "a church" when it has lost its "churchliness," because it has lost its relation with the Christ-event and the world. "Churchliness" does not refer only to the dimension of community of "church" but to the whole reality in all its dimensions. Consider, for example, "institution" and "community" as two polar dimensions of the church. Churchliness is to be evident in both dimensions. A church is therefore "becoming church" through its re-living and re-enacting of the Christ-narrative in its present "world" context. It must bear "testimony" to its churchliness, both as an institution and as a community.

Testimony becomes an index of the church's churchliness or worldliness. It is possible that a church's testimony is not of its churchliness but of worldliness, that is of the same orientation as others in the world, without evidence of faith, in its structures or life as corporate body, that distinguishes it from other communities in the same context.

The question may now be put: What is it about the Church of Uganda that makes it a church? In terms of the "church in the world" construct and in the context of this study, this question requires reflection on the content of the preposition "in" in "the Church of Uganda *in* Uganda," and in particular turbulent post-independence Uganda.

---

35. H. Richard Niebuhr has used the same term in his *The Purpose of the Church*, 25.

The Ecclesiology of the Church of Uganda

There are at least four features that emerge in the account of the Church of Uganda, which explicate its being and becoming church in post-independence turbulent Uganda: authenticity, identity, sacramental presence and paradox.

Authenticity

In the discussion on the indigenization, it was shown that the Church of Uganda is an indigenous church. The issue therefore is not to show that the church of Uganda is an indigenous church but rather to identify the features of its indigeneity which authenticate it as "true church." By utilizing the notion of "testimony," expounded above as both the substantive process of indigenization and the expression of its result, it should be possible to determine what these features are. The Church of Uganda will be authenticated as "true church" by its testimony in the various historical eras. The content of that testimony will indicate whether the process of indigenization yielded churchliness or worldliness.

The ecclesiological significance of the schismatic and Revival movements in the decades of 1910s, 1920s and 1930s, lies in their questioning of the Church's authenticity as "true church." Each of the movements emerged with their own versions of testimony to churchliness, a divergence from what it perceived to be a loss of churchliness in the Church.

The two characteristic features of *Ekibina kya 'Katonda Omu Ayinza Byona (KOAB)* discussed in chapter 3, of repudiating medicine and the medical profession, and of baptism *en masse*, were meant to be a corrective to what they judged as unbiblical practice in the Church. This judgement was based on the vernacular Scriptures. KOAB emerged with a testimony of healing-faith and as a people's movement. The testimony of KOAB, though inspired by indigenous ethos, was problematic because it was not sufficiently inbetween the reality of the world and the Christ-event. Their baptism was so inclusive that in the end there was no qualitative distinction between KOAB adherents and the others who were not baptized.

Mabel Ensor's reaction to the worldliness in the Church was to separate from it. The formation of Mengo Gospel Church was based on the notion of withdrawal from the world in order to preserve churchliness.

Unfortunately for Ensor, the alternative church she formed could only continue to be a church when rooted in the world. A testimony is validated by the world because the world is the locus of faith praxis. Therefore, withdrawal from the world as a faith response was bound to be self-defeating because there cannot be a church unless it relates to a concrete world. Hence the demise of Mengo Gospel Church.

The Revival movement's corrective genius lay in its pointing back to the Christ-event without withdrawing from the world, as the basis for a testimony of "real Christianity." Although there were tendencies in the movement towards withdrawal, the predominant thrust was one of maintaining the tension and balance necessitated by faith-life, "*in* the world" and not "*of* the world." J. Church's explanation on the character of faith-life is worth quoting again:

> It does *not* necessarily mean the life of an ascetic, or to shut oneself up in a monastery. But spiritually, for the true Christian it means the power to live "in the world, but not of the world," i.e. the desire for worldly things and pleasures is replaced and overcome by the new nature of Christ, which fills the heart. Compromise with evil in any form hinders blessings for the Christian.[36]

It has been argued, sufficiently, how this disposition to the world produced a truly indigenous Christianity, rooted in both the Christ narrative and the religio-cultural context.

Indigeneity as a quality of the Church has to be redefined if the Church is to manifest its churchliness. It is not to be thought of only as originating from "belonging naturally" to a historical-cultural-political community, but also originating from *belonging by faith* to the narrative of Christ. Faith in Christ becomes second nature. The blending of both "natures" may be called "redeemed indigeneity." In the account of the social-political turbulence in Buganda, redeemed indigeneity was to be reflected in the understanding of the church as "the family of Christ"; and in the Teso account, redeemed indigeneity was manifested in prayer, preaching and the work of reconciliation.

---

36. Church, *Every Man a Bible Student*, 61 (emphasis in original).

This focus of the churches and individuals on prayer, the Word of God, and social concern, that runs though the entire account of the Church in turbulence, as a reaction and response to the chaos and suffering, manifest the disposition of redeemed indigeneity as a primary mark of the church. The important point here is that faith becomes second nature to an individual or community with a testimony of faith-encounter with Christ. Devotion to prayer, the ministry of the Word of God and social service, become the marks of faith. Catechist Mujabi of Luwero put it thus, in recounting the response and survival of the Church during the so-called bandit war in Luwero Triangle: "*Twasabanga buli kiseera, kubanga buli kiseera kyali nga kya kabi eri abantu* (we prayed all the time because each moment brought with it danger for the people)"[37].

Similar examples are rife in the account, as told in chapters 4–7. There was Canon Lubwama, in Namirembe Cathedral, passionately praying for the safety of the Kabaka and the defeat of the central government forces, as the battle for the Lubiri raged on. In Lango, during the plunder and carnage of the Idi Amin Regime, there were overcrowded church services, singing and praying, and the Bible reading groups that proliferated all over Lira. In the Luwero account, the catechists, in their work and service in the refugee camps, took preaching as a priority. Prayer, the ministries of the Word and relief service are what distinguished these communities as the church. And in Teso, there were calls to prayer by Bishop Ilukor, the Bible study groups in the camp at Ngora and the immunisation of the children. Confidence in God was manifested in prayer, preaching and the work of reconciliation that Bishop Ilukor spearheaded.

The question as to what authenticates a community that calls itself a church as "true church" has been contentious throughout the centuries of Christendom.[38] The credal statement of "one, holy, catholic, and apostolic church" as an affirmation of the marks or, as Hans Kung calls them, "dimensions,"[39] of the true church has attracted the most reflection

---

37. Amunoni Mujabi, quoted in chapter 6, 256–257.
38. Eric Jay's monumental work, *The Church: Its Changing Image through Twenty Centuries* (London: SPCK, 1977), among other ecclesiological issues surveys the several approaches to the question of the marks of a true church.
39. Hans Kung, *The Church* (London: Burns and Oates, 1967), 263–359.

especially within Anglican and Roman Catholic circles. A cursory reading of the exposition of these concepts by various theologians, however, shows that there is no unanimity on how they should be understood, because different assumptions, ecclesiastical traditions and theologies have determined their meaning. Consequently, they are used differently with varying ontological content.[40] It is Luther and Calvin who added to the "one, holy, catholic and apostolic" marks, and posited that: "Wherever we see the Word of God purely preached and heard, and the sacraments administered according to Christ's institution, there, it is not to be doubted, a church of God exists."[41] In the case of turbulent Uganda, however, it is legitimate to conclude that it was devotion to prayer, the ministry of the Word of God and service to society that evidenced the marks of the church. Devotion to prayer, the Word of God and social concern were the communities' visible expression of faith, a testimony to a faith-response in turbulence.

Prayer, the devotion to the Word of God, and social service are human acts, by which a community of faith reflects its heritage and reliance on the narrative of Christ. By its devotion to the word in its various forms, while rooted in the written Word, the community affirms that it belongs within the historical tradition of the narrative of Christ, beginning with the first witnesses. By prayer, the community attests to the existential reality of that narrative in the here and now, in the crisis moment of faith-decision. In its service to the society, the Church affirms the Lordship of Christ over all. The ecclesiological question as to *how* that faith was exercised and manifested in indigenous idiom is answered: by devotion to prayer, the Word, and social service.

---

40. Eric Jay in his *The Church*, outlines some of the content assigned to these marks by the different generations of theologians and churchmen from the time of the early church fathers when the apostles creed was framed. Colin Gunton has made this point as well in his "The Church on Earth: The Roots of Community" in *On Being the Church: Essays on the Christian Community*, eds. Colin E. Gunton and Daniel W. Hardy (Edinburgh: T & T Clark, 1989), 48.

41. John Calvin, *The Institutes of the Christian Religion*, ed. John T. McNeill, trans. Ford L. Battles (Philadelphia: Westminster Press, 1960), Book IV, Section 1.9, 1023. A shorter discussion of both Luther and Calvin's discussion in Eric Jay, *The Church*, 161–176.

Identity

The story of the Church of Uganda is one long quest of corporate identity. The Protestant-established identity characteristic of the Church up to the time of independence was formed in a social political context defined in Protestant-Catholic terms. However, when the "question of Buganda"[42] increasingly took centre stage as the critical defining element of the social-political climate of Uganda, heightened by the Mengo Crisis, the Protestant identity receded in importance. The crucial identity question was the Church's internal structural relations as a church in Uganda, with one identity incorporating the diversity of regional identities. The crisis arising from the conflict between the dioceses in Buganda with the Provincial Assembly Executive was a manifestation of this identity crisis.

Idi Amin's regime transformed the social political scene with the "establishment" of Islam and the institutionalization of violence. As in the Lango account, the specifically Protestant testimony became irrelevant because of the shared consciousness of "united through common suffering ... against the Muslims, their common enemy"[43] cut across the Protestant-Catholic divide; therefore this time the definition of "us" included Catholics. In this case they defined themselves as "the persecuted" because the whole Christian community, both Catholics and Protestants, considered themselves as the targets of the Muslims, as their "persecutors." But soon this Christian-Muslim distinction became irrelevant once the Muslims shared the experience of suffering. Suffering diminished the distinction church and world; therefore suffering could not be a testimony of churchliness, but of the fact that the church's life was rooted in the real world.

What is evident from the story of the Church is that there is not one enduring feature of its corporate identity in the rapidly changing social-political climate. This matter of the transitional nature of its corporate identity can be appreciated once identity is seen as testimony.

Paul Avis has argued that the concept of identity incorporates the twin themes of continuity and individuality.[44] In discussing what he calls

---

42. This is the complex issue about the place of the Kabaka and the kingdom of Buganda in the new independent nation-state of Uganda, discussed in chapter 4, 132–137.
43. Olal, "Church and Politics in Lango-Uganda," 37.
44. Paul Avis, *Anglicanism and the Christian Church* (Edinburgh: T & T Clark, 1989).

structures of corporate identity,⁴⁵ which result from the community's instinct to preserve itself, he outlines the conditions that these structures ought to fulfil.

> The first condition of corporate identity is naturally *continuity*, either of individual or of office. The second is that each member of the group should have a definite *idea* of the nature, composition, functions and the capacities of the group. Durkheim defined the identity of a society as "the idea which it forms of itself." The third requirement is *interaction* – especially in form of conflict of rivalry – of the group with other similar groups "animated by different ideals and purposes and swayed by different traditions and customs." Fourthly the group needs *traditions*, customs or habits, that delineate the role of an individual in the group. And finally, group identity demands a definite *structure* expressed in "the differentiation and specialisation of functions of its constituents."⁴⁶

The capacity of the Revival notion of testimony, in elucidating the quest of identity in the Church of Uganda, is vindicated, because it encompasses all five conditions outlined: continuity, the group's idea of itself, interaction, traditions, and structure were part of what the testimony served.

The oral version of a testimony was intended to tally with faith-life. In other words, the essence of the testimony in its fullness was continuity of faith. By it an individual qualified to be a witness, a responsibility for every one; and its quality differentiated roles in the fellowship. It is this that distinguished one as a *Mulokole*, a real Christian, from *Omukristayo*, a "nominal" Christian. The structures of corporate identity that evolve in a church's history are testimony of its identity in the present, and could be evaluated as to whether they manifest churchliness in that historical epoch.

Positing static church identity results in a prescriptive ecclesiology. However, since both the church and the world are dynamic, each new experience of "church in the world" must yield a fresh testimony, a re-enacting and renewing of its testimony of yesteryears. A church is therefore

---

45. Ibid., 8.
46. Ibid.

in a perpetual search for its identity; each realized identity is tentative. There are two directions of movement in the church's quest for identity. The first movement is in the direction of its relation to the "world," the cultural-social-political context of which it is a part and to which it must bear its testimony. The second is a movement in the direction of the Christ-event, as it strives to be true to the Christ narrative, again, of which it is a part. Churchliness is maintaining both movements simultaneously. It is the continual living and re-enacting the Christ-narrative, telling and retelling it to succeeding generations of the world, as each moment and generation presents new opportunities and challenges of faith-decision, to be "in the world but not of the world."

This precludes positing a static church identity as a comprehensive definition of what a church is. For example the argument for an "Anglican identity" manifested in liturgy, episcopacy and parochial structure[47] is valuable in so far as it refers to historical origins, but is not a testimony of churchliness. During the years of the Luwero Triangle war, there was no proper Anglican administration of the sacraments; the bishop visited twice in the span of four years; and the parochial structure was non-existent, due to the dislocation and scattering of entire populations. And yet there was a church. What sustained the Church in Luwero were the catechists and pastors that traversed the length and breadth of the Triangle, bringing help and hope to all the people. The Episcopal identity of the ministry, with its three-fold order of bishop, priest and pastor, was inadequate as a testimony of churchliness. This begs the question: What is the chief work and purpose of the ministry? Rather than begin with a predetermined identity, which is not easily justified, an exploration of the corporate identity of the ministry operative in the Church is what will clarify the nature of ministry that is a testimony of churchliness.

H. Richard Niebuhr has argued convincingly, from church history, that each era has had a conception of ministry oriented towards a particular focus, leading to different perspectives as to what the primary work and purpose of the ministry is.

---

47. Ibid., 9–12.

Since the days described in the New Testament Christian ministers have preached and taught; they have led worship and administered sacraments; they have presided over the church and exercised oversight over its work; they have given pastoral care to individuals in need. Though at times these functions have been distributed among specialised orders of clergy, still each minister, in his domain, has needed to exercise them all. Yet whenever there has been clear conception of the office one of these functions has been regarded as central and the other functions have been ordered so as to serve, not indeed it, but the chief purpose that it served directly.[48]

Niebuhr has identified four major types of ministry orientation. The first is the pastoral ruler in the early church, who directed his work toward the care of the souls. The second is the preacher of the churches of the Reformation, whose main work was to preach the gospel of forgiveness, declaring God's love for man as revealed in Jesus Christ. The third is the evangelist of the Wesleyan, Evangelical and Pietist movements represented as a variation of the Protestant idea of the preacher. And fourth is the Catholic priesthood marked by emphasis on the importance and greatness of the work of administering the sacraments.[49] Niebuhr has rightly pointed out that a conception of the chief work of the ministry helps in providing cohesion in ministry by relating each function to it, as well as "directing each function to a chief, though still proximate end."[50] In order to determine the corporate identity of the ministry in the Church of Uganda, it is crucial to identify the chief work of the ministry as exercised in the different epochs of the story of the Church of Uganda.

In terms of ministry orientation, there are two distinguishable eras in the story of the Church of Uganda. The first era spans the period of the planting of the churches covered in chapter 1, throughout the time of developing of the infrastructure, to the election of Erica Sabiti as Archbishop. During this era, the chief work of the ministry was what Niebuhr identified

---

48. Niebuhr, *The Purpose of the Church*, 58–59 (emphasis added).
49. Ibid., 58–63.
50. Ibid., 62–63.

as the Protestant preacher of the Reformation, and the evangelist of Pietism. The hero of the account during this era is the evangelist-preacher. Louise Pirouet's study, *Black Evangelists*, highlights the central role African agents played in the planting of the churches all over Uganda, and shows that these Africans were first and foremost evangelists. John Poulton, writing about the Church of Uganda in the first half of the twentieth century, made the observation that:

> The emphasis on preaching-for-conversion remains a feature of the Church of Uganda. Her hymn-book is full of the mission-service style of hymns. Her best preachers and most faithful pastors are unlikely to stray far from the one theme in their public ministry.[51]

The Revival's norm that "every Mulokole is a witness,"[52] with its strong bias to preaching, added value to the idea of the chief work of the ministry as preaching.

The second era is associated with the social-political turbulence of the post-independence period. During this epoch, the chief work of the ministry became pastoral. This was especially the case among the communities that experienced social turmoil; and as the turbulence moved from region to region, covering the entire country, the Church became dominated by the pastoral orientation of the ministry. All other aspects of the ministry served this primary work: of care, comfort and consolation, amidst pain and trauma. Although the ministry function of preaching remained central, it was to serve pastoral concerns. For example, in the camps for the displaced, during the Luwero Triangle war, preaching was always central in the work of all those who served in the camps. However, as pointed out in chapter 6, in the context of war and death it was considered urgent to present the gospel of salvation, as preparation for eternity. No wonder the response was phenomenal. The idea of eternal life brought solace and comfort to those for whom death had become part of their daily experience.

Pastor-ship, as the chief work of the ministry, has two further implications on the exercise of ministry: first, in the structuring order in the

---

51. Poulton, "Like Father, Like Son," 300.
52. Katarikawe and Wilson, "East African Revival Movement," 185.

ministry, and second, in determining what constitutes the primary tasks. For instance, in the Luwero account, because of the primacy of pastoral work, the canonical order of bishop-priest-deacon was abandoned in practice, because it is based on the idea of ministry that posits the administration of the sacraments as the primary work. The *de facto* order was unitary – pastor-ship – rather than three-fold distinction of orders. In the "pastor-ship" idea of the order of the ministry, the bishop is recognized as first among equals, the elder pastor, or to use the early fathers' terminology, the pastoral-ruler. Pastor-ship is the testimony to churchliness in the leadership of the church.

Focusing on the pastoral service as the chief work of the ministry shifts the leadership paradigm from a hierarchical form to an egalitarian one. The Revival concept of leadership parallels this, and gives further insight into the testimony of churchly leadership. The leadership concept in the Revival was egalitarian, where fellowship leadership was not hierarchical but rather that of a team. All the members of the team were "fellow brethren," and the leaders were among them as elders, having distinguished themselves by the quality of their testimony. What therefore distinguishes churchly leadership is the quality of testimony, of pastoral service.

The implications, of taking pastoral work as the chief work of the ministry, are evident in the three accounts of the Church in Lango, Luwero and Teso. They are all unanimous that the constitutive "works" of pastoral work were prayer, the ministry of the Word and relief distribution. By these three, the pastors attended to the needs of the communities. They were the visible forms by which the ministers communicated the gospel of Christ and the testimony of churchliness; meeting both spiritual and physical needs of the people.

This conceptual perspective may shed some light on how to interpret Luwum's involvement in what Amin judged as clandestine treasonable acts. Luwum, by supporting initiatives to remove Amin, was fulfilling his ministry as pastor, seeking the welfare and protection of the people he served. Luwum's pastoral experiences, of the pain and agony of bereavement among those he served, first as bishop of Northern diocese and then later as Archbishop, seem to have led him to the conclusion that the best pastoral service to the people of Uganda was the removal of Amin. He could have fled the country, and saved his life. In fact on the previous day before that fateful day of his death, his wife pleaded with him to get out of Uganda. But Luwum refused. And on the day of his death, she pleaded again and told him that if he went for the meeting at the International Conference Centre, he would not return, to which Luwum replied, "If I die, my blood will save Uganda."[53]

It is significant that Luwum did not say, "If I die my blood will *save the Church.*" Given his Revival heritage, he knew better whose blood saves the church. Therefore the salvific value that he attached to his suffering was pastoral rather than ontological. This signifies Luwum's awareness of his pastoral call. It posits a distinct identity of the one who dies from the community for which he dies. Luwum, as pastor, undertook the ultimate duty of pastoral-leadership responsibility: taking upon himself the whole burden of the identity of the community, in order to save it.

In the same vein, Bishop Ilukor's crusade for peace and reconciliation during the Teso insurgency war should be interpreted as a pastoral act motivated by a vision of care and concern for the Iteso. It was his pastoral vision that inspired his plea to "tell the rebels to tell the people that *we* should stop fighting."[54] He therefore traversed the entire Teso, pleading with the Iteso to end rebellion and pave the way for the rebuilding of their lives that had been shattered by the plunder of their cattle, their symbol of identity.

Luwum, Odurukami, Serubidde, Ilukor, Mujabi – the bishops, clergy and catechists of turbulent Uganda – demonstrate that the testimony of churchliness in turbulence is not priesthood but pastor-ship. In their dedication and service to all the people, not just members of the Church of Uganda, they mirror the lordship of Christ. In their service Christ is manifested not just as Lord of the church, but Lord of all, because he is Lord of life. These leaders became a testimony to the lordship of Christ over all, and through their mission and ministry they extended his grace to all.

---

53. These are some of Luwum's last words, in Henry Okullu, in "The Role of a Church Leader," as quoted in this thesis, p. 218.
54. Bishop Gershom Ilukor, quoted on p. 219.

Sacrament

In a church where the sacraments have historically played a central role as symbols of faith and means that signify the mission of the church, a discussion of its ecclesiology would be incomplete without considering the meaning of the sacraments in the context of turbulent Uganda.

A distinction needs to be made between intrinsic meaning and existential meaning. Although these two meanings are not mutually exclusive, they originate from two distinct hermeneutical positions. The intrinsic meaning is derived from the standpoint of the elements and the ritual as prescribed, while existential meaning is that given by the administrator and partaker. The former is inherent in the ritual irrespective of context, and the latter is dynamic and posited in a subjective faith-experience.

It was pointed out in chapter 6 that the existential functional value of the sacraments of Baptism and Holy Communion during the war in Luwero Triangle was the same as the traditional concept of sacrament, whereby the material objects mediate the blessing and favour sought. This is similar to the Vatican II Catholic[55] understanding of sacrament as a sign and instrument of that which it signifies, as Dulles has expounded:

> A sacrament is, in the first place, a sign of grace. A sign could be a mere pointer to something that is absent, but a sacrament is a "full sign," a sign of something that is really present. Hence the Council of Trent could rightly describe a sacrament as "the visible form of an invisible grace." Beyond this, a sacrament is an efficacious sign; the sign itself produces or intensifies that of which it is a sign. Thanks to the sign, the reality signified achieves an existential depth; it emerges into solid, tangible existence . . . Thus the Councils can say that the sacraments contain the grace they signify, and confer the grace they contain.[56]

---

55. Walter M. Abbott, ed., *The Documents of Vatican II* (New York: Guild Press, 1966); the sections on The Dogmatic Constitution of the Church, and The Pastoral Constitution of the Church.
56. Dulles, *Models of the Church*, 70.

For the people of Luwero, Baptism and Holy Communion were believed to contain and confer blessing. These services were to the ministers and the people testimony, an experience in the Christ narrative. The elements used were ordinary – water for Baptism, sugared-water, as "wine," and regular cassava as "bread" – but to the people these elements when consecrated mediated hope, grace and protection amidst turbulence, and preparation for death. Being baptized and receiving Communion were therefore acts of faith, a participation and appropriation of the grace of Christ mediated by the ritual. Baptism and Communion therefore were testimony to churchliness, because they mediated the presence of the Christ event in their world of pain and trauma.

It was not only Baptism and Communion that mediated blessing and protection, but every church service. This is evidenced in accounts of the churches in Teso and Luwero; the Church's leading role in relief and medical service, the ministers work of burying the dead in the camps, and the ministry of peace-making, were all testimony of the grace mediated by the Church. The mass movement into the churches reflected in the large numbers of those who attended worship, prayer and Bible study services, manifests a faith-search of the blessings believed to be inherent in the Church. The ministries of Bishop Ilukor in Teso, Scrubidde in Luwero, the clergy and catechists in the camps, were real blessings in concrete terms. Dulles has expressed this testimony of churchliness explicated in a church's work and presence as sacrament:

> Where the Church as sacrament is present, the grace of Christ will not be absent. That grace, seeking its appropriate form of expression – as grace inevitably does – will impel men to prayer, confession, worship, and other acts whereby the Church externally realises its essence. Through these actions the Church signifies what it contains and contains what it signifies. In coming to expression, the grace of the Church realises itself as grace. The Church therefore confers the grace that it contains, and contains it precisely as conferring it. The Church becomes an event of grace as the lives of its members

are transformed in hope, in joy, in self-forgetful love, in peace, in patience, and in all Christ-like virtues.[57]

Churchliness is the sacramentality of the faith-community in the world. "Church becomes Church in so far as the grace of Christ, operative within it, achieves tangibility through the actions of the Church as such"[58]. The argument here is that the testimony of churchliness was manifested in the sacramental presence of the Church manifested in its diverse pastoral ministry and embodied in its pastors and people. This was particularly so in the leadership: Archbishop Luwum in Amin's Uganda; Odurukami in Lango; Serubidde and the other clergy and catechists in Luwero; Bishop Ilukor and the clergy and catechists in Teso, were all sacraments to the people.

The mission of the Church in sacramental terms was not primarily the multiplication of converts and churches, but rather incarnational presence. In a sense there was no need to symbolize the presence of the suffering Christ, in bread and wine, as the locus of faith. The sufferings of the pastors and catechists embodied the sufferings of Christ. The church's presence in the world is to mediate the grace and values of the kingdom of God in Jesus Christ. This is the church's mission.

Paradox and Mystery

The paradox or mystery[59] of the efficacious presence of the church in the world is explicated in the bipolar "in-between" nature of churchliness. There are four pairs of polarities in the "church in the world" existence: catholicity and particularity; eternity and temporality; "from above" and "from below"; and the subject-object relation in its testimony of the love of the Christ-event. Herein lies the paradox: neither catholicity nor particularity is churchliness or worldliness; and neither eternity nor temporality is churchliness or worldliness; and neither is life "from above" nor "from below."

---

57. Ibid., 74.
58. Ibid., 73.
59. Emil Brunner, *The Word and the World* (London: SCM Press, 1931), 6–7. Brunner uses the word "paradox" in referring to this bipolar existence, and Dulles calls it "mystery." Dulles, *Models of the Church*, 21–24.

Churchliness is sustained in paradox, the continual co-existence of apparent opposites in one historical reality; for if a church should lose the balance and tumble towards either of the poles, its testimony ceases to be of churchliness. For example, in the case of the two poles of eternity and temporality: if the church should exist in time and lose its eternal dimension engendered by the Christ-event, its testimony is of worldliness; and if it tumbles toward the historical Christ-event, its testimony is ethereal, archaic and irrelevant. Consequently for a church to continue becoming church, it will always be in tension, in a perpetual moment of decision, seeking to maintain the tension and balance dictated by its quest to be true to its bipolar dimensional life.

The tension and struggle in maintaining the bipolar eternity-temporality existence is evident in the story of the Revival. Although Revival ethos espoused maintaining the tension and balance, the tendency among the Balokole was to emphasize more the eternal dimension at the expense of the temporal; leading to a testimony that was often ethereal and irrelevant. John Wilson's testimony[60] of how he declined an appointment to become Ambassador illustrates this. President Obote invited him, in 1964, to consider becoming the ambassador of Uganda to the United States of America or Britain. His initial reaction was excitement and joy at the prospect. He writes:

> I imagined being driven round in London in a black Austin Princess with the Uganda flag flying on top of the body, a big double-story house or apartment as the ambassador's home I would be living in, my children going to the best schools in London; and on the other hand, I imagined if I were to choose the USA, a big Chrysler or Cardillac; why not? With the Uganda flag flying in Washington! The embassy prestige and the grandeur of diplomat banquets really fascinated me.[61]

However, after much struggle and reflection, he declined the invitation, having concluded:

---

60. John Wilson's life story, entitled "Testimony: John Wilson" is in James Katarikawe and John Wilson, "East African Revival Movement," 232–252. Wilson was one of the elders in the Revival in the late 1960s and 1970s.

61. Ibid., 247–248.

> I belonged to Jesus. I can never sing another person's song or indulge in earthly politics, I thought to myself. I was chosen by grace and saved by grace. I had gone back and become lustful and sinful yet Jesus had given me another chance. How quickly was I (sic) getting imprisoned again.[62]

Wilson equated accepting the ambassadorial job with worldliness, "singing another person's song," and therefore antithetical to serving Jesus to whom he belonged. And yet Wilson could have repented his initial worldly excitement and proceeded to accept the invitation with a different disposition. The challenge for Wilson was whether to "sing Jesus' song" or "sing another person's song." He tumbled to singing only Jesus song. Wilson's tendency was typical in the Revival, and it is what gave birth to *Re-awakening*, discussed at the end of chapter 3.

The struggle to maintain the bipolar catholicity-particularity existence was mirrored in the tension and struggle over the question of Buganda in chapter 4. It is instructive to contrast the way the "question of Buganda" was dealt with in the Church, and in the political arena. Both the central and Buganda governments were uneasy with the tension of two governments co-existing. Instead of living with the reality, and seeking to maintain equilibrium through persuasion and compromise, force was used to impose resolution; on the one hand the Central government troops forcing "universality," a Republic of Uganda, on locality, a kingdom of Buganda; and on the other, Mengo government's fight to retain particularity in isolation from catholicity.

In the arena of the Church, there were tendencies in the Church in Buganda to push for particularity without catholicity, manifested in the various memoranda to secede. Similarly there were tendencies in the Provincial organs to force catholicity, manifested in the provincial Assembly of December 1970 at which resolutions were made on the contentious issues, without the participation of the dioceses in Buganda.[63] The Church was then faced with a faith-decision, either to accommodate to the

---

62. Ibid., 248.
63. See p. 161–165 in chapter 4.

Buganda-Uganda divide as in the political arena or bear testimony to its national Uganda identity without denying its local Buganda identity.

The testimony to churchliness was the process of struggle through prayer, negotiation and persuasion with a view to maintaining particularity and catholicity, and the recognition that though antithetical they are complementary. Moreover it was not achievable that the "churchliness" of the Church of Uganda become manifest nationally without being evident locally. Testimony presupposes indigeneity; indigeneity demands locality; and locality justifies catholicity. Churchliness must therefore be both local and catholic. The settlement arrived at in 1971 over the question of the place of Namirembe Cathedral, one of the contentious issues, affirmed both locality and catholicity in resolving that "the Cathedral would continue to be the Cathedral of Namirembe Diocese and also the Provincial Cathedral."[64]

One other consideration in the Sabiti-Nsubuga conflict is a clash of perspectives of the Church that Archbishop Sabiti and Bishop Nsubuga respectively represented, which heightened the level of conflict and delayed resolution. Sabiti had a vested interest, as Archbishop, to keep the Church together, while Nsubuga, leading the Church in Buganda, was striving for the retention of the distinct and pre-eminent identity of the Church in Buganda. Sabiti was oriented towards catholicity and Nsubuga towards locality. The point here is that historical experience informs and increases propensity to tip the balance on one side and not the other.

Should a church fall to either side, churchliness is not lost irredeemably. Falling is not the last word, because the option of repentance is always available to it. According to the Revival, what sustains the balance and tension of the inbetween life is a perpetual disposition of repentance, a "daily coming back to the cross with a broken and contrite heart."[65] As John Wilson asserted: "All those who find repentance impossible soon revert to a life of works and churchgoing, the nominal Christianity so common all over the world."[66] A feature of the testimony to churchliness is therefore repentance. Festo Kivengere's *I Love Idi Amin,* after the brutal murder of

---

64. Archbishop's Papers, "Report on Conference of Bishops," 3.
65. Church, *Quest for the Highest*, 126.
66. Katarikawe and Wilson, "East African Revival Movement," 156.

Luwum and evident threat to Kivengere's life, was for him a testimony of repentance, a faith decision, which he narrated thus:

> I had to face my own attitude towards Amin and his agents. The Holy Spirit showed me that I was getting hard in my spirit, and that my hardness and bitterness towards those who were persecuting us could only bring spiritual loss. This would take away my ability to communicate the love of God, which is the essence of my ministry and *testimony*.
>
> So I had to ask for forgiveness from the Lord, and for grace to love President Amin more, because these events had shaken my loving relationship with all those people. He gave me assurance of forgiveness on Good Friday, when I was one of the congregation that sat for three hours in All Souls' Church in London, meditating on the redeeming love of Jesus Christ. Right there the Lord healed me, and I hurried to tell Mera about it. This was fresh air for my tired soul. I knew I had seen the Lord and been released: love filled my heart.[67]

Bishop Kivengere was convinced that this was "the spirit in which brother Janani met his death."[68] Kivengere is here suggesting that Luwum faced his killers without bitterness. His disposition was one of repentance leading to forgiveness. Only the repentant can forgive. A predisposition of forgiveness would connote the idea that it was only Amin that was in need of forgiveness, positing a "holier than thou" attitude *vis-a-vis* Amin. In positing a "spirit of repentance" as the inspiration to suffering without bitterness, Kivengere is acknowledging the possibility of becoming like Amin, reverting to the way "of the world."

It was the same disposition, in the Luwero account, that led Bishop Kawuma to the recognition that the sufferings inflicted on his people by the "Northerners" was not a result of "northern-ness," but rather a result of "the sinful nature, which we share." He discovered:

> So it was not a tribe; it was not an ethnic sin. It was a human problem. And I said that since I could not call all the Baganda,

---

67. Kivengere, *I Love Idi Amin*, 62 (emphases added).
68. Ibid.

The Church in the World: Toward an Ecclesiology

I said [to Melchisedek] on behalf of the Baganda who live in Namirembe Diocese, I just want to say sorry about the things the Baganda did for the northerners.[69]

The testimony to the common identity and participation in the Christ narrative among what were otherwise a warring people, the Baganda and Langi, was manifested in Kawuma's plea for forgiveness from Bishop Otim of Lango diocese. Notably, as in the case of Kivengere, Kawuma does not pronounce forgiveness to Otim and the Langi, but rather he asks for forgiveness, taking responsibility for the "worldly" way of responding to their oppressors with bitterness.

The awareness of the capacity to fall is in itself a result of faith. Decision is preceded by uncertainty, a manifestation of the lack of confidence in the sufficiency of human capacity to make the right choice. This is what yielded the disciplines of prayer and the word, that were characteristic of the Church in turbulence. By prayer, the community bears testimony to its tension and uncertainty in making a decision and acknowledges its dependence on "Another"; and through the discipline of the word the community testifies to its indebtedness and belonging to a "tradition" of the narrative of Christ to which it must refer.

Thus the church is both subject and object of this "tradition," to which it bears testimony. The title of Festo Kivengere's book that narrates some of the experience of the Church during Idi Amin's regime and his flight to exile – *I Love Idi Amin* – echoes this paradoxical subject-object identity of the church. Kivengere was one of the last bishops in the company of Luwum hours before his death, and thereafter fled for his life after receiving information that he too may suffer the same end. He says he wrote *I Love Idi Amin* to "share what God has done for ordinary Christians in an ordinary church in the middle of storms and stresses – because Christ does shine brighter when all around is darker."[70] While in exile he wrote:

> We look back with great love to our country. We love President Idi Amin. We owe him a debt of love, for he is one of those for whom Christ shed His precious blood. As long as he is still

---

69. Kawuma, OI, Nsangi, Kampala, 20 April 1997.
70. Kivengere, *I Love Idi Amin*, 7.

alive, he is still redeemable. Pray for him, that in the end he may see a new way of life, rather than a way of death.[71]

Kivengere's unequivocal attestation to the redeemability of Amin is a statement of faith. It reaffirms that the *raison d'être* of the church is to bear witness to the love of God as it was manifested in the Christ-event. It also expresses the paradox of that testimony at three levels. The first level is the apparent contradiction in the subject-object relation of the testimony of the church to the world. The Church as subject had to bear its witness to the love of God for the people of Uganda, by defending those traumatized by Idi Amin and his regime. But it had also to bear witness to the love of God *even* for Idi Amin and the perpetrators of carnage in his regime.

The second level of the paradox in the testimony of the church is in its means. Kivengere's "we" suggests that Luwum was among those who loved President Idi Amin. While Kivengere pledges prayer as the means of the Church's testimony, Luwum seemed to have pledged Amin's removal. Both "prayer" and "removal" bear testimony of the love of God for the people of Uganda, Idi Amin and his agents.

At the third level, the Church is subject and at the same time object of God's love. As subject, it bears witness to the world, but as object it is a recipient of the love of God. The church is in the world as subject and object, judge and plaintiff, and agent of the kingdom of God and not the kingdom itself.

The paradoxical inbetween nature of the church is necessary for sustaining a holistic view of the mission of the church; mission refers to that work and service of the church that is directed primarily to the world. The church is in the world as prophet and pastor. By prophet we mean one who speaks as from "above" as contrasted with from "below"; who announces judgement to the oppressor with the dictum "repent or perish," what Gustavo Gutierrez has called denunciation and annunciation,[72] without working along side the oppressor to bring about the change in him or her. By pastoral type we mean one who speaks from "below" as contrasted with

---

71. Ibid., 63.
72. Gustavo Gutierrez, "The Church: Sacrament of History," in *Liberation Theology: An Introductory Reader*, ed. Curt Cadorette et al. (Maryknoll, New York: Orbis Books, 1994), 176–179.

the one from "above"; who with empathy, stands along side the oppressor and leads him on to repentance. The pastoral dimension is explicated in the incarnational-sacramental presence, and the prophetic in denunciation, annunciation and proclamation.[73]

The Luwum-Wani succession shows the reality of the tension and struggle to maintain the inbetween tension of prophet-pastor. If Luwum's and Wani's service to the Amin regime were to be categorized according to the two polar missions, of the prophetic and pastoral type, Luwum was of the prophetic type, standing in opposition to the powers that were – Idi Amin and his regime; and Wani of the pastoral type. It was hoped that since Wani was Amin's "uncle," he could gently and firmly rebuke him, without provoking him to rain his fury on the Church. These two types are borne out when one examines the two types of Memoranda, the hard hitting ones during Luwum's leadership, and the gentle and pleading ones characteristic of Wani's period. The significance of the story is not just the opposition of Luwum to the regime or the empathetic disposition of Wani; these postures were also present in the world. But it is that the House of Bishops elected a pastoral-type leader in an age of "prophets," at a time when the momentum of opposition to the Amin regime was mounting towards a climax. The testimony to churchliness was the faith-choice of Wani, the pastoral-type, to balance Luwum, the prophetic-type, thereby keeping the two otherwise antithetical services complementary.

Conclusion

Erica Sabiti's statement of his vision for the future of the Church of Uganda, in his "Charge to the Church of Uganda, Rwanda and Burundi" in the December 1970 Provincial Assembly, will serve to bring this study to a conclusion. Daunted by the internal conflicts in the leadership of the Church then, and looking toward the celebration of the Church's centenary, Sabiti stated:

---

73. It is common to posit evangelism against social responsibility in discussions about the mission of the church. However if the church is to maintain its mystery, both evangelism and social concern have to be held in tension and balance, as essential components of the nature of Christian mission.

What then is the will of God for us? What charge does He lay upon us as we begin this assembly? Serve the poor and suffering, unify the people and bring them to the knowledge of God. He said these words to our fathers and He says them to us. He says also to us, dare to search for new ways of doing those things. Dare to make your ministry more effective even if it means painful change; even if it means giving up things you have learned to value and love.[74]

This book has reflected on some of the history that was in Sabiti's future. How right he was that the quest for identity would continually be at the heart of the testimony of the churchliness of the Church of Uganda, as a faith community in Uganda. The account has vindicated Sabiti further by showing that the Church's ministry emphasis was on the primacy of pastoral work, as the integrating function of all other activities of its ministers; a sacramental presence, a testimony of the church's mission in the world. The disciplines of prayer and the word of God, in the context of turbulence continually informed, formed and transformed the Church's apprehension of the gospel, the narrative of Christ. Prayer and the Word of God were the primary ways that connected the Church to the historical Christ-event, thereby incorporating it into the Christ-narrative. "What then is the will of God" except for the Church of Uganda to strive to maintain the balance and tension of the paradoxical faith-life as a "church *in* the world."

This study has shown that though the missionary roots of the Church were Anglican, it is not the Anglican identity that defined its "being church," but rather an ethos that emerged as the Anglican inheritance was blended with the historical, religio-cultural, and socio-political context. What has emerged is a church *in* Uganda, whose identity is marked by indigenous Ugandan traits; showing that to prescribe a precise ecclesiology for the Church of Uganda is not defensible. For example "being church" in Uganda meant redefining the corporate identity of ministry, from the canonical Anglican bishop-priest-deacon order to pastor-ship. Therefore, although at the institutional level, the canonical order has been maintained,

---

74. Erica Sabiti, "The Archbishop's Charge to the Church of Uganda, Rwanda and Burundi," Provincial Assembly Papers, COU Archives, December 1970, 7.

the reality at the grassroots life is different. A pro-active indigenizing step for the Church would be to take the bold stride and recognize the *de-facto* order by making it *de-jure*. How that would be structured, is left for further study and discussion.

There are five other areas in the study of the Church of Uganda, which this book has only touched upon, that warrant further research in the future: the impact of pre-Christian traditional customs, norms, rituals and values on hymnody; Muslim-Christian relations; the Church in West Nile and Acholi areas during the post-independence turbulent times; the ethics of violence; and, the internal conflicts in some dioceses in the Church of Uganda.

At different points in this study, the importance of the pre-Christian tradition and culture in shaping to a large extent the ecclesiological orientation of the Church of Uganda was pointed out. Although there are already some studies that examine its impact on worship and liturgy,[75] none has dealt with the development of hymnody in the light of this tradition. In the process of the field research for this study many songs, choruses and hymns with traditional ethos were found to be in use. It would also be of immense benefit to ecclesiological study if such material were collected and stored in a retrievable manner.

Islam has shaped the image and identity of the Church of Uganda, especially in two historical epochs: the genesis period, from the 1870s to early 1890s; and, during the Idi Amin regime, in the 1970s. Between the two epochs is a period of about one hundred years. It is significant that in each of these periods Christian-Muslim relations were tainted with violence. There is need for an indepth historical study and an appraisal of the prospects for dialogue, rather than confrontation. It does not have take another one hundred years for the Church to acknowledge Islam as a major force in shaping the image and identity of the Church, if some deliberate reflection on Christian-Muslim relations is not undertaken.

---

75. They include: Mutebi, "Towards an Indigenous Understanding"; Joachim Sentongo, "The Traditional Concept of Worship among the Ganda People of Uganda in Relation to the Concept of Worship in the Bible," Makerere University, unpublished Diploma in Theology dissertation, 1988; and Kyewalyanga, *Traditional Religion*.

The two other regions in Uganda that experienced turmoil, of the magnitude manifested in the Luwero Triangle and Teso, are West Nile and Acholi. Case studies of the life and mission of the Church of Uganda in these regions would complete the circuit of turbulent post-independence Uganda.

The post-independence story of the Church has highlighted the issue of violence from within the Church. It was argued that it was more likely than not that Archbishop Luwum was party to a plan to remove Idi Amin from power through the agency of military means; Archbishop Okoth identified with the so called liberation army that overthrew the Idi Amin regime; and in both Luwero and Teso accounts there was a tacit support given to the insurgents based in those areas. The question that these case studies raise, that this study has not addressed, is whether and under what circumstances it is legitimate for a church to be involved in destabilizing political authority through the use of violence, in a context where that authority is using violence against the populace.

The discussion, in chapter 4, on the Church of Uganda in the context of an emerging republic, highlighted some issues that shaped the internal dynamics and self-consciousness of the Church as it dealt with internal conflicts that arose from the socio-political configuration of Uganda at the time. During the course of archival research, there were other situations of internal conflict in the Church, at diocesan level, that were encountered, notably in Busoga, Kigezi, Mbale, and Rwenzori dioceses. Further research in those situations will contribute to the study of the history of the Church of Uganda and might give more insights into its ecclesiology, especially in regard to church polity.

Beyond contributing to the study of the Church of Uganda, this thesis presents a historical-theological methodological approach for the study of African church history and ecclesiology. The merits of the "church in the world" paradigm for historical study lie in its insistence in taking both church and society together in writing a church history. It gives premium to "historical context" in the study of church history. By "historical context" we mean the religio-cultural-socio-political context as it evolves in the process of history: in one word – "the world." The point has been made that story of the church is not complete without the story of the world in which the church explicates its faith-life. Church history should therefore not be confined to ecclesiastical history that focuses only on ecclesial concerns, but rather be seen as an interdisciplinary historical endeavour that takes into account other aspects of history.

From the theological angle, the "church in the world" paradigm demands that the historical context provide essential raw material for constructing a theology of the church. But the paradigm also posits a distinct identity of the church from its "world" arising from its faith-relation with the Christ-event. What has been said of the Church of Uganda, that to prescribe a precise ecclesiology is indefensible, could to be extended to other ecclesiological studies. The dynamic nature of "historical context" and the consequent dynamic apprehension of the Christ-event imply that any church's ecclesiological identity is always tentative. Thus the question, "What is the church?" is perpetual, and its answers always provisional, as each generation of the Christian community lives and defines itself in action *vis-à-vis* the world. Prescriptive ecclesiology, whether it is "Anglican ecclesiology" or the credal "One, Holy, Apostolic and Catholic Church" does not fully account for the ecclesiological identity of a church. It is imperative that the contextual experience of the church is taken into account.

To this end, by utilizing the conceptual paradigm of the "church in the world," this book has constructed a broad framework for the ecclesiology of the Church of Uganda, that could be utilized in other studies. The four motifs – authenticity, identity, sacrament and mystery – that explicate the corporate faith, ministry, mission and presence of the Church in Uganda's historical context, are offered as pillars for constructing an African ecclesiology.

CHAPTER 9

Continuing the Story: The Church in the Museveni-NRA/M Regime, 1993 to the Present

It is nearly twenty years since the work on *The Church in the World: A Historical-Ecclesiological Study of the Church of Uganda With Particular Reference to Post-Independence Uganda, 1962–1992* was submitted and accepted for the award of the degree of Doctor of Philosophy. Anyone demanding that the account of the Church of Uganda "in the world" of Uganda be brought up-to-date, would be making a legitimate demand. A lot has happened during the last twenty-year period in the country and in the Church, as well as in my life, including serving as the Assistant Bishop of Kampala Diocese (Church of Uganda).[1] I hope that other researchers will undertake to fill this gap, in addition to the other five areas recommended in chapter 8, namely: the impact of pre-Christian traditional customs, norms, rituals and values on hymnody; Muslim-Christian relations;

---

1. When I worked on the PhD study and research in the 1990s I was serving with the International Fellowship of Evangelical Students (IFES) as the Regional Secretary for the work in English- and Portuguese-speaking countries in Africa. In 2001, I moved on to serve with the Church Mission Society, as Regional Director for the work in Africa. It is in 2005 that I moved on, was ordained bishop in the Church of Uganda in January 2005 and served as Assistant Bishop of Kampala Diocese until the end of June 2012, when I took an early retirement. During the latter period, I served the Church and the country, seconded by the Uganda Joint Christian Council (UJCC) to the African Peer Review Mechanism (APRM) National Commission and its successor, the National Governing Council (NGC), where I was Vice-Chairperson and Chairperson respectively. Two important reports from this work: APRM National Commission, *The Country Self-Assessment Report, 2007,* Kampala: National Planning Authority (NPA), 2007; and, APRM, *Republic of Uganda APRM Country Review Report No. 7,* Midrand South Africa: APR Secretariat, 2009.

the Church in West Nile and Acholi areas during the post-independence turbulent times; the ethics of violence; and the internal conflicts in some dioceses in the Church of Uganda. Space and time do not permit to do the important work of bringing the study up-to-date. This postscript sketches a few incidents that highlight the nature of "church in the world" over that period. I follow the same logic as in the previous chapters: outline the historical-religio-cultural-socio-political context and identify what I consider significant shifts in the Church's image and identity, as it sought to shape or readjust to the context.

What is distinctive about the religio-cultural and socio-political context after the 1962–1992 timeline of the research, is the fact that Uganda has not had any change of regime; it is still the same Museveni-NRA/M regime throughout the period, giving to Museveni the accolade of the longest serving President of post-independence Uganda. The longevity of the Museveni-NRA/M regime entrenched the Museveni factor in the political economy of Uganda but the same narrative of turbulence, which characterized the thirty years of independence, continued to define the next twenty years. Any work on Uganda during this latter period has to grapple with the prolonged conflict and war in Northern Uganda and its impact on the psyche of Uganda. However, my considered view is that the two critical milestones in the political governance over this period were: the promulgation of a new Constitution in 1995; and the transition from Movement-cum-single-party to a multi-party dispensation. The latter was enabled by the former, which provided for democratic processes for political contestation thereby changing the terrain of conflict and turbulence in Uganda. However, military means, which were the primary arbitrator of conflicts – often leading to more violence, as the research of the thirty-year period showed – remains central in the story of turbulence. The 1995 Constitution did not shift arbitration from violent means; it added a new dimension – "Rule by Law,"[2] rather than rule of law; a case of having a Constitution, without constitutionalism.

---

2. This is the title of an Amnesty International Report on human rights abuses in Uganda: *Rule by Law: Discriminatory Legislation and Legitimized Abuses in Uganda* (London: Amnesty International, 2014).

The Church of Uganda's image and identity interacted with and shifted in response to this context, bringing forth new expressions of being "church in context." It is noteworthy that over this period, the Church of Uganda has had three archbishops succeeding Archbishop Yona Okoth: Bishops Livingstone Mpalanyi-Nkoyoyo (installed December 1994); Henry Luke Orombi (installed January 2004); and the incumbent Stanley Ntagali (installed December 2012), hailing from the Buganda, Northern and Western regions, respectively. The four motifs developed in chapter 8 for developing an ecclesiology, demand that we reframe the questions we pose on "being church" of the Church of Uganda. Does the Church's testimony reflect authenticity to its dual location, "in the world and not of the world": in Christ-in-Uganda? Or is it more biased, reflecting more truly to be worldly? Does its life and ministry reflect the mystery of its identity – true to the Christ-narrative, in the turbulence of Uganda? Do the actions of the Church, as institution and community, reflect a tangible presence of the grace of Christ (as sacrament), operative within and through it? These are the questions to grapple with in reflecting on the life and ministry of the Church of Uganda in turbulent Uganda.

Continuing Turbulence under Museveni-NRA/M regime, 1993 to-date (2015)

The report by the Refugee Law Project, of the "Findings of the National Reconciliation and Transitional Justice Audit (NRTJ)," entitled *Compendium of Conflicts in Uganda*, which chronicles all the major conflicts in Uganda since the colonial period, is a valuable one-stop centre for the story of turbulence since 1993.[3] For the period under review in this chapter, the *Compendium* considers it to span two phases of the Museveni regime: "Museveni's No Party System Regime (1986–2006)" followed by the "Return to Multi-Party System, Restoration of Kingdoms (1996–present)." There is a tacit assumption in this periodization that the *Compendium* adopts, that politics and political contestation are the defining factors for

---

3. A quick count of the number of conflicts reported in the Refugee Law Project, "Compendium of Conflicts in Uganda," Kampala: School of Law Makerere University, 2014, which involved the use of military means, gives at least twenty during the period 1992–2012.

conflict and turbulence in Uganda. What the *Compendium* does not include is how the promulgation of the 1995 Constitution changed the terrain of conflict and turbulence. My view is that from 1996, there is a combination of military and pseudo-democracy means as the primary drivers of conflict and violence in Uganda. The reintroduction of multiparty politics in 2005 "ostensibly permitted electoral competition" while the Museveni-NRA/M government initiated various legal and institutional processes "simultaneously restricting free expression and peaceful assembly."[4]

As the adage goes, "violence breeds violence." The Museveni regime, having come to power through violent means, has been reliant on the same means to maintain and keep power. This was bound to evoke armed rebellions. In the "Museveni's No Party System Regime (1986–2006)" phase, the most notable violent conflicts (which are typical of the same cycle of armed rebellions) were[5]: the continuing war against the insurgency in the North by the Lord's Resistance Army (LRA), which spilled over to Eastern Uganda (1986–2006); rebel insurgency in West Nile, by the West Nile Bank Front (1995–1998) and the Uganda National Rescue Front II (1998–2002); and the Allied Democratic Forces (ADF) insurgency in Western Uganda (1998–2003). In the "Return to Multi-Party System, Restoration of Kingdoms (1996–present)" phase, the most notable turbulence arose from "restricting free expression and peaceful assembly," notably: electioneering related conflicts leading to demonstrations and violent confrontations with security forces, including the now infamous "Walk to Work" protests following after the contested 2011 General Elections; the tensions and conflicts between Museveni and the Buganda Kingdom that culminated in bloody riots in 2009; and, the protracted protests led by civil society groups and leaders against the sale of Mabira Forest Reserve, from 2007 to 2010, which turned violent (now known as Mabira Riots). It is noteworthy that the conflicts in the latter period did not follow the same logic, as previous ones that were occasioned by armed rebellion against

---

4. Amnesty International, *Rule by Law*, 12. The entire report chronicles specific laws that were passed with the sole intention of suppressing free expression, association and peaceful assembly.
5. Aili Mari Tripp in her book, *Museveni's Uganda: Paradoxes of Power in a Hybrid Regime*, (London: Lynne Rienner Publishers, 2010), 152, lists eleven major rebellions.

government, based in particular regions. The turbulence of the latter period had Kampala as its epicentre; and they involved more actors beyond regional or ethnic lines.

The war in Northern Uganda demands more space and attention. Not only was it the longest sustained violent intra-conflict in Uganda[6] – more than two decades – its impact both horizontally and vertically is unparalleled in the post-independence history of Uganda. Robert Senath Esuruki has summarized the destruction of the war succinctly:

> The horrendous atrocities inflicted by the LRA and UPDF held back and cause total destruction in, the northern Uganda regions and, more specifically the Acholi sub-region and the districts of Apac, Lira, Katakwi and Soroti. More than 38,000 children were abducted and forcefully recruited into the rebel army. More than 1.8 million people were forced into internally displaced persons' (IDPs) camps throughout northern Uganda and parts of West Nile and eastern Uganda for more than two decades. Women and young girls were abducted and taken as wives and sex slaves for the LRA commanders. Some widely documented serious crimes include murder, abduction, forced marriage, sexual assault and horrific mutilation including amputating limbs, noses and lips.[7]

The war resulted in the destruction of the social fabric of society in the Greater Northern Uganda (the sub-regions of West Nile, Acholi, Lango, Karamoja and Teso); and total breakdown of social, economic and other infrastructures, to the extent that nearly one-third of chronically poor people in Uganda coming from this northern region alone[8]. Jon Egelund, the UN's undersecretary for humanitarian affairs, described it in 2003 as

---

6. Aili Mari Tripp, in her book *Museveni's Uganda*, 160, notes that by 2015 this conflict had become the longest standing conflict in Africa.
7. Robert Senath Esuruku, "The Peace Recovery and Development Plan for Northern Uganda," in *Where Law Meets Reality: Forging African Transitional Justice*, eds. Moses Chrispus Okello, Chris Dolan, et al. (Cape Town: Pambazuka Press, 2012), 147–150.
8. Ibid., 150.

"the biggest neglected humanitarian emergency in the world" and a "moral outrage."[9]

No doubt, like all the conflicts in Uganda, the turbulence in Northern Uganda has its antecedents in the colonial period and "the issues of inequality and exclusion from important state appointments and development opportunities, which have marginalised a large proportion of vulnerable groups in the northern region."[10] However, the immediate cause was the ruthless actions of NRA/M soldiers, a "war on the citizens in Northern Uganda"[11] (apparently avenging for the "Skulls of Luwero," who "plundered the area and committed atrocities, including rape, abductions, confiscating livestock and killing unarmed civilians; the destruction of granaries, schools, hospitals and bore holes"[12] after they had demobilized the bulk of the UNLA Acholi soldiers. In addition, as we saw in the account of the war in Teso, the "NRA/M also allowed Karamajong cattle raiders to loot with impunity as far west as Gulu town, sometimes participating in the looting themselves."[13] In response, the majority of the former UNLA soldiers fled to the bushes of Northern Uganda and others to South Sudan, from where they regrouped to form rebel groups, and were later joined by many youth and adults seeking to resist the NRA atrocities.

The first was the Uganda Peoples' Democratic Movement/Army (UPDM/A) led by Professor Justine Odong Latek and Otema Alimadi (previously Foreign Affairs Minister in the Obote II Regime); then the Holy Spirit Mobile Forces of Alice Auma Lakwena, which was succeeded by the Holy Spirit Movement II led by her Severino Lukoya. After the defeat of the latter in 1987, the Lord's Resistance Army (LRA) led by Joseph Kony, a cousin to Alice Lakwena[14] took over its leadership. The war with

---

9. Tripp, in her book, *Museveni's Uganda*, 159, notes this.
10. Senath Esuruku, "The Peace Recovery and Development Plan," 150.
11. This is how it is described in the Refugee Law Project, *Compendium of Conflicts in Uganda*, 138.
12. Senath Esuruku, "The Peace Recovery and Development Plan," 146. There was also "wide spread rape of men (tek gungu), defecating in food and drinking water, burning houses in villages" according to the Refugee Law Project, *Compendium of Conflicts in Uganda*, 139.
13. Senath Esuruku, "The Peace Recovery and Development Plan," 146.
14. For a chronicle of these rebel groups and more that arose in Acholi, read the Refugee Law Project, *Compendium of Conflicts In Uganda*, 138–155.

LRA continued for the next twenty years. It was the negotiations between the leaders of LRA and the Government of Uganda that culminated in the signing of the Cessation of Hostilities Agreement on 26 August 2006 that ended the war.

As the Northern Uganda war was raging on, another "war" was launched with the promulgation of 1995 Constitution, arising from government's contradicting actions in "restricting free expression and peaceful assembly" (contrary to Constitutional provisions). As already highlighted, the 1995 Constitution introduced new processes and mechanisms for political contestation, which were intended to build democratic governance. Justice Benjamin Odoki, the Chairman of the Constitutional Commission that managed the process and drafting of the Constitution, expressed it well: "The new Constitution was intended to promote a fundamental change in the politics of Uganda and give the country a fresh start."[15]

The Preamble of the 1995 Constitution captures the sentiment for the Constitution to work as a cure to a history that had been "characterised by political and constitutional instability," struggles against "forces of tyranny, oppression and exploitation." It commits Ugandans to "building a better future by establishing a socio-economic and political order through a popular and durable national Constitution based on the principles of unity, peace, equality, democracy, freedom, social justice and progress."[16] While the same Constitution outlines the terms and processes for fulfilling these aspirations, in real terms, the implementation was dependant on the political will of Yoweri Museveni,[17] whose desire to hold on to power at all costs became Uganda Achilles' heel in the pursuit for establishing a peaceful and democratic socio-economic and political order. The fact that Museveni came to power through the barrel of the gun also meant that the use of repression and violence or the threat of violence were to remain important means of sustaining political control.

---

15. Benjamin J. Odoki, *The Search for a National Consensus: The Making of the 1995 Uganda Constitution* (Kampala: Fountain Publishers, 2005), 292.
16. Preamble to *The 1995 Constitution of the Republic of Uganda* (Kampala: Government Printers, 1995).
17. The Constitution centralized power in the office and person of the President.

The first elections in 1996 under the new Constitution were marred with violence across the country particularly in areas where President Museveni was unpopular. The entry of Kizza Besigye as a presidential contestant – a man that had been part of the NRA/M machinery, as a minister and political commissar of the NRM – against Museveni in 2001, escalated levels of violence in elections. They are reckoned to have been the most violent, with all the military and paramilitary forces deployed in the campaigns[18]. Moreover, given that the entire Greater North of the country was engulfed in the LRA insurgency during this time, the heightened presence of the military was a given. A Report by the Parliamentary Committee on Election Violence of July 2002 "noted that violence had increased since 1996,"[19] and recorded more than 2,000 cases of election violence. The first multiparty elections held under the Museveni-NRA/M government of 2006, took place in the context of President Museveni's decision to amend the 1995 Constitution, scrapping the two-term limit for President. The return of Kizza Besigye in October 2005 from exile to contest again against Museveni in the 2006 elections created a dynamic that added to the tension in the country.[20] Thus a situation was developing in which President Museveni and his cronies were oppressing dissenting voices, manipulating processes, extending the patronage machinery, using violence and enacting legislation that would ensure his hold on to power.

The country was increasingly relapsing back into fear of violence triggered by elections, as happened in 1980s. Commenting on result of the opinion survey conducted by Afrobarometer in 2010 – as the country prepared for the 2011 elections, Nicolas de Torente in his review of the survey remarked, "One of the most striking findings is would-be voters' fear of violence associated with political contest. The majority of Ugandans (57%) said that competition 'always' or 'often' leads to violent conflict, and

---

18. A. M. Tripp lists: Presidential Guard Brigade (PGB) [today's Special Forces Command (SFG)], the Chieftaincy of Military Intelligence (CMI), the Violent Crime Crack Unit (VCCU), the Kalangala Action Plan (KAP), the Civic Defence Team, the Joint Anti Terrorism Task Force and the Black Mamba Squad. See Tripp, *Museveni's Uganda*, 136–140.

19. Tripp, *Museveni's Uganda*, 94.

20. A chronicle of the harassment of Kizza Besigye by the Museveni regime, in Charles Ochen Okwir, *Portrait of a Despot* (Milton Keynes: AuthorHouse, 2011), 157–162.

a sizeable minority (38%) stated that politicians 'always' or 'often' use violence during elections."[21] More over the refusal by the Museveni regime to undertake major political and electoral reforms, which were demanded by political parties, civil society and even development partners,[22] meant that from the outset those challenging the incumbent government had little or no confidence in the credibility of 2011 elections to deliver a legitimate outcome. As a matter of fact, "the opposition in general anticipated flawed elections and vowed not to go to the courts of law to contest the electoral results but called on its supporters to be ready to take to the streets, thereby creating fear of post-electoral violence."[23] What the population feared, the security services anticipated and prepared for; the police are said to have imported massive riot equipment in January 2011. When the results of the elections were announced naming Museveni as the winner of the presidential contest, all the party leaders that participated in the contest rejected them, except Beti Kamya of the Federal Alliance. Barely two months after the results were announced, protests and violence broke out on the streets of Kampala. A newly formed activist group, Activists for Change (A4C) launched a Walk to Work (W2W) campaign on 11 April 2011.

The immediate triggers of the W2W demonstrations were the commodity price hikes following the rise in inflation from 11 percent in March to 39.9 percent in April.[24] However the public perception was that the rampant inflation was driven by the reckless expenditure by the Museveni-NRM machinery during the 2011 elections. This brings to the fore one other feature of the Museveni-NRA/M regime over the last twenty years,

---

21. Nicolas de Torente, "Opinion Polls in the Spotlight: Opinion Polls, NRM's Strengths," in *Elections in a Hybrid Regime: Revisiting the 2011 Uganda Polls*, eds. S. Perrot, S. Makara, J. Lafargue, and M. Fourere (Kampala: Fountain Publishers, 2014), 42.
22. Sabiti Makara gives the account of this push towards 2011 Elections in his "Managing Elections in a Multiparty Political Dispensation: The Role of the Electoral Commission in Uganda's 2011 Elections," in *Elections in a Hybrid Regime: Revisiting the 2011 Uganda Polls*, eds. S. Perrot, S. Makara, J. Lafargue, and M. Fourere (Kampala: Fountain Publishers, 2014), 117–123.
23. Makara, "Managing Elections," 111.
24. Ibid., 135. Also a more detailed account by Sandrine Perrot, "From February 2011 Elections to the Walk-to-Work Protests. Did Uganda Really Want 'Another Rap,'" in *Elections in a Hybrid Regime: Revisiting the 2011 Uganda Polls*, eds. S. Perrot, S. Makara, J. Lafargue, and M. Fourere (Kampala: Fountain Publishers, 2014), 423–441.

which has been a major factor to turbulence in the county: corruption.[25] It is now an established fact that the vice of corruption has been increasing over the years and is manifest in all sectors of Ugandan society today.[26] Although one the Ten-Point Program of the NRA/M on capturing power was the "Elimination of corruption and misuse of power," corruption seems to be an agency for regime survival and longevity. Consequently, corruption has grown exponentially over the twenty-year period, 1992–2012. The African Peer Review Mechanism (APRM) process outcomes reported documentary evidence indicating that "corruption is most rife in procurement, privatisation, administration of public expenditure and revenue, and the delivery of public services."[27] The same report pointed out that, although there was a reputable legal and institutional framework,[28] corruption continued to grow to the extent that in 2008 the country was losing more to corruption each year than it was receiving in total international aid.[29] Tripp's argument in her book *Museveni's Uganda: Paradoxes of Power in a Hybrid Regime* is compelling: "Corruption feeds patronage and clientelistic networks to build and maintain political loyalty."[30] Patronage and political loyalty are the primary drivers of corruption. Hence, Museveni shields and protects loyal political and civil service leaders who are implicated

---

25. The study and report by the Institute for Economics and Peace (based in Sydney Australia), *Peace and Corruption 2015*, shows that although corruption and peace do not have a linear relationship, "after a certain threshold the degeneration of the governing institutions from corruption nurtures violent behavior." (7)

26. Uganda was listed as No. 1 in East Africa in overall likelihood of bribery in 2013. See Transparency International-Kenya, "The East African Bribery Index 2013," available at http://www.tikenya.org/index.php/the-east-african-bribery-index, 1. Uganda was also listed among the top 14 countries with the highest Bribery reporting, higher than 50%. See also Transparency International, *Global Corruption Barometer 2013*, available at http://www.transparency.org/gcb2013, 10.

27. APRM, *Republic of Uganda: APRM Country Review Report No. 7*, 298.

28. Among the laws are: The Whistle Blower's Act 2010; The Audit Act 2009; Access to Information Act 2009; and the Anti-Corruption Act 2009. The institutions include: The Inspectorate of Government (IG); the Ministry of Ethics and Integrity in the President's Office; the Anti-Corruption Court, the Office of the Auditor General.

29. APRM, *Republic of Uganda: Country Review Report No. 7*, 298.

30. Tripp, *Museveni's Uganda*, 128. Tripp dedicates an entire chapter, entitled "The Carrot and the Stick," on how both the military machinery and excessive corruption serve the purpose of regime survival and longevity (p. 127–147).

in corruption scandals provided they are committed to his continuing in power.[31] Electoral corruption is part of this narrative.

The fraud-ridden 2011 elections[32] must therefore also be understood as part and parcel of corruption machinery and misuse of power by the Museveni regime to maintain hegemony. In its call to all the town and city dwellers to "walk to work," A4C was calling upon the wider population not only to protest against the sky-rocketing prices, but also against the regime, with a view to bringing it on its knees. All the leaders of the opposition political parties – Kizza Besigye of FDC, Nobert Mao of DP; Olara Otunnu of UPC; Ken Lukyamuzi of CP; Asumani Basalirwa of JEEMA, including some MPs – got involved in the W2W, although clearly the leader was Kizza Besigye. The Arab Spring, which had led to the collapse of the dictatorships in Tunisia, Egypt and Libya, and the fall of Laurent Gbagbo's government in Ivory Coast, all of which happened in 2010 through popular people uprising, was part of the inspiration. Aware of all this, Museveni and his security machinery responded decisively, "using excessive brutality and extrajudicial means to curb the rising anti-government sentiments triggered by the riots."[33] Besigye was shot in the hand on the second day of the demonstrations; "police fired live bullets at demonstrators throwing stones";[34] and many were arrested, detained and charged with disobeying lawful orders, committing traffic offences and inciting violence. The climax was on 28 April 2011, when a plainclothes security agent smashed the window of Besigye's car and sprayed a poisonous substance in his eyes[35].

---

31. The President defended the former Permanent Secretary, who is the accounting officer in the Office of the Prime Minister, Mr Pius Bigirimana, as a "whistle blower," in the highly publicized corruption scandal where more than 50 billion shillings from donors meant for the war ravaged Northern Uganda was stolen. See http://www.monitor.co.ug/News/National/OPM-scam--Museveni-explains-why-he-stood-by-Bigirimana/-/688334/2418294/-/12kb68/-/index.html (accessed August 2014). However, he was transferred to the Ministry of Gender, Labour and Community Development in the same position.
32. For a thorough review of the 2011 Elections, see S. Perrot, S. Makara, J. Lafargue, and M. Fourere, eds., *Elections in a Hybrid Regime: Revisiting the 2011 Uganda Polls* (Kampala: Fountain Publishers, 2014).
33. Makara, "Managing Elections," 135.
34. Perrot, "From February 2011 Elections," 426.
35. A more detailed description of this in Daniel K. Kalinaki, *Kizza Besigye and Uganda's Unfinished Revolution* (Kampala: Dominant Seven Publishers, 2014), 291–292.

Besigye was effectively taken out of action for a while. He was hospitalized in Nairobi.

Although, the protests lost their steam momentarily under the repressive Museveni machinery, upon his return a few weeks later, on the day of President Museveni's swearing in on 12 May 2011, crowds thronged the entire road from Entebbe airport to Kampala to welcome Kizza Besigye back.[36] What would typically have been a one-hour ride to Kampala lasted nine hours, with crowds engaging in running battles with troops from the elite Presidential Guard Brigade, which dispersed the crowds with live ammunition. The beginning of Museveni's march towards the thirty-year mark as President was welcomed with violence and turbulence. Thus although the guns are silent and there has been no war in any part of Uganda since the 2011 elections, turbulence did not cease. The *Compendium* chronicles turbulence across the country, occasioned in particular by conflicts over natural resources.[37] The other turbulence that has characterized the last five years is political in nature, the State's suppression of dissent and freedoms of speech, association and assembly.[38] It is not an overstatement to say that the country is gripped with fear of another violent transition[39].

Continuing the Story of the Church of Uganda in the Museveni regime, 1992 to the present

All we can attempt here is a cursory view of the story of the Church of Uganda in this period, from a historical and theological perspective; not

---

36. It was estimated that there were bigger crowds welcoming Kizza Besigye than those at the swearing in ceremony at Kololo Independence grounds. Kalinaki, *Kizza Besigye*, 316.

37. Refugee Law Project, "Compendium of Conflicts in Uganda" identifies violent conflicts in Acholiland over land (156–157) and in Bunyoro and Rwenzori regions over oil (206–210).

38. Amnesty International, *Rule by Law*, chronicles Government clampdown of demonstrations and protests, harassment of anti-corruption activists, and restrictions to freedoms of association, assembly and speech. Also, Uganda Human Rights Commission (UHRC), *17th Annual Report* (Kampala: UHRC, 2015), 121–128.

39. G. M. Sseruwagi, *Our Greatest Fear is the Transition of Power: An Open Letter to the President* (Bloomington, IN: AuthorHouse, 2013); "Uganda: No Resolution to Growing Tensions," The International Crisis Group, Africa Report N°187 – 5 April 2012, (Also available on the web: http://www.crisisgroup.org/-/media/Files/africa/horn-of-lafrica/uganda/187-uganda-no-resolution-to-growing-tensions.pdf)

just the story, but its meaning. The question to grapple with is in what ways the entity named as "Church of Uganda" acted, responded, shaped and was shaped by the socio-political context of the last twenty years of the Museveni regime, animated by the dictates of its faith-relation with the Christ-event. Did the engagement and actions of the Church and her actors, as institution and community, reflect a church-as-sacrament? In terms of the language of the East African Revival movement, the issue is the testimony of the Church. Is it a testimony of "churchliness" or "worldliness"? Does the life of the Church of Uganda in its expressions, both at national and local levels, authenticate it as community animated by its devotion to the faith in Jesus? To what extent was the Church prevented or able to do God's bidding as a mystery and sacrament, in its "continuing struggle to break down the walls that divide men; a struggle to transcend the divisions of tribe, clan, language, culture and race."[40]

The first place to begin in this reflection is the Church's Archiepiscopal leadership: to ponder how the different archbishops led in the "struggle to break down the walls that divide" in the Church and country; the extent to which they lived the reality of the "broken walls" and/or engaged as "sacrament" in breaking those walls. Consider and contrast the character of the leadership of the three Archbishops of the Museveni era – Livingstone Mpalanyi-Nkoyoyo, Henry Luke Orombi and Stanley Ntagali – with that of the previous Ugandan Archbishops. Erica Sabiti, faced with the Buganda-Uganda divide; Janani Luwum, faced with a military tyrant, "de-establishing" Church of Uganda; Silvanus Wani, leading a traumatized Church after the murder of Luwum, and faced with the same tyrant who also happened to be a kinsman; and Yona Okoth, leading a divided Church in a divided country, at war.

In keeping with Archbishop Sabiti's metaphorical language of "struggle to break down the walls that divide," the account of the Church in chapters 2 and 5, one can conclude that Sabiti and Luwum confronted the walls with the express desire to break them, while Okoth was conflicted

---

[40]. "The Proceedings of the Second Meeting of the Second Provincial Assembly Held at Bishop Tucker College, Mukono, December 9, 10, and 11, 1970; Appendix 'B': The Archbishop's Charge to the Church of Uganda, Rwanda and Burundi, December 1970." Provincial Assembly Papers, COU Archives, 3.

by the walls. In chapter 5, I characterize the epoch of Wani's leadership as "ceasefire," a no-confrontation stance against the "walls that divide." The historic meeting of the House of Bishops with Idi Amin, on 17 March 1977 after Wani's election and one month after the murder of Luwum is telling. The Government daily reported that Idi Amin "was extremely happy to receive the Church leaders, whom he described as the true sons of Uganda and leaders of the Church of Uganda, who were dedicated to preach the word of God to their followers as well as people of Uganda in general."[41] One could therefore locate the character of leadership of the Mpalanyi-Nkoyoyo, Orombi and Ntagali in the Wani-model: accommodation, "ceasefire" and non-confrontational.

The disposition of the three Archbishops in the way they engaged President Museveni was non-confrontational. There is here a sense of *déjà vu*. In that sense the 17 March 1977 meeting between the House of Bishops and Idi Amin is proverbial – a situation of accommodation, cordiality and courtesy, in spite of conflict, violence and turbulence in the population. Mpalanyi-Nkoyoyo's disposition to the Museveni-NRA/M regime was one of accommodation, loyalty and cordiality. He did not consider or see ways in which the Church would engage with the Museveni regime to end the war and carnage raging in Northern Uganda at the time, in spite of evidence of atrocities committed by both the rebel and government troops.[42] Orombi, although hailing from the North, maintained a similar stance. Although he constantly preached a peaceful end to the conflict and war in the North, he was always non-committal on the path to achieve that end.[43] Orombi's biographer narrated:

---

41. *Voice of Uganda*, 18 March 1977, 1.
42. In an interview with Episcopal News Service after his retirement in 2004, as to what he thought would bring a peaceful end to the conflict in Northern Uganda, his answer was simply "I don't know" and called for the international community to send soldiers to support the Uganda government troops. http://archive.episcopalchurch.org/3577_37377_ENG_HTM.htm (accessed May 2015).
43. See news report on his first visit to Acholi during the first quarter of his service as a new Archbishop: "Orombi Entourage Weep on Tour of Pabbo Camp in Northern Uganda," by Joe Nam, on http://webarchive.cms-uk.org/news/2004/8_03_2004.htm (accessed May 2015). See also, "Archbishop Orombi Noncommital on Anti-LRA Offensive," available on http://ugandaradionetwork.com/a/story.php?s=19620 (accessed May 2015).

Orombi was on talking terms with the president. It was easy to talk to someone who knew you were working to help him. He spoke one-on-one with the president when it was just the two of them in one room. Museveni was honest and if he did not agree with Orombi he would ask the archbishop questions. Once Orombi had even slept over at Rwakitura (Museveni's country home).[44]

President Museveni himself acknowledged, when Orombi retired, "he has worked closely with me and I have not had any problem with him. He has never given me lectures in public, which some religious leaders do, and I have never counter-lectured him."[45] Although Ntagali has only served two years, his public remarks and disposition indicate that he will follow the same model. In one of his first public statements on his engagement with issues of a political nature, he stated that he was not political[46] and that his approach to politics and politicians was to "preach the gospel to all people including politicians so they can have good morals. The church has a big role to change peoples' morals and turn politicians into morally upright citizens . . . I don't believe in attacking leaders and I will advocate for dialogue. Confrontation and attacks are not my way, dialogue is the best."[47]

The question as to how the House of Bishops as a body-corporate, under the leadership of the Mpalanyi-Nkoyoyo, Orombi and Ntagali, engaged with the conflicts and turbulence of the day, should be of interest to researchers and students of the story of the Church of Uganda. As an ordained minister in the Church throughout most of this time,[48] and

---

44. Joseph Jabo and Julia Kushemererwa, *Orombi: The Biography of His Grace Henry Luke Orombi, Archbishop of the Church of Uganda (2004-2012)* (Kampala: WASP Ltd., 2012), 13.
45. *New Vision*, Thursday, 23 August 2012, as quoted in Jabo and Kushemererwa, *Orombi*, 149.
46. Joseph Baguma and Pascal Kwesiga, "I Am Not a Political Archbishop – Ntagali," *New Vision*, available on http://www.newvision.co.ug/news/632294-i-am-not-a-political-archbishop-ntagali.html (accessed May 2015).
47. Interview with *New Vision* Reporter on 24 June 2014, "I Want a Vibrant, United Church – Ntagali," available on http://www.newvision.co.ug/news/632286-i-want-a-vibrant-united-church--ntagali.html (accessed May 2015).
48. I was ordained Deacon and Priest in the Church of Uganda by the Bishop of the Diocese of Muhabura, in 1995 and 1996 respectively; consecrated Bishop in 2005, and assigned to be Assistant Diocesan Bishop for the Arch-bishopric Diocese of Kampala,

part of the House of Bishops during most of the tenure of the Archbishop Orombi's leadership, I was keenly following and involved in the work of the Church. One of the challenges for the House of Bishops was the fact that confronting "the walls that divide" the country would demand an honest self-critique of the Church's roots in the turbulence and its contribution to that narrative. Could the House create the space, and harness the necessary resources – intellectual, spiritual and otherwise – to address its own internal contradictions? Did the Archbishops have the conviction and capacity to provide leadership in this direction? Did the evangelical-revivalist orientation of the Church bias the leadership against engaging in political discourse? These and other questions should interest researchers. The two issues that preoccupied the House of Bishops were: first, internal wrangles and conflicts in several dioceses, mostly to do with Episcopal succession (notably in the Diocese of Busoga,[49] Muhabura, North Mbale, Masindi-Kitara and Kitgum); and second, conflicts and wrangles in the Anglican Communion over human sexuality, occasioned by the Lambeth Conference 1998 Resolution 1.10[50] and the consecration of Bishop Gene Robinson, an openly gay man, by the Episcopal Church in the United States (ECUSA), as Bishop of New Hampshire.[51] What is ironic is how President Museveni often took advantage of these internal contradictions, positioning himself as a champion for the good of the Church, either indirectly through his emissaries, or directly. The latter stance more clearly a *déjà vu*, remembering the role of Idi Amin in the resolution of the Namirembe Diocese–Church of Uganda rift during the time of Archbishop Erica Sabiti, with the creation of Kampala Diocese!

---

serving directly under Archbishop Orombi as the Diocesan. I took an early retirement from the Assistant Bishop role in 2012, to focus on the civic-political work of social justice, human dignity and good governance.

49. The Busoga Diocese crisis has received some scholarly attention. See Paul Gifford, *African Christianity: Its Public Role in Uganda and other African Countries* (Kampala: Fountain Publishers, 1999), 69–78; and Emmanuel Katongole, *The Sacrifice of Africa: A Political Theology of Africa* (Grand Rapids: Eerdmans, 2011), 48–49.

50. The Resolution among others, rejected "homosexual practice as incompatible with Scripture" and advised against "the legitimising or blessing of same sex unions nor ordaining those involved in same gender unions."

51. Joseph and Kushemererwa, *Orombi*, 129–133, identify these two as key issues of the Orombi era.

The accommodation-collaboration stance of the three Archbishops contrasts with the way the local Church leadership in the North related to the Museveni-NRA/M regime. Bishops Nelson Onono Onweng of Northern Uganda Diocese and Macleord Baker Ochola II of Kitgum Diocese were vocal over the atrocities of the LRA, the government, the NRA and its excesses in the war against the rebels. Another *déjà vu*; something of the same experience of the Churches in Lwero Triangle and Teso, as we saw in chapters 6 and 7 respectively. The most significant development in the region was the founding of the Acholi Religious Leaders' Peace Initiative (ARLPI) in 1997, an interfaith organization, bringing together leaders from six different religious traditions: Church of Uganda (Anglican), Roman Catholic, Muslim, Orthodox, Pentecostal and Seven Day Adventist Union. ARLPI was a proactive response of the religious leaders in the region to act together to confront the war and conflict. The Church of Uganda leadership in the region were at the forefront of this initiative. It is noteworthy that the first Chair of ARLPI was Bishop Nelson Onono Onweng. ARLPI became the foremost champion for a peaceful resolution of the conflict, urging both the LRA and the Museveni regime to embrace the peace talks. The peace talks between the Museveni regime and the LRA, which began on 14 July 2006 in the Southern Sudan capital of Juba, was in part the success of the work of ARLPI. However, the failure to sign the Comprehensive Peace Agreement (CPA) means that the cloud of uncertainty on the conclusive resolution of the Northern Uganda conflict remains. As we have already indicated, it is an uncertainty shared across the country.

The ARLPI model of engagement was also present at the national level. It is instructive that while the Archbishops employed the accommodation-collaboration model with the Museveni regime, the Church found new institutional spaces to confront the "walls that divide." The Uganda Joint Christian Council (UJCC)[52] and the later, the Inter-Religious Council of Uganda (IRCU)[53], became significant actors during this period of

---

52. Founded in 1963, the UJCC is an umbrella organization bringing together Roman Catholic Church, Church of Uganda [Anglican] and Uganda Orthodox Church.
53. IRCU was founded in 2001 as an umbrella body adding to the UJCC membership the Uganda Muslim Supreme Council and the Seventh Day Adventist Church Uganda Union.

turbulence and political transition uncertainty. The work of these two institutions deserves attention[54].

It was at the UJCC plenary of June 1993, under the chairmanship of Cardinal Emmanuel Wamala and executive leadership of Canon James Ndyabahika (a Church of Uganda clergyman), that the story begins. Although UJCC was founded as early as 1963, hitherto it only worked as an agency for advocating and brokering government constructive engagement with the churches on education and healthcare. With the prospect of the making of a new constitution, however, UJCC became a civic education platform, as well as for holding the Museveni-NRA/M regime accountable towards a political transition. Father John Mary Waliggo, an NRM ideologue (then Secretary of the Uganda Constitutional Commission (UCC)[55]), made a presentation at the plenary on the "Role of the Church in the Making of the New Constitution of Uganda." Among the resolutions made at the end of the plenary, was one that mandated UJCC to engage in civic education beginning with the Constitution-making process, in particular the establishment of a Constituent Assembly (CA). Subsequently, a ten-member Civic Education and Election Monitoring Team was appointed to "develop and coordinate a nation-wide civic education and election monitoring programme to run up to the election of delegates to the CA, to participate in the CA elections from an informed perspective."[56] The UJCC civic education efforts[57] in the run up to the first elections under the 1995 Constitution significantly contributed making the population aware of the regime's agenda for perpetuating itself in power. UJCC, under the leadership of Rev Canon Grace Kaiso[58], scaled up the civic education

---

54. This section draws heavily on research work supported by the African Research and Resource Forum (ARRF), which I did towards a yet to be published paper, "Religion, Religious Identity and Democratic Transition: Challenges and Prospects for Uganda".
55. According to Benjamin Odoki's account, in his work *The Search for a National Consensus*, President Museveni appointed the Uganda Constitutional Commission in February 1989 on the basis of a statute that mandated the Commission to traverse the country, collect views from the people and draft a new Constitution.
56. *UJCC 45th Anniversary Commemoration Magazine* (Kampala: UJCC, 2008), 20.
57. UJCC teamed up with the National Council of Election Monitors (NOCEM), Action for Development (ACFODE) and the Uganda Manufactures Association (UMA) to form the Civic Education Joint Coordination Unit (CEJOCU), for effective civic education.
58. Rev Canon Grace Kaiso, another Church of Uganda clergyman, succeeded Rev Canon James Ndyabahika as the Executive Director of UJCC in January 1999.

and election monitoring initiatives of the churches. UJCC was one of the leading voices in the campaign to change the political system of governance from the Movement to multiparty system of governance. For the first time, the churches together raised the issue of dialogue with the aim of building consensus. In a paper released at the time, the position of the churches was unequivocal: "Dialogue is the only means that can guarantee a peaceful and orderly transition. The Church in Uganda is committed to the policy of dialogue and will strive to promote dialogue at all levels."[59]

However, UJCC did not carry forward its promise of promoting dialogue. The space was taken by the IRCU. The immediate cause of the founding of IRCU was to create a mechanism through which international development support to interfaith-based HIV and AIDS programs could be channelled.[60] It should surprise any observer that even while the memory of the persecution of the Church under Idi Amin's Islamic regime was still fresh, the Church of Uganda under the leadership of Archbishop Mpalanyi Nkoyoyo embraced the idea of collaborating with Muslims in a cause of national concern – the HIV/AIDS pandemic. However, the organization later took on the agenda for dialogue, peace and national reconciliation. The crucial milestone event was the first *National Conference on National Reconciliation, Justice and Peace*, held in September 2009.[61] The conference took place against the backdrop of heightened tensions between Buganda Kingdom and the Museveni/NRM government, sparked off by the government's refusal to let the Kabaka visit his subjects in Kayunga district.[62]

---

59. Uganda Joint Christian Council, *Facing the Challenges of Political Transition in Uganda: Key Issues in the White Paper* (Kampala: UJCC, 2004), 3–4.

60. The Vision of the organization includes HIV/AIDS, namely "IRCU work to have a peaceful, prosperous and AIDS free Uganda." All IRCU Annual reports to the 2006 one report primarily report on HIV/AIDS work, because the other aspects of its work were yet to be developed.

61. Prior to this, regional interfaith initiatives with social-political mandates had been active. The Acholi Religious Leaders Peace Initiative (ARLPI) is the better known of all. Formed in 1997, the ARLPI was interfaith response to the conflict in Northern Uganda. Based in Acholi, it brings together leaders of six different religious denominations with adherents: Church of Uganda (Anglican), Roman Catholic Church, Muslim, Orthodox, Pentecostal and Seventh Day Adventist Church (Uganda Union) and was very instrumental in getting the Lord's Resistance Army and the Government of Uganda to hold peace talks (http://www.arlpi.org/about-us, accessed October 2014).

62. It is estimated 40 people were killed in riots protesting the Government's blockage of the Kabaka's visit to Kayunga district (http://www.hrw.org/news/2010/09/10/uganda-

According to the report of the conference, key among the objectives of the conference was promoting "peace-building as a foundation for sustainable development and peaceful co-existence irrespective of ethnicity, faith and political affiliation."[63] The Conference resolutions are worth highlighting as they are unprecedented in the history of Uganda, notably:

- An appropriate legal framework should be enacted by the Parliament of Uganda to regulate and enhance national reconciliation in the country;
- A Truth and Reconciliation Commission should be set up expeditiously to deal with both historical and current wrongs with a view of promoting reconciliation and healing among different groups and individuals in Uganda;
- A credible process of electoral reforms, including the review of membership of the Electoral Commission, should be undertaken to enhance transparency and credibility in our electoral system, hence prevent election-related violence in the country[64].

Among the five commitments by the religious and cultural leaders were:

- Offer ourselves as mediators in conflict resolution and reconciliation processes at different levels.
- Offer ourselves to organize an annual forum for interactions and dialogue among different stakeholders in the country.[65]

To implement the above resolutions and commitments, and as the political temperature was rising towards the 2011 general Elections, the Council of Presidents (CoP) – constituting the heads of the IRCU constituent religious bodies and its apex leadership organ – created the *National Task for Peace and Conflict Transformation during the Electoral Process 2011*. It was created as "an institutional mechanism to coordinate all IRCU initiatives for peace building, mediation, reconciliation, and dialogue among

---

investigate-2009-kampala-riot-killings accessed October 2014).

63. IRCU, *Report on the Conference on Sustainable National Reconciliation, Justice and Peace*, Kampala: IRCU, September 2009, 5. 468 people attended. Among the participants at the conference were all the national leaders of the religious denominations constituting IRCU; Regional and district leaders from across the county; and, cultural leaders from all the traditional and cultural institutions recognized at the time.

64. Ibid., 34.

65. Ibid.

stakeholders during and after the 2011 electoral process, in order to prevent election related violence."[66] The Task Force commenced its work in November 2010 and was inaugurated at the second *National Conference for Sustainable Peace Justice and National Reconciliation* at the beginning of December 2010.[67] Its activities were focused on areas considered to be violence hot-spots, creating mechanisms to mediate in conflicts arising between and among political parties or candidates, ethnic, cultural and religious groups and institutions, as well as intervening where necessary. The Task Force also organized prayer and peace rallies, across the country in which leaders from across the religious spectrum participated.

Although IRCU initiatives toward peace building and conflict transformation in the 2011 General Elections were applauded by both internal and external observers, the consensus also was that the country was and is still vulnerable to violent transition. The IRCU Post-Elections Conference acknowledged that the intervention through the Task Force mechanism had contributed to the overall violence-free general elections. However, subsequent statements by IRCU indicated the elections had not contributed in any significant way to democracy development but rather "the conduct and process of those elections had left Ugandans more divided"[68] than had been hoped. The leaders therefore argued that "an all inclusive national dialogue for all political groups and other key stakeholders would go a long way in providing a more inclusive framework for deeper reflection and action on the post-election challenges."[69] They further asserted:

> It is our view that the current President of Uganda has a personal responsibility to ensure that the country goes through

---

66. IRCU, *Report on the Work of the National Task Force for Peace and Conflict Transformation during the Electoral Process, 2011,* Kampala: April 2011, 3. The author was appointed as its Chairman.
67. The Task Force created regional teams across the country, as a way of decentralizing its work. It organized national dialogue meetings for the CoP among the critical stake holders: presidential candidates, heads of security agencies, Electoral Commission, the leadership of the Judiciary, media house owners and proprietors, captains of industry (private sector), international development partners, and leaders of civil society organisation with governance and human rights mandates.
68. IRCU, *The Message of the Council of Presidents of the IRCU to Political Leaders and People of Uganda, Kampala*: IRCU, August 2012, 15.
69. Ibid.

a peaceful transition from the current leadership to the next in 2016. This will greatly help diffuse the current political tension and anxiety and prevent the eruption of violence in our country.[70]

By this IRCU was admitting that efforts towards peace building and conflict transformation had only succeeded in dealing with symptoms and not causes. The *Envisioning the Uganda We Want* three-year project, launded by the IRCU in September 2011, was intended to mobilize religious leaders both to reflect on the "state of Uganda" and review their role in "constructing and promoting a shared vision, values and moral standards for Uganda."[71] However, the project was not implemented due to failure by IRCU to mobilize the requisite resources, internally and externally.

The Church of Uganda's engagement in processes of peace and democratic governance through the two networks, UJCC and IRCU, was a self-definition of it being church *vis-a-vis* its traditional rivals, notably the Catholic Church and Islam. It represents the Church's rediscovery of its ecumenical identity, as part of the wider Christian movement, through its partnership in UJCC and its civic consciousness – a belongingness to all of Uganda, as it acted with other bodies in IRCU, in particular the Uganda Muslim Supreme Council (UMSC) with whom it did not share any doctrinal convergence. It remains to be seen however, whether the Church will sustain it in its self-consciousness, especially when political actors seek to resurrect the "walls that divide" for their selfish ends. Since IRCU's call for a process to negotiate a new consensus, for a "National Consensus Building Convention to Mark Jubilee Year"[72] was not heeded, it remains to be seen whether the Church of Uganda leadership believed enough in the agenda for social and political harmony in Uganda and therefore finds a new way of pursuing that cause, towards "the Uganda we want."

---

70. Ibid.

71. IRCU, *Envisioning the Uganda We Want: Our Commitment, a Report on Regional Consultations on the Role of Religious Leaders in Nation-building*, Kampala: IRCU, August 2012, 3.

72. IRCU, *The Message of the Council of Presidents of the IRCU to Political Leaders and People of Uganda, Kampala*: IRCU, 19 August 2012.

Conclusion

The overall purpose of this entire study was to construct a theology of the church, taking the Church of Uganda in the turbulent "world" of Uganda as a case study. The study was premised on the thesis that all theology is contextual; hence an ecclesiological study must of necessity take the historical-cultural-social-economic-political context into account. Uganda's history from its beginnings in the pre-colonial period is chequered with conflict, violence and turbulence to this day. It is in this "world" of conflict and turbulence that the Church of Uganda has been shaped. As the study has also shown, the Church itself contributed to what that "world" became and has become. However, although the Church of Uganda is part of the narrative of conflict and turbulence of Uganda, as a church, it is both a social and theological reality. That is why the narrative of the East African Revival is crucial, delineating the theological parameters of "churchliness," providing us with the tools for theological reflection. Thus, as it would be expected, the endogenous and exogenous impetus of the church was distinct from that of the "world," due to its paradoxical identity – "in the world, but not of the world." But, as the study has shown, there were times when the church's action and inaction was typical of the "world"; when the church simply mirrored the world.

A common thread that runs through the account of the Church of Uganda is how it is more authentically church in times and places when its leadership identified with the people, in their material context, particularly in their sufferings. To use the language that Erica Sabiti used, reframing the mission of the Church in terms of the "struggle to break down the walls that divide," the church is more true to her identity when it engages in the struggle "together with" those suffering the consequences of the erected walls. Ministry is authentic to the extent that those ordained or commissioned are present among the people, journeying with them in their sufferings as well as their dying. The stories of the work and ministry of bishops and archbishops shows that authentic episcopal and archiepiscopal ministry was distinguished by its identification with the people through bold and courageous pastoral work among the people, as well as speaking truth and love to those who wield political power. It was sometimes the case that episcopal and archiepiscopal leadership shied away from the latter calling, acquiescing to the power schemes and designs of "the world." There were some who defined their ministry in terms of solidarity with their "kin" – their ethnic, regional, religious or denominational identities. However, even then the church's testimony is not all lost, because the church's presence as sacrament among the people emerges through other forms, animated by its devotion to the gospel.

There are arguments that suggest that "the walls that divide" are the diverse ethnic, tribal, regional and religious identities, and that therefore the roots of conflict and turbulence is the plurality. However, while it is true that Uganda is a country of many nationalities (ethnic and tribal groups), many of whom were independent kingdom-nations or chieftainships prior to the advent of the British missionaries and colonists, ethno-regional-religious identities are not the primary roots of the conflict. The problem is political leadership, the structuring of political power, and the structuring of the Ugandan state. The character of the Ugandan state is what has been termed neo-patrimonial, whereby public officials exercise their powers as a form "not of public service but of private property," and "public office has been accepted as the route to personal wealth and power."[73] Neo-patrimonial regimes do not consider it their obligation to allocate benefits to the citizens according to recognized criteria of justice, efficiency or need, but rather do so to encourage political support. Since the creation of Uganda in the colonial times, those who control political power and therefore control the magnitude and distribution of economic and political resources of the state, rather than directing resources for the benefit of all, direct the access to those who will ensure they keep their grip on power. The structure of the colonial and independent state was such that it serves the interest of those in power rather than the citizens. Consequently, politics of patronage and clientelism dominate political order. The power relationship between the rulers and the ruled is a relationship of exchange; those in power providing social-economic and political security in exchange for political support of those being ruled. Those who wield political power utilize existing ethnic and regional identities, and create new ones for building patronage system. Religious affiliation is one of the group identities utilized in positioning

---

73. Gifford, *African Christianity*, 6.

for taking, negotiating and retaining political power. The result is ethnic, regional, religious and other polarizations of the society and wider body politic, resulting in violent contestation for political power. Therefore the turbulence has an ethnic, religious and regional hue because political leadership, the structuring of power and therefore injustice is along religious, regional and ethnic lines.

The historical-theological question for the Church of Uganda was as to whether it would locate itself, or be captured and co-opted into the patron-client structuring of Ugandan politics and society, or whether the Church could resist patronage politics and be an antidote to the politics of clientelism, providing a different vision of leadership and society. But the historical and theological roots of Church of Uganda – a church within the Anglican tradition and as the quasi-established religion of Uganda – made the Church of Uganda vulnerable to the politics of patronage and clientelism. In fact the account gives credence to the fact that Church of Uganda was an integral part of structuring of patron-client politics of Uganda. As the account showed, religion in general and Christianity in particular were key instruments in drawing the lines in the patron-client structure of state and society. As we saw, the operating principle is what Professor Mazrui enunciated, which we referred to in chapter 5: "The religion of the ruler is the official religion of the state."[74] Consequently, the Church of Uganda, in particular its archbishops, were constantly under the pressure of this "worldliness" – Uganda's socio-political history and Church's orientation of "establishment" to pander to the neo-patrimonial character of the state and its political leadership. Successive regimes took advantage of this social history, and were constantly aligning and realigning their relationship with the Church and her establishment, to ensure full co-optation into the patron-client framework.

There is a sense in which it could be said that President Museveni achieved fully where previous regimes had only partially succeeded, in subtly incorporating the archiepiscopal and episcopal (as a body corporate) leadership of the Church of Uganda into his patronage network. From the Church's perspective, one could say that the archbishops of the Church of

---

74. This is Ali A. Mazrui's argument in "Religious Strangers in Uganda," 21–38.

Uganda succumbed to the pressure of history, the Church's orientation to establishment and Museveni's patronage machinery. However, as in other epochs of the life of the Church of Uganda, even under the Museveni era, there was a different narrative: authentic sacramental pastoral mission and ministry in the high-density regions of conflict and turbulence (in Teso and Northern Uganda); the Church's rediscovery of its ecumenical identity and ministry (in UJCC); and its recovery of its civic-prophetic calling of "breaking the walls that divide" (in the IRCU formation). History will tell whether the Church of Uganda will make the most of the moment, to rewrite history (beyond the turbulence that has characterized Uganda's history hitherto), defy patron-client politics and contribute to a new era of peace and national reconciliation, reflecting its authentic identity "in Christ in the world." The Church of Uganda has a unique and rich social-theological history, from which it could draw to become an authentic reflection and sacramental presence of Christ in Uganda and beyond.

APPENDIX A

Chronology of the Creation of Dioceses, 1960–1992

In May 1960, the synod of the Uganda diocese and the Diocesan Council of the Upper Nile diocese and agreed to form one Province to be called the Church of Uganda, Ruanda-Urundi.[1] An agreement was also reached on the constitution of the Province. Eight new dioceses were to be carved out of the two existing ones. The Uganda diocese was to be partitioned into five: Namirembe, to cover Busoga and East Buganda; Ankole-Kigezi, covering Ankole and Kigezi; Rwanda-Urundi, covering the two countries of Rwanda and Burundi; Rwenzori, to cover Toro, Bunyoro, and Mboga; and, West Buganda, covering Masaka and Mubende. The Upper Nile diocese was to be partitioned into another three: Mbale, covering Bugisu and Bukedi; Soroti, to cover Teso and Karamoja; and, Northern Uganda, covering Acholi, Lango and West Nile. The Church of the Province of Uganda, Ruanda-Urundi was inaugurated on 16 April 1961.[2] With the creation of the Francophone Province, covering Rwanda, Burundi and Boga-Zaire in November 1979, Uganda became a separate Province, with the official

---

1. Ruanda-Urundi was at the time one country under Belgium colonial Administration. However after independence in 1962, the territory became two separate countries, Rwanda and Burundi. Thereafter the name of the Province became "the Church of Uganda, Rwanda and Burundi." In 1972, the name of the province changed to the Province of the Church of Uganda, Rwanda, Burundi and Boga Zaire. Minutes of the Provincial Assembly, August 1972, Provincial Assembly Papers, COU Archives.
2. "Service of the Inauguration of the Church of the Province of Uganda and Rwanda-Urundi, 11 April, 1961." Archbishop's Papers, COU Archives.

name of "The Church of the Province of Uganda" or just "The Church of Uganda."³

---
3. The Church of Uganda, Rwanda, Burundi and Boga-Zaire, Minutes of the Provincial Assembly, 2 January 1980, p. 4.

Chronology of the Creation of Dioceses, 1960–1992

Namirembe, carved out of Uganda diocese	1960
Ankole-Kigezi, carved out of Uganda diocese	1960
Ruwenzori, carved out of Uganda diocese	1960
Ruanda-Urundi, carved out of Uganda diocese	1960
West Buganda, carved out of Uganda diocese	1960
Mbale, carved out of Upper Nile diocese	1961
Northern Uganda, carved out of Upper Nile diocese	1961
Soroti, carved out of Upper Nile diocese	1961
Kigezi, carved out of Ankole-Kigezi diocese	1967
Ankole, carved out of Ankole-Kigezi diocese	1967[4]
Madi/West Nile, carved out of Northern Uganda diocese	1969
Bukedi, carved out of Mbale diocese	1972
Bunyoro-Kitara, carved out of Rwenzori diocese	1972
Busoga, carved out of out of Namirembe diocese	1972
Kampala, carved out of Namirembe diocese	1972
Karamoja, carved out of Soroti diocese	1976
Lango, carved out of Northern Uganda diocese	1976
Mityana, carved out of West Buganda diocese	1977
West Ankole, carved out of Ankole diocese	1977
East Ankole, carved out of Ankole diocese	1977[5]
North Kigezi, carved out of Kigezi diocese	1981
South-Rwenzori, carved out of Rwenzori	1984
Mukono, carved out of Namirembe diocese	1984
Muhabura, carved out of Kigezi diocese	1990
North Mbale, carved out of Mbale diocese	1992

Dioceses as at December 1992

Note: The diocesan boundaries are the same as the boundaries of the districts indicated.

---

4. The name Ankole-Kigezi was dropped in preference for the two names of Ankole and Kigezi coterminous with the District administration units.
5. The name Ankole was dropped in preference for the two names of West Ankole and East Ankole coterminous with the District administration units.

Bukedi diocese, Pallisa and Tororo districts
Bunyoro-Kitara diocese, Hoima and Masindi districts
Busoga diocese, Iganga, Jinja and Kamuli districts
East Ankole diocese, Mbarara and Ntungamo districts
Kampala Dioces, Kampala District
Karamoja diocese, Kotido and Moroto districts
Kigezi diocese, Kabale district
Lango diocese, Apach and Lira districts
Luwero diocese, Luwero district
Madi/ West Nile, Arua, Moyo and Nebbi districts
Mbale diocese, Kapchorwa and Mbale district
Mityana diocese, Mubende and Kiboga districts
Muhabura diocese, Kisoro district
Mukono diocese, Mukono and Kalangala districts
Namirembe diocese, part of Mpigi and Kampala districts
Northern Uganda diocese, Acholi and Kitgum districts
North Kigezi, Rukungiri district
North Mbale[6]
Rwenzori diocese, Kabarole and Kibale districts
Soroti diocese, Kumi and Soroti districts
South Rwenzori diocese, Bundibugyo and Kasese districts
West Ankole diocese, Bushenyi district
West Buganda diocese, Masaka and Rakai Districts

---

6. Covers the counties of Budadiri, Buginyanya, Buhugu, Bulambuli, and Buwalasi.

APPENDIX B

Sample Questions Used in Oral Interviews

Personal Information
1. Name
2. Address
3. Occupation
4. Age
5. Marital status
6. Local church
7. Local language spoken
8. Ethnicity
9. Highest level of Education

Personal Christian History
10. When were you baptized?
11. Are you confirmed?
12. Are you a Mulokole/saved?
13. When did you get saved?
14. Are you a leader in the church? Clergy or lay leader?
15. What leadership positions have you held in the church and when?
16. How were you chosen to be a leader in the first instance?
17. What motivated you to accept/consider ordination or whatever leadership postion you hold?

Turbulent Periods and Areas

18. Were you physically present during any of the following times or areas of crises and conflicts?

    Periods: The Mengo crisis 1966–1967; Asian expulsion 1972; Rebel invasion and massacres 1972; UNLF Governments 1979/80; Election 1980; and Okello Lutwa period 1985–1985.

    Areas: Luwero Triangle war 1980–1985; West Nile 1980/81; Acholi–Lango war 1986–1991; and Teso war 1986–1991

19. Describe briefly what happened in your area/period during those times:

    i. *The Mengo crisis 1966–1967*

    Was the fighting confined to Mengo? Did people die outside the Kabaka's palace? What was the response of the Buganda public? What about the rest of Uganda?

    ii. *Asian expulsion 1972*

    What was the response of the general public? Was there any protest response from any group or Church of Uganda?

    iii. *Rebel invasion and massacres 1972*

    To what extent were the massacres confined to the barracks? Were there any particular ethnic groups targeted in the killings? What groups?

    iv. *UNLF governments 1979/80*

    What kind of instability was there during these times? How did it affect people's normal routine? Were there any mass killings? Who was responsible? Who suffered most? Were any killings ethnically or religiously motivated?

    v. *Elections 1980*

    How important were these elections? How did the church members participate? On what basis do you think people voted – ethnic, language, religion, region, education, political party?

vi. *Okello Lutwa period 1985–1986*
How was lawlessness manifested? Who were the killers? Who was responsible? Who was targeted? Were any killings ethnically or religiously motivated?

vii. *Luwero Triangle war 1980–1985*
Who was fighting? How did it affect people's normal routine? Were there any mass killings? Who was largely responsible? Who was being targeted? Were any killings ethnically, religiously or politically motivated?

viii. *West Nile 1980/81*
Who was fighting? How did it affect people's normal routine? Were there any mass killings? Who was responsible? Who was targeted? Were the killings ethnically, religiously or politically motivated?

ix. *War in Lango and Acholi 1986–1991*
Who was fighting? How did it affect people's normal routine? Were there any mass killings? Who was largely responsible? Who was targeted? Were any killings ethnically, religiously or politically motivated?

x. *Teso war 1986–1991*
Who was fighting? How did it affect people's normal routine? Were there any mass killings? Who was largely responsible? Who was targeted? Were any killings ethnically, religiously or politically motivated?

20. Describe briefly what you did in the church during those difficult times? Some aspects to consider:

    i. *Leadership.* Were there any leadership arrangements, strategies or structures set up?

    ii. *Relations with other denominations.* How did you relate to other Christians of other religious traditions, particularly the Roman Catholics?

    iii. *Worship and liturgy.* Did this change in any way? Examine form, style, content and variability. Any linkages with primal religious practice? Any hymns and prayers that may have developed in response to the crises?

 iv. *Church Services.* How was church attendance affected by the crises?

 v. *Church Attendance.* How was church attendance affected by the crises?

 vi. *Mission and Ministry.* Are there any forms and focus of work that relate to the crises, and human suffering? Are there any ways to help people cope? Any specific services or work that were developed?

 vii. *Devotion.* What aspects of church life did you focus on as the most important? (Prayer, evangelism, Bible study, etc.)

 viii. *Spirituality.* How did being a Christian help you in coping with the challenges? What spiritual discipline did you find most helpful? Quiet time, prayer, attending church, attending fellowship, etc.

 ix. *Community.* What community was closest to you in hard times? (Fellowship, church members, church leaders, relatives, etc.)

 x. *Impact.* Did the crises and sufferings shape or change your understanding of being a Christian? In what ways?

Personal involvement

21. How did the troubles affect you, your family and relatives? Was any of your family killed? Lost jobs? Who? When? Where?
22. What did you do for yourself, family, or relatives? (Runaway, went abroad, fought etc.)
23. Did the church do anything for you and your family?

General

24. What do you understand the church to be?
25. What is the work of the church?
26. What is the work of the clergy? (Preach, evangelize, priest, comfort, etc.)

Sample Questions Used in Oral Interviews

27. What is the work of the ordinary Christian?
28. What is unique or special about the Church of Uganda?
29. Was the church true to itself and its mission during the difficult times referred to above? In what ways would you say the church was faithful/unfaithful?

Bibliography

Oral Sources

This section is organized according to the eras of the history of the Church for which the sources were relevant. The name of the interviewee is given together with birthdate, where known, in parenthesis; and the place and date of the interview are given in square brackets. A brief summary of the interviewee's involvement in the Church and the personal impact of the civil-political crisis (where applicable) follows. For those with whom I had more than one interview, the date indicated is of the first interview.

Spanning More than One Era of the Church of Uganda

Baganizi (1940–), Rev Canon Dr Wilson, [Namirembe, 16 January 1997]: saved 1960; catechist 1962–64; attended Bishop Tucker College 1964–66; ordained deacon 1966, priest 1967; Director, Christian Rural Service 1972–77; Provincial Secretary 1977–84; Diocesan Secretary, Kigezi and Muhabura, 1984–90 and 1990–95, respectively; Executive Secretary, Church Commissioners 1995 to-date.

Bikangaga (1920–), Canon John, [Makindye, Kampala, 17 January 1997]: saved 1945; lay-leader in Church since 1940s as Deanery Council member for Kigezi, Deanery Representative to the Mengo Church Council in 1940s. Provincial level: member of Provincial Assembly since the 1950 to 1980s; Chairman, House of Laity 1970s and 80s; pioneer lay member of the Anglican Consultative Council (1971); Chairman, Ten Year Plan 1966/67, and Canon Law and Constitution Committee, 1968–1971.

Gonahasa (1930–), Rt Rev (Retired Bishop) Lucas, [Kadama, Pallisa, 22 April 1997]: saved 1952; attended Buwalasi Theological College 1952–53; catechist 1954–55; ordained deacon 1957, priest 1959; Army Chaplain 1961–68; Bishop, Bukedi 1977–79; acting Bishop, Mbale 1979–81; Provost, All Saints Cathedral Kampala 1981–84; Bishop, Kampala 1984–96.

Kabaza (1919–), Mr Zebulon, Kansanga, [Kampala, 15 January 1997]: saved in 1936; he is one of the few surviving Balokole saved during that period; Schoolteacher and Headmaster, 1950s and 1960s; Evangelist, African Evangelistic Enterprise 1970–79; first Provincial Missions Coordinator, 1979–1987.

Kawuma (1929–1997), Rt Rev (Retired Bishop) Misaeri, [Nsangi, Kampala, 20 April 1997]: Saved 1948; Schoolteacher 1954–62; attended Buwalasi Theological College 1962–64, Bishop Tucker College, 1964–65 and Durham University in UK, 1965–68; Assistant Provincial Secretary, 1968–69; All Africa Council of Churches Refugee Secretary 1970–1972; Principal, Bishop Tucker Theological College, 1973–75; Assistant Bishop, Namirembe 1975–85; Bishop, Namirembe 1985–1995.

Kigozi (1914–), The Rev Canon Simon Peter, [Ntinda, Kampala, 20 December 1996]: married the widow of Kabaka Daudi Chwa; saved 1948; catechist, early 1950s; Provincial Sunday School Organiser 1957–67; ordained deacon 1968, priest 1969; Canon Missioner and Archdeacon, Kampala diocese 1972–83 and 1975–83.

Mukasa (1917–), Rt Rev (Retired Bishop) Yokana, [Kampala, 24 April, 1997]: saved 1947; attended Bishop Tucker College 1938–40, and 1953–54; ordained deacon 1954, priest 1955; Tutor, Bishop Tucker College 1966–68; Dean, Namirembe Cathedral 1968–72; General Secretary, Bible Society of Uganda 1972–77; Bishop, Mityana 1977–88.

Okoth (1927–), The Most Rev (Retired Archbishop) Yona, [Tororo 16 January 1997]: catechist, late 1940s; saved 1947; attended Buwalasi Theological College 1951–53; ordained deacon 1953, priest 1955; Diocesan Treasurer, Upper Nile Diocese 1958–61; Diocesan Treasurer, Mbale Diocese 1961–1963; Provincial Treasurer 1964–1965; Provincial Secretary 1965–1966 and 1969–1972; first Bishop, Bukedi Diocese 1972–1983; Archbishop 1984–1994.

Ruhindi (1926–), The Rt Rev (Retired Bishop) Yustus, [Kampala, 2 March 1994]: Saved in the 1950s; attended Bishop Tucker Theological College for teacher training and ordination course; attended Yale University in the USA in the early 1960s, after which taught at BTTC and later its Principal 1970–72; Bishop, Bunyoro-Kitara, 1972–81; first bishop of North Kigezi, 1981–1996.

Sabiti (1912–), Mrs Geraldine, [Kinoni, Mbarara, 18 December 1996]: married in 1934 to Erica Sabiti, later the first African Archbishop of the Church of Uganda, Ruanda-Urundi; saved in 1937.

Wani (1914–), The Most Rev (Retired Archbishop) Silvanus, [Kyambogo, Kampala, 15 January 1997]: saved 1937; schoolteacher, in the 1930s until 1940; attended Buwalasi Theological College, 1940–43; ordained deacon 1943, priest 1944; Chief Army Chaplain 1943–1979; Diocesan Secretary/ Treasurer, Northern Uganda 1960–1964; Bishop, Northern Uganda 1964–1969; first Bishop, Madi/ West Nile Diocese 1969–1977; Archbishop 1977–84.

Namirembe Crisis, 1965–1971

Lubwama (1901–), Rev Canon Daniel, Mengo, [Kampala, 13 Jan 1997]: catechist and schoolteacher, 1916–1939; attended Bishop Tucker College; ordained deacon 1940, priest 1944; acting Rural Dean Namirembe 1944–45; Inspector of Church accounts 1945–52; Sub-Dean, Namirembe Cathedral 1952–58 and 1972–75; Archdeacon Buganda 1958–72; Diocesan Secretary, Namirembe 1961–75; saved 1989.

The Church in Lango and the Idi Amin Regime, 1971–1979

Apelo (1932–), Rev Opolo Y, [Lira, 27 September 1996]: saved 1953; catechist, 1956–57; attended Buwalasi Theological College 1954–60; ordained deacon 1960, priest 1961; Parish priest Lira Town 1968–79; Archdeacon, Lira 1977–79; Lango Diocese Auditor 1990–92. He was arrested once in 1978 and taken to the army barracks.

Atyamu (1954–), Mrs Christine, [Lira, 27 September 1996]: active member of Lira Town Parish 1975–to date; Warden 1991–to date. Lived in Lira during from 1975–78; witnessed 24 deaths In neighbourhood; she was arrested twice in 1978, and later fled to Kenya in 1978 with family.

Obonyo (1944–), Mr Julius Peter, [Lira, 27 September 1996]; saved in 1981; active as lay-man, Chairman, Laity Lira Town Parish 1980s and early 1990s; owned a business in Lira during the Amin regime and knew personally many of the businessmen that were killed during that time.

Odongo (1943–), Haj Musa, [Lira, 27 September 1996]: Muslim, son of the Lango District at the time the Obote regime was overthrown; narrowly escaped, with a bullet wound, but his father arrested in 1974 and detained with several other district Muslim leaders.

Odurukami (1953–), Rev Canon Charles, [Kampala 27 August 1996]: saved in the 1970s; Attended Church Army College in Nairobi in mid 1970s; Warden, St Augustine Community Centre in Lira, 1976–79; Archbishop's Chaplain 1986 to-date. Amin Regime killed many of his relatives.

Odwe (1952–), Rev Willy Okello, [Lira, 28 September 1996]: saved in the 1980s; catechist, 1981–1982; ordained deacon, 1984 and priest, 1986; was in Lango during the Idi Amin regime.

Okodi, Mr Levi Macpio, [Lira, 27 September 1996]: active layman in Lira Town Parish. From 1972–76 working as a Cooperatives' extension worker in Lango.

Ongom (1951–), Mrs Caroline, [Lira, 27 September 1996]: wife of Ben Ongom who was accused together with Archbishop Luwum and later executed by firing squad in 1977; active in Lira Town Parish; not saved

Otim (1935–), Rt Rev Melchisedek, [Boroboro, Lira, 27 September 1996]: saved 1968; attended Bishop Tucker College 1967–69; ordained deacon 1970, priest 1972; Diocesan Secretary/ Treasurer, Northern Uganda 1975–1976; first Bishop of Lango 1976 to-date. Fled to exile in 1977 after the death of Janani Luwum.

The Church in Luwero and the Obote II Regime, 1981–1985

Kampujja (1935–), Rev Henry, [Nakaseke, Luwero, 20 September 1995]: catechist, 1955–1984; saved 1985; attended Namugongo Seminary 1984–1985; ordained deacon 1985, priest 1986. He stayed in Luwero until he and his family were displaced to Singo in 1983. His two brothers and mother were killed in the war.

Kayima (1917–), Mr Yedediya, [Mengo, Kampala, 29 April 1997]: saved 1940; licensed preacher 1942. His home is near Matuga in Luwero, where the Luwero insurgency found him. He assisted Museveni and the rebels during the Luwero war.

Mujabi (1932–), Mr Amunoni Salongo, [Kiwoko, Luwero 20 September 1995]; saved 1952; catechist since 1970 to-date. He attended a primary Teacher Training College. He was in Luwero for the whole time of the Luwero war. Three of his sister's children were shot and killed before him.

Sajjabi (1901–), Rev Can Blassio, [Semuto, Luwero, 20 September 1995]: not saved; attended Bishop Tucker College mid 1930s; ordained deacon 1937, priest 1939; Rural Dean Kako late 1940s and in Luwero 1953–1965. He stayed at Semuto in Luwero throughout the Luwero war, saw 7 men shot, and was host to over 1000 rebels in his compound for about 6 months in 1983.

Serubidde, Rev Canon Daudi, [Namirembe, Kampala, 17 January 1995]: saved 1964; attended Bishop Tucker College; ordained deacon 1967, priest 1968. He was Archdeacon of Luwero during the first half of 1982 and 1983–90.

The Church in Teso and the NRA/M Regime, 1986–1992

Adupu, Mr Thomas, [Serere, 2 March 1996]: catechist at Serere.

Angois (1949–), Rev Yeku, Odudui, [Soroti, 1 March 1996]: saved 1983; catechist 1981–1988; attended Buwalasi Theological College, 1988–90;

Bibliography

ordained deacon 1990, priest 1992. Family lost 107 cows during the insurgency; he served among displaced in Soroti during the Teso War.

Ariko, Mr John Steven, [Odudui Parish, Soroti, 1 March 1996]: catechist in Odudui parish; was detained by NRA during the Teso war.

Arutu, Rev Naboth Hannington, [Serere, 2 March 1996]; Vicar at St Mark Serere.

Egadu, Mr Kenan, [Soroti, 2 March 1996]: active lay Christian, Soroti Cathedral.

Engwau, Rev Enos, [Serere, 2 March 1996]: Archdeacon of Serere, 1987–89: was attacked by NRA soldiers in his house during the Teso war.

Ilukor (1935–), Rt Rev Gershom, [Soroti Diocese Office, Soroti, 19 March 1996]: catechist, 1956–63; attended Buwalasi Theological College 1963–64 and St John's College, Nottingham, UK; ordained deacon 1964, priest 1966; Diocesan Secretary/ Treasurer, Soroti Diocese 1972–75; Bishop, Soroti 1976 to-date; saved 1983. He was in Teso throughout the period of the insurgency and spearheaded peace initiatives.

Obaikol (late 1940s–), The Ven Rev Canon Charles, [Serere, 2 March 1996]. Saved 1960s; Acting Principal Bishop Tucker College 1980–82; Provincial Secretary 1982–88; Principal, Buwalasi Theological College 1988–95. Lost many relatives and friends during the war.

Odwar (1934–), Mr Joel Enabi, Pamba, [Soroti, 18 March 1996]: elder in Pamba village. Odwar was in Bukedea during the period of the Teso Insurgency where he acted as informer to rebels; his son was killed by NRA in 1987; saved in 1995.

Oguli (1929–), Mr George, Soroti, 18 March 1996: licensed catechist but not in full-time Church work; active as layman in councils and synods; was delegate to the World Anglican Assembly Canada 1980s; Chairman of the Electoral Commission 1985. During the Teso insurgency, he was detained for one year by the NRA, 1987–88; and later was part of the Teso Commission in 1990.

Okalebo (1928–), Rev Othniel, [Ngora, 18 March 1996]: attended Bishop Tucker College 1978–81; saved 1983; ordained deacon 1981, priest 1982; He was Headmaster of Ngora Girls High School during the Teso insurgency, 1988–1993. He was detained and tortured for three months by NRA.

Okare (1927–), Rev Canon Yesero, [Soroti, 1 March 1996]: catechist 1960s and early 1970s; attended Buwalasi Theological College; Rural Dean Soroti 1979–83; Archdeacon Soroti, 1984 to-date; saved 1989. The NRA detained him over night at the barracks in Soroti.

Okodu (1966–), Rev George R, [Soroti, 1 March 1996]: saved 1990; catechist 1992–94; attended Buwalasi Theological College 1994–96; ordained deacon 1996. During the Teso insurgency he was an informer for the rebels.

Okwii (c.1958–), The Ven Rev Charles, [Ngora, 2 March 1996]: saved 1976; he was based in Ngora during the peak period of the insurgency, 1987–91. Father killed during the war. He was in charge of the camp at Ngora.

Olupot (1945–), Mr Joash O, [Kumi, 19 March 1996]; not saved; Headmaster of Ngora High School, 1982 to-date; on various Church councils, parish and diocesan. He was in Ngora throughout the period of the insurgency in Teso, and lost 51 cows.

Opwata, Rev Naphtali, [Soroti Diocese Office, Soroti, 1 March 1996]: Diocesan Mission Coordinator; was not in Teso during the insurgency, but lost relatives.

Osuret (1935–), The Ven Rev Job, [Kumi, 19 March 1996: saved in 1980]; was parish priest in Ngora, 1983–90, during the Teso war and lost 48 cows.

Group of local parish Church leaders interviewed as a group and discussed issues of the Teso War, [Odudui Parish, Soroti Archdeaconry, Soroti, on 1 March 1996]:

Angois, Rev Yeku (Parish Priest)	Ariko, Mr Steven (Catechist)
Acibu, Mr David	Elelu, Mr Steven
Elobu Mr Robert	Emolu, Mr John
Eten, Mr Justine	Ojuli, Mr Justine
Omaje, Mr Nelson	Osegel, Mr Washington

Archival Sources[1]

African Evangelistic Enterprise Archives, Kampala

African Evangelistic Enterprise, Kumi Displaced Peoples' Project Report, dated 30 June 1990.

Letter from the Office of the Deputy Minister, Ministry of Relief and Social Rehabilitation, to Donor Agencies, dated 3 July 1990.

Centre for Basic Research Archives (CBR), Kololo Kampala

Kato, Wycliffe, *An Escape from Kampala*, n.d. PF 320.9 KAT (1992).

Ocan, Charles, "The Political Situation in Teso," an unpublished paper delivered at the Seminar on Political and Economic Situation in Uganda" at the Commonwealth Institute, London, 1992. PF 320.9 OCA (1992) 1.

---

1. Archival Sources are sorted by date.

Ochyengh, Dan M, "Proposals on the Restoration of Stability, Peace and Progress to Teso (15 December 1991)" to the Chairman, Presidential Commission of Teso. PF 320.9 (1992) 1.
Otai, Peter, "Uganda: The Skulls of Luwero and the Legacy of Terror," October 1988, unpublished document. PF 320.9 OTA (1992) 1.
Otai, Peter, "Political and Security Situation in North and Eastern Uganda," an unpublished paper presented at the Seminar on the Political, Economic and Security situation in Uganda at the Commonwealth Institute, London, June 1992. PF 320.9 OTA (1992) 1.

Church of Uganda Archives, Provincial Secretariat, Namirembe

Archbishop's Papers
Brown, Leslie, "Bishop's Charge to Uganda Diocesan Synod, 1958."
Brown, Leslie, "Bishop's Charge," Synod of the Church of Uganda, 1960.
Cathedral Church of St Paul, Namirembe. "Service of the Inauguration of the Church of the Province of Uganda and Ruanda-Urundi," Namirembe, 16 April 1961.
Cathedral Church of St Paul, Namirembe. "Service of the Enthronement of the Archbishop of Uganda, Rwanda and Burundi," Namirembe, 25 January 1965.
Sabiti, Erica, "The Archbishop's Charge: Enthronement of the Most Rev Erica Sabiti," St. Paul's Cathedral, Namirembe, 25 January 1966.
Flinn, J Seymour, "Church of Uganda, Rwanda and Burundi," unpublished paper, February 1967.
"Report on Conference of Bishops and Diocesan Councils, called by H. E. the President of Uganda, General Idi Amin Dada, International Conference Centre, Kampala, 26–28 November 1971, and State House, Entebbe, 29 November, 1971."
Letter and Report to General Idi Amin, from Archbishop Janani Luwum, on "The Commission of Enquiry into land possessed, owned, acquired or otherwise held by the Church of Uganda, or any Diocese thereof for Ecclesiastical Purposes: 1973."
Letter to His Excellency, Life President of Uganda, from Rt Rev Dr D Nsubuga, Dean of the Province, dated 24 March 1977.
Letter to His Excellency, Life President of Uganda, from Silvanus Wani, Archbishop Elect, dated 24 March 1977.
"The Dedication and Consecration of St Paul's Church of Simba Mechanised Regiment, Mbarara, Uganda Army," 25 June 1978.

Okoth, Archbishop Yona, "The present situation after the NRA took over the government on January 25, 1986."

Letter to His Excellency the President, from Archbishop Yona Okoth, dated 30 December 1986.

Letter to His Excellency the President, from Archbishop Yona Okoth, dated 2 June 1987.

Letter to His Excellency the President, from Archbishop Yona Okoth, Re: "Insecurity Surrounding some Church of Uganda Leadership," dated 24 September 1987.

House of Bishops' Papers

"The Constitution of the Church of the Province of Uganda and Ruanda-Urundi, 1960."

"An Open Statement by the Bishops of the Church of Uganda to His Excellency, the President of the Republic of Uganda, Al-Hadji General Idi Amin Dada."

Letter to His Excellency, Life President of Uganda, from the House of Bishops dated 5 February 1977.

Letter to His Excellency, Life President of Uganda, from the House of Bishops dated 10 February. 1977.

Letter to His Excellency, Life President of Uganda, from the House of Bishops, signed by the Rt. Rev Dr D Nsubuga, Dean of the Province, dated 23 March 1977.

Prepared Response of the House of Bishops of the COU, to His Excellency on Wednesday 16 February 1977.

Yona Okoth, "Communication from the Chair at the House of Bishop's Special Meeting on 23 August 1985."

Otim, Rt Rev Melchisedek, "Address to the Members of House of Bishops at Lweza Training and Conference Centre."

Memorandum of the House of Bishops of COU, presented to His Excellence Y. K. Museveni, Kampala 23 April 1987.

Letter to His Excellency the President, from House of Bishops, dated 4 June 1987.

"Memorandum to His Excellency the President of Uganda Yoweri Kaguta Museveni at State House on 23 February 1989."

Provincial Assembly Papers

Minutes of the Provincial Assembly meeting of April 1961.

Brown, Leslie, "Opening address to the Assembly by His Grace, Provincial Assembly," Provincial Assembly, September 1964.

Minutes of the Provincial Assembly meeting of January 1964.

Minutes of the Provincial Assembly meeting of January 1966.

Sabiti, Erica, "Opening Address by the Chairman," Provincial Assembly, 26 January 1966.
Minutes of the Provincial Assembly meeting of January 1967.
Sabiti, Erica, "Archbishop's Address to the Provincial Assembly," Provincial Assembly, January 1967.
Minutes of the Provincial Assembly meeting of October 1968.
Minutes of the Provincial Assembly meeting of December 1970.
Sabiti Erica, "The Archbishop's Charge to the Church of Uganda, Rwanda and Burundi," Provincial Assembly, December 1970.
"The Proceedings of the Second Meeting of the Second Provincial Assembly Held at Bishop Tucker College, Mukono, December 9, 10, and 11, 1970; Appendix 'B': The Archbishop's Charge to the Church of Uganda, Rwanda and Burundi, December 1970." Provincial Assembly Papers, COU Archives.
Minutes of the Provincial Assembly meeting of January 1972.
Minutes of the Provincial Assembly meeting of August 1972.
Minutes of the Provincial Assembly meeting of August 1979.

PAE Papers

Provincial Assembly Executive, Minutes of the meeting of 22 October 1964, 30 March 1965.
Provincial Assembly Executive, Minutes of the meeting of 31 January 1965.
Provincial Assembly Executive, Minutes of the meeting of 31 January 1966.
Provincial Assembly Executive, Minutes of the meeting of 13 May 1966.
Provincial Assembly Executive, Minutes of the meeting 29 November 1966.
"Report of Adhoc Committee on the Provincial Secretariat," 1966.
Provincial Assembly Executive, Minutes of the meeting of 4,5,6 January 1967.
"Report by Provincial Literature and Radio Board, Provincial Advisory Board, COU," October 15, 1968.
Letter from Namirembe Diocese to the PAE, dated 29 November 1968.
Letter from PAE to Namirembe Diocesan Council, dated 18 February 1969.
Provincial Assembly Executive, Minutes of the meeting of 6, 7 February 1969.
A Memorandum from the Diocesan Council Retreat at Mukono, dated 3 May 1970.
Letter from PAE to Namirembe Diocesan Council, dated 18 February 1969.
Letter from Namirembe Diocese to the Provincial Secretary, dated 26 January 1971.
Letter from West Buganda Diocese to the Provincial Secretary, dated 12 March 1971.
Provincial Assembly Executive, Minutes of the meeting of 2 February 1971.
Report of Meeting between PAE and Delegates of Namirembe and West Buganda Dioceses, held on 20 October 1971.

Provincial Assembly Executive, Minutes of the meeting with the House of Bishops present, 16 September 1972.

Namirembe Diocese Archives
Minutes of the Namirembe Diocesan Council, 19 September 1969. Diocesan Secretary Files.

"The Interim Constitution of the Province of Namirembe, Church of Uganda: The Articles of the Constitution," November 1970.

Personal Archives
Zebulon Kabaza, Personal Diary, 1952, 1953, Kansanga, Kampala.

Newspapers

New Day: 9 September 1960; and, 4 December 1965.

The New Vision: 27 June 1989; 7 July 1989; 19 July 1989; 24 July 1989; and 28 August 1989.

Taifa Empya: 18 November 1971.

Uganda Argus: 13 November 1965; 16 November 1965; 22 November 1965; 28 May 1966; 22 January 1968; 1 February, 1970; 2 April 1970; 18 January 1971; 12 February 1971; 5 April, 1971; 27 April 1971; 27 November 1971; 17 January 1972; 21 February 1972; 3 August 1972; 15 August 1972; 13 September 1972; 13 February 1973; 4 February 1974; and 29 April 1975.

Uganda Times: 4 July 1979; 1 April 1981; 12 June 1981; 24 October 1981; 6 February 1982 and, 2 March 1982.

Voice of Uganda: 12 February 1977; 15 February 1977; 17 February 1977; and, 18 March 1977.

Note: *The New Vision*, *Uganda Times*, and *Uganda Argus* were government sponsored newspapers. They are held in the Africana Section of Makerere University Library and the Uganda Management Institute Library. Makerere University Library holds copies of *Uganda Argus* published between January 1955 and July 1976; *Voice of Uganda*, between August 1976 and April 1979; and *Uganda Times* between April 1979 and January 1986; and, *The New Vision*, from January 1986 to-date.

Official Publications

Church of Uganda Publications
The Upper Nile Magazine 3, no. 2 (1960).
The Upper Nile Magazine 4, no. 1 (1961).

The Crisis in the Christian Ministry in Uganda. Kampala: Uganda Bookshop Press, 1964.
The Ten Year Plan. Kampala: Uganda Bookshop Press, 1967.
Survey on Administration and Finance of the Church in Uganda. Namirembe: Uganda Bookshop Press, 1969.
Information about the Church of Uganda. Kampala: Research Unit, Planning and Advisory Office, 1978.
Evangelism and Development: 1985 PIM Consultation Report. Namirembe: Mission Department, 1985.

Uganda Government Publications
Uganda: The Case for the Second Republic. Entebbe: Government Printer, 1971.
The First 366 Days. Kampala: Ministry of Information and Broadcasting, 1972.
Uganda's Economic War. Kampala: Ministry of Information and Broadcasting, January 1975.
Documentary History of the Boundary of Uganda and Administrative Divisions 1900 and those of 1976. Entebbe: the Republic of Uganda, 1976.
Public Holidays Act, Decree no. 10. Entebbe: Government Printers, 1978.
The 1991 Population and Housing Census (National Summary) Uganda. Entebbe: Statistics Department, Ministry of Finance and Economic Planning, Uganda, April 1994.
The 1995 Constitution of the Republic of Uganda. Kampala: Government Printers, 1995.

Others
The Kabaka's Government. *Buganda's Independence*. Mengo: The Information Department of the Kabaka's Government, 1960.
Kiwanuka Joseph. *Church and State: Guiding principles, Pastoral Letter of Archbishop Joseph Kiwanuka*. Kampala, November 1961.
Violation of Human Rights and the Rule of Law in Uganda. Geneva: International Commission of Jurists, 1974.
The Commonwealth Observer Group. *Uganda Elections, December 1980: The Report of the Commonwealth Observer Group*. London: Commonwealth Secretariat, 1980.
Uganda Joint Christian Council. *Facing the Challenges of Political Transition in Uganda: Key Issues in the White Paper*. Kampala: UJCC, 2004.
APRM National Commission. *The Country Self-Assessment Report, 2007*. Kampala: National Planning Authority (NPA), 2007.
APRM. *Republic of Uganda APRM Country Review Report No. 7*. Midrand South Africa: APR Secretariat, 2009.

Transparency International, *Global Corruption Barometer 2013*, available at http://www.transparency.org/gcb2013

Transparency International-Kenya, "The East African Bribery Index 2013," available at http://www.tikenya.org/index.php/the-east-african-bribery-index.

Amnesty International. *Rule by Law: Discriminatory Legislation and Legitimized Abuses in Uganda.* London: Amnesty International, 2014.

Refugee Law Project. "Compendium of Conflicts in Uganda." Kampala: School of Law Makerere University, 2014.

Uganda Human Rights Commission (UHRC). *17th Annual Report.* Kampala: UHRC, 2015.

Unpublished Works

Theses

Adraa, E. "The Growth and Impact of Chosen Evangelical Revival in Ayivu County, West Nile." Makerere University, Kampala, DipTh dissertation, 1986.

Aquir, Brainy. "The Revival Movements in the Church of Uganda with Specific Reference to Boroboro Parish, Lango Diocese." Makerere University, Kampala, DipTh dissertation, May 1990.

Atine, Wilson. "The Effects of Civil Wars, since 1977, on the Anglican Diocese of Northern Uganda, with Particular Reference to the Headquarters at Gulu." Makerere University, Kampala, DipTh dissertation, 1988.

Bamunoba, Yoram R. K. "The Development of the Anglican Church in West Ankole 1900 to 1990." Leeds University, MPhil thesis, 1992.

Bukenya, Dunstan K. "The Development of Neo-Traditional Religion: the Buganda Experience." University of Aberdeen, MLit dissertation, December 1980.

Gong, Kenneth. "The History of the Revival Movement in Kitgum Church of Uganda Parish, Northern Uganda Diocese." Makerere University, Kampala, DipTh dissertation, 1985.

"How Christianity came to Teso (1900-40) with Special Reference to the Church Missionary Society." Makerere University, Kampala, DipTh dissertation, n. d. and no author named.

Irigei, Thomas E. "The Social Change and its Effects on the Morals of Iteso with Specific Reference to Ngora, COU Archdeaconry Soroti Diocese." Makerere University, Kampala, DipTh dissertation, 1990.

Bibliography

Kalimi, John. "The Life and Contribution of Dunstan Nsubuga (Bishop of Namirembe 1964–85) to the Church of Uganda." Makerere University, Kampala, DipTh dissertation, 1988.

Kasangaki, George. "The Revival Movement in Hoima Archdeaconry, Bunyoro-Kitara Diocese Uganda, 1937–1987, its Impact and People's Response." Makerere University, Kampala, DipTh dissertation, 1988.

Katarikawe, James, and John Wilson. "The East African Revival Movement." Fuller Theological Seminary, MTh and MA Theses, 1975.

Kermu, S. "The Life and Times of Bishop Silvanus Wani." Makerere University, Kampala, BD dissertation, 1987.

Kigundu, D. "The Fears and Attitudes of Ordinary Christians to the Revival Movement." Makerere University, Kampala, DipTh dissertation, 1987.

Kizito, Elias L. "The Church of Uganda's Role towards the Displaced Christians in Mityana Diocese 1980-1984." Makerere University, Kampala, DipTh dissertation, 1984.

Komakech, William. "The Impact of Alice Lakwena on Christianity in Acholi Land." Makerere University, Kampala, DipTh dissertation, 1989.

Kyakulagira, S. K. "The Work of the Church in Luwero C.O.U. Archdeaconry, Uganda during the Guerrilla War 1981-1986." Makerere University, Kampala, DipTh dissertation, 1988.

Lockard, Kathlene. "Religion and Political Development in Uganda, 1962-72." University of Wisconsin, PhD dissertation, 1974.

Max-Olet, Ameri. "The impact of the Wars on the Diocese of Lango, With Specific Reference to Lira Town Parish, Church of Uganda, between 1976-1989." Makerere University, Kampala, DipTh dissertation, 1990.

Mukibi, Paul. "The Impact of the Guerrilla War (1981-85) and the Challenge of Rehabilitation for the Church in Kiboga area Singo Uganda." Makerere University, Kampala, DipTh dissertation, 1987.

Mukungu, Frederick N. "A Survey of the Anglican Church of Uganda Archives Documents in Britain." Loughborough University, MA dissertation, 1995.

Mutebi, Wilson. "Towards an Indigenous Understanding and Practice of Baptism amongst the Baganda, Uganda." Makerere University, Kampala, MA thesis, 1982.

Muhanguzi, John. "The Spread of the Revival movement at Burunga in Nyabushozi County, East Ankole, Uganda." Makerere University, Kampala, DipTh dissertation, 1985.

Muhima, Edward B. "'The Fellowship of His Suffering': A Theological Interpretation of Christian Suffering under Idi Amin." North Western University, Evanston Illinois, PhD dissertation, 1981.

Muhima, Edward B. "Church and State." Kampala: unpublished paper presented at Salt and Light Conference, Kampala, November 1992.

Muyinde, Mande Wilson. "An Ethics for Leadership Power and the Anglican Church in Buganda." Aberdeen University, PhD thesis, 1996.

Ndahiro, Peter S. "The Impact of the Abalokole Revival on the Church of Uganda with Particular Reference to the Diocese of Namirembe, 1940-1992." Makerere University, Kampala, BD dissertation, 1992.

Niringiye, David Zac. "Prolegomena to an African Theology: An Examination of the Sources and Methodology of Mbiti's Theology." Wheaton Graduate School, MA thesis, 1987.

Obote, O. "Why the Revival Movement has Failed in Teso." Makerere University, Kampala, DipTh dissertation, 1978.

Okwii, Michael E. "The Economic Revolution in Teso and its Effects on the Life and Mission of the Church during the 1980s with particular Reference to Serere Parish." Makerere University, Kampala, DipTh dissertation 1990.

Ogwok, Jacob. "The Causes and Effects of Insecurity on the People of Lango Diocese with Specific Reference to Aber Archdeaconry, Church of Uganda (1985-1992)." Makerere University, Kampala, BD dissertation, 1982.

Olal, Tom K. "Church and Politics in Lango-Uganda (1971-1981)." Makerere University, Kampala, DipTh dissertation, 1982.

Petersen, R. Anker. "A Study of the Spiritual Roots of the East African Revival with Special Reference to its Use of Confession of Sin in Public." Aberdeen University, MTh thesis, 1988.

Robins, Catherine. "'Tukutendereza': A Study of Social Change and Sectarian Withdrawal in the Balokole Revival of Uganda." Columbia University, PhD dissertation, 1975.

Sebalugga-Kalimi, John. "The Life and Contribution of Dunstan Nsubuga (Bishop of Namirembe 1964-85) to the Church of Uganda." Makerere University, Kampala, DipTh dissertation, 1988.

Sentongo, Erisa. "The Conflicts Surrounding the Creation and Development of an Anglican Diocese of West Buganda (Uganda), 1960-1976." Makerere University, Kampala, DipTh dissertation, 1981.

Sentongo, Joachim. "The Traditional Concept of Worship among the Ganda people of Uganda in Relation to the Concept of Worship in the Bible." Makerere University, Kampala, DipTh dissertation, 1988.

Waliggo, John Mary. "The Catholic Church in the Buddu Province of Uganda 1879-1925." Cambridge University, PhD thesis, 1976.

Weeks, David. "The Growth of Christianity in the Kingdom of Nkore (Ankole) in Western Uganda before 1912." University of Aberdeen, MTh dissertation, 1979.

Wilson, John. "Beliefs and Practices of the East African Revival Movement," Fuller Theological Seminary, unpublished MA thesis, 1975.

Zodia, Kefa. "The Revival in West Nile." Makerere University, Kampala, DipTh dissertation, 1978.

Manuscripts, Public Lectures and Seminar Papers

Hansen, Holger B. "Religion and Politics in Independent Uganda: the Role of the Religious Factor in Ugandan Politics and a Discussion of the Conceptual Framework." University of Copenhagen: paper prepared for the Workshop on Religion and Politics, E.C.P.R. Joint Session, Brussels, April 1979.

Mande, Wilson. "Anglicanism and Ethnic Identity in Uganda." Namirembe, Kampala, n.d.

Mujabi, Amunoni Salongo. "*Ebyafaayo by'Olutalo Dekabusa.*" Memoirs of the Luwero Triangle War, unpublished manuscript, Kiwoko, 1996 (copy in my possession).

Mujaju, Akiiki B. "Church and State Relations in Rapidly Changing Societies." Makerere University, a public lecture in memory of Archbishop Janani Luwum, Kampala, February 1989.

Mutava, Musimi. "Church and State in Africa Today." paper presented at Worldview'88, Nairobi, June 1988.

Niringiye, D. Zac. "Ecclesiology in African Theological Scholarship; a Survey." Kampala, 1993.

Okullu Henry. "The Role of a Church Leader in Society Today." Janani Luwum Lecture, Kampala, 16 February 1985.

Pirouet, Louise M. "The Churches and Human Right in Kenya and Uganda since Independence." A paper submitted at a conference at Copenhagen University, 1990.

Serubidde, Daudi. "The Pastor's Experience." Unpublished manuscript, Kampala, 1992.

Wani, Silvanus. "How to Make Christ Relevant to my People: The Story of the Church of Uganda." A seminar paper, n.d.

Ward, Kevin. "The Church and the Exile of Kabaka Mutesa II of Buganda (1953-55)." A seminar paper presented at CSCNWW, New College, Edinburgh University, October 1993.

Articles in Books and Journals

Billington, Roy. "Early Years of Medical Work in the Church of Uganda." In *A Century of Christianity in Uganda 1877-1977*, edited by T. Tuma and P. Mutibwa. Nairobi: Uzima Press, 1978.

Buthelezi, Manas. "Toward Indigenous Theology in S. Africa." In *The Emergent Gospel*, edited by S. Torres and V. Fabella, 56–75. Maryknoll, New York: Orbis Books, 1978.

———. "In Christ - One Community." *Africa Theological Journal* 7, no. 1 (1979).

Fashole-Luke, Edward. "Ancestral veneration and the Communion of Saints." In *New Testament Christianity for Africa and the World*, edited by M. Glasswell and E. Fashole-Luke, 209–221. London: SPCK, 1974.

Getui, N. N. "The Family, the Church and Development of the Youth." In *The Church in African Christianity: Innovative Essays in Ecclesiology*, edited by J. N. K. Mugambi and L. Magesa. Nairobi: Initiatives Publishers, 1990.

Gingyera-Pinycwa, A. G. "Is there a Northern Question?." In *Conflict Resolution in Uganda*, edited by Kumar Rupesinghe. Oslo: International Peace Research Institute, 1989.

Gunton, Colin E. "The Church on Earth: The Roots of Community." In *On Being the Church: Essays on the Christian Community*, edited by Colin E. Gunton and Daniel W. Hardy, 48–80. Edinburgh: T & T Clark, 1989.

Gutierrez, Gustavo. "The Church: Sacrament of History." In *Liberation Theology: An Introductory Reader*, edited by Curt Cadorette et al., 170–179. Maryknoll: Orbis Books, 1994.

Hamidullah. "Islam in Uganda and its Contribution to National Development." In *The Role of Religious Organisations in Development of Uganda*, edited by A. H. Abidi Syed, 83–85. Kampala: Foundation for African Development, 1991.

Hansen, Holger B. "Church and State in a Colonial Context." In *Imperialism, the State and the Third World*, edited by Michael Twaddle, 95–123. London: British Academic Press, 1992.

Hansen, Holger B. "Church and State in Early Colonial Uganda." *African Affairs* 85, no. 338 (1986): 55–74.

Hansen, Holger B. "Pre-colonial Immigrants and Colonial Servants. The Nubians in Uganda Revised." *Africa Affairs* 90, no. 361 (1991): 559–580.

Hastings, Adrian. "On African Theology." *Scottish Journal of Theology* 37, no. 3 (1984): 359–374.

Hutagalung, Sutan M. "The Church in the World." *Africa Theological Journal* 10, no. 2 (1981): 46–64.

Karugire, Samwiri. "Arrival of European Missionaries." in *A Century of Christianity in Uganda 1877-1977*, edited by T. Tuma and P. Mutibwa. Nairobi: Uzima Press, 1978.

Kasozi, A. B. K. "Christian-Muslim Inputs into Public Policy Formulation in Kenya, Tanzania and Uganda." In *Religion & Politics in East Africa*, edited by Holger H. Hansen and Michael Twaddle, 223–246. London: James Currey, 1995.

Kokole, Omari H. "Idi Amin, 'The Nubi' & Islam in Ugandan Politics 1971-1979." In *Religion & Politics in East Africa,* edited by Holger H. Hansen and Michael Twaddle, 45–55. London: James Currey, 1995.

Low, D. A. "Converts and Martyrs in Buganda." In *Christianity in Tropical Africa,* edited by C. G. Baeta, 329–347, 152–163. London: Oxford University Press, 1968.

Makara, Sabiti. "Managing Elections in a Multiparty Political Dispensation: The Role of the Electoral Commission in Uganda's 2011 Elections." In *Elections in a Hybrid Regime: Revisiting the 2011 Uganda Polls,* edited by S. Perrot, S. Makara, J. Lafargue, and M. Fourere. Kampala: Fountain Publishers, 2014.

Mazrui, Ali. "Religious Strangers in Uganda: From Emin Pasha to Amin Dada." *African Affairs* 76, no. 302 (1977): 21–38.

Mbiti, John. "The Ways and Means of Communicating the Gospel." In *Christianity in Tropical Africa,* edited by C. G. Baeta, 329–347. London: Oxford University Press, 1968.

———. "Christianity and Traditional Religions in Africa." *International Review of Missions* 59 (1970): 430–440.

———. "Christianity and African Culture." *Journal of Theology for Southern Africa* 20 (1977): 26–40.

———. "Christianity and African Religion." In *Facing the New Challenges: The Message of PACLA,* edited by M. Cassidy, and L. Verdinden, 308–313. Kisumu, Kenya: Evangel Publishing House, 1978.

Mshana, Eliewaha E. "Church and State in the Independent States of Africa." *Africa Theological Journal* 5 (1972): 46–58.

Mudoola, Dan. "Religion and Politics in Uganda: The Case of Busoga, 1900-1962." *African Affairs* 77, no. 306 (January 1978): 22–35.

———. "Political Transitions since Idi Amin: A Study in Political Pathology." In *Uganda Now: Between Decay and Development,* edited by Holger H. Hansen and Michael Twaddle, 280–298. London: James Currey, 1988.

Mujaju, Akiiki. "The Political Crisis of Church Institutions in Uganda." *African Affairs* 75, no. 298 (1976): 67–85.

Murray, Jocelyn. "A Bibliography on the East African Revival Movement." *Journal of Religion in Africa* 8, no. 2 (1975): 144–147.

Museveni, Yoweri K. "Address to Makerere University students and Staff at Freedom Square, Makerere University, Kampala, June 1991." In *What is Africa's Problem?,* edited by Yoweri K. Museveni. Kampala: NRM Publications, 1992.

Nasimiyu-Wasikye, Anne. "African Women's Legitimate Role in Church ministry." In *The Church in African Christianity: Innovative Essays in Ecclesiology,* edited by J. N. K. Mugambi and L. Magesa, 57–70. Nairobi: Initiatives Publishers, 1990.

Nthamburi, Zablon. "The Donatist Controversy as a Paradigm for Church and State." *Africa Theological Journal* 7, no. 3 (1988): 196–206.

———. "Toward Indigenisation of Christianity in Africa: A Missiological Task." *International Bulletin of Missionary Research* 13, no. 3 (1989): 112–118.

Nyamiti, Charles. "The Church as Christ's Ancestral Mediation: An essay in African Ecclesiology." In *The Church in African Christianity: Innovative Essays in Ecclesiology*, edited by J. N. K. Mugambi and L. Magesa, 129–177. Nairobi: Initiatives Publishers, 1990.

Padilla, Rene. "The Contextualisation of the Gospel." *Journal of Theology for Southern Africa* 24 (1978): 12–30.

Payne, Roland J. "The Influence of the Concept of the Traditional African Leadership on the Concept of Church Leadership: Some Personal Impressions, I." *Africa Theological Journal* 1 (1968): 69–74.

Perrot, Sandrine. "From February 2011 Elections to the Walk-to-Work Protests. Did Uganda Really Want 'Another Rap'." In *Elections in a Hybrid Regime: Revisiting the 2011 Uganda Polls*, edited by S. Perrot, S. Makara, J. Lafargue, and M. Fourere. Kampala: Fountain Publishers, 2014.

Pirouet, Louise. "Religion in Uganda under Idi Amin." *Journal of Religion in Africa* 11, no. 1 (1980): 13–29.

———. "The Church and Human Rights in Kenya & Uganda." In *Religion and Politics in East Africa*, edited by Holger H. Hansen and Michael Twaddle, 251. London: James Currey, 1995.

Poulton, John. "Like Father, Like Son: Some Reflections on the Church of Uganda." *International Review of Mission* 50 (1961): 297–307.

Rowe, John A. "Islam under Idi Amin: a case of deja vu?" In *Uganda Now: Between Decay and Development*, edited by Holger H. Hansen and Michael Twaddle, 267–279. London: James Currey, 1988.

Rutiba, Eustace G. "Religions in Uganda, 1960-1993." In *Uganda: Thirty Years of Independence, 1962-1992 – Assessments*, edited by Khiddu E. Makubuya, V. M. Mwaka and P. G. Okoth, 378–405. Makerere University: The Committee for the Workshop, 1994.

Sanneh, Lamin. "The Horizontal and Vertical in Mission: An African Perspective." *International Bulletin of Missionary Research* 7, no. 4 (1983): 165–171.

Senath Esuruku, Robert. "The Peace Recovery and Development Plan for Northern Uganda." In *Where Law Meets Reality: Forging African Transitional Justice*, edited by Moses Chrispus Okello, Chris Dolan, et al., 147–150. Cape Town: Pambazuka Press, 2012.

Shenk, Wilbert R. "Missionary Encounter with Culture." *International Bulletin of Missionary Research* 15, no. 3 (1991): 104–109.

Shejavali, Abisai. "The Influence of the Concept of the Traditional African Leadership on the Concept of Church Leadership: Some Personal Impressions, II." *Africa Theological Journal* 1 (1968): 75–82.

Smoker, Dorothy E. W. "Decision-making in East African Revival Movement Groups." In *African Initiatives in Religion,* edited by D. Barret, 96–108. Nairobi: East African Publishing House, 1971.

Son, B. "The power and Egoism of the Modern State: A Christian Perspective." *Transformation Magazine* 6, no. 3 (1989): 1–5.

Stanley, Brian. "The East African Revival – African Initiative within a European Tradition." *Evangelical Review of Theology* 2, no. 2 (1978): 188–207.

Sweeting, Rachael. "The Growth of the Church in Buwalasi-I." *The Bulletin of the Society for African Church History* II no. 4 (1968): 334–49.

———. "The Growth of the Church in Buwalasi-II." *The Bulletin of the Society for African Church History* III, no. 1–2 (1969-70): 15–27.

Torente, Nicolas de. "Opinion Polls in the Spotlight: Opinion Polls, NRM's Strengths." In *Elections in a Hybrid Regime: Revisiting the 2011 Uganda Polls,* edited by S. Perrot, S. Makara, J. Lafargue, and M. Fourere. Kampala: Fountain Publishers, 2014.

Trites, A. A. "Witness, Testimony." In *New Testament Theology,* edited by Colin Brown, 1038–1051, Vol. 3: Pri-Z. Exeter: The Paternoster Press, 1978.

Tuma, T. "Church Expansion in Buganda." In *A Century of Christianity in Uganda 1877–1977,* edited by T. Tuma and P. Mutibwa. Nairobi: Uzima Press, 1978.

Turner, Philip. "The Wisdom of the Fathers and the Gospel of Christ." *Journal of Religion in Africa* 4, no. 1 (1972): 46–68.

Waliggo, John Mary. "The African Clan as the True Model of the African Church." In *The Church in African Christianity: Innovative Essays in Ecclesiology,* edited by J. N. K. Mugambi and L. Magesa, 111–127. Nairobi: Initiatives Ltd., 1990.

Walls, Andrew F. "Africa and Christian Identity." In *Mission Focus: Current Issues* edited by W. R. Shenk, 212–221. Ontario: Herald Press, 1980.

Wandira, Asavia. "Missionary Education in Uganda Revisited." In *A Century of Christianity in Uganda 1877-1977,* edited by T. Tuma and P. Mutibwa. Nairobi: Uzima Press, 1978.

Ward, Kevin. "A History of Christianity in Uganda." In *From Mission to Church* edited by Z. Nthamburi, 81–112. Nairobi: Uzima Press, 1982.

———. "'Tukutendereza Yesu': The Balokole Revival in Uganda." In *Mission to Church* edited by Z. Nthambuli, 113–144. Nairobi: Uzima Press, 1982.

———. "Catholic-Protestant Relations in Uganda: An Historical Perspective." *Africa Theological Journal* 13, no. 3 (1984): 176–185.

———. "'Obedient Rebels' - The Relationship between the Early "Balokole' and the Church of Uganda: The Mukono Crisis of 1941." *Journal of Religion in Africa* XIX, no. 3 (1989): 194–227.

———. "The Church of Uganda amidst Conflict: the Interplay between Church and Politics in Uganda since 1962." In *Religion and Politics in East Africa*, edited by Holger H. Hansen and Michael Twaddle, 72–105. London: James Currey, 1995.

Warren, Max. "The Missionary Expansion of Ecclesia Anglicana." In *New Testament Christianity for Africa and the World; Essays in Honour of Harry Sawyerr*, edited by Mark E. Glasswell and Edward W. Fashole-Luke, 124–140. London: SPCK, 1974.

Waruta, D. W. "Towards an African Church: A Critical Assessment of Alternative Forms and Structures." In *The Church in African Christianity: Innovative Essays in Ecclesiology*, edited by J. N. K. Mugambi and L. Magesa, 29–42. Nairobi: Initiatives Publishers, 1990.

Williams, Trevor. "The Coming of Christianity to Ankole." *The Bulletin of the Society for African Church History* II, no. 2 (1966): 155–173.

Winter, Mark. "The Balokole and the Protestant Ethic – A Critic." *Journal of Religion in Africa* XIV, no. 1 (1983): 58–73.

Books

Abbott, Walter, M., ed. *The Documents of Vatican II*. New York: Guild Press, 1966.

Adoko, Akena. *From Obote to Obote*. Kampala: Vikas Publishing House, 1983.

Ajayi, J. F. *Christian Missions in Nigeria 1841-1891*. London: Longmans, 1965.

Amnesty International. *Rule by Law: Discriminatory Legislation and Legitimized Abuses in Uganda*. London: Amnesty International, 2014.

Andersson, Efraim. *Churches at the Grass-root*. London: Lutterworth Press, 1969.

Apter, David E. *The Political Kingdom in Uganda*. London: Oxford University Press, 1961.

Ashe, Robert. *Two Kings of Uganda* (2nd ed.). London: Frank Cass & Co. Ltd., 1970.

———. *Chronicles of Uganda* (2nd ed.). London: Frank Cass & Co. Ltd., 1971.

Avirgan, Tony, and Martha Honey. *War in Uganda: The Legacy of Idi Amin*. Dar es Salaam: Tanzania Publishing House Ltd, 1982.

Avis, Paul. *Anglicanism and the Christian Church*. Edinburgh: T & T Clark, 1989.

Ayandele, E. A. *The Missionary Impact on Modern Nigeria, 1842-1914: A Political and Social Analysis*. London: Longmans, 1966.

Bibliography

Barth, Karl. *Theology and the Church*. London: SCM Press, 1962.

Bebbington, David. *Patterns in History: A Christian Perspective on Historical Thought*. Leicester: Apollos, 1990.

Bethge Eberhard, et al., eds. *Dietrich Bonhoeffer: A Life in Pictures*. London: SCM Press, 1986.

Book of Common Prayer of 1662. London: Collin Publishers, 1968 edition.

Brown, Colin, ed. *New International Dictionary of New Testament Theology*, Vol 3. Exeter: The Paternoster Press, 1978.

Brown, Leslie. *Three Worlds: One Word*. London: Rex Collings, 1981.

Brunner, Emil. *The Word and the World*. London: SCM Press, 1931.

Bujo, Benezet. *African Theology in its Social Context*. Maryknoll, New York: Orbis Books, 1992.

Bukenya, Alex B. *Inside Luwero Triangle*. Kampala: Kitaka Publishing and Trading Co. Ltd, 1992.

Bujo, B. *African Theology in its Social Context*. MaryKnoll, New York: Orbis Books, 1992.

Butler, Bill. *Hill Ablaze*. London: Hodder & Stoughton, 1976.

Calvin, John. *The Institutes of the Christian Religion*. Edited by John T. McNeill, translated by Ford L. Battles. Philadelphia: Westminster Press, 1960.

Church, Joe E. *Awake Uganda! The Story of Blasio Kigozi and His Vision for Revival*. Kampala: The Uganda Bookshop Press, 1957.

Church, Joe E. *Jesus Satisfies: An Account of Revival in East African*. Revised Edition. London: Africa Christian Press, 1973.

Church, Joe E. *William Nagenda: A great Lover of Jesus*. London: Ruanda Mission, 1973 (a pamphlet published in Memory of Nagenda).

———. *Every Man a Bible Student* (rev. ed.). Exeter: The Paternoster Press, 1976.

———. *Quest for the Highest*. Exeter: The Paternoster Press, 1981.

Coomes, Anne. *Festo Kivengere*. Eastbourne: Monarch, 1990.

Dulles, Avery. *Models of the Church*. Garden City, New York: Image Books, 1978.

Ebyeshongoro Eby'Okujunwa. London: SPCK, 1951.

Fashole-Luke, E. et al., eds. *Christianity in Independent Africa*. London: Rex Collings 1978.

Faupel, John F. *African Holocaust: the Story of the Uganda Martyrs*. Africa: St. Paul Publications, 1984.

Ford, Margaret. *Janani: The Making of a Martyr*. London: Marshal, Morgan & Scott, 1978.

Forstman, H. Jackson. *Christian Faith and the Church*. St Louis, Missouri: The Bethany Press, 1965.

Fowler, H. W., F. G. Fowler, and Della Thompson, eds. *The Concise Oxford Dictionary* (ninth edition). London: Oxford University Press, 1996.

Gifford, Paul. *African Christianity: Its Public Role in Uganda and Other African Countries*. Kampala: Fountain Publishers, 1999.

Giles, Kevin. *What on Earth is the Church? A Biblical and Theological Inquiry*. London: SPCK, 1995.

Gingyera-Pinycwa, A. G. *Northern Uganda in National Politics*. Kampala: Fountain Publishers, 1992.

Grahame, Ingram. *Amin and Uganda: A Personal Memoir*. London: Granada, 1980.

Gukina, Peter M. *Uganda: A Case Study in African Political Development*. Notre Dame: University of Notre Dame Press, 1972.

Gunton, Colin E., and Daniel W. Hardy, eds. *On Being the Church: Essays on the Christian Community*. Edinburgh: T & T Clark, 1989.

Gwyn, David. *Idi Amin: Death-Light of Africa*. Boston: Little, Brown and Co., 1977.

Hansen, Holger B. *Mission, Church and State in a Colonial Setting: Uganda 1890-1925*. London: Heinemann, 1984.

Hansen, Holger B. and Michael Twaddle, eds. *Uganda Now: Between Decay and Development*. London: James Currey, 1988.

———. *Changing Uganda*. London: James Currey, 1991.

———. *Religion and Politics in East Africa*. London: James Currey, 1995.

Hastings, Adrian. *Church and Mission in Modern Africa*. London: Burns & Oates, 1967.

———. *The Faces of God: Essays on Church and Society*. London: Geoffrey Chapman, 1975.

———. *African Christianity: an Essay in Interpretation*. London: Geoffrey Chapman, 1976.

———. *A History of African Christianity, 1950-1975*. Cambridge: Cambridge University Press, 1979.

———. *African Catholicism*. London: SCM, 1989.

———. *The Church in Africa, 1450-1950*. Oxford: Clarendon Press, 1994.

Hauerwas, Stanley, and Gregory Jones, eds. *Why Narrative? Readings in Narrative Theology*. Grand Rapids: Eerdmans, 1989.

Hallencreutz, C., and A. Mayo, eds. *Church and State in Zimbabwe*. Gweru: Mambo Press, 1988.

Henige, David. *Oral Historiography*. London: Longman, 1982.

Hewitt, Gordon. *The Problem of Success: A History of the Church Missionary Society, 1910 – 1942*. London: SCM Press, 1971.

Ibingira, Grace. *The Forging of an African Nation*. New York: The Viking Press, 1973.

———. *African Upheavals since Independence*. Boulder: West View Press, 1980.

Idowu, Bolaji. *African Traditional Religion: A Definition*. London: SCM Press, 1973.
———. *Towards an Indigenous Church*. London: Oxford University Press, 1965.
Ingham, Kenneth. *Obote, A Political Biography*. London: Routledge, 1994.
Ingrams, Harold. *Uganda: A Crisis of Nationhood*. London: Her Majesty's Stationery Office, 1960.
Jabo, Joseph, and Julia Kushemererwa. *Orombi: The Biography of His Grace Henry Luke Orombi, Archbishop of the Church of Uganda (2004-2012)*. Kampala: WASP Ltd., 2012.
Jay, Eric. *The Church: Its Changing Image Through Twenty Centuries*. London: SPCK, 1977.
Jorgensen, Jan Jelmert. *Uganda: A Modern History*. London: Croom Helm, 1981.
The Kabaka of Buganda. *The Desecration of My Kingdom*. London: Constable, 1967.
Kalinaki, Daniel K. *Kizza Besigye and Uganda's Unfinished Revolution*. Kampala: Dominant Seven Publishers, 2014.
Kalu, Ogbu, ed. *The History of Christianity in West Africa*. London: Longman, 1980.
Karugire, Samwiri R. *A Political History of Uganda*. Nairobi: Heinemann Educational Books, 1980.
———. *Roots of Instability in Uganda*. Kampala: Fountain Publishers, 1996.
Kasfir, Nelson. *The Shrinking Political Arena: Participation and Ethnicity in African Politics, with a Case Study of Uganda*. London: University of California Press, 1976.
Kasozi, Abdu B. *The Spread of Islam in Uganda*. Nairobi: Oxford University Press, 1986.
Katongole, Emmanuel. *The Sacrifice of Africa: A Political Theology of Africa*. Grand Rapids: Eerdmans, 2011.
Kavulu, David. *The Uganda Martyrs*. Kampala: Longman, 1969.
Kavuma, Paulo. *Crisis in Buganda 1953-55*. London: Rex Collings, 1979.
Kibira, Josiah. *The Church, Clan and the World*. Upsala: Almenist and Wiskell, 1974.
Kilega Par Jo Ducu, Wer Me Pako Lubanga, (Lwo Prayer Book and Hymnal, Revised). Kampala: Centenary Publishing House, 1979.
King, N., A. Kasozi, and A. Oded. *Islam and the Confluence of Religions in Uganda 1840-1966*. Florida: American Academy of Religion, 1973.
Kisembo, B., L. Magesa, and A. Shorter, eds. *African Christian Marriage*. London, Geoffrey Chapman, 1977.
Kivengere, Festo. *I Love Idi Amin*. London: Marshal Morgan & Scott, 1977.
Kiwanuka, Semakula. *A History of Buganda*. London: Longman, 1971.
Kung, Hans. *The Church*. London: Burns and Oates, 1967.

Kyemba, Henry. *A State of Blood: The Inside Story of Idi Amin*. London: Corgi Books, 1977.

Kyewalyanga, Francis-Xavier. *Traditional Religion, Custom and Christianity in Uganda*. Freiburg im Breisgau: Internationales Katholishes Missionswerk, 1979.

Lawrence, J. C. D. *The Iteso: Forty Years of Change in a Nilo-Hamitic Tribe of Uganda*. London: Oxford University Press, 1957.

Listowel, Judith. *Amin*. New York: IUP Books, 1973.

Lloyd, Margaret. *Wedge of Light: Revival in North West Uganda*. Rugby: Margaret Lloyd, n.d.

Low, D. Anthony. *Religion and Society in Buganda 1875-1900*. Kampala: East African Institute of Social Research, 1956.

———. *Political Parties in Uganda 1949-62*. University of London: The Athlone Press, 1962.

———. *Buganda in Modern History*. London: Weidenfeld and Nicolson, 1971.

———. *The Mind of Buganda: Documents of the Modern History of an African Kingdom*. London: Heinemann, 1971.

Low, D. Anthony, and R. Cranford Pratt. *Buganda and British Overrule 1900-1955*. London: Oxford University Press, 1960.

Luck, Anne. *African Saint: The Story of Apolo Kivebulaya*. London: SCM Press, 1963.

Mahmood, Mamdani. *Imperialism and Fascism in Uganda*. London: Heinemann Educational Books, 1983.

Makubuya, Khiddu E., V. M. Mwaka and P. G. Okoth, eds. *Uganda: Thirty Years of Independence, 1962–1992 – Assessments*. Makerere University: The Committee for the Workshop, 1994.

Martin, David. *General Amin*. London: Faber and Faber, 1974.

Mazrui, Ali. *Soldiers and Kinsmen in Uganda: The Making of a Military Ethnocracy*. London: Sage Publications, 1975.

Mbiti, John S. *African Traditional Religions and Philosophy*. London: Heineman, 1969.

———. *The Crisis in Mission in Africa*. Kampala: Uganda Church Press, 1971.

Melady, Thomas P., and Margaret B. Melady. *Uganda: The Asian Exiles*. Maryknoll, New York: Orbis Books, 1976.

Moon, Karen. *St Paul's Cathedral Namirembe: A History and Guide*. Richmond, England: Karen Moon, 1994.

Muddola, Dan M. *Religion, Ethnicity and Politics in Uganda*. Kampala: Fountain Publishers, 1993.

Mugambi, J. N. K., and L. Magesa, eds. *The Church in African Christianity: Innovative Essays in Ecclesiology*. Nairobi: Initiatives Publishers, 1990.

Mukulu, Alex. *Thirty Years of Bananas*. Nairobi: Oxford University Press, 1993.

Museveni, Yoweri K. *What is Africa's Problem?* Kampala: NRM Publications, 1992.

———. *Sowing the Mustard Seed: The Struggle for Freedom and Democracy in Uganda.* London: Macmillan Publishers, 1997.

Mutibwa, Phares. *Uganda since Independence: A Story of Unfulfilled Hopes.* Kampala: Fountain Publishers, 1992.

Nabudere, Wadada D. *Imperialism and Revolution on Uganda.* London: Onyx Press Ltd., 1980.

National Resistance Movement. *Mission to Freedom: The Story of NRM-NRA.* Kampala: NRM Secretariat, 1990. (This is a compendium of *The Uganda Resistance News* from 1981-1985.)

Neill, Steven. *Anglicanism.* London and Oxford: Mowbrays, 1977.

Niebuhr, Richard H. *Christ and Culture.* New York: Harper and Row Publishers, 1951.

———. *The Purpose of the Church and its Ministry.* New York: Harper and Brothers, 1956

Niebuhr, Richard H., W. Pauck, and F. P. Miller. *The Church against the World.* New York: Willett, Clark & Co., 1935.

Nthamburi, Zablon. *The Methodist Church in Kenya.* Nairobi: Uzima Press, 1982.

———, ed. *From Mission to Church.* Nairobi: Uzima Press, 1982.

Nzita, Richard and Mbaga-Niwampa. *Peoples and Cultures of Uganda.* Kampala, Fountain Publishers Ltd., 1993.

O'Brien, B. *That Good Physician: Cook of Uganda.* London: Hodder and Stoughton, 1962.

Ochen Okwir, Charles. *Portrait of a Despot.* Milton Keynes: AuthorHouse, 2011.

Oded, Arye. *Religion and Politics in Uganda: A Study of Islam and Judaism.* Nairobi: East African Educational Publishers, 1995.

Odoki, Benjamin J. *The Search for a National Consensus: The Making of the 1995 Uganda Constitution.* Kampala: Fountain Publishers, 2005.

Oliver, Roland. *The Missionary Factor in East Africa.* London: Longmans, 1952.

Omara-Otunnu, Ammi. *Politics and the Military in Uganda, 1890-1985.* London: Macmillan Press, 1987.

Osborn, H. *Revival: A Precious Heritage.* Winchester: Apologia, 1995.

Parratt, John, ed. *A Reader in African Christian Theology.* London: SPCK, 1987.

Perrot, S., S. Makara, J. Lafargue, and M. Fourere, eds. *Elections in a Hybrid Regime: Revisiting the 2011 Uganda Polls.* Kampala: Fountain Publishers, 2014.

Pirouet, Louise M. *Strong in the Faith: the Witness of the Uganda Martyrs.* Mukono, Uganda: Church of Uganda Literature Centre, 1969.

Pirouet, Louise M. *Black Evangelists.* London: Rex Collings, 1978.

Rheenen, Van G. *Church Planting in Uganda*. Pasadena: William Carey Library, 1976.

Robertson, A. F. *Community of Strangers*. London: Scolar Press, 1978.

———. *Uganda's First Republic: Chiefs, Administrators and Politicians 1967-1971*. Cambridge: Cambridge University Press, 1982.

Roscoe, John. *The Baganda: Their Customs and Beliefs*. London: Frank Cass & Co Ltd., 1965.

Rupesinghe, K., ed. *Conflict Resolution in Uganda*. London: James Currey, 1989.

Russell, Keith J. *Men without God? A Study of the Impact of the Christian Message in the North of Uganda*. London: Highway Press, 1966.

Sanneh, Lamin. *Translating the Message: The Missionary Impact on Culture*. New York: Orbis Books, 1991.

———. *West African Christianity: The Religious Impact*. Maryknoll, New York: Orbis Books, 1983.

Schnackenburgh, Rudolph. *The Church in the New Testament*. New York: Herder & Herder, 1965.

Sempangi, Kefa. *A Distant Grief*. Glendale, California: Regal Books, 1979.

Smith, George I. *Ghosts of Kampala*. London: Weidenfeld and Nicolson, 1980.

Smith, Stanley. *Road to Revival*. London: Church Missionary Society, 1946.

Smoker, D. W. *Ambushed by Love: God's Triumph in Kenya's Terror*. Fort Washington: Christian Literature Crusade, 1994.

Sseruwagi, G. M. *Our Greatest Fear is the Transition of Power: An Open Letter to the President*. Bloomington, IN: AuthorHouse, 2013.

St John, Patricia. *Breath of Life*. London: The Norfolk Press, 1971.

Stanley, Brian. *The Bible and the Flag: Protestant Missions and British Imperialism in the Nineteenth and Twentieth Centuries*. Leicester: Inter-Varsity Press, 1990.

Syed, Abidi A. H., ed. *The Role of Religious Organisations in the Development of Uganda*. Kampala: Foundation for African Development, 1991.

Taylor, John V. *The Growth of the Church in Buganda*. London: SCM Press, 1958.

———. *Processes of Growth in an African Church* (International Missionary Council Research Pamphlets 6). London: SCM Press, 1958.

Tripp, Aili Mari. *Museveni's Uganda: Paradoxes of Power in a Hybrid Regime*. London: Lynne Rienner Publishers, 2010.

Tuma, Tom A. D. *Building a Ugandan Church: African Participation in Church Growth and Expansion in Busoga 1891-1940*. Nairobi: Kenya Literature Bureau, 1980.

Tuma, Tom A. D., and Phares Mutibwa, eds. *A Century of Christianity in Uganda 1877-1977*. Nairobi: Uzima Press, 1978.

Tumusime, James, ed. *Uganda 30 Years, 1962-1992*. Kampala: Fountain Publishers, 1992.

Twaddle, Michael. *Kakungulu and the Creation of Uganda, 1868-1928*. London: Currey, 1993.

———, ed. *Expulsion of a Minority: Essays on Ugandan Asians*. London: Athlone Press, 1975.

Vansina, Jan. *Oral Tradition: A Study in Historical Methodology*, translated by H. M. Wright. London: Routledge and Kegan Paul, 1965.

———. *Oral Tradition as History*. London: James Currey, 1985

Wallis, Roy. *The Elementary Forms of the New Religious Life*. London: Routledge & Kegan Paul, 1984.

Walls, Andrew F. *The Missionary Movement in Christian History: Studies in the Transmission of Faith*. Maryknoll, New York: Orbis Books, 1996.

Ward, Kevin. *Called to Serve: Bishop Tucker Theological College, Mukono: A History, 1913-1989*. Mukono: Bishop Tucker Theological College, 1989.

Warren, Max. *Revival: An Enquiry*. London: SCM Press, 1954.

———. *Problems and Promises in Africa Today*. London: Hodder and Stoughton, 1964.

Webber, Robert E. *The Church in the World: Opposition, Tension, or Transformation*. Grand Rapids: Zondervan Publishing House, 1986.

Welbourn, F. B. *The East African Rebels*. London: SCM Press, 1961.

———. *Religion and Politics in Uganda 1952-62*. Nairobi: East African Publishing House, 1965.

Wooding, Dan and Ray Barnett. *Uganda Holocaust*. London: Pickering & Inglis, 1980.

Wright, Michael. *Buganda in the Heroic Age*. Nairobi: Oxford University Press, 1971.

Online Sources

Acholi Religious Leaders Peace Initiative, The. "About us." Available on http://www.arlpi.org/about-us (accessed October 2014).

Baguma, Joseph, and Pascal Kwesiga. "I Am Not a Political Archbishop – Ntagali." *New Vision*. Article available on http://www.newvision.co.ug/news/632294-i-am-not-a-political-archbishop-ntagali.html (accessed May 2015).

Human Rights Watch. "Uganda: Investigate 2009 Kampala Riot Killings." 10 September 2010. Available on https://www.hrw.org/news/2010/09/10/uganda-investigate-2009-kampala-riot-killings (accessed October 2014).

Kwesiga, Pascal. "I Want a Vibrant, United Church – Ntagali." *New Vision*. Article available on http://www.newvision.co.ug/news/632286-i-want-a-vibrant-united-church--ntagali.html (accessed May 2015).

Nam, Joe. "Orombi Entourage Weep on Tour of Pabbo Camp in Northern Uganda." *The New Vision Newspaper*. Available on http://webarchive.cms-uk.org/news/2004/8_03_2004.htm (accessed May 2015).

Uganda Radio Network. "Archbishop Orombi Noncommital on Anti-LRA Offensive." 17 December 2008. Available on http://ugandaradionetwork.com/a/story.php?s=19620 (accessed May 2015).

Langham Literature and its imprints are a ministry of Langham Partnership.

Langham Partnership is a global fellowship working in pursuit of the vision God entrusted to its founder John Stott –

> *to facilitate the growth of the church in maturity and Christ-likeness through raising the standards of biblical preaching and teaching.*

Our vision is to see churches in the majority world equipped for mission and growing to maturity in Christ through the ministry of pastors and leaders who believe, teach and live by the Word of God.

Our mission is to strengthen the ministry of the Word of God through:
- nurturing national movements for biblical preaching
- fostering the creation and distribution of evangelical literature
- enhancing evangelical theological education

especially in countries where churches are under-resourced.

Our ministry

Langham Preaching partners with national leaders to nurture indigenous biblical preaching movements for pastors and lay preachers all around the world. With the support of a team of trainers from many countries, a multi-level programme of seminars provides practical training, and is followed by a programme for training local facilitators. Local preachers' groups and national and regional networks ensure continuity and ongoing development, seeking to build vigorous movements committed to Bible exposition.

Langham Literature provides majority world preachers, scholars and seminary libraries with evangelical books and electronic resources through publishing and distribution, grants and discounts. The programme also fosters the creation of indigenous evangelical books in many languages, through writer's grants, strengthening local evangelical publishing houses, and investment in major regional literature projects, such as one volume Bible commentaries like *The Africa Bible Commentary* and *The South Asia Bible Commentary*.

Langham Scholars provides financial support for evangelical doctoral students from the majority world so that, when they return home, they may train pastors and other Christian leaders with sound, biblical and theological teaching. This programme equips those who equip others. Langham Scholars also works in partnership with majority world seminaries in strengthening evangelical theological education. A growing number of Langham Scholars study in high quality doctoral programmes in the majority world itself. As well as teaching the next generation of pastors, graduated Langham Scholars exercise significant influence through their writing and leadership.

To learn more about Langham Partnership and the work we do visit **langham.org**

www.ingramcontent.com/pod-product-compliance
Lightning Source LLC
Chambersburg PA
CBHW071355300426
44114CB00016B/2070